EAST ANGLIAN ARCHAEOLOGY

Frontispiece. Wiggenhall St Peter: this fine Perpendicular church, serving a small Marshland hamlet, was abandoned in 1929. Photo: the author.

The Ruined and Disused Churches of Norfolk

by Neil Batcock

surveying by
Philip Williams,
Steven Ashley, Tom Loader,
Stephanie Rickett, Andrew Rogerson

illustrations by
Philip Williams,
Steven Ashley, Hoste Spalding, Sue White

photographs by
Neil Batcock,
Hallam Ashley, Derek Edwards

East Anglian Archaeology
Report No. 51, 1991

Norfolk Archaeological Unit
Norfolk Museums Service

EAST ANGLIAN ARCHAEOLOGY
REPORT NO.51, 1991

Published by
The Norfolk Archaeological Unit
Union House
Gressenhall
Dereham
Norfolk NR20 4DR

in conjunction with
The Scole Archaeological Committee Ltd.

Editor: Peter Wade-Martins
EAA Managing Editor: Susie West

Scole Editorial Sub-Committee:
David Buckley, County Archaeologist, Essex Planning Department
Peter Wade-Martins, County Field Archaeologist, Norfolk Museums Service
Stanley West, County Archaeological Officer, Suffolk Planning Department

Typeset in Plantin by Spire Origination, Norwich
Printed by

© THE NORFOLK ARCHAEOLOGICAL UNIT 1991
ISBN 0 905594 03 7

For details of *East Anglian Archaeology*, see last page

This volume is published with the aid of a grant from
the Historic Buildings and Monuments Commission for England
and a grant from the Marc Fitch fund

Cover Illustration
Bawsey, St James (Photo: D. A. Edwards, NAU/ALK 15).

Contents

Table of contents	v
List of Plates	vi
Contents of Microfiche	x
List of Figures	xiii
Index of Sites	xiii
Acknowledgements	xvi
Summary	1

Chapter 1. Introduction
I. Purpose of the Survey	1
II. Range of the Survey	1
III. Rate of Deterioration	5
IV. Causes of Abandonment	7
V. Quality of Buildings	23
VI. Quality of Church Contents	33
VII. Churchyards	41
VIII. Condition of Remains	42
IX. Recommendations	44
X. Format of Catalogues	47
XI. Format of Reports	48
XII. Historical Sources	48
Endnotes	49

Chapter 2. Catalogue: Summary Reports
I. Category I	50
II. Category II	51
III. Category III	52
IV. Category IV	52
V. Category V	53
VI. Category VI	53

Chapter 3. Category I, Full Reports
I. Barningham North, St Peter	56
II. Brandiston, St Nicholas	60
III. West Harling, All Saints	65
IV. West Tofts, St Mary	72
V. Wiggenhall, St Mary the Virgin	76
VI. Great Yarmouth, St George	79

Chapter 4. Category II, Full Reports
I. Babingley, St Felix	83
II. Burlingham, St Peter	88
III. Great Hautbois, St Mary	94
IV. Kempstone, St Paul	97
V. Sco Ruston, St Michael	101
VI. Tivetshall, St Mary	108

Chapter 5. Category III, Full Reports
I. Bawsey, St James	114
II. Mintlyn, St Michael	116
III. West Raynham, St Margaret	119
IV. Saxlingham Thorpe, St Mary	123
V. Snarehill	127
VI. Surlingham, St Saviour	131

Chapter 6. Category IV, Full Reports
I. Egmere, St Edmund	134
II. Godwick, All Saints	136
III. Hindolveston, St George	138
IV. Panxworth, All Saints	140
V. Pudding Norton, St Margaret	142
VI. Wallington, St Margaret	144

Chapter 7. Category V, Full Reports
I. Burnham Sutton, St Ethelbert	146
II. Eccles-next-the-Sea, St Mary	148
III. Hackford, All Saints	149
IV. King's Lynn, St James	149
V. Great Walsingham, All Saints	152
VI. Weeting, All Saints	154

Chapter 8. Category VI, Full Reports
I. Ashby, St Mary	156
II. Fincham, St Michael	157
III. Holverston, St Mary	158
IV. Itteringham, St Nicholas	159
V. Ormsby, St Peter	160
VI. Thetford, St Giles	161

Glossary	163
Appendix I: Parish Churches and Chapels-of-Ease founded after AD 1800	166
Appendix II: Parish Churches of Norfolk founded before AD 1800	170
Appendix III: Disused/ruined/disappeared medieval churches within the city walls of Norwich	175
Appendix IV: Erroneous attributions of parochial status	176
Appendix V: Statistics for the diocese of Norwich	177
Appendix VI: Major building operations	177
Appendix VII: Quality of church architecture (excluding City of Norwich)	178
Appendix VIII: Quality of church contents	179
Appendix IX: Condition of churches	180
Appendix X: Dates of the abandonment of parish churches	180
Appendix XI: Causes of abandonment of churches	185
Appendix XII: Additional sites	187
Bibliography	188
Index	192
Microfiche	

List of Plates

Cover:	Bawsey	
Frontispiece:	Wiggenhall St Peter	

Introduction
Plate I	Hindolveston, Ladbrooke print	13
Plate II	Hindolveston, tower	13

Category VI
Plate III	Itteringham, cropmarks	14

Category V
Plate IV	Quarles	14

Category IV
Plate V	Wallington	15
Plate VI	Heigham, St Bartholomew	15

Category III
Plate VII	Castle Rising	16

Category II
Plate VIII	Appleton	16

Category I
Plate IX	Moulton St Mary	17

Causes of Abandonment
Plate X	Barmer *Isolated site*	17
Plate XI	Southery, Ladbrooke *Inconvenient site*	18
Plate XII	Eccles *Disaster*	18
Plate XIII	Roudham *Disaster*	19
Plate XIV	Islington *Shrunken village*	19
Plate XV	Thetford, Martin's map *Urban decline*	20
Plate XVI	Reepham, aerial view *2 or more churches*	20
Plate XVII	Antingham, Ladbrooke *2 or more churches*	21
Plate XVIII	Great Melton *2 or more churches*	21
Plate XIX	Reepham Church, Martin *2 or more churches*	22
Plate XX	Babingley *DMV*	22

Quality of Buildings
Plate XXI	Kempstone (window) *Romanesque*	25
Plate XXII	Pudding Norton (window) *Romanesque*	25
Plate XXIII	Shingham (door) *Romanesque*	25
Plate XXIV	Hales (Cotman print) *Romanesque*	26
Plate XXV	Hales (door, Cotman print) *Romanesque*	26
Plate XXVI	Coston (whole church) *E.English*	27
Plate XXVII	Buckenham Ferry (tower) *E.English*	27
Plate XXVIII	Feltwell (arcading) *E.English*	27
Plate XXIX	Islington (internal view with vaulting) *E.English*	28
Plate XXX	W.Walton (tower) *E.English*	28
Plate XXXI	Hockwold (window and arcading) *Decorated*	28
Plate XXXII	E.Ruston (arcarding) *Decorated*	29
Plate XXXIII	Shingham (interior) *Decorated*	29
Plate XXXIV	Wiggenhall St Peter (exterior *Perpendicular*	30
Plate XXXV	Wolterton (tower) *Perpendicular*	30
Plate XXXVI	Feltwell (exterior) *Perpendicular*	30
Plate XXXVII	Hockwold (roof) *Perpendicular*	31
Plate XXXVIII	Gunton (front) *Post-Med.*	31
Plate XXXIX	Gunton (side) *Post-Med.*	32
Plate XL	Gunton (door) *Post-Med.*	32
Plate XLI	Gunton (interior) *Post-Med.*	32

Contents
Plate XLII	Crownthorpe (interior, before)	36
Plate XLIII	Crownthorpe (interior, after)	36
Plate XLIV	Frenze (brasses, x 2)	37
Plate XLV	W.Harling (brasses, x 2)	37
Plate XLVI	Wiggenhall (eagle lectern detail)	38
Plate XLVII	Moulton (wall painting)	38
Plate XLVIII	Moulton (font)	38
Plate XLIX	Buckenham Ferry (font)	38
Plate L	N.Barningham (medieval floor)	39
Plate LI	Moulton (monument)	39
Plate LII	Hockwold (monument)	39
Plate LIII	Tottington (benches)	40
Plate LIV	Morton (door)	40
Plate LV	Frenze (pew)	40
Plate LVI	Moulton (pulpit)	41
Plate LVII	Tottington (screen)	41

Churchyard
Plate LVIII	Cockthorpe (gravestones)	41

Condition of Remains
Plate LIX	Feltwell (Ladbrooke)	43
Plate LX	Feltwell (now)	43
Plate LXI	Morton (before)	43
Plate LXII	Morton (after)	43
Plate LXIII	Southwood (Ladbrooke)	44
Plate LXIV	Southwood (ruin)	44

Main Text

Category I
Plate LXV	N.Barningham (Ladbrooke print)	56
Plate LXVI	N.Barningham (exterior)	58
Plate LXVII	Brandiston (exterior)	61
Plate LXVIII	West Harling (Ladbrooke print)	66
Plate LXIX	West Harling (exterior)	69
Plate LXX	West Tofts (exterior)	73
Plate LXXI	West Tofts (Ladbrooke print)	75
Plate LXXII	Wiggenhall St Mary (exterior)	78
Plate LXXIII	Yarmouth St George (exterior)	80
Plate LXXIV	Yarmouth St George (interior)	81

Category II
Plate LXXV	Babingley (Ladbrooke print)	83

Plate LXXVI	Babingley (view)	83
Plate LXXVII	Babingley (interior, 1947)	85
Plate LXXVIII	Babingley (detail)	86
Plate LXXIX	Burlingham St Peter (exterior)	89
Plate LXXX	Burlingham St Peter (Ladbrooke print)	89
Plate LXXXI	Burlingham St Peter (interior, 1945)	93
Plate LXXXII	Burlingham St Peter (interior, today)	93
Plate LXXXIII	Great Hautbois (Ladbrooke print)	94
Plate LXXXIV	Great Hautbois (exterior)	95
Plate LXXXV	Great Hautbois (interior)	96
Plate LXXXVI	Kempstone (Ladbrooke print)	98
Plate LXXXVII	Kempstone (detail arch)	99
Plate LXXXVIII	Sco Ruston (Ladbrooke print)	102
Plate LXXIX	Sco Ruston (exterior)	102
Plate XC	Tivetshall St Mary (aerial view)	108
Plate XCI	Tivetshall St Mary (exterior)	108

Category III
Plate XCII	Bawsey (tower)	114
Plate XCIII	Bawsey (tower arch)	115
Plate XCIV	Bawsey (detail of tower)	115
Plate XCV	Bawsey (tower, c.1900)	115
Plate XCVI	Mintlyn (detail of doorway)	117
Plate XCVII	Mintlyn (Cotman of doorway)	118
Plate XCVIII	Mintlyn (architectural fragment)	118
Plate XCIX	Mintlyn (exterior)	119
Plate C	West Raynham (Ladbrooke print)	120
Plate CI	West Raynham (interior)	120
Plate CII	Saxlingham Thorpe (interior)	124
Plate CIII	Saxlingham Thorpe (detail)	124
Plate CIV	Snarehill (exterior)	128
Plate CV	Snarehill (detail of long and short work)	129
Plate CVI	Snarehill (interior of barn showing roofline)	129
Plate CVII	Surlingham (Ladbrooke print)	132
Plate CVIII	Surlingham (exterior)	132

Category IV
Plate CIX	Egmere (exterior with cows)	135
Plate CX	Egmere (interior)	135
Plate CXI	Godwick (tower)	137
Plate CXII	Panxworth (Ladbrooke print)	140
Plate CXIII	Panxworth (exterior)	141

Category V
Plate CXIV	Pudding Norton (exterior)	143
Plate CXV	Burnham Sutton (Ladbrooke print)	147
Plate CXVI	Eccles (Ladbrooke print)	148
Plate CXVII	Eccles (today)	148
Plate CXVIII	Hackford (print)	149
Plate CXIX	King's Lynn, St James (today)	150
Plate CXX	King's Lynn, St James (print)	151
Plate CXXI	King's Lynn, St James (print)	151

Category VI
Plate CXXII	Great Walsingham (aerial view)	153
Plate CXXIII	Ashby (aerial view)	156
Plate CXXIV	Holverston (aerial view)	159
Plate CXXV	Ormesby St Peter (aerial view)	161
Plate CXXVI	Thetford, St Giles (Wilkinson print)	162

Appendix I: 19th century foundations
Plate CXXVII	Heigham (exterior)	167
Plate CXXVIII	Heigham (interior)	168
Plate CXXIX	Thorpe (exterior)	169
Plate CXXX	Thorpe (interior)	169

Microfiche Plates

Category I
Plate CXXXI	Bagthorpe (exterior)
Plate CXXXII	Bagthorpe (interior)
Plate CXXXIII	Bagthorpe (view)
Plate CXXXIV	Bagthorpe (Ladbrooke print)
Plate CXXXV	Bagthorpe (exterior)
Plate CXXXVI	Bagthorpe (detail)
Plate CXXXVII	Barmer (exterior)
Plate CXXXVIII	Barmer (exterior)
Plate CXXXIX	Barmer (Ladbrooke print)
Plate CXL	N.Barningham (exterior)
Plate CXLI	N.Barningham (exterior)
Plate CXLII	N.Barningham (detail)
Plate CXLIII	N.Barningham (detail)
Plate CXLIV	N.Barningham (detail)
Plate CXLV	Barton Bendish (exterior)
Plate CXLVI	Barton Bendish (interior)
Plate CXLVII	Barton Bendish (interior)
Plate CXLVIII	Barton Bendish (Cotman, of doorway)
Plate CXLIX	Barton Bendish (Ladbrooke print)
Plate CL	Brandiston (interior)
Plate CLI	Brandiston (interior)
Plate CLII	Brandiston (exterior)
Plate CLIII	Brandiston (interior)
Plate CLIV	Brandiston (Martin)
Plate CLV	Buckenham Ferry (exterior)
Plate CLVI	Buckenham Ferry (interior)
Plate CLVII	Buckenham Ferry (exterior)
Plate CLVIII	Buckenham Ferry (exterior)
Plate CLIX	Buckenham Ferry (interior)
Plate CLX	Buckenham Ferry (Cotman)
Plate CLXI	Cockthorpe (exterior)
Plate CLXII	Cockthorpe (Ladbrooke print)
Plate CLXIII	Cockthorpe (interior)
Plate CLXIV	Cockthorpe (detail)
Plate CLXV	Corpusty (exterior)
Plate CLXVI	Corpusty (exterior)
Plate CLXVII	Corpusty (Ladbrooke print)
Plate CLXVIII	Corpusty (window)
Plate CLXIX	Corpusty (exterior)
Plate CLXX	Coston (Ladbrooke print)
Plate CLXXI	Coston (interior)

Plate CLXXII	Coston (interior)
Plate CLXXIII	Crownthorpe (exterior)
Plate CLXXIV	Crownthorpe (exterior)
Plate CLXXV	Crownthorpe (exterior)
Plate CLXXVI	Crownthorpe (Ladbrooke print)
Plate CLXXVII	Crownthorpe (detail)
Plate CLXXVIII	Crownthorpe (interior)
Plate CLXXIX	Crownthorpe (interior)
Plate CLXXX	Crownthorpe (interior)
Plate CLXXXI	Crownthorpe (detail)
Plate CLXXXII	Crownthorpe (detail)
Plate CLXXXIII	Dunton (exterior)
Plate CLXXXIV	Dunton (exterior)
Plate CLXXXV	Dunton (exterior)
Plate CLXXXVI	Dunton (interior)
Plate CLXXXVII	Dunton (exterior)
Plate CLXXXVIII	Dunton (interior)
Plate CLXXXIX	Feltwell St Nicholas (interior)
Plate CXC	Feltwell (arcade)
Plate CXCI	Feltwell (north arcade)
Plate CXCII	Feltwell (exterior)
Plate CXCIII	Feltwell (tower arch)
Plate CXCIV	Feltwell (tower arch)
Plate CXCV	Feltwell (exterior)
Plate CXCVI	Frenze (exterior)
Plate CXCVII	Frenze (interior)
Plate CXCVIII	Frenze (brass)
Plate CXCIX	Frenze (brass by Cotman)
Plate CC	Frenze (brass by Cotman)
Plate CCI	Frenze (Jane Blenerhaysett brass)
Plate CCII	Frenze (Johann Braham brass)
Plate CCIII	Frenze (font)
Plate CCIV	Frenze (pulpit)
Plate CCV	Frenze (detail)
Plate CCVI	Gunton (Ladbrooke print)
Plate CCVII	Hales (exterior)
Plate CCVIII	Hales (arcading)
Plate CCIX	Hales (interior)
Plate CCX	Hales (doorway by Cotman)
Plate CCXI	Hales (tower)
Plate CCXII	Hales (Ladbrooke print)
Plate CCXIII	Hales (font)
Plate CCXIV	W.Harling (interior)
Plate CCXV	W.Harling (interior)
Plate CCXVI	W.Harling (interior)
Plate CCXVII	W.Harling (interior)
Plate CCXVIII	W.Harling (exterior)
Plate CCXIX	W.Harling (interior)
Plate CCXX	W.Harling (piscina)
Plate CCXXI	W.Harling (porch)
Plate CCXXII	W.Harling (porch)
Plate CCXXIII	W.Harling (tower)
Plate CCXXIV	W.Harling (painted plaster)
Plate CCXXV	W.Harling (Gipps monument)
Plate CCXXVI	W.Harling (reredos)
Plate CCXXVII	Hockwold (exterior)
Plate CCXXVIII	Hockwold (interior)
Plate CCXXIX	Hockwold (interior)
Plate CCXXX	Hockwold (interior)
Plate CCXXXI	Hockwold (interior)
Plate CCXXXII	Hockwold (Ladbrooke print)
Plate CCXXXIII	Hockwold (interior)
Plate CCXXXIV	Hockwold (detail)
Plate CCXXXV	Hockwold (monument)
Plate CCXXXVI	Hockwold (brass by Cotman)
Plate CCXXXVII	Hockwold (painted plaster)
Plate CCXXXVIII	Langford (exterior)
Plate CCXXXIX	Langford (south door)
Plate CCXL	Langford (interior)
Plate CCXLI	Langford (detail)
Plate CCXLII	Langford (Ladbrooke print)
Plate CCXLIII	Moulton (exterior)
Plate CCXLIV	Moulton (Ladbrooke print)
Plate CCXLV	Moulton (interior)
Plate CCXLVI	Moulton (exterior)
Plate CCXLVII	Moulton (interior)
Plate CCXLVIII	Moulton (altar rails)
Plate CCXLIX	Rackheath (Ladbrooke print)
Plate CCL	Rackheath (exterior)
Plate CCLI	Rackheath (chancel)
Plate CCLII	Rackheath (chancel)
Plate CCLIII	Rackheath (interior)
Plate CCLIV	Rackheath (exterior)
Plate CCLV	Rackheath (interior)
Plate CCLVI	Rackheath (tower)
Plate CCLVII	W.Rudham (exterior)
Plate CCLVIII	W.Rudham (interior)
Plate CCLIX	W.Rudham (interior)
Plate CCLX	W.Rudham (interior)
Plate CCLXI	W.Rudham (detail)
Plate CCLXII	E.Ruston (exterior)
Plate CCLXIII	E.Ruston (chancel)
Plate CCLXIV	E.Ruston (interior)
Plate CCLXV	E.Ruston (Ladbrooke print)
Plate CCLXVI	E.Ruston (exterior)
Plate CCLXVII	E.Ruston (interior)
Plate CCLXVIII	E.Ruston (interior)
Plate CCLXIX	E.Ruston (interior)
Plate CCLXX	E.Ruston (detail)
Plate CCLXXI	E.Ruston (screen)
Plate CCLXXII	Snetterton (exterior)
Plate CCLXXIII	Snetterton (interior)
Plate CCLXXIV	Snetterton (interior)
Plate CCLXXV	Snetterton (interior)
Plate CCLXXVI	Snetterton (interior)
Plate CCLXXVII	Snetterton (Ladbrooke print)
Plate CCLXXVIII	Stanford (exterior)
Plate CCLXXIX	Stanford (interior)
Plate CCLXXX	Stanford (exterior)
Plate CCLXXXI	Thurgarton (exterior)
Plate CCLXXXII	Thurgarton (chancel)
Plate CCLXXXIII	Thurgarton (interior)
Plate CCLXXXIV	Thurgarton (exterior)
Plate CCLXXXV	Thurgarton (interior)
Plate CCLXXXVI	Thurgarton (exterior)
Plate CCLXXXVII	Thurgarton (interior)
Plate CCLXXXVIII	Thurgarton (interior)
Plate CCLXXXIX	Thurgarton (Cotman)
Plate CCXC	Thurgarton (detail)
Plate CCXCI	Thurgarton (porch corbel)
Plate CCXCII	Thurgarton (Ladbrooke print)
Plate CCXCIII	Tottington (exterior)
Plate CCXCIV	Tottington (Ladbrooke print)
Plate CCXCV	Tottington (exterior)
Plate CCXCVI	Tottington (interior)
Plate CCXCVII	Tottington (interior)
Plate CCXCVIII	Tottington (exterior)
Plate CCXCIX	Tottington (exterior)
Plate CCC	West Tofts (exterior)
Plate CCCI	West Tofts (exterior)

Plate CCCII	West Tofts (exterior)
Plate CCCIII	West Tofts (exterior)
Plate CCCIV	West Tofts (interior)
Plate CCCV	West Tofts (interior)
Plate CCCVI	West Tofts (interior)
Plate CCCVII	West Tofts (tower)
Plate CCCVIII	West Tofts (glass)
Plate CCCIX	Wiggenhall (exterior)
Plate CCCX	Wiggenhall (interior)
Plate CCCXI	Wiggenhall (lectern)
Plate CCCXII	Wiggenhall (Kervil monument)
Plate CCCXIII	Wiggenhall (benches)
Plate CCCXIV	Wiggenhall (benches)
Plate CCCXV	Wiggenhall (font cover)
Plate CCCXVI	Yarmouth (interior)
Plate CCCXVII	Yarmouth (bell cupola)
Plate CCCXVIII	Yarmouth (font)
Plate CCCXIX	Yarmouth (pulpit)

Category II

Plate CCCXX	Appleton (exterior)
Plate CCCXXI	Appleton (exterior)
Plate CCCXXII	Appleton (Ladbrooke print)
Plate CCCXXIII	Appleton (exterior)
Plate CCCXXIV	Appleton (tower)
Plate CCCXXV	Babingley (exterior)
Plate CCCXXVI	Babingley (exterior)
Plate CCCXXVII	Babingley (chancel)
Plate CCCXXVIII	Babingley (exterior)
Plate CCCXXIX	Babingley (exterior)
Plate CCCXXX	Babingley (nave)
Plate CCCXXXI	Babingley (exterior)
Plate CCCXXXII	Bayfield (exterior)
Plate CCCXXXIII	Bayfield (exterior)
Plate CCCXXXIV	Bircham Tofts (exterior)
Plate CCCXXXV	Bircham Tofts (tower arch)
Plate CCCXXXVI	Bircham Tofts (tower)
Plate CCCXXXVII	Bowthorpe (exterior)
Plate CCCXXXVIII	Bowthorpe (Ladbrooke print)
Plate CCCXXXIX	Bowthorpe (exterior)
Plate CCCXL	Burlingham (exterior)
Plate CCCXLI	Burlingham (exterior)
Plate CCCXLII	Burlingham (interior)
Plate CCCXLIII	Fulmodestone (exterior)
Plate CCCXLIV	Fulmodestone (Ladbrooke print)
Plate CCCXLV	Hargham (exterior)
Plate CCCXLVI	Hargham (Ladbrooke print)
Plate CCCXLVII	Hargham (exterior)
Plate CCCXLVIII	Great Hautbois (exterior)
Plate CCCXLIX	Great Hautbois (interior)
Plate CCCL	Great Hautbois (nave detail)
Plate CCCLI	Great Hautbois (nave arcade)
Plate CCCLII	Great Hautbois (exterior)
Plate CCCLIII	Great Hautbois (Cotman)
Plate CCCLIV	Hopton (exterior)
Plate CCCLV	Hopton (exterior)
Plate CCCLVI	Hopton (tower)
Plate CCCLVII	Houghton (exterior)
Plate CCCLVIII	Houghton (window)
Plate CCCLIX	Houghton (nave window)
Plate CCCLX	Houghton (nave quoins)
Plate CCCLXI	Houghton (exterior)
Plate CCCLXII	Houghton (Ladbrooke print)
Plate CCCLXIII	Islington (interior)
Plate CCCLXIV	Islington (exterior)
Plate CCCLXV	Kempstone (exterior)
Plate CCCLXVI	Kempstone (chancel arch)
Plate CCCLXVII	Mannington (exterior)
Plate CCCLXVIII	Mannington (exterior)
Plate CCCLXIX	Mannington (exterior)
Plate CCCLXX	Morton (Ladbrooke print)
Plate CCCLXXI	Morton (interior)
Plate CCCLXXII	Morton (nave)
Plate CCCLXXIII	Morton (exterior)
Plate CCCLXXIV	Morton (tower)
Plate CCCLXXV	Morton (interior)
Plate CCCLXXVI	Oxwick (Ladbrooke print)
Plate CCCLXXVII	Little Ringstead (exterior)
Plate CCCLXXVIII	Roudham (exterior)
Plate CCCLXXIX	Roudham (exterior)
Plate CCCLXXX	Roudham (exterior)
Plate CCCLXXXI	Roudham (Ladbrooke print)
Plate CCCLXXXII	Roudham (exterior)
Plate CCCLXXXIII	Sco Ruston (chancel)
Plate CCCLXXXIV	Sco Ruston (nave)
Plate CCCLXXXV	Sco Ruston (tower)
Plate CCCLXXXVI	Shotesham (Ladbrooke print)
Plate CCCLXXXVII	E.Somerton (Ladbrooke print)
Plate CCCLXXXVIII	E.Somerton (exterior)
Plate CCCLXXXIX	Southery (exterior)
Plate CCCXC	Southery (interior)
Plate CCCXCI	Southery (nave)
Plate CCCXCII	Southery (exterior)
Plate CCCXCIII	Thorpe-by-Norwich (Ladbrooke print)
Plate CCCXCIV	Tivetshall (Ladbrooke print)
Plate CCCXCV	Tunstall (exterior)
Plate CCCXCVI	Tunstall (exterior)
Plate CCCXCVII	Tunstall (Ladbrooke print)
Plate CCCXCVIII	S.Walsham (general view)
Plate CCCXCIX	S.Walsham (exterior)
Plate CD	S.Walsham (exterior)
Plate CDI	S.Walsham (exterior)
Plate CDII	S.Walsham (Ladbrooke print)
Plate CDIII	Wiggenhall (exterior)
Plate CDIV	Wiggenhall (interior)
Plate CDV	W.Wretham (Ladbrooke print)
Plate CDVI	W.Wretham (tower)

Category III

Plate CDVII	Antingham (exterior)
Plate CDVIII	Antingham (interior)
Plate CDIX	Antingham (tower)
Plate CDX	Bawsey (exterior)
Plate CDXI	Bawsey (exterior)
Plate CDXII	Beachamwell (exterior)
Plate CDXIII	Beachamwell (exterior)
Plate CDXIV	Beachamwell (exterior)
Plate CDXV	Bickerston (Martin)
Plate CDXVI	Burgh Parva (Ladbrooke print)
Plate CDXVII	Castle Rising (exterior)
Plate CDXVIII	N.Elmham (exterior)
Plate CDXIX	Gasthorpe (exterior)
Plate CDXX	Gasthorpe (tower)
Plate CDXXI	Gasthorpe (piscina and font)
Plate CDXXII	Gasthorpe (Martin)
Plate CDXXIII	Kirby Bedon (nave and tower)
Plate CDXXIV	Kirby Bedon (tower)
Plate CDXXV	Mintlyn (exterior)
Plate CDXXVI	Oxborough (exterior)
Plate CDXXVII	Oxborough (Martin)

Plate CDXXVIII	W.Raynham (exterior)
Plate CDXXIX	Little Ryburgh (Ladbrooke print)
Plate CDXXX	Saxlingham Thorpe (Ladbrooke print)
Plate CDXXXI	Great Snarehill (quoins)
Plate CDXXXII	Great Snarehill (quoins)
Plate CDXXXIII	Great Snarehill (window)
Plate CDXXXIV	Stanninghall (tower)
Plate CDXXXV	Stanninghall (Ladbrooke print)
Plate CDXXXVI	Surlingham (interior)
Plate CDXXXVII	Surlingham (Blomefield)
Plate CDXXXVIII	E.Walton (exterior)
Plate CDXXXIX	E.Walton (exterior)
Plate CDXL	E.Walton (interior)
Plate CDXLI	Whitlingham (Ladbrooke print)
Plate CDXLII	Wood Norton (exterior)
Plate CDXLIII	Wood Norton (interior)
Plate CDXLIV	Wood Norton (exterior)

Category IV

Plate CDXLV	Bastwick (Ladbrooke print)
Plate CDXLVI	Beachamwell (exterior)
Plate CDXLVII	Burgh (Ladbrooke print)
Plate CDXLVIII	W.Caister (exterior)
Plate CDXLIX	W.Caister (exterior)
Plate CDL	W.Caister (nave and tower)
Plate CDLI	W.Caister (Ladbrooke print)
Plate CDLII	Edgefield (Ladbrooke print)
Plate CDLIII	Garboldisham (tower)
Plate CDLIV	Garboldisham (Ladbrooke print)
Plate CDLV	Gillingham (exterior)
Plate CDLVI	Gillingham (tower)
Plate CDLVII	Gillingham (tower)
Plate CDLVIII	Gillingham (Ladbrooke print)
Plate CDLIX	Hainford (exterior)
Plate CDLX	Hainford (Ladbrooke print)
Plate CDLXI	Heigham (Holl brass)
Plate CDLXII	Hindolveston (tower)
Plate CDLXIII	Hindolveston (exterior)
Plate CDLXIV	Hindolveston (interior)
Plate CDLXV	Great Melton (Ladbrooke print)
Plate CDLXVI	Great Melton (Ladbrooke print)
Plate CDLXVII	Panxworth (tower)
Plate CDLXVIII	Pudding Norton (nave)
Plate CDLXIX	Pudding Norton (tower)
Plate CDLXX	Pudding Norton (tower quoins)
Plate CDLXXI	Great Ringstead (exterior)
Plate CDLXXII	Great Ringstead (tower)
Plate CDLXXIII	Rockland (exterior)
Plate CDLXXIV	Rockland (tower)
Plate CDLXXV	Rockland (Ladbrooke print)
Plate CDLXXVI	Thorpe Parva (Ladbrooke print)
Plate CDLXXVII	Wallington (exterior)
Plate CDLXXVIII	Wolterton (exterior)
Plate CDLXXIX	Wolterton (tower)

Category V

Plate CDLXXX	E.Beckham (Ladbrooke print)
Plate CDLXXXI	W.Beckham (Ladbrooke print)
Plate CDLXXXII	Burnham Sutton (exterior)
Plate CDLXXXIII	Burnham Sutton (tower)
Plate CDLXXXIV	Foulden (exterior)
Plate CDLXXXV	Hackford (exterior)
Plate CDLXXXVI	Hempton (corner)
Plate CDLXXXVII	Rockland (general view)

Category VI

Plate CDLXXXVIII	Fincham, St Michael (tomb by Martin)
Plate CDLXXXIX	Markshall (Martin)
Plate CDXC	Sidestrand (Ladbrooke print)
Plate CDXCI	Thetford (fragments)

Contents of Microfiche

Category 1

1. Bagthorpe, St Mary 1:A10
2. Barmer, All Saints 1:35
3. Barningham, North, St Peter 1:B12
4. Barton Bendish, St Mary 1:C3
5. Brandiston, St Nicholas 1:D2
6. Buckenham Ferry, St Nicholas 1:D7
7. Cockthorpe, All Saints 1:E4
8. Corpusty, St Peter 1:F1
9. Coston, St Michael 1:F10
10. Crownthorpe, St James 1:G5
11. Dunton, St Peter 2:A8
12. Feltwell, St Nicholas 2:B5
13. Forncett, St Mary 2:C4
14. Frenze, St Andrew 2:C8
15. Gunton, St Andrew 2:D8
16. Hales, St Margaret 2:D13
17. Harling, West 2:E11
18. Hockwold, St Peter 2:F10
19. Illington, St Andrew 2:G14
20. Langford, St Andrew 3:A3
21. Moulton, St Mary 3:A12
22. Narford, St Mary 3:B8
23. Rackheath, All Saints 3:B12
24. Rudham, West, St Peter 3:C10
25. Ruston, East, St Mary 3:D6
26. Shimpling, St George 3:57

27. Shingham, St Botolph 3:E11
28. Snetterton, All Saints 3:E14
29. Stanford, All Saints 3:F12
30. Thurgarton, All Saints 3:G6
31. Tottington, St Andrew 4:A11
32. West Tofts, St Mary 4:B9
33. Wiggenhall, St Mary the Virgin 4:C4
34. Yarmouth, Great, St George 4:C11

Category 2

35. Appleton, St Mary 4:D1
36. Babingley, St Felix 4:D11
37. Bayfield, St Margaret 4:E4
38. Bircham Tofts, St Andrew 4:E10
39. Bowthorpe, St Michael 4:F2
40. Burlingham, St Peter 4:F9
41. Croxton, St John the Baptist 4:F12
42. Fulmodeston, St Mary 4:G1
43. Hargham, All Saints 4:G7
44. Hautbois, Great, St Mary 5:A1
45. Hopton, St Margaret 5:A7
46. Houghton-on-the-Hill 5:A14
47. Islington, St Mary 5:B10
48. Kempstone, St Paul 5:C4
49. Mannington 5:C6
50. Morton-on-the-Hill 5:C13
51. Oxwick, All Saints 5:D9
52. Ringstead, Little, St Andrew 5:D14
53. Roudham, West, St Peter 5:E4
54. Sco Ruston, St Michael 5:F1
55. Shotesham, St Martin 5:F4
56. Somerton, East, St Mary 5:F9
57. Southery, St Mary 5:F13
58. Southwood, St Edmund 5:G9
59. Thorpe-by-Norwich 5: G12
60. Tivetshall, St Mary 6:A2
61. Tunstall, St Peter and St Paul 6:A3
62. Walsham, South, St Laurence 6:A9
63. Wiggenhall, St Peter 6:B4
64. Wretham, West, St Lawrence 6:B11

Category 3

65. Antingham, St Margaret 6:C3
66. Bawsey, St James 6:C10
67. Beachamwell, All Saints 6:C12
68. Bickerston, St Andrew 6:D6
69. Buckenham, New, St Mary 6:D9
70. Burgh Parva, St Mary 6:D12
71. Castle Rising 6:E3
72. Elmham, North, 1 6:E6
73. Gasthorpe, St Nicholas 6:E12
74. Kirby Bedon, St Mary 6:F5
75. Mintlyn, St Michael 6:F11
76. Mundham, St Ethelbert 6:F12
77. Oxborough, St Mary Magdalen 6:F14
78. Raynham, West, St Margaret 6:G6
79. Ryburgh, Little, All Saints 6:G7
80. Saxlingham Thorpe, St Mary 6:G11
81. Snarehill 6:G12
82. Stanninghall 7:A1
83. Surlingham, St Saviour 7:A5
84. Walton, East, St Andrew 7:A7
85. Whitlingham, St Andrew 7:A13
86. Wood Norton, St Peter 7:B4

Category 4

87. Bastwick, St Peter 7:B9
88. Beachamwell, St John 7:B12
89. Burgh, St Mary 7:C2
90. Caister, West, St Edmund 7:C6
91. Edgefield, Saints Peter and Paul 7:C13
92. Egmere, St Edmund *see full Report*
93. Garboldisham, All Saints 7:D4
94. Gillingham, All Saints 7:D9
95. Godwick, All Saints *see full Report*
96. Hainford, All Saints 7:E1
97. Heigham, St Bartholomew 7:E6
98. Hindolveston, St George 7:E10
99. Melton, Great, St Mary 7:E13
100. Panxworth, All Saints 7:F4
101. Pudding Norton, St Margaret 7:F5
102. Ringstead, Great, St Peter 7:F8
103. Rockland, St Andrew 7:F13
104. Snoring, Little 7:G6
105. Testerton, St Remigius 7:G8
106. Thorpe Parva, St Mary 7:G11
107. Wallington, St Margaret 7:G14
108. Walton, West 8:A1
109. Wolterton, St Margaret 8:A3

Category 5

110. Barnham Broom, St Michael 8:A8
111. Barwick, Great, St Mary 8:89
112. Beckham, West, All Saints 8:A11
113. Beckham, West, All Saints 8:A14
114. Burnham Sutton, St Ethelbert 8:B3
115. Carleton, East, St Peter 8:B5
116. Colveston, St Mary 8:B6
117. Creake, North, St Michael 8:B8
118. Eccles, St Mary *see full Report*
119. Foulden, St Edmund 8:B10
120. Hackford, All Saints 8:B13
121. Hempton, St Andrew 8:B14
122. Letton, All Saints 8:C3
123. Leziate, All Saints 8:C5
124. Lynn, King's, St James *see full Report*
125. Pensthorpe 8:C8
126. Quarles 8:C10
127. Rockland St Mary, St Margaret 8:C12
128. Shotesham, St Botolph 8:C14
129. Tattersett, St Andrew 8:D2
130. Thorpland, St Thomas 8:D4
131. Walsingham, Great, All Saints *see full Report*
132. Weeting, All Saints *see full Report*

Category 6

133. Alethorpe 8:D6
134. Algarsthorpe, St Mary Magdalen 8:D8
135. Alpington/Apton, St Martin 8:D9
136. Ashby, St Mary *see full Report*
137. Barton Bendish, All Saints 8:D10
138. Barton Turf, B 8:D12
139. Bedingham, St Mary 8:D13
140. Beeston, St Andrew 8:D14
141. Bittering, Great, St Nicholas 8:E1
142. Blo Norton, St Margaret 8:E2
143. Bracondale, St Nicholas 8:E4
144. Bradcar, St Andrew 8:E6

145. Breccles, Little 8:E6
146. Broomsthorpe 8:E7
147. Brundall, St Clement 8:E8
148. Buckenham, Old, St Andrew 8:E9
149. Buckenham Tofts, St Andrew 8:E10
150. Burnham, St Andrew 8:E11
151. Burnham Westgate, St Edmund 8:E12
152. Burnham Thorpe, St Peter 8:E13
153. Caldecote, St Mary 8:E14
154. Cantelose, All Saints 8:F2
155. Carleton, Rode, B 8:F3
156. Carbrooke, Little 8:F4
157. Carrow 8:F6
158. Choseley 8:F7
159. Clenchwarton, South 8:F8
160. Cockley Cley, St Peter 8:F9
161. Congham, All Saints and St Mary 8:F10
162. Congham, All Saints and St Mary 8:F10
163. Cressingham, Great, St George 8:F12
164. Dereham, West, St Peter 8:F13
165. Doughton 8:F14
166. Dunham, Great, St Mary 8:G1
167. Dykesbeck 8:G3
168. Fincham, St Michael 8:G4
169. Foston, St Peter 8:G5
170. Gowthorpe, St James 8:G6
171. Guist Thorpe, All Saints 8:G7
172. Hardwick 8:G9
173. Harleston 1 8:G10
174. Harling, Middle 8:G12
175. Hautbois, Little, St Mary 8:G14
176. Helmingham, St Mary 9:A1
177. Hempnall, St Andrew 9:92
178. Herringby, St Ethelbert 9:93
179. Hockham, Little, St Mary 9:A4
180. Holm, St Andrew 9:95
181. Holverston, St Mary *see full Report*
182. Irmingland, St Andrew 9:A6
183. Itteringham, St Nicholas *see full Report*
184. Kenningham 9:A7
185. Kenwick, St Thomas 9:A8
186. Kerdiston, St Mary 9:A9
187. Keswick, St Clement 9:A11
188. Langhale, St Christopher 9:A12
189. Langham Parva, St Mary 9:A13
190. Lynford 9:A14
191. Lynn, North, St Edmund 9:B1
192. Marham, St Andrew 9:B3
193. Markshall, St Edmund 9:B4
194. Massingham, Great, All Saints 9:B7
195. Methwold Hythe 9:G8
196. Moulton, Little, All Saints 9:B9
197. Nelonde, St Peter 9:B10
198. Oby 9:B11
199. Ormesby, St Andrew 9:B12
200. Ormesby, St Peter *see full Report*

201. Overstrand, St Martin 1 9:B13
202. Palgrave, Little 9:B14
203. Pattesley, St John the Baptist 9:C2
204. Pickenham, South, St Andrew 9:C3
205. Poringland, West, St Michael 9:C4
206. Rackheath, Little, Holy Trinity 9:C5
207. Roxham, St Michael 9:C6
208. Saxthorpe, St Dunstan 9:C7
209. Scratby, All Saints 9:C8
210. Seething, B 9:C9
211. Setchey 9:C10
212. Shipden 9:C11
213. Shouldham, St Margaret 9:C12
214. Sidestrand, St Michael 9:C13
215. Snetterton, St Andrew 9:D1
216. Stiffkey, St John the Baptist 9:D2
217. Stoke Holy Cross, B 9:D3
218. Stratton, St Peter 9:D4
219. Sturston, Holy Cross 9:D5
220. Summerfield, All Saints 9:D6
221. Swainsthorpe. St Mary 9:D7
222. Thetford, All Saints 9:D8
223. Thetford, St Andrew 9:D9
224. Thetford, St Benet 9:D10
225. Thetford, St Edmund 9:D11
226. Thetford, St Etheldreda 9:D13
227. Thetford, St George 9:E1
228. Thetford, St Giles *se full Report*
229. Thetford, St Helen 9:E3
230. Thetford, Holy trinity 9:E4
231. Thetford, St John 9:E6
232. Thetford, St Lawrence 9:E8
233. Thetford, St Margaret 9:E9
234. Thetford, St Martin 9:E11
235. Thetford, Great St Mary 9:E12
236. Thetford, St Michael 9:E14
237. Thetford, St Nicholas 9:F1
238. Thetford, Red Castle site 9:F4
239. Thetford, Gas Works site 9:F5
240. Thetford, St Michael's Close site 9:F6
241. Thorpe-by-Norwich, Old Thorpe Church 9:F12
242. Thorpeland, St Thomas 9:F14
243. Thurketeliart 9:G1
244. Topcroft, St Giles 9:G2
245. Wacton, Little, St Mary 9:G3
246. Warham, St Mary the Virgin 9:G4
247. Waxham, Little, St Margaret 9:G5
248. Weasenham, St Paul 9:G6
249. Wicklewood, St Andrew 9:G7
250. Windle, St Andrew 9:G8
251. Winston, St Andrew 9:G10
252. Worstead, St Andrew 9:G11
253. Wreningham, Little, St Mary 9:G12
254. Yarmouth, Great, St Benedict 9:G13
255. Yarmouth, Southtown 9:G14

List of Figures

Fig. 1	Location map of catalogue entries.	3
Fig. 2	Medieval parish churches in Norfolk.	2
Fig. 3	Medieval and post-medieval parish churches in Norfolk.	5
Fig. 4	Rate of abandonment of Norfolk parish churches.	6
Fig. 5	Causes of abandonment of Norfolk parish churches.	6
Fig. 6	North Barningham, St Peter: plan.	57
Fig. 7	North Barningham, St Peter: phase plan.	59
Fig. 8	Brandiston, St Nicholas: plan.	62
Fig. 9	Brandiston, St Nicholas: phase plan.	64
Fig. 10	West Harling, All Saints: plan.	67
Fig. 11	West Harling, All Saints: elevation of nave, re-set window.	68
Fig. 12	West Harling, All Saints: phase plan.	70
Fig. 13	Babingley, St Felix: plan.	84
Fig. 14	Babingley, St Felix: phase plan.	87
Fig. 15	Burlingham, St Peter: plan and south elevation.	90
Fig. 16	Burlingham, St Peter: 1. Nave north window. 2. Nave south window. 3. Chancel south window. 4. South porch doorway.	91
Fig. 17	Burlingham, St Peter: phase plan.	92
Fig. 18	Great Hautbois, St Mary: plan.	95
Fig. 19	Great Hautbois, St Mary: phase plan.	97
Fig. 20	Kempstone, St Paul: plan.	98
Fig. 21	Kempstone, St Paul: 1. Chancel south window. 2. Nave south window.	99
Fig. 22	Kempstone, St Paul: nave south wall, double-splayed window.	100
Fig. 23	Kempstone, St Paul: phase plan.	100
Fig. 24	Sco Ruston, St Michael: plan.	103
Fig. 25	Sco Ruston, St Michael: elevations of north and south walls.	104
Fig. 26	Sco Ruston, St Michael, windows.	105
Fig. 27	Sco Ruston, St Michael, doorways and east window.	106
Fig. 28	Sco Ruston, St Michael: phase plan.	107
Fig. 29	Tivetshall, St Mary: plan.	109
Fig. 30	Tivetshall, St Mary: elevation of south wall.	111
Fig. 31	Tivetshall, St Mary: phase plan.	112
Fig. 32	West Raynham, St Margaret: plan.	121
Fig. 33	West Raynham, St Margaret: phase plan.	122
Fig. 34	Saxlingham Thorpe, St Mary: plan.	124
Fig. 35	Saxlingham Thorpe, St Mary: phase plan.	126
Fig. 36	Snarehill: plan.	128
Fig. 37	Snarehill: phase plan.	130
Fig. 38	Panxworth, All saints: elevation of tower; plan including 1847 nave and porch.	141
Fig. 39	Panxworth, All Saints: phase plan.	142
Fig. 40	Burnham Sutton, St Ethelbert: plan, as revealed by excavation in 1985.	146
Fig. 41	Burnham Sutton, St Ethelbert: phase plan.	147
Fig. 42	Weeting, All Saints: plan.	155

Index of Sites

Numbers 1 to 255 refer to the site reports contained within this volume, and located on the map (Fig. 1). The prefix 'N' refers to the Norwich churches listed in Appendix III, the prefix 'A' to the additional churches of Appendix XII (neither group is located on Fig. 1).

133	Alethorpe, All Saints
134	Algarsthorpe, St Mary Magdalen
135	Alpington/Apton, St Martin
35	Appleton, St Mary
65	Antingham, St Margaret
136	Ashby, St Mary
36	Babingley, St Felix
1	Bagthorpe, St Mary
2	Barmer, All Saints
110	Barnham Broom, St Michael
3	Barningham, North, St Peter
137	Barton Bendish, All Saints
4	Barton Bendish, St Mary
138	Barton Turf, B
111	Barwick, St Mary
87	Bastwick, St Peter
66	Bawsey, St James
37	Bayfield, St Margaret
67	Beachamwell, All Saints
88	Beachamwell, St John
112	Beckham, East, St Helen
113	Beckham, West, All Saints
139	Bedingham, St Mary
140	Beeston, St Andrew
68	Bickerston, St Andrew
38	Bircham Tofts, St Andrew
141	Bittering, Great, St Nicholas
142	Blo Norton, St Margaret
A1	Booton, St Michael

39	Bowthorpe, St Michael		43	Hargham, All Saints
143	Bracondale, St Nicholas		173	Harleston
144	Bradcar, St Andrew		174	Harling, Middle, St Andrew
5	Brandiston, St Nicholas		17	Harling, West, All Saints
145	Breccles, Little		44	Hautbois, Great, St Mary
146	Broomsthorpe		175	Hautbois, Little, St Mary
147	Brundall, St Clement		97	Heigham, St Bartholomew
6	Buckenham Ferry, St Nicholas		176	Helmingham, St Mary
69	Buckenham, New, St Mary		177	Hempnall, St Andrew
148	Buckenham, Old, St Andrew		121	Hempton, St Andrew
149	Buckenham Tofts, St Andrew		178	Herringby, St Ethelbert
89	Burgh, St Mary		98	Hindolveston, St George
70	Burgh Parva, St Mary		179	Hockham, Little, St Mary
40	Burlingham, St Peter		18	Hockwold, St Peter
150	Burnham, St Andrew		180	Holm, St Andrew
151	Burnham, St Edmund		181	Holverston, St Mary
114	Burnham Sutton, St Ethelbert		45	Hopton, St Margaret
152	Burnham Thorpe, St Peter		46	Houghton-on-the-Hill, St Mary
90	Caister, West, St Edmund		19	Illington, St Andrew
153	Caldecote, St Mary		182	Irmingland, St Andrew
154	Cantelose, All Saints		47	Islington, St Mary
156	Carbrooke, Little		183	Itteringham, St Nicholas
155	Carleton Rode, B		48	Kempstone, St Paul
115	Carlton, East, St Peter		184	Kenningham
157	Carrow		185	Kenwick, St Thomas
71	Castle Rising		186	Kerdiston, St Mary
158	Choseley		187	Keswick, St Clement
159	Clenchwarton, South		74	Kirby Bedon, St Mary
160	Cockley Cley, St Peter		20	Langford, St Andrew
7	Cockthorpe, All Saints		188	Langhale, St Christopher
116	Colveston, St Mary		189	Langham Parva, St Mary
161	Congham, All Saints		122	Letton, All Saints
162	Congham, St Mary		123	Leziate, All Saints
8	Corpusty, St Peter		190	Lynford
9	Coston, St Michael		124	Lynn, King's, St James
117	Creake, North, St Michael		191	Lynn, North, St Edmund
163	Cressingham, Great, St George		A3	Lynn, West, St Peter I
41	Croxton, St John the Baptist		49	Mannington
10	Crownthorpe, St James		192	Marham, St Andrew
164	Dereham, West, St Peter		193	Markshall, St Edmund
165	Doughton		194	Massingham, Great, All Saints
166	Dunham, Great, St Mary		99	Melton, Great, St Mary
11	Dunton, St Peter		195	Methwold Hythe
167	Dykebeck		75	Mintlyn, St Michael
118	Eccles, St Mary		50	Morton-on-the-Hill, St Margaret
91	Edgefield, SS Peter and Paul		21	Moulton, St Mary
92	Egmere, St Edmund		196	Moulton, Little, All Saints
72	Elmham, North, I		76	Mundham, St Ethelbert
12	Feltwell, St Nicholas		22	Narford, St Mary
168	Fincham, St Michael		197	Nelonde, St Peter
13	Forncett, St Mary		198	Oby
169	Foston, St Peter		199	Ormesby, St Andrew
119	Foulden, St Edmund		200	Ormesby, St Peter
14	Frenze, St Andrew		201	Overstrand, St Martin I
42	Fulmodestone, St Mary		77	Oxborough, St Mary Magdalen
93	Garboldisham, All Saints		51	Oxwick, All Saints
73	Gasthorpe, St Nicholas		202	Palgrave, Little
94	Gillingham, All Saints		100	Panxworth, All Saints
95	Godwick, All Saints		203	Pattesley, St John the Baptist
170	Gowthorpe, St James		125	Pensthorpe
171	Guist Thorpe, All Saints		204	Pickenham, South, St Andrew
15	Gunton, St Andrew		A4	Poringland, East I
120	Hackford, All Saints		205	Poringland, West, St Michael
96	Hainford, All Saints		101	Pudding Norton, St Margaret
16	Hales, St Margaret		126	Quarles
172	Hardwick		23	Rackheath, All Saints

206	Rackheath, Little, Holy Trinity		230	Thetford, Holy Trinity
78	Raynham, West, St Margaret		231	Thetford, St John
102	Ringstead, Great, St Peter		232	Thetford, St Lawrence
52	Ringstead, Little, St Andrew		233	Thetford, St Margaret
103	Rockland, St Andrew		234	Thetford, St Martin
127	Rockland, St Mary, St Margaret		235	Thetford, Great St Mary
53	Roudham, St Andrew		236	Thetford, St Michael
207	Roxham, St Michael		237	Thetford, St Nicholas
24	Rudham, West, St Peter		238	Thetford, Church at Red Castle Site
25	Ruston, East, St Mary		239	Thetford, Church on Site of Gas Works
79	Ryburgh, Little, All Saints		240	Thetford, Church on Site of St Michael's Close
80	Saxlingham Thorpe, St Mary		59	Thorpe-by-Norwich, St Andrew I
208	Saxthorpe, St Dunstan		241	Thorpe-by-Norwich, Old Thorpe Church
54	Sco Ruston, St Michael		242	Thorpeland, St Thomas
209	Scratby, All Saints		106	Thorpe Parva, St Mary
210	Seething, B		130	Thorpland, St Thomas
211	Setchey		30	Thurgarton, All Saints
26	Shimpling, St George		243	Thurketeliart
27	Shingham, St Botolph		60	Tivestshall, St Mary
212	Shipden		244	Topcroft, St Giles
128	Shotesham, St Botolph		A5	Tottenhill
55	Shotesham, St Martin		31	Tottington, St Andrew
213	Shouldham, St Margaret		61	Tunstall, St Peter and St Paul
214	Sidestrand, St Michael		245	Wacton, Little, St Mary
81	Snarehill		107	Wallington, St Margaret
28	Snetterton, All Saints		A2	Walpole, St Andrew
215	Snetterton, St Andrew		62	Walsham, South, St Laurence
104	Snoring, Little		131	Walsingham, Great, All Saints
56	Somerton, East, St Mary		84	Walton, East, St Andrew
57	Southery, St Mary		108	Walton, West
58	Southwood, St Edmund		246	Warham, St Mary the Virgin
29	Stanford, All Saints		247	Waxham, Little, St Margaret
82	Stanninghall		248	Weasenham, St Paul
216	Stiffkey, St John the Baptist		132	Weeting, All Saints
217	Stoke Holy Cross, B		32	West Tofts, St Mary
218	Stratton, St Peter		85	Whitlingham, St Andrew
219	Sturston, Holy Cross		249	Wicklewood, St Andrew
220	Summerfield, All Saints		33	Wiggenhall, St Mary the Virgin
83	Surlingham, St Saviour		63	Wiggenhall, St Peter
221	Swainsthorpe, St Mary		250	Windle, St Andrew
129	Tatterset, St Andrew		251	Winston, St Andrew
105	Testerton, St Remigius		109	Wolterton, St Margaret
222	Thetford, All Saints		86	Wood Norton, St Peter
223	Thetford, St Andrew		252	Worstead, St Andrew
224	Thetford, St Benet		253	Wreningham, Little, St Mary
225	Thetford, St Edmund		64	Wretham, West, St Lawrence
226	Thetford, St Etheldreda		254	Yarmouth, Great, St Benedict
227	Thetford, St George		34	Yarmouth, Great, St George
228	Thetford, St Giles		255	Yarmouth, Southtown
229	Thetford, St Helen			

Acknowledgements

The author wishes to thank the following organisations: the Council for British Archaeology, English Heritage, the Norfolk Archaeological Unit and the Norwich Diocesan Board of Finance; and the following individuals for their help and support: Steven Ashley, Alan Davison, Lt Colonel Haddock, Richard Morris, Andrew Rogerson, Edwin Rose, Peter Wade-Martins, Philip Williams.

Thanks are also due to Philip Williams, who surveyed the churches in Figs 6-14, 17-20, 23, 28, 31-37, 39, 42; Andrew Rogerson and Tom Loader for Figs 15, 16, 21, 22, 24-27, 38; Andrew Rogerson and Stephanie Rickett for Figs 29, 30; Andrew Rogerson and Steven Ashley for Figs 40, 41; and to the illustrators: Hoste Spalding for Fig.1, Sue White for Figs 4, 5; Steven Ashley for Figs 40, 41, and especially to Philip Williams for all the remaining figures. For the plates, thanks belong to the Royal Commission on the Historical Monuments of England for Plates VI, XII, XIX, XXXIII, XXXVIII-XLII, XLIV, XLV, XLVII-XLIX, LI, LIII-LVII, LXI, LXII, LXXIV, LXXVII, LXXVIII, LXXXI, XCV, XCVI, XCIX, CXIV, CXXVII-CXXX; to Derek A. Edwards for Plates III, XIV, XVI, XVIII, XC, CX-XIV; to the Cambridge University Collection of Air Photographs for Plates CXXII, CXXIII, CXXV; and to Hallam Ashley for Plate CXI. David Wicks processed the author's plates. Thanks too to Joy Lodey for typing the original reports, and to Joan Daniells for typing the main text of the volume.

Chapter 1. Introduction

Summary

Over the last thousand years, more than a thousand parish churches have been built in Norfolk. About one third of these are no longer in use, and this volume is a record of those churches, whether redundant, ruined or disappeared.

If this record were to be published in full, it would require several volumes. Therefore, it has been decided to contain it within a single volume by confining most of the site reports to microfiche, whilst retaining summary reports within the main text.

In order to indicate the degree of ruination of each church, the reports are classified in six categories, from Fully Intact (Category I) to Disappeared (Category VI). As a sample, six reports from each category are published in full in the main text.

There is a brief consideration in the Introduction of relevant issues, such as the rate of deterioration of fabrics, the causes of abandonment, the quality of churches and contents, and some tentative recommendations for future management.

The many monastic sites and non-parochial chapels are not included here, nor are the partly ruined parish churches which remain in current use.

I. Purpose of the survey
(Figs. 1, 2, 3, 4, 5; Plates I, II)

This survey was initiated in 1976, at the prompting of the Council for British Archaeology and the Diocese of Norwich, because of the need to assess the extent of abandonment and ruination of parish churches in a large rural county such as Norfolk. Further support was given by the Department of the Environment, who wanted to establish priorities for preservation, and the Royal Commission on the Historical Monuments of England, with its interest in assembling a comprehensive record of these buildings. It was considered that, since the process of decay is continuous, and very little was known about the ruined sites in the county, the survey was necessary primarily as a record of important deteriorating monuments. Later, it was decided to include the fully-standing but disused parish churches, so that the historic context of church abandonment would be fully up-to-date. The reasons for abandoning churches in the past could therefore be considered alongside the causes of church disuse today. It would then be possible to evaluate the rate of decline of the rural parish church in this county, set within its historic context.

The biggest procedural change occurred in 1968, when the *Pastoral Measure* came into force. Whereas before, a disused church may have been simply abandoned and left to deteriorate (although this can still happen today), the *Pastoral Measure* of 1968 made provision for churches no longer needed or used for regular worship to be declared Redundant. There could be three possible outcomes for a redundant church: appropriation for another use, preservation as a monument, or demolition. How this has been applied to Norfolk can be seen in the Recommendations (p.44). This section sets out some recommendations for the future which are purely personal. Nevertheless, it is to be hoped that the survey provides a factual base for future decisions on disused or ruined churches. It must be borne in mind that the survey is frozen in time: all entries are accurate up to December 1987, but the process of decay goes on. However, provision has been made, through the Norfolk Archaeological Unit, to keep the survey updated in the years ahead[1].

II. Range of the survey

Norfolk churches or chapels-of-ease founded in the 19th or 20th centuries have not been included in the survey; but some brief notes on them are contained in Appendix I. Of seventy-nine churches built during this period sixty-eight are still in use, six have been demolished, two converted to houses, one converted to offices, and two are disused[2]. All remaining parish churches in the county are of medieval foundation, with the single exception of St George's at Great Yarmouth. This is only one of seven parish churches built in Norfolk in the two centuries from 1600-1800. Six of them (Yarmouth being the exception) were constructed on the site of medieval predecessors[3]. Out of the seven, only two are no longer in use (Gunton and St George's Yarmouth). A full list of all parish churches founded by 1800, with a breakdown by deanery of those in use and those ruined, is supplied in Appendix II.

At least 928 parish churches existed in Norfolk between the 11th century and the 16th century. Some 620 of these are still in use today, over two-thirds. Of the 308 (or one-third) no longer in use[4], a total of fifty-four are fully intact but redundant, a further 101 are in ruins, and at least 153 have disappeared completely (see Fig. 2). Thus Norfolk possessed more medieval parish churches than any other county, and equally, more ruined and demolished medieval churches than any county. Compare, for example, Essex, which had only 415 parishes prior to 1750, of which thirty-nine are ruined or demolished and a further thirty-six totally rebuilt (Rodwell 1977a). The figures are greater for Suffolk, which possessed some 580 medieval parish churches, of which thirty are redundant, fifteen ruined and about seventy-five have left no trace above ground (figures taken from Cautley and Northeast in Cautley 1982). Not only are the Norfolk figures substantially higher, but the number of churches surviving as ruins (101 in Norfolk, fifteen in Suffolk) demonstrates that the task of caring for the ruined churches of Norfolk is of a different order of magnitude from other counties.

The overall figures for parish churches in Norfolk, including post-medieval churches and chapels-of-ease are set out in Fig. 3. Norfolk therefore becomes the county of 1004 churches, although only 685 are still in use. These statistics embrace the whole county, including Norwich.

However, since the brief for this survey is to report on the churches of Norfolk excluding the city of Norwich[5], there are no entries on the fifty city churches (nineteen redundant, four ruined, twenty-seven disappeared) in the catalogue, but a list is supplied in Appendix III (p.179).Thus the number of catalogue entries in this volume comes to a total of 254 churches[6], of which only two (St George's Yarmouth and Gunton) are post-medieval.

The parochial status of the church is the single criterion for establishing which sites to include and which to leave out. In other words, it has to be reasonably certain that the site is that of a parish church or parochial chapel, with full rights of baptism, marriage and burial. All non-Anglican churches or chapels are excluded. Previous lists of ruined churches in the county have included many chapels of dubious parochial status. On careful examination, they have often been found to be chantry or guild chapels, or to have monastic or private status. Appendix IV (p.180)is a list of such erroneous attributions. Of course, it is not always easy to be certain about the status of a church or chapel demolished many centuries ago; however, it should be noted that the list of ruined churches published by Messent (1931) differs considerably from this volume.

There is a complication with the geographical range of this survey. Both the catalogue and list of sites, as well as the statistical information (Figs 2-5), are based on sites within the county of Norfolk (*i.e.* its present boundaries). Until the late 19th century, the whole county formed part of the diocese of Norwich. However, today the diocese of Norwich does not extend to the three south-western deaneries of Feltwell, Fincham and Lynn Marshland (now in the diocese of Ely)[7]; and the Norwich deanery of Lothingland is almost entirely in Suffolk. None of the Suffolk sites are entered in the catalogue[8], but the figures for the diocese of Norwich, distinct from the county of Norfolk, are noted in Appendix V. Boundaries of dioceses, archdeaconries and deaneries can be followed on the map, Fig. 1. Since the completion of the catalogue, five further sites have come to my notice (see Appendix XII), alas, too late to be included in the catalogue or maps; nevertheless, they have been incorporated into the statistical data of Figs 2-5 and the Appendices.

Diocese	Archdeaconry	Deanery	In use	I	II	III	IV	V	VI	Total	Ruined/Disused as % of total
Norwich	Norwich	Blofield	27	3	4	—	1	—	2	37	27%
		Flegg	23	—	1	—	3	—	8	35	34%
		Ingworth	27	1	2	—	2	—	4	36	25%
		Norwich North	12	—	—	1	—	—	1	14	17%
		Norwich South	4	—	1	—	1	—	2	8	50%
		Norwich East	12	19	1	1	1	2	28	64	81%
		Repps	25	3	—	1	—	—	3	32	19%
		Sparham	24	2	1	1	1	1	3	33	27%
		Tunstead	32	—	1	—	—	—	3	36	11%
		Waxham	15	1	—	—	—	1	1	18	17%
	Norfolk	Depwade	28	1	1	1	—	1	8	40	30%
		Hingham and Mitford	31	1	—	1	—	2	—	35	11%
		Humbleyard	26	1	—	—	1	1	9	38	32%
		Loddon	44	1	—	4	1	1	10	61	28%
		Lothingland (in Norfolk)	1	—	1	—	—	—	—	2	50%
		Redenhall	27	2	1	—	1	—	1	32	16%
		Thetford and Rockland	29	5	3	3	2	—	26	68	57%
	Lynn	Breckland	32	2	1	1	—	2	10	48	33%
		Brisley and Elmham	39	—	2	2	1	—	5	49	20%
		Burnham and Walsingham	36	3	2	1	4	8	7	61	41%
		Heacham and Rising	25	1	4	1	1	1	2	35	29%
		Holt	34	1	1	1	1	2	2	42	19%
		Lynn	22	1	—	3	—	2	6	34	35%
Ely	Wisbech	Feltwell	7	2	—	—	—	1	1	11	36%
		Fincham	24	2	1	1	2	—	9	39	38%
		Lynn Marshland	8	2	2	—	—	—	2	14	43%
		Wisbech (in Norfolk)	4	—	—	—	—	—	—	4	0%
		March (in Norfolk)	1	—	—	—	—	—	—	1	0%
St Edmundsbury and Ipswich	Sudbury	Mildenhall	1	—	—	—	—	—	—	1	0%
Total			620	54	30	23	23	25	153	928	33%

Figure 2. Medieval parish churches in Norfolk.

Diocese	Arch-Deaconry	Deanery	In Use	Disused/Ruined	Total
Norwich	Norwich	Blofield	29	10	39
		Flegg	31	14	45
		Ingworth	29	9	38
		Norwich North	20	2	22
		Norwich South	13	5	18
		Norwich East	18	54	72
		Repps	28	9	37
		Sparham	26	9	35
		Tunstead	32	4	36
		Waxham	15	3	18
	Norfolk	Depwade	30	12	42
		Hingham and Mitford	31	4	35
		Humbleyard	28	14	42
		Loddon	44	17	61
		Lothingland (in Norfolk)	2	1	3
		Redenhall	29	5	34
		Thetford and Rockland	29	39	68
	Lynn	Breckland	32	16	48
		Brisley and Elmham	39	10	49
		Burnham and Rising	38	25	63
		Holt	38	8	46
		Lynn	24	14	38
Ely	Wisbech	Feltwell	8	4	12
		Fincham	28	15	43
		Lynn Marshland	11	6	17
		Wisbech (in Norfolk)	4	—	4
		March (in Norfolk)	1	—	1
		Ely (in Norfolk)	1	—	1
St Edmundsbury and Ipswich	Sudbury	Mildenhall (in Norfolk)	1	—	1
			685	319	1004

Figure 3. Medieval and post-medieval churches in Norfolk.

III. Rate of deterioration

(Fig. 4)
The following statements may seem blindingly obvious, but they need saying for all that: firstly, buildings deteriorate continuously, especially when abandoned; secondly, buildings may decay at a gradual, even rate; or they may collapse more rapidly. The fall of the tower at Hindolveston (Pls I, II) amply illustrates the last point. Nonetheless, the general pattern is one of gradual, continuous decay, as the data of Fig. 4 indicate: the Category I (fully intact) and Category II (largely intact) sites preponderate on the lower part of the graph (more recently abandoned), whilst Category V (fragmentary remains) and Category VI (no above-ground remains) sites tend more to the top (long abandoned). There are some interesting exceptions which will be discussed below.

One factor which greatly affects the durability of an abandoned church is whether an alternative use can be found, usually conversion to a barn, although sometimes towers were kept on as dove-houses. This is clearly shown with some of the Category II, III and IV sites mentioned below. Before proceeding with a breakdown of Fig. 4 category by category, it should be made clear that the categories have been selected according to the quantity of church fabric surviving, and not according to date of abandonment.

Category VI (disappeared)
(Plate III)
It is clear that if there is no trace of the church above ground, the overwhelming probability is that it was abandoned before 1600 A.D. Of 153 Category VI sites, only ten disappeared after 1600. We can be sure that these ten were deliberately demolished. Indeed, we know precisely the fate of seven of them: two were bombed in 1942; three were demolished to build a new church on a different site (two of these were about to fall into the sea); and two were in small villages which possessed two and three churches respectively.

Category V (fragmentary remains)
(Plate IV)
It is most noticeable that the vast majority (seventeen out of a total of twenty-five) from this category date to the 16th century; only one predates these. On the whole, one expects more than fragmentary remains from a post-1600 abandonment. There are seven of the latter, of which six were deliberately demolished, and one was crushed by its tower collapsing.

Category IV (tower)
(Plate V, VI)
There is only one tower surviving from before the 16th century: Little Snoring. The rest of the church appears to have collapsed and been rebuilt on an adjacent site. From that time on there is a fairly even survival rate century by century. It may seem surprising to find as many as eight surviving abandonments as early as the 16th century; one would expect them to have been maintained in some alternative use for a while. In fact, we know that four of those abandoned in the 16th century were being used as barns, and another was used as a dove-house. Leaving all but the tower must always suggest deliberate but careful demolition, and this seems to have been the case in the majority of sites in this category; even the two that were bombed had their towers left as landmarks after the destroyed shells of the churches had been dismantled (Pl.VI).

Category III (substantial ruin)
(Plate VII)
If the 16th century is the period in which we may 'expect' Category V ruins, then the 17th and 18th centuries provide the period in which we might 'expect' Category III ruins. No Category III ruin is found after the 18th century; and those found before the 17th century all owe their survival to their re-use (mainly as barns) after abandonment. Most extraordinarily, there are two which were abandoned as early as the 12th century: North Elmham, which was the parish church of the village from its demotion from cathedral status in the 1070s to the construction of the new parish church in the 1100s, owing its survival to its re-use as part of the bishop's manor (or, as Heywood 1982, argues, its interim rebuilding as a bishop's chapel); and Castle Rising, partly engulfed by the castle bank c. 1150, forming an out-building to the castle for a while, and more recently excavated. A similar conversion took place c. 1240, when St Mary's at New Buckenham became chapel to the castle after the construction of the new parish church, and continued in use as a barn from the 16th century.

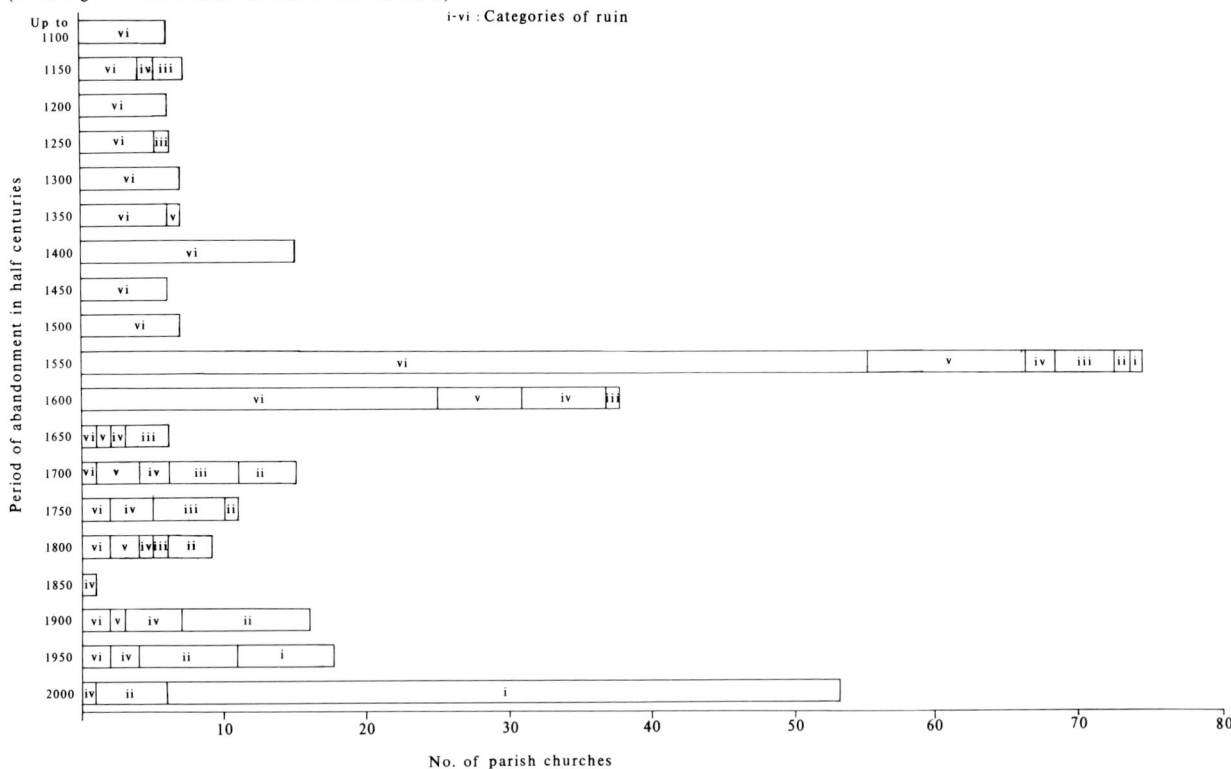

Figure 4. Rate of abandonment of Norfolk parish churches.

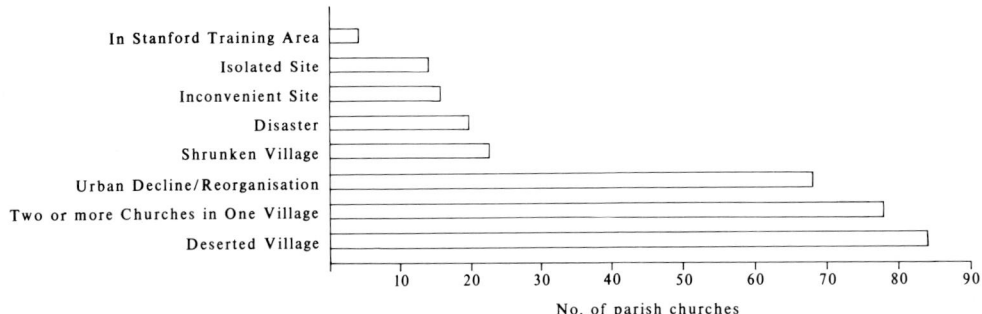

Figure 5. Causes of abandonment of Norfolk parish churches.

Category II (largely intact)
(Plate VIII)
There is no doubt about the golden age of the Category II ruin: from 1850 to the present day. In other words, most churches abandoned over the last hundred years or so, if left to deteriorate naturally, are likely to be in the Category II range (which allows quite a variation in the degree of ruination, as examination of the catalogue will confirm). It is almost certain that the pre-19th century Category II sites have been at some time 'artificially' preserved, either by conversion to barn, or maintained as an attractive monument within a park (*e.g.* Mannington, East Somerton, Appleton, West Wretham, Bayfield). The most remarkable survival is that of Little Ringstead, which was only kept up as a chapel from the second half of the 14th century, and became a barn at the end of the 16th century.

Category I (completely intact)
(Plate IX)
In 1968 we arrive at the age of the Redundant church as a formal category of legal status. Category I churches are all roofed and are mostly kept in good repair; they are therefore free from the spiral of deterioration by which a Category I becomes a Category II, which becomes a Category III and so on. The outstanding anomaly in this Category is St Mary-the-Less in Norwich, abandoned in the first half of the 16th century but given to the French-speaking protestant congregation of the city.

In general, to judge from the Norfolk data, it would seem to take up to 100 years for a church to become a Category II ruin, about 200 to 300 years to become a Category III or IV ruin, some 400 years to become a Category V ruin, and 400 to 500 years will normally suffice to obliterate all trace of the church above ground (Category VI). Although a generalisation, it is surprising how often this 'law' of the rate of deterioration of churches works; and while there are many exceptions to the rule, these often draw attention to special local circumstances ensuring preservation, such as re-use as a barn.

IV. Causes of Abandonment
(Figs. 4, 5; Plates LXXIX-LXXXII)

Abandonment of a church occurs when it ceases to be used for regular worship. It is of course possible for the fabric of the church to be kept up after abandonment, as, for example, when an alternative use is found. The precise date of abandonment is sometimes hard to identify, but the evidence is set out in Appendix X.

The rate of abandonment of parish churches has varied greatly from century to century, as a glance at Fig. 4 will confirm. Until the 16th century, the pattern is fairly steady, with an abandonment rate of about seven for every half-century. It may be significant that the exception is the half-century 1350-1400, which, with fifteen abandonments, is twice the 'norm'. This is probably an effect of the recurrent pestilences of that century; a proportion of them might have been caused by the Black Death, but only three of them can be unequivocally attributed to that notorious plague of 1349.

There can be little doubt that the 16th century was a period of dramatic change, not least of all for the history of the parish church. That century saw the demise of 112 of them throughout the county. The vast majority of such closures were a result of the ecclesiastical reorganisation associated with the Reformation. In particular, the Act of 1535/6 permitting the consolidation of parishes had a profound impact on a county with such a multiplicity of churches as Norfolk, since it allowed adjacent parishes to be united and one church abandoned, provided that the churches were less than a mile apart and one of the churches valued at less than £6 a year. This led to the abandonment of the poorer church in many of the Norfolk villages in possession of two parish churches, and the amalgamation of parishes in the towns of Norwich, Thetford and Lynn. The 16th century was also a period of economic change, which led to further depopulation and desertion of villages in some areas, and the concomitant growth of towns. Village desertion almost invariably resulted in the abandonment of parish churches in Norfolk. Of course, many of the churches abandoned after 1536 stood in villages which may have begun to decline in the 14th century.

The same processes continued at a very much slower rate in the 17th and 18th centuries. By the first half of the 19th century, church abandonments had all but ceased. A sizeable increase occurred in the second half of the 19th century, although it should be noted that twelve of the seventeen abandonments in that half-century were due to a new church being built on a more convenient site, often incorporating material from the old church.

This century looks like being as dramatic for the history of the parish church as was the 16th century; there have already been seventy-one abandonments of churches founded before 1800, and a further eleven amongst those founded since 1800. We are witnessing a half-century of far-reaching parochial reorganisation, with many parishes already amalgamated, with team ministries serving wide groups of parishes, and with one full-time minister to four or more parishes being quite commonplace. Village depopulation is still an important factor; for whereas towns and large villages continue to grow, small villages are still declining. It seems likely that, given that these conditions will continue, the rate of abandonment of the second half of the 20th century may continue for another fifty or so years to come.

Underlying historic factors need to be borne in mind when we come to examine the causes of abandonment in more detail. Fig. 5 represents an attempt to identify specific causes. Clearly, depopulation, with the resultant desertion of villages, has been one of the more important causes, along with a problem more specific to Norfolk, that of villages having more places of worship than could reasonably be kept up. Before going through the eight causes of abandonment represented in Fig. 5, it is important to make clear that there is usually more than one cause which leads to the closure of a church. Take, for example, Burlingham St Peter (Pls LXXIX-LXXXII)): the diminution of village population, the collapse of the tower, and the existence of a second parish church in the same village, were all factors leading to its abandonment. In other words, Fig. 5 gives an indication of principal causes, and the list assigning a specific church to a principal cause of abandonment can be found in Appendix XI.

Stanford Training Area: Four sites
(Plate LXXI)
Four churches ceased to function in 1942, when a large part of the Breckland including the villages of Stanford, Tottington and West Tofts were evacuated to make way

for an army training area. The villagers have never been allowed to return. In recent years considerable effort has been made to keep the churches in reasonable condition, but their future is uncertain.

Isolated Site: Fourteen sites
(Plates X, LXIII, LXIV)
Hales, that paradigm of the Norman parish church in Norfolk, has been vested in the Redundant Churches Fund since 1974. The village of Hales is far from being in decline, and would normally be able to support its parish church with ease; the village, however, is a good 1.5km from the church which stands in total isolation. Faced with the same problem 100 years ago, the church at Southwood is now a ruin (Pls LXIII, LXIV); in fact, the villagers found that the neighbouring church at Limpenhoe was actually nearer than their own parish church.

It is paradoxical that, in the age of the motor-car, distances as small as 1.5km should be such a problem; but then it is just as easy to drive 2km to the larger neighbouring church and enjoy the fellowship of a larger congregation. Of the fourteen churches for which isolation is the principal cause of abandonment, twelve were declared Redundant this century; and in Norfolk there are many isolated churches in current, if sporadic, use. But for how much longer?

Inconvenient site: Sixteen sites
(Plate XI)
When W.H.Marcon became rector of Edgefield in 1875, he found that all was not well. The parish church of SS Peter and Paul stood isolated a good half-mile from the centre of the village, and needed substantial repairs. Marcon himself described it thus: 'Its broken and moss-covered walls, its miserable seating, its chancel arch with a threatening bend in it, its wretched altar old and stained, its font with its Early English bowl remaining, without pedestal or footpace, were enough to try the stoutest heart'. (NCT 'Edgefield'). Rather than carry out expensive repairs and ask the people to continue to make a journey to the church, Marcon decided it would be better to take the church to the people. He therefore set out energetically raising funds, and in 1884 had most of the old church dismantled and re-erected as a new church nearer the centre of the village. This was a peculiarly late-19th century solution to the problem of the isolated church; the 20th century solution is rather different (see above). 'Church moving' became a minor craze between 1850 and 1900, with eleven of the sixteen entries in this section being moved at that time. An even more cunning solution was found at Croxton and Fulmodestone in 1881, where neighbouring isolated churches were both abandoned and a single new church built half-way between the two. An identical proposal had previously been made for Southwood and Limpenhoe, but had been rejected by the parishioners in 1874.

Not all 'church moving' was prompted by the isolation of the site. Sidestrand church was moved because it was perched on a rapidly eroding cliff and in danger of falling into the sea; the site of the old church, dismantled and moved further inland in 1880, was indeed engulfed by the sea twenty-six years later. The churches of Harleston and Thorpe St Andrew were moved because they were too small. In the case of Harleston, the site was so cramped that further expansion was indeed impossible. Thorpe St Andrew, an attractive but small rural medieval church had found itself, by the second half of the 19th century, engulfed by one of the most rapidly expanding suburbs of Norwich; it would have been very difficult to enlarge the church without destroying much of the original fabric, and so a vast new church was built at the northern end of the churchyard, and the old church left to decay as a picturesque ruin.

Perhaps the oddest case is that of Southery (Pl.XI), where a small medieval church, enlarged in 1828, was abandoned in 1858 and replaced by a church of more or less the same size, a mere 200m away. One of the reasons given is that the then rector was very keen to buy the land between the Rectory and the church for 'access'; this had not proved possible, and so he had a new church built on a site which did give access. However, one suspects that the underlying reason for the abandonment of the old church lies elsewhere: that its design no longer fulfilled the ecclesiological aspirations of the rector and the congregation. Much had changed in the field of church design in the thirty years since the enlargement of the old church in 1828; since then, with its short chancel and boxy nave with gallery, the old church no doubt resembled a modern non-conformist chapel rather than a medieval parish church. It was probably considered impractical to restore the old church to its earlier medieval form: better to start again, with a new 'medieval' design. Occasionally churches are abandoned for very odd reasons.

Disaster: Twenty sites
(Plates I, II, XIII)
Sometimes the abandonment of a church was abrupt. South Clenchwarton, Eccles, Keswick (near Bacton), North Lynn, West Lynn, Overstrand and Shipden, were all washed away to sea after violent storms. It is interesting to reflect that these seven churches are the only ones in the whole county for which a *single* reason is sufficient to explain their abandonment. Whilst the remaining thirteen churches in this section have never been in use since the day of their disastrous demise, none were completely destroyed; it would theoretically have been possible to salvage and rebuild. Certainly the outer shells of St Julian's and St Benedict's at Norwich and St Bartholomew's at Heigham survived the Norwich 'blitz' of 1942, but only St Julian's was rebuilt (the other two have been demolished apart from their towers); the two other bombed churches in Norwich were St Paul's and St Michael's at Thorn, of which no trace of their site remains.

Structural failure put paid to only three churches, illustrated most dramatically by Hindolveston (Pls I, II), but was a contributory factor in the abandonment of many more (*e.g.* North Burlingham, Feltwell, South Walsham, Whitlingham). It is worth noting that the ruins of Hindolveston were incorporated into a new church built nearer the centre of the village. Fire destroyed a further five churches, but only that at Hopton was replaced by a new church on a new site. It is a particular irony that in 1734 the church at Roudham was being put into good repair after years of neglect, when, as the 'workmen were repairing the lead on the top of the tower, one of them blew the ashes carelessly out of his pipe, which fell on the thatch, and not being seen in time burned the church and the chancel, so that the walls only are standing, in a ruinous condition, at this time'. (Blomefield 1805-10, I, 432). The parishioners, very few in number, had been struggling for many years to keep the church going until this calamity; they had recently sold one of the church bells to help pay for vital repairs; the burning of the thatch roof was literally the last straw (Pl.XIII).

So far this century, there have been no churches destroyed by urban riot. The same cannot be said of the turbulent 13th century, when the cauldron of discontent between the citizens of Norwich and the monks of the cathedral priory finally boiled over. In June 1272 a mob laid siege to the priory and set fire to it, in the course of which the church of St Ethelbert was destroyed. It is the only church in the county known to have been abandoned because of destruction by riot.

Shrunken village: Twenty-three sites
(Plate XIV)

The relationship of the church to the shrunken village varies from place to place: it could be a small cluster of houses around the church as at Frenze or Islington, or a more isolated church with a tiny scattering of houses across the parish as at Buckenham Ferry. Whatever the situation, these are churches set within villages that are too small to support their church materially, spiritually, or both. They represent a continuation of the pattern of rural decline which will be dealt with in more detail in the section on Deserted Villages (p.11). As an indication of the level of population within these shrunken villages, Bagthorpe and Barmer together can only muster forty-five souls, Brandiston seventy-two, Cockthorpe thirty-four, Coston twenty-four and Frenze 126 (1982 figures). Parishes with populations of less than fifty are in greatest danger (there are twenty-two such parishes whose churches still remain in use), and even populations of over 100 can be insufficient to support a church. Of course, much depends on local circumstances. A very small parish can be kept going by a generous benefactor or enthusiastic parishioners. Other parishes may find their parishioners attending a neighbouring church, either out of convenience or preference. This can cut both ways; for example, Salle has one of the tiniest villages, and a parish population totalling eighty, very few of whom regularly attend church; however, the church is kept 'in business' by a group which drives out from neighbouring Reepham, preferring the unchanging 1662 service which they unfailingly receive at Salle.

It is significant that twenty of the twenty-three churches in this section were abandoned this century. The process is likely to continue, unless there is a reverse in demographic trends. For the parishes in which the population continues to decline, the eventual abandonment of the church is almost inevitable.

Urban decline/reorganisation: Sixty-nine sites
(Plate XV)

Excluding the Norwich sites already referred to, this section comprises a further forty-seven Norwich (and suburbs) sites, nineteen sites from Thetford, one from King's Lynn and two from Yarmouth. With its nine parish churches in the Middle Ages, it is tempting to classify the Burnhams as a town, but it really cannot be characterised as urban in the sense of Norwich, Yarmouth or Lynn.

Since the 11th century Norwich has possessed an exceptionally large number of parish churches, exceeded only by London throughout the Middle Ages. There were already between forty-nine and fifty-four churches and chapels at the time of *Domesday* (of which two were demolished to make way for the new cathedral and precinct), and about sixty parish churches by c. 1200 (Tanner 1984, 3). Cities are always changing, expanding in some areas and declining in others. In Norwich, it appears that the Conesford area was in decline by the late 13th century, when the parish church of St John Conesford was abandoned and replaced by a tavern (Hudson 1908-10, 104). Also in the 13th century, St John the Baptist (Colegate) was absorbed into the Dominican Friary, and St Ethelbert's was destroyed during the Tombland riot. Several other churches went during the 14th century, including St Christopher's, St Edward's, St Anne's, St Olave's Conesford, and St Michael's Conesford (the latter absorbed into the Augustinian Friary). Some parishes were seriously depopulated by the Black Death of 1348-9, including St Winwaloy's, St Margaret's at Newbridge and St Matthew's.

Whilst there was a certain shrinkage of the overall numbers of parish churches, there was also a great deal of rebuilding; indeed, almost every parish church in the city was rebuilt on a larger scale between the 14th and early 16th centuries (Tanner 1984, 4). Of the parishes that had amalgamated before the 16th century, most dispensed with one of their churches after the Act of 1535/6 (p. 7), reducing the total by a further eleven. From the 16th to the 20th century, the pattern remained very stable; St Peter's Southgate was the sole abandonment, demolished in 1887. The first half of the 20th century witnessed the first parish church being made redundant and reused as an ecclesiastical museum: St Peter Hungate in 1932; and four churches were bombed in 1942. The most dramatic changes have occurred since 1950, since when no fewer than twenty parish churches have been made Redundant. This has been largely due to the fundamental changes in living patterns over the last 100 years; before then, most inhabitants of Norwich lived within or near the city walls; now, only a small percentage live within this area, most now inhabiting the suburbs. As a consequence, the ten parish churches remaining in use within the area of the old city are more than adequate for parochial needs.

Whereas reorganisation is the term which most happily applies to the history of the parish church in Norwich, decline is the word which most readily springs to mind with Thetford. Out of a total of twenty-two medieval parish churches, only three remain today; the remaining nineteen have been all but obliterated. From a population of about 4,500 in the 11th century, the town's diminishing prosperity resulted in a population of about 1,500 by the 16th century (Crosby 1986, 49), and the history of its parish churches is a small catalogue of closure. Great St Mary's became the new cathedral in the 1070s; St George's, St Martin's and the church excavated at St Michael's close had all gone out of use by the end of the 12th century; St Benet's, St John's and St Margaret's by the end of the 13th century; St Helen's and All Saints by the end of the 14th century; St Lawrence's, St Edmund's, St Michael's and St Giles' by the end of the 15th century; and four in the 16th century, St Andrew's, St Etheldreda's, St Nicholas's and Holy Trinity. Although the town has expanded greatly since 1958, the three surviving parish churches seem sufficient for present day needs.

It is extraordinary to compare the history of the parish church in towns of Saxon foundation such as Norwich and Thetford, and the Norman creations of Yarmouth and Lynn. Both the latter had but one parish church each, founded by the first Bishop of Norwich,

Herbert de Losinga. Bishop's Lynn (called King's Lynn since 1536) was the creation of de Losinga north of the already existing village of South Lynn; he founded the church of St Margaret in the late 11th century, which he placed under the control of the priory of Norwich. With the expansion of the town, de Losinga's successor, Eborard (1121-45), built a new church (St James) in the eastern part of the town; although on the same scale as St Margaret's, the new structure was not given the status of a parish church in its own right, but was made a parochial chapel dependent on St Margaret's. As Lynn continued to grow, another parochial chapel, dedicated to St Nicholas, was built in the 'Newland' north of St Margaret's, by Eborard's successor, Turbe (1146-74). Thus King's Lynn (excluding South Lynn), because of the bishops' control of the parochial development of the town, possessed but one parish church and two parochial chapels right up to the 19th century. The town has therefore, unlike Norwich, not suffered from a superfluity of churches; indeed, the only loss has been that of the chapel of St James, abandoned in the 16th century[9].

The same degree of parochial control was exercised by the bishops of Norwich at Yarmouth. It was again de Losinga who founded, soon after 1100, the sole parish church of the town[10]. As Yarmouth grew, so the parish church of St Nicholas grew with it, until it became the largest parish church in the country. Unlike Lynn, Yarmouth had to wait until 1714 before gaining its first parochial chapel (St George's). It is ironical that, because of the many new parish churches founded in Yarmouth in the 19th century, St George's found itself devoid of parishioners and was declared Redundant in 1971.

Villages with two or more churches: Seventy-nine sites
(Plates XVI-XIX)
When one considers the great number of medieval villages in Norfolk, it is not surprising that there are also a great number of medieval parish churches. However, it is much harder to explain why so many villages were at one time in possession of more than one parish church. Density of settlement must be one reason: some were large sprawling villages, such as Beachamwell, with its three churches (Davison 1988), or the Burnhams with their nine parish churches (four survive today). Others appear to have been subdivided from a single earlier parish *e.g.* South Walsham; and some resulted from later expansion or replanning *e.g.* the Marshland parishes (Terringtons, Tilneys etc.), or New Buckenham. Patterns of manorial holding and the possession of churches no doubt hold equally important clues. Dymond (1985, 82) has pointed out that the provision of villages with more than one church 'seems to be the rural equivalent of the numerous closely spaced churches which appeared in Late Saxon towns, such as Thetford and Norwich'.

There are twenty-six entries of more than one church recorded by *Domesday Book*. Of these, sixteen are simply entered as 'two churches', with the rest having the two churches appearing under separate entries (three churches in the cases of Barsham and Burlingham)[11]. It seems therefore possible to argue, like Dymond, that 'the provision of multiple churches was common before the Norman Conquest' (Dymond 1985, 82). Whilst it is possible to agree with this in principle, the figures supplied by *Domesday* do present a few problems. Many of the 'two church' entries refer to churches which are actually quite a distance apart, as much as 3km in the case of the Tuddenhams (now North Tuddenham and East Tuddenham) and the Wheatacres (now Wheatacre and Burgh St Peter). Some were churches with a subsidiary parochial chapel, as with Tivetshall (St Mary and St Margaret), Worstead (St Mary and St Andrew), Wroxham (whose chapel of Salhouse became a parish in its own right) and Hethersett (with its chapel at Cantelose, 2km away). Others belong to subdivided villages: Barsham (East, North and West), Burlingham (North and South), Cressingham (Great and Little), Langham (Episcopi and Parva), Rudham (East and West), Tuddenham (East and North), Waxham (Great and Little). Some of the remaining examples have become villages with different names: Foulsham (and Themelthorpe), Helmingham (and Morton-on-the-Hill), Stoke Ferry (and Wretton). There are still two churches at Hoveton (1.4km apart), and there are remains of a second church at East Carlton and Tattersett; and there certainly used to be a second church at Hempnall, Shouldham, and Shotesham (indeed, by the 13th century Shotesham possessed four churches). Having sifted through all these, we are left with four churches for which the *Domesday Book* is virtually the only evidence for the village possessing a second church: Barton Turf, Carleton Rode, Seething and Stoke Holy Cross (although the last three all possessed chapels later on, which may have been the same as the churches recorded in *Domesday*). Of these *Domesday* double-churched villages, East Carlton is the only example to have had both churches in the same churchyard.

During the medieval period, East Carlton was one of twelve Norfolk villages to have had two churches in one churchyard. Standing remains of the second church can also be found at Antingham (Pl.XVII), Barnham Broom, Great Melton (Pl.XVIII), Rockland St Mary and South Walsham, whilst at Reepham the two churches are still in use (Pls XVI, XIX), and remains of a third church can be found in the churchyard. We have to rely on documentary evidence for two churches in one churchyard at Bedingham, Blo Norton, West Dereham, Stiffkey and Wicklewood. Others had practically adjoining churchyards, such as Gillingham and Shotesham St Martin[12].

An extract from the Calendar of Papal Letters[13], referring to St Margaret's church at Blo Norton, makes it clear why so many of these churches have been abandoned:

'1401 Confirmation at the recent petition of Robert de Brome, patron, and all the parishioners of St Margaret, Norton, in the diocese of Norwich, of the union and consolidation of their church made by Bishop Henry. Exemplification is given of the bishop's letter *Univ. Sancte etc. Suggestion delectorum filiorum*, which, dated at Norwich 13 May 1394, the 25th year of his consecration, relates the statement made by the above Robert de Brome, patron of St Margaret's Norton in the deanery of Rokelonde, and all the parishioners to the effect that lately the church was able to support its burdens, but that now, by reason of pestilences and mortalities, barrenness of lands, ruin of buildings, the malice of the times, and especially the fewness and poverty of the parishioners, it is too poor to maintain a priest of its own, that the repair and building of the nave pertains to them, that the church is so ruined in roof and wall that it almostly daily threatens to fall, and their means are unequal to such repair and building; and that in the cemetery of St Margaret's is another church of St Andrew, very near and almost contiguous, and very easy of access. At their petition the Bishop, having found the above to be true from an enquiry made by Master Henry Welle his corrector, unites and consolidates St Margaret's to St Andrew's, the same to take effect on the violence [?] of the former, and the two to be held as a single benefice by a single rector.'

Blo Norton is one of the earlier of such abandonments, which became particularly common in the 16th century.

Tom Martin, Blomefield's contemporary, was able personally to witness to his disgust, the demolition of one of these 'superfluous' churches. The village of Gillingham was one of very few to retain two churches in adjacent churchyards, when Martin went to view them in 1748. To his horror, All Saints was at that very moment being dismantled:

> 'If the sight of so mean a fabrick being demolish'd, could give me the uneasy thoughts, this has done. Good God, what could bear to see the noble structures of our monasteries [sic] laid level with the ground, considering their pious founders intentions, their exquisite and costly buildings, sumptuous monuments, rich vestments, invaluable plate, books etc.etc... The church was desecrated in 1748. The battlements of the steeple, the whole porch, the roof of the church and the chancel, the east gable, are pull'd down, all the windows beaten out so that only the base walls (in a shatter'd condition) are now remaining and are likewise threatened'. (Martin 1771, II, 155).

At the time when Martin was writing, there were only two remaining villages with two churches in one churchyard: St Mary and St Lawrence at South Walsham continued in use until 1890, and St Mary and St Michael at Reepham remain in use to this day (although only St Mary's is used for services, St Michael's being effectively used as a church hall/Sunday School). Reepham is remarkable not only in possessing three churches in one churchyard (All Saints was destroyed by fire in 1543), but also in having each church belonging to a separately named parish *i.e.* Reepham, Hackford and Whitwell (not Reepham All Saints, Reepham St Mary and Reepham St Michael); indeed, Whitwell church stands within the parish of Hackford, linked to its own parish 200m to the south by a finger of land 3m wide. This serves to illustrate that the boundaries of multiple-churched villages can be very complex, as can their parochial history (Pl. XIX).

The majority of villages with more than one church did not have churches in the same or adjacent churchyards. Most were like Langham Parva, whose church stood just 300m west of the church of Langham Episcopi, or like Guist Thorpe, whose church was 1km away from the church of Guist St Andrew. Many such villages abandoned their second church in the 16th century, taking advantage of the new Act permitting consolidation of parishes; thus the church at Guist Thorpe was abandoned in 1551: the 1552 Inventory of Church Goods records:

> 'the churchwardens certify thatt there were ij Chyrches in Gests and on' paryche and on paturne and on person and both Chyrches in grett decae. In concederacyon whereof the paturne and person Sir Roger Tounesend wyth the consent of the Inhabitantes there hath unyd on' Chyrche to Repare the other the ij daye of October laste paste' (Walters 1941, 13).

Using one church to repair the other was a common solution to the problem of maintaining two churches from pre-Reformation times to the end of the 18th century.

Deserted village: Eighty-four sites
(Figs. 1, 2, 4; Plate XX)

The most common cause of church abandonment is the desertion of the village in which the church stands: a parish church needs to have parishioners. The 14th and 15th centuries were a period of general depopulation in Norfolk; and from the 16th century to the present day there have been many local areas of depopulation.

It is commonly assumed that many villages were deserted and churches abandoned because of the Black Death in 1349. However, whilst it is true that the Black Death, and other plagues, were an important cause of depopulation in the later Middle Ages, very few villages were entirely deserted as a result. A probable exception is Little Ringstead, where the village appears to have been abruptly deserted between 1332 and 1352 (Allison 1955, 130); it is possible that the church continued, reduced in size and status, as a chapel until the 16th century (thereby indicating that churches need not necessarily be abandoned after village desertion). Several Norwich parishes were also abandoned at the time of the Black Death, including St Winwaloy and St Margaret at Newbridge; St Matthew's parish was so depleted by plague that it was left to ruin soon after, the remaining parishioners attending St Martin at Palace[14]. A glance at Fig. 4, showing a doubling of the number of churches abandoned between 1350 and 1400, compared to the half-centuries either side of it, suggests that the misfortunes of the 14th century, including the ravages of pestilence, but especially the series of poor harvests (largely due to worsening climatic conditions), were a notable cause of village desertion and church abandonment. In some cases the effects were delayed for more than a century; it is recognised that 'the 14th and 15th centuries were the main period of village decline' (Cushion *et al.* 1982, 40).

Underlying economic change caused the desertion of far more villages (and concomitant abandonment of churches) than did a pestilence such as the Black Death. Godwick, a village already poor in the 14th century, declined further during the 15th and 16th centuries. As depopulation continued, there was 'a parallel progression of enclosure and acquisition of holdings' (Cushion *et al.* 1982, 67). As sheep farming became more profitable from the 14th to the 16th century, so there was ever-increasing demand for grazing land. The problem was not so much that arable land was being converted to sheep pasture (although Choseley may be an exception: Allison 1955, 133); the main difficulties came as a result of the overstocking or enclosing of common land. With certain aggressive landlords, this could lead to a loss of livelihood for poorer tenants. Particularly unscrupulous landlords might even evict tenants and demolish their houses to make way for sheep pasture, as at Bawsey, Leziate, Mintlyn and Sturston in the second half of the 16th century (Allison 1955, 136-7). Some were more stealthy, gradually acquiring more and more land until the whole village was owned by one landlord. The new estates might then be depopulated, as at Hargham (1681-1708), Stanninghall and West Wretham. Davison (Cushion *et al.*

1982, 54-59) has carefully documented the decline and depopulation of the village of Roudham in the 17th and 18th centuries, combined with the buying-in of tenants' lands by the lord.

Sometimes the village was moved to make way for the landlord's park, and the church allowed to fall into ruin, as at Wolterton in the 1740s and at West Wretham in the 1790s. In 1793 a Faculty was obtained to abandon West Wretham church; the Bond (N.R.O. FCB4,7,5) records that William Colhoun owned all the houses in the village, that he intended to pull all of them down for the 'improvement of his estate' and to rehouse the parishioners in East Wretham; therefore, since West Wretham would be devoid of parishioners, it made sense to abandon the church, especially since East Wretham church was 'large enough to contain both parishes'; Colhoun offered a further bribe of £300 for the upkeep of East Wretham church if the diocese should accede to his offer (which it did). However, unscrupulous behaviour does not always pay off: owing to the destruction of the nave and chancel of Wolterton church by the Walpoles in the 1740s, along with the sale of tombstones, legend has it that the ghost of one of the ladies of the Scammler family, whose tombs were in the chancel, haunts the church ruins, searching for the remains of her relations; former Earls of Orford, at their burial, were driven three times round the ruins before being buried at neighbouring Wickmere, with a view to placating this troubled spirit. An even worse fate befell Judge Gawdy of Wallington Hall, who cleared his estate of tenants and had the church demolished (apart from the tower) in the late 16th century. Blomefield (1805-10, VII, 412) tells with relish how, after Gawdy had died in London in 1606,

> 'and having made his appropriate parish church a hay-house, or a dog-kennel, his dead corps being brought from London to Wallington, could for many days find no place of burial, but growing very offensive, he was at last conveyed to Runcton, and buried there without any ceremony, and lyeth yet uncovered with so small a matter as a few paving stones'.

Whilst it is clear that unscrupulous landlords (at risk to their souls!) could be responsible for the desertion of villages and abandonment of churches, it is equally evident that some parts of the county were more prone to village desertion than others. This indicates that long-term economic and demographic change had a more profound impact on parish life than a number of ruthless individual landlords. Fig. 1 shows that there are more abandoned churches in west and south-west Norfolk than in other parts. Looking at the figures in more detail in Fig. 2, it can be seen that, on average, each deanery has lost 33% of its churches; however, this figure includes the towns of Norwich and Thetford, with a combined loss of seventy-four urban churches; if the figures for these urban areas are removed, we are left with an average loss of 27% in the rural deaneries. The deaneries with a below-average percentage of abandonments are in the north-east (Holt and Repps at 19%, Tunstead at 11%, Waxham at 17%), in mid-Norfolk (Brisley and Elmham at 20%, Hingham and Mitford at 11%), and the extreme south (Redenhall at 16%). Those with an average percentage are largely in the eastern half of the county (Blofield at 27%, Ingworth at 25%, Sparham at 27%, Depwade at 30%, Loddon at 28%), and an outlier in the north-west (Heacham and Rising at 29%). The areas with the greatest percentage of abandoned churches are in the south-west, mainly the Breckland, Marshland and Fen-edge deaneries (Thetford and Rockland at 57% (44% excluding Thetford), Breckland at 33%, Lynn at 35%, Lynn Marshland at 43%, Fincham at 38%, Feltwell at 36%), with further areas in the north (Burnham and Walsingham at 41%), in the south (Humbleyard at 32%) and in the east (Flegg at 34%). It is highly significant that the areas with the greatest percentage of church abandonment are the same as the areas with the greatest number of deserted villages, as shown in Allison's figures (1955, 125): the hundreds of Grimshoe and South Greenhoe, corresponding to the deaneries of Fincham and Breckland, have the highest percentage of deserted villages; whereas there are hardly any deserted villages in north-east Norfolk. Allison (1955, 138) has pointed out that the areas with most deserted villages are those with the lighter, more marginal soils in the west and south-west of the county. Poorer areas such as the Breckland may have been too intensively colonized at an earlier date. The 'thinning-out' process may have been a factor in other, densely settled areas, such as Flegg, Humbleyard, and Burnham and Walsingham.

The growth of the towns, especially Norwich, Yarmouth and Lynn has been a further factor in the depopulation and desertion of villages. The vast majority of new inhabitants in these growing towns came from the villages of Norfolk (a process which continues to this day). The success of the three main towns may partly explain the high percentage of abandonment in some of the neighbouring deaneries (Flegg, Lynn, Humbleyard). It may also explain the apparent ring of deserted villages and abandoned churches around some of the towns: Bowthorpe, Stanninghall, Beeston St Andrew, Whitlingham and Markshall around Norwich; Babingley, Appleton, Bawsey, Leziate, Mintlyn, Hardwick and Setchey around Lynn; and it might help to explain why so large a number of deserted villages surround Fakenham (although only a small town), such as Pudding Norton, Testerton, Little Ryburgh, Pensthorpe, Alethorpe, Thorpland and Hempton.

Plate I. Hindolveston church by Ladbrooke (1832).

Plate II. Hindolveston, St George: an ill-fated church: the south aisle burned down after being struck by lightning in 1804; then in 1892 half of the tower collapsed and demolished the nave. All photos by the author unless credited otherwise.

Plate III. Itteringham, St Nicholas: a Category VI site, with no above-ground remains; cropmarks revealed by aerial photographs in 1986. South of the apsidal church is the rectangular outline of a late medieval manorial hall. Norfolk Archaeological Unit TG 1530/A/DB M8.

Plate IV. Quarles church: a Category V ruin, showing low walling belonging to the west end of the church.

Plate V. Wallington, St Margaret: a Category IV ruin. Judge Gawdy emparked the village and turned the church into a barn in 1589. When he died, he could not be buried in the church or churchyard since he had profaned them. He was therefore buried without ceremony in a neighbouring parish.

Plate VI. Heigham, St Bartholomew: bombed in 1942, the rest was demolished, apart from the tower, after 1951. BB52/214 copyright Royal Commission on Historical Monuments (England).

Plate VII. Castle Rising, church in the castle bailey: a Category III ruin, this served as the parish church until the construction of the castle in the middle of the 12th century. Along with the castle, it is now in the care of English Heritage. Norfolk Archaeological Unit 1980 TF6624/AE/APE4.

Plate VIII. Appleton, St Mary: a Category II ruin, with the walls mostly standing to full height; 14th-century south arcade of the church. St Mary's was abandoned towards the end of the 17th century.

Plate IX. Moulton St Mary: a completely intact Category I, in the care of the Redundant Churches Fund since 1980. It contains superb wall paintings, monuments and furnishings. The village is over 1km away.

Plate X. Barmer, All Saints: an isolated site on a hill above the tiny village. The church has been in the care of the Norfolk Churches Trust since 1977.

Plate XI. Southery church by Ladbrooke (1832). This was replaced in 1858 by a church only 200m away but in a more 'convenient' location, *i.e.* next door to the Rectory.

Plate XII. Eccles-next-the-Sea, St Mary: the distinctly curved masonry of the round tower exposed after a storm. Most of the village was engulfed by the sea in 1604, leaving only the church tower; the latter fell after a storm in 1895. Copy print held in Sites and Monuments Record, Norfolk Archaeological Unit.

Plate XIII. Roudham, St Andrew: a workman repairing the tower in 1734 carelessly blew the ashes out of his pipe, which set fire to the thatched roof of the church. It has remained a disused ruin ever since.

Plate XIV. Islington, St Mary: an abandoned church in a shrunken village. Norfolk Archaeological Unit 1983 TF 5716/A/ATS 12.

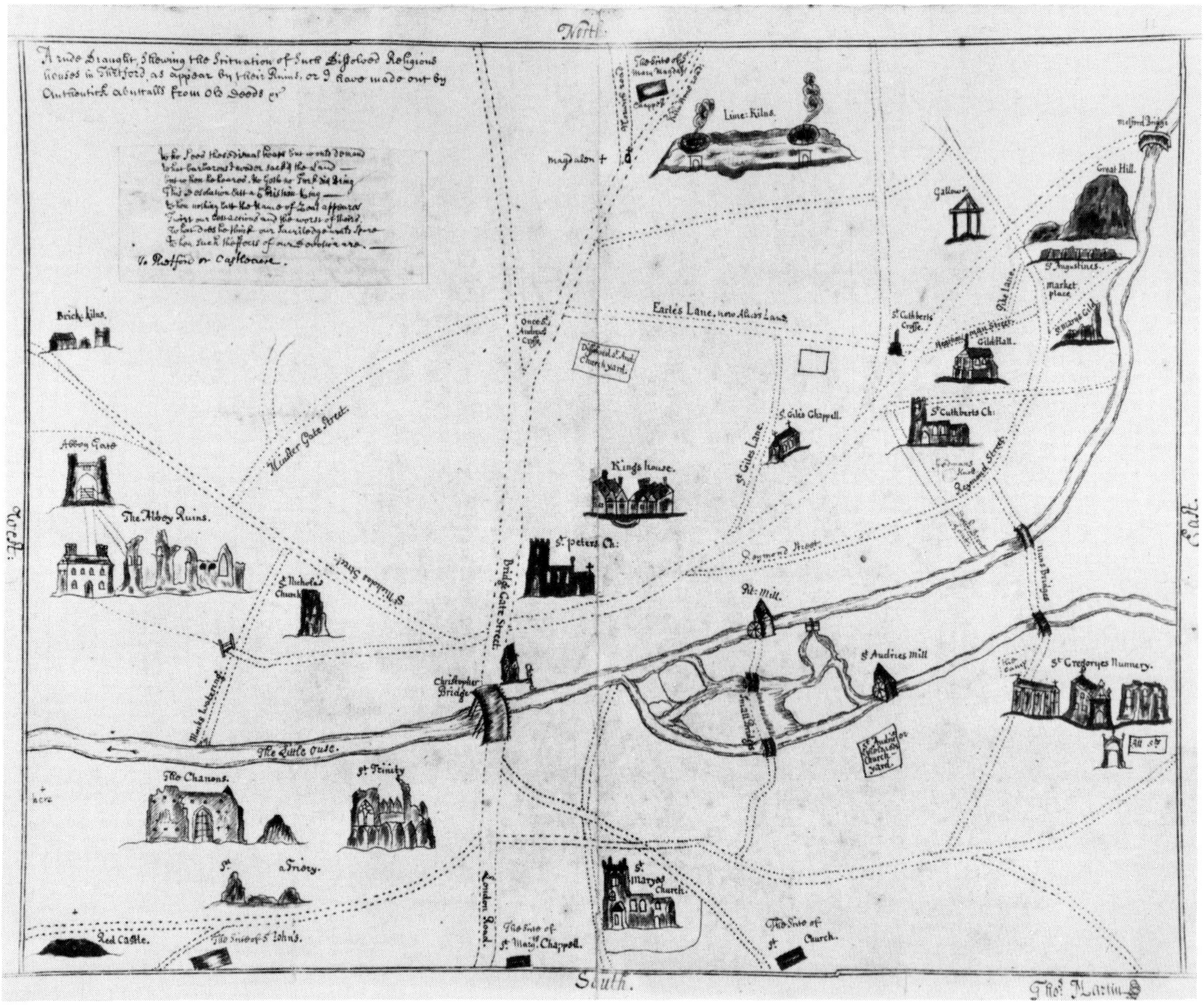

Plate XV. Martin's map of Thetford (c. 1750): nearly all the sites of churches and monastic remains have been built over during the expansion of the town since the 1950s.

Plate XVI. Reepham churchyard, with Reepham St Mary standing north-east of Whitwell St Michael; formerly, Hackford All Saints stood south of Whitwell church. Norfolk Archaeological Unit 1984 TG1022/C/AVR3.

Plate XVII. Antingham St Margaret and St Mary by Ladbrooke (1823): one of twelve Norfolk villages having two churches in the same churchyard.

Plate XVIII. Great Melton, All Saints (to north) and St Mary (tower only): curiously, All Saints had been in ruins from the early 18th century, but was rebuilt in 1883 while St Mary's was being demolished. Norfolk Archaeological Unit 1983 TG1406/F/ATB2.

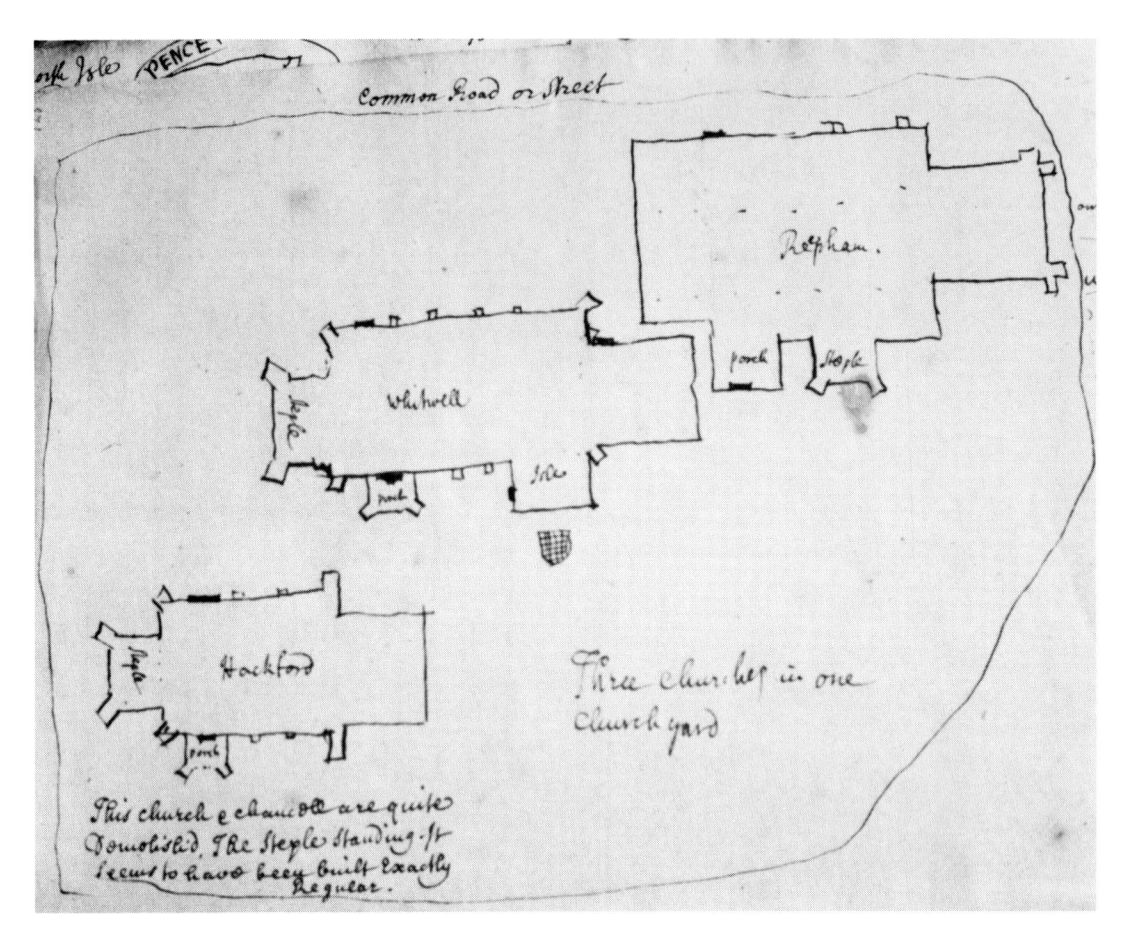

Plate XIX. Reepham churchyard by Martin (c. 1750), showing the outline of the parish church of Hackford as well as Whitwell and Reepham; the former was largely destroyed by fire in 1549. The three parishes each made use of separate parts of the churchyard.

Plate XX. Babingley, St Felix: by the 16th century, the village had been deserted apart from the landlord's farm and a few labourers' cottages. There were only eight communicants in 1603, so the church was reduced to a third of its size and struggled on until 1895.

V. Quality of Buildings

Since it excludes central Norwich, this survey catalogues thirty-four fully standing churches and ninety-eight ruined churches. They are a broadly representative sample of the the ecclesiastical architecture of Norfolk as a whole, and there are many buildings of outstanding quality.

Major building operations (*i.e.* more than the insertion of windows *etc.*) have been grouped according to broad (and overlapping) stylistic frameworks: Romanesque, *c*. 1040 - *c*. 1180; Transitional and Early English, *c*. 1170 - *c*. 1310; Decorated, *c*. 1280 - *c*. 1380; Perpendicular, *c*. 1350 - *c*. 1540; Post-medieval, *c*. 1540 - 1800 (see Appendix VI).

Romanesque *c*. 1040 - *c*. 1180
(Plates XXI-XXV, LXVI, XCIII, CIV, CV)
Romanesque building phases can be found at fifty-two sites. Early Romanesque features such as double-splayed windows survive at Houghton-on-the-Hill, Kempstone (Pl. XXI), Morton-on-the-Hill and Saxlingham Thorpe, and (uniquely in Norfolk) there are remains of a salient tower with upright-and-flat quoins at Snarehill (Pl. CIV-CV). Romanesque fabric is most commonly identified by the quality of the masonry, usually with clear horizontal courses of flint rubble separated by wide mortar joins, and quoins of large flints or conglomerate blocks, as at North Barningham (Pl. LXVI).

Romanesque builders showed greater inventiveness in church planning than their later medieval counterparts, for whom the rectangular chancel, rectangular nave and square west tower became the rule. We have that Norfolk speciality, the round tower, at Appleton, Brandiston, Burgh St Mary, Feltwell, Hales, Great Hautbois, Kirby Bedon, Morton-on-the-Hill, Great Ringstead, Stanford and Whitlingham. An apsidal chancel survives only at Castle Rising and Hales, although excavations (*e.g.* at Bawsey) have revealed that apsidal east ends were common in this period. The axial tower between chancel and nave substantially survives at Bawsey (Pl. XCIII), although it also clearly existed at Castle Rising and Surlingham. The square west tower, as at Pudding Norton, was a yet further possibility (the latter with upright-and-flat window jambs) (Pl. XXII).

The late Romanesque period provides the most spectacular churches. With the increasing use of freestone, stone-carvers were able to create more sumptuous features. There are notable portals at Buckenham Ferry, Langford, Shingham (Pl. XXIII) and a superb, very late example with beakhead and dogtooth at Barton Bendish (Rogerson *et al.* 1987, fig. 42). Langford also possesses a fine chancel arch, and Feltwell and Stanford have good tower arches. The tower at Bawsey has excellent nave and chancel arches, and remnants of belfry openings (Pl. XCV); there is also a triangular-headed doorway above the chancel arch which led into a chamber above the vault of the chancel (a semi-circular scar of masonry is all that survives of the vault). But when it comes to quality, arguably the finest Romanesque church in Norfolk is St Margaret's, Hales (Pl. XXIV). Firstly it is unique in retaining its entire 12th-century plan and elevation; secondly, it possesses two magnificent portals, the north doorway being the finest (Pl. XXV); thirdly, all the dressings, corners, string-courses and edgings are of carved and shaped limestone, enriching and sharpening the features of the church; and fourthly, Hales has been little affected by later insertions and alterations. It is correctly described by Pevsner (1962, b, 183) as 'A perfect Norman village church'.

Transitional and Early English *c*. 1170 - *c*. 1310
(Figs. 11, 19; Plates XIV, XXVI-XXX)
Early English building phases can be found at twenty-nine sites. At only one, Coston, does the church survive substantially unaltered since its construction in the 13th century (Pl. XXVI): a small, unaisled church, lacking the rich carving of Hales and the magnificent scale of contemporary churches such as Grimston. Much finer detail can be found at Buckenham Ferry, with its sumptuously carved north doorway and elegant octagonal west tower (Pl. XXVII). There are also good doorways at Wiggenhall St Mary the Virgin and at West Rudham; the latter also possesses a four-bay arcade with octagonal piers, and two plate-tracery windows (albeit reset) in the south aisle; another plate-tracery window survives (again reset) on the site of the Berdewell chapel at West Harling (Fig. 11). Remains of Early English arcades can also be found at Feltwell (Pl. XXVIII; note quatrefoil piers with keeled shafts) and East Walton. But more intriguing, if less spectacular, is the south transept projecting from the chancel at Great Hautbois, built in all probability to house the relic of St Theobald (Fig. 19). Transepts, added to earlier naves, are also a feature of Marshland churches, notably at Islington where the north wall of the north transept is pierced by stepped lancets (Pls XIV, XXIX).

Undoubtedly the finest example of Early English architecture described in this volume is the tower at West Walton (vested in the Redundant Churches Fund, although the church remains in use). The lavish use of limestone allows a wealth of carved detail in the form of shafts, capitals, arcading and the ubiquitous dog-tooth decoration, paralleling work in Lincoln Cathedral of the 1240s (Pl. XXX).

Decorated *c*. 1280 - *c*. 1380
(Plates XIII, XXXI-XXXIII, LXXV-LXXVIII, XCI)
Decorated building phases are not only more numerous (with a total of thirty-nine sites) than Early English, but there is also much more work of high quality. If one were to choose the 'Hales' of the 14th century, it would have to be St Mary's at Barton Bendish, with its delightful chancel of *c*. 1340 complete with reticulated tracery and carved label-stops, and its late Decorated (*c*. 1370) nave with charmingly rustic attempts at flowing tracery (see Rogerson *et al.* 1987, pls XIII-XV). In second place comes Babingley (Pls LXXV-LXXVIII), a splendid and intriguing ruin in which three building phases rapidly followed one another in the decades between *c*. 1300 and *c*. 1340. Although the arcades (now blocked) are only of two bays, the work throughout is of exceptional quality; the aisles terminate in tomb canopies which are integral to the arcades, an arrangement which focuses attention on the links between the financing of the new nave and the funereal aspirations of its patron. Grander in scale and more ornately decorated than the Babingley tombs is the canopy of the double piscina and sedilia at North Barningham, where a dark mortar filling forms a flushwork pattern on the pinnacles.

Several churches have arcades of four or more bays. There is a good early example (*c*. 1300) at West Tofts with piers of clustered shafts; the arcade had been blocked in the 18th century, but was reopened by Pugin a century later. Nearby Stanford has even more complex shafts (although only a three-bay arcade), while at Brandiston the piers have a simple quatrefoil plan. Usually the piers were octagonal, as at Appleton, Great Hautbois, Hockwold (Pl. XXXI) and East Ruston (Pl. XXXII); the latter has a five-bay arcade of giant proportions, with no clerestorey. This 'hall-church' arrangement was originally in evidence also at Rackheath, where the blind clerestorey was decorated with flushwork panelling.

The Decorated style is renowned for its inventive window tracery design, and there are many interesting examples here. There are many examples of the ubiquitous Y-tracery, as in the belfry at Babingley or Roudham (Pls LXXVI, XIII; it is worth noting that the Y-tracery coexists with more complicated forms). A more complex version of Y-tracery, often used in larger windows, is intersecting tracery, as at Tivetshall St Mary (Pl. XCI). Reticulated tracery can be found at Babingley, Barton Bendish and Shingham (Pl. XXXIII), and intersecting ogees at North Barningham and Hockwold (Pl. XXXI). That there was an overlap between the use of Decorated forms and the introduction of Perpendicular types is demonstrated, amongst other places, at Brandiston, where Perpendicular windows alternate with Decorated (Pl. XXII).

Perpendicular *c*. 1350 - *c*. 1540
(Frontispiece, Plates XXXIV-XXXVII, LXVII, LXIX, LXXI, LXXII)
Covering over twice the number of decades as the Decorated period, it is not surprising to find over twice the number of building programmes (eighty-two). Very few churches were newly built or rebuilt during this period; but equally, few were untouched to some degree by Perpendicular rebuilding or restoration. It was a period of adding an aisle, clerestorey or porch, or inserting a large new window. Against this background Wiggenhall St Peter's is something of an exception. Rebuilt in the 1420s from end to end, it receives the author's nomination as the 'Hales' of the 15th century (Pl. XXXIV). Although now roofless, and having had its aisle demolished since 1840, it still retains most of its window tracery owing to the high quality of its stonework (Frontispiece). Despite being greater in scale, the neighbouring church of Wiggenhall St Mary the Virgin is undeniably less lively in terms of its architecture (Pl. LXXII); fortunately the interest of the latter is lifted by the quality of its furnishings.

Both these Wiggenhall churches have piers similar in section to the quatrefoil of the Decorated style; but in the transition from Decorated to Perpendicular a more slender type of pier comes into vogue, as at Tottington, where the pier is distinctly narrower along its east-west axis. The process has gone a stage further at Snetterton in the 15th century, where pier and arch are fused by a continuous hollow chamfer moulding, and capitals have been banished from the nave side. Perpendicular tracery has often been compared unfavourably with that of the Decorated period; certainly it has greater rectilinearity than the former, but it is by no means without variety. Window arches could be four or two-centred (as at Wiggenhall St Peter); archlets could be two- centred or ogee (as at West Harling; Pl. LXIX); there could be supermullions and inverted daggers (as at Wiggenhall St Peter; Frontispiece) or supertransoms (as at Brandiston; Pl. LXVII).

In many cases it is the tower which provides the most exhilarating architectural features. That at West Tofts (Pl. LXXI) is a good example, made more memorable by the survival of donor plaques around the base, confirming its date of construction in the decades from 1480-1520. The 14th and 15th centuries also saw the revival of an old East Anglian form, the round tower. That at Wolterton (Pl. XXXV) was built *c*. 1390, and is unusual in possessing an integral spiral staircase (in brick). The late medieval round towers, as at Wolterton, commonly possess an octagonal belfry stage; and octagonal belfries were often added to older towers, as at Stanford. Indeed, the octagonal belfry became so popular (*cf*. monastic towers, *e.g.* Wymondham) that there are several, such as West Wretham, where an octagonal belfry surmounts a tower of square plan. Full play is made of the decorative potential of the unpierced faces of the octagon with imaginative flushwork; and flushwork panels enliven the crenellated parapet. This decorative device is taken a step further at Feltwell (Pl. XXXVI), where some of the flushwork panels (re-set in the restored clerestorey) are donor plaques.

By the nature of this volume, there are not many roofs to report on. Good arch-braced roofs survive at North Barningham, Shimpling and Snetterton; but the finest is undoubtedly at Hockwold, where arch-braced tie-beams alternate with hammer-beams exquisitely carved with angels (Pl. XXXVII).

Post-Medieval *c*. 1540 to today
(Plates XXXVIII-XLI, LXXI, LXXIII-LXXIV, CXI)
That there are only twenty-two sites with post-medieval building campaigns is a reflection on the rarity of church building in the 450 years since the Reformation. However, there are three churches built within this period which admirably match in quality the best in the medieval period: Yarmouth St George, Gunton and West Tofts.

The later 16th and 17th centuries saw very little rebuilding; mainly repairs to churches reduced in size (as at Babingley) or the restoration of 'romantic' ruins, such as the tower at Godwick (Pl. CXI) or west wall at Beachamwell All Saints. St George's at Yarmouth (Pls LXXIII, LXXIV) was the first church to be erected on a new site since the Reformation[15]. Built by John Price in 1714-16 and based on the Wren church of St Clement Danes in London, St George's is in fact a Wren city church imported to Norfolk. But however imitative the design, the quality of execution cannot be faulted; it is regrettable that all the original furnishings have been removed. Fortunately St Andrew's at Gunton (Pls XXXVIII-XLI) has retained its furnishings, and is unquestionably the 'Hales' of the 18th century. It remains one of the few churches built by Robert Adam, replacing the medieval church in 1769. Its fine four-column portico directly faces Gunton Hall, giving the appearance of a garden temple in the manner of Stowe. Inside, the gallery and much of the panelling and plasterwork is original, but the seating and other furnishings were changed in the 19th century.

Of 19th-century churches, Norfolk has very few outside the towns. As in the 18th century, new building resulted only from having an enthusiastic incumbent or patron. Such is the case at West Tofts (now in the Battle Training Area), where Sir Richard Sutton was patron, his eldest son, John, was a close friend of A.W.N. Pugin, and his fifth son, Augustus, became the rector in 1849. The family set about building a vast new chancel and family chantry, and rebuilding the north aisle; all to designs by Pugin. The result is one of Pugin's finest churches, and probably the best example of 19th-century ecclesiastical architecture in the county (Pl. LXXI).

Appendix VII is an attempt to classify those churches with standing remains in order of importance.

Plate XXI. Kempstone, St Paul: double-splayed window in south wall of nave.

Plate XXII. Pudding Norton, St Margaret: single-splayed window of the second half of the 11th century.

Plate XXIII. Shingham, St Botolph: nave south doorway.

Plate XXIV.   Hales, St Margaret, by Cotman (1838).

Plate XXV.   Hales, St Margaret, by Cotman (1838): nave north doorway. The arch has five principal bands of ornamentation consisting of chevron, zig-zag, star pattern, bobbin and roundels.

Plate XXVI. Coston, St Michael: unusually for Norfolk, a church virtually unaltered since the 13th century.

Plate XXVII. Buckenham Ferry, St Nicholas: an elegant Early English octagonal tower.

Plate XXVIII. Feltwell, St Nicholas: 13th-century south arcade.

Plate XXIX. Islington, St Mary: transept, looking north in 1946; the plaster vault was destroyed after thieves stole lead from the roof in 1971. AA47/3793 copyright Royal Commission on Historical Monuments (England).

Plate XXX. West Walton, detached tower: although the neighbouring church of St Mary is still in use, the tower was declared redundant in 1974.

Plate XXXI. Hockwold, St Peter: looking west, with Decorated west window and arcade, but Perpendicular clerestorey and roof.

Plate XXXII. East Ruston, St Mary: giant octagonal piers and no clerestorey windows.

Plate XXXIII. Shingham, St Botolph: looking east; note the reticulated east window and the Jacobean furnishings.
BB78/8059 copyright Royal Commission on Historical Monuments (England), 1974.

Plate XXXIV. Wiggenhall St Peter: from the north-east; a complete (but roofless) Perpendicular church of the 1420s.

Plate XXXVI. Feltwell, St Nicholas: re-set flushwork panels in the clerestorey.

Plate XXXV. Wolterton, St Margaret: a round tower of c. 1390 with integral brick stairway. The rest of the church was demolished c. 1740, leaving the tower as a 'picturesque' ruin in the grounds of Wolterton Hall.

Plate XXXVII. Hockwold, St Peter: magnificent early 16th-century nave roof of arch-braced tie-beams alternating with hammer-beams.

Plate XXXVIII. Gunton, St Andrew: Doric west front facing Gunton Hall, a rare Robert Adam church of 1769. CC56/706 copyright Royal commission on Historical Monuments (England).

Plate XXXIX. Gunton, St Andrew: view from south-east. The 18th-century church is built on the site of its medieval predecessor. BB77/5944 copyright Royal Commission on Historical Monuments (England).

Plate XL. Gunton, St Andrew: looking east. This plaster ceiling collapsed in 1976 but has been replaced. AA49/6063 copyright Royal Commission on Historical Monuments (England), 1948.

Plate XLI. Gunton, St Andrew: nave west door looking west, showing 18th-century woodwork and plaster frieze. AA49/6067 copyright Royal commission on Historical Monuments (England), 1948.

VI. Quality of Church Contents
(Plates XVII-LVII, LXXV)

The term 'contents' is preferred to 'furnishings', since the former term includes everything in the church apart from the architectural framework. Contents have been grouped according to material: ceramic, glass, metal, paint, stone and wood. Even the least inspired of contents can make their contribution (Pls XLII, XLIII).

Ceramic
Many churches have tiled floors. The best set of medieval tiles to be included in this volume are those from Barton Bendish, All Saints (Rogerson *et al.* 1987, 41), where a number of yellow and green Flemish tiles (14th to mid-16th century) were recovered. There are also a few churches with good 19th-century tiles, notably West Tofts.

Other uses of ceramic are rare. An interesting cusped panel in terracotta was discovered on the site of Middle Harling church. Still more unusual is the terracotta infill of the floor monument in North Barningham church (see below, Pl. L).

Glass
Several churches have fragments of medieval painted glass, as can be found at Brandiston, West Harling and Wiggenhall St Mary the Virgin. Shimpling has some 14th-century canopy work, and some good 15th-century angels. But for quantity and quality, the best range of medieval painted glass is St Peter's at West Rudham. The three nave north windows contain two figures of Christ, one of the Virgin, two angels, and St Mark with a lion. According to King (1974, 35) they date to 1430-40. They 'stand comparison with the best glass of the period in any country' (King 1974, 5). The St Peter Hungate Museum in Norwich contains a late medieval depiction of God the Father brought from West Tofts.

Nineteenth-century glass is much more common; there are good examples at Bagthorpe, West Harling, East Ruston and West Tofts. At the latter, Pugin incorporated in his chancel glazing four 14th-century figures of saints from Leoben in Austria. They are no longer in the church.

It is worth noting that the earliest painted glass in the county (*c.* 1250) at Saxlingham Nethergate may well have come from Saxlingham Thorpe after its abandonment in 1688 (King 1974, 25).

Metal (Bells, brasses, crucifixes, lecterns)
Bells survive in only a few of the churches recorded in this volume; and even these are not easy to examine without the aid of a very long ladder. However, some of the bells can be studied at ease, as they have been removed to the safety of museums. At the King's Lynn Museum there is a bell made by Thomas de Lenne at the Lynn foundry in the 14th century; it formerly hung in the tower of Hales church[16]. The St Peter Hungate Museum in Norwich houses the full set of bells from Burlingham St Peter, made in 1450 by Richard Brasyer of Norwich.

Figure brasses survive in only four of the churches recorded in this volume. Undoubtedly the most important church for brasses is Frenze, with ten altogether of which five have effigies; they mostly commemorate the Blenerhaysett family. The oldest depicts Ralph Blenerhaysett (d. 1475), in plate armour, feet on a lion (Pl. XLIV a); also in plate armour, John Blenerhaysett (d. 1510), and next to it an effigy of his wife Jane (d. 1521). The remaining two figure brasses are of Thomas Hobson (in a shroud, undated; Pl. XLIVb) and the vowess Johanna Braham (d. 1519). Unfortunately the finest brass in the church, with enamel colouring, to Sir Thomas Blenerhaysett (d. 1531), was stolen from the church after Cotman's illustration of 1816 and before 1864.

The oldest brass at West Harling is that of the priest, Ralph Fuloflove (d. 1479). There are also two man and wife brasses of the Berdewell family: William Berdewell and Elisabeth (d. 1490; Pl. XLVa), and William Berdewell and Margaret (d. 1508; Pl. XLVb).

The Palgrave family are represented at North Barningham, with a brass depicting not only Henry Palgrave (d. 1516) and his wife Anne, but also their five sons and seven daughters. St Peter's at Hockwold used to have a brass of Amfelicie Tendall (d. 1532) and her nine daughters but it has long been missing. That of Thomas Holl (d. 1630) remained in St Bartholomew's at Heigham until it was bombed in 1942; it is now in the Bridewell Museum, Norwich. Other brasses include a heart brass at Wiggenhall St Mary the Virgin, and a palimpsest at Moulton St Mary, with on one side the figure of Thomasine Palmer (d. 1544).

In 1840, a crucifix (and an alabaster slab; see below) was found hidden 2ft below the chancel floor of the church of Buckenham Ferry. 13th century in date, made of gilded and enamelled copper, it is a rare survival, and can be seen in the St Peter Hungate Museum in Norwich. It was carefully wrapped in sedge, and therefore probably hidden in the hope of later reinstatement. Thus it may fit into the wider context of images and altar slabs secreted within churches during the Reformation. Could further discoveries of this nature await the archaeologist's investigation?

There are two brass eagle lecterns. The one at West Harling is unremarkable for 1890, imitating late medieval originals. That at Wiggenhall St Mary the Virgin is the real thing (Pl. XLVI); it is the latest of the three dated ones in the county, and bears the inscription: 'Orate p'aia fratis Robti Barnard, gardiani Walsingham Annon Domini 1518'.

Paint
Most medieval wall-painting consisted of decorative patterning, as at West Harling. Some figurative work survives too. At Hales both can be found, with some bands of 13th-century decorative work as well as later figures of St James the Great and St Christopher. St Christopher also adorns the nave north wall of Moulton St Mary, with the Seven Works of Mercy on the south wall (Pl. XLVII: Drink to the Thirsty, Clothing the Naked), both late 14th-century. There is a depiction of St Catherine in St Mary's at Barton Bendish.

Stone (Fonts, wall monuments, wall tablets, floor slabs, panels)
North-west Norfolk is famous for its Norman fonts; one of the plainer examples can be found in Bagthorpe church, with decoration confined to engaged shafts at the angles and interlacing circles on one face. A much more elaborate example was found at Great Hautbois in 1805, buried under the floor of the church, and moved into the new church of Holy Trinity in 1864; it has an elaborate stem carved with interlacing plants and animals.

As with a large number of 13th-century fonts, that at Moulton St Mary has blind arcading along the bowl and is made of Purbeck marble (Pl. XLVIII). The remaining fonts recorded in this volume are mainly octagonal in form, and 14th or 15th-century in date. One of the most fascinating is that at Frenze. It is octagonal with a reeded stem, and each of the eight faces of the bowl is carved with a different type of window tracery, all of them current in the first half of the 14th century: two-light intersecting; Y-tracery; two-light reticulated with cusping; two-light with mouchettes; three-light reticulated; two-light with 'petal' motif; three lancets set within an arch. Thus the font is virtually a pattern-book of late Early English and Decorated tracery styles. One of the best Perpendicular fonts is at Shimpling, with lions guarding the stem and Evangelist symbols and Instruments of the Passion carved on the bowl. Good Perpendicular fonts can also be found at Buckenham Ferry (Pl. XLIX: good figures of saints and apostles), West Harling, Shingham and East Ruston, the latter with carved heads at the base. That at West Tofts is a 19th-century copy of nearby Mundford.

Some churches are full of the funerary monuments of a particular family, such as the Blenerhaysett's at Frenze, or the Berdewell's at West Harling (see above). Other churches are bereft, save the occasional floor slab forming part of the paving. In St Peter's at North Barningham, we have a church that is decidedly in the former category: it is the funerary 'pantheon' of the Palgrave family, with a 16th-century brass and three superb early 17th-century marble wall monuments. In fact, there are few churches which provide such an object lesson in late medieval and post-medieval funerary monuments.

The first tomb to be encountered is in the middle of the nave, where a trapezoidal black stone sepulchral slab is set into the floor (Pl. L); it is inset with a small brass inscription to Robert Bakon (d. 1472). Contiguous with this tomb slab is an extraordinary area of stone inlay; its design is not unlike a rose window, about 1.5m in diameter, set into the floor and filled with brick and terracotta rather than glass. It certainly appears to draw attention to the Bakon tomb; if the funerary connection is not the reason for this terracotta and stone wheel, it is very difficult to find a more plausible explanation. Figure brasses were used to commemorate Henry and Anne Palgrave (d. 1516, see above), buried in the north aisle. Next to this is another grave slab whose inset brass inscription has now gone; it was that of James Bacon (d. 1531).

We now come to the magnificent post-medieval monuments to the Palgrave family. Against the north wall of the chancel is the black marble tomb chest to John Palgrave (d. 1611); above the tomb are three allegorical figures (defaced) of Justice, Toil and Peace, and above them an elaborate pink and white marble architectural framework. West of this is an even finer monument, that to Margaret Pope (d. 1624), John Palgrave's daughter; her cloaked effigy is kneeling at prayer, within a baldachino whose curtains are pulled aside by two angels. Perhaps even more spectacular is the monument in the north aisle to Sir Austin Palgrave (d. 1633) and Elizabeth his wife, where the large architectural framework which rises from the tomb chest contains the marble busts of Sir Austin and his wife, both very fine portraits. The only other monument is the large floor slab to Sir Augustine Palgrave (d. 1790) in the chancel, just to show that the church is equipped with at least one example of every type of funerary monument.

There is, within the scope of this survey, only one other monument to compare with the Palgrave tombs: that to Sir Henry Kervile (d. 1624) and his wife Mary at Wiggenhall St Mary the Virgin. The alabaster life-size figures are recumbent on a panelled chest, whose central panel contains figures of their two children; against the wall is a black marble inscription surrounded by an imposing architectural framework of paired Corinthian columns and arched entabulature. Another fine early 17th-century monument can be found at Moulton St Mary, carved in alabaster and depicting the kneeling figures of Edmund Anguishe (d. 1628) and his wife and two children (Pl. LI); the tympanum contains a carved bust of Edmund, hands resting on a skull. Less spectacular, but not without interest, is the Calthorpe tomb and monument in Cockthorpe church. The tomb chest to Sir James Calthorpe (d. 1615) stands against the south wall of the small south aisle, while against the east wall is the marble inscription to Sir James and his wife Barbara (d. 1639); they seem to have been a more fruitful family than the Kerviles, since, by the time Barbara died, she had lived to see no less than 193 of her children and their offspring.

About a century intervenes before we encounter a monument comparable to these of the Kerviles or Palgraves in quality or scale. In the tiny church of Langford, whose windows are boarded to protect them from damage by the army (it is within the Stanford Training Area), is the exceptional marble monument to Sir Nicholas Garrod (d. 1727). Sculpted by Christopher Horsnaile senior, it depicts the almost life-size figure of Sir Nicholas in Roman costume, reclining on a large pedestal; behind him, the two standing figures of his father and grandfather flank an urn. Whilst interesting, the Hungerford monument at Hockwold is not really in the same class; flanked by cherubs are the marble busts of Maria and John Hungerford (d. 1719), with a relief of musical instruments above, and a winged skull below (by R. Singleton of Bury). Staying in the same church but moving on sixty years, we find in the monument to Cyrill Wyche (d. 1780) by John Ivory of Norwich (Pl. LII) that portraiture has given way to sentimental imagery, with a weeping putto leaning against a broken column. This contrasts strikingly with the dignified simplicity of the monument to Richard Gipps in West Harling church by Joseph Wilton (dated to 1780), a superb marble bust on a pedestal.

Whilst in no way rivalling the quality of the North Barningham monuments, those in the church of All Saints at Rackheath are not without interest. They cover two centuries, firstly those of the Pettus family: John (d. 1698), Thomas (d. 1723), Horatio (d. 1730; by J.Chapling), Sir Horatio (d. 1772; by Thomas Rawlins); and the Straceys: Elizabeth (d. 1808) and Harriet (d. 1817; both by Cushing). Finally, at West Tofts we have the finest 'gothic' tomb in the county, that of Mary Sutton (d. 1832) by Pugin: the tomb-chest is decorated with enamel shields on the sides and a brass foliate cross on top, and surmounted by a vaulted canopy with cusped arches, crockets and finials.

The only carved panel of interest is the medieval alabaster depiction of the martyrdom of St Erasmus, found in 1840 beneath the floor of Buckenham Ferry church, and now displayed in the St Peter Hungate Museum.

Wood (Altar rails, benches, biers, chests, commandment boards, cupboards, doors, font canopies, pews, pulpits, reredos, royal arms, screens)

Four churches have altar rails of quality: North Barningham, Morton-on-the-Hill, Moulton St Mary and Shingham. The 17th-century oak rails in these churches are supported by turned balusters. The rails at North Barningham were brought recently from St Mary Coslany in Norwich.

In addition, North Barningham possesses eight medieval bench-ends, carved with poppy-heads; Shimpling also retains some carved bench-ends. Thurgarton has far more, and of much higher quality; there is a striking variety of design, with carved figures, dragons, barrels, fighting dogs, and even an elephant and castle. At Shingham not only are the bench-ends carved (with poppyheads, one with a figure), but also the bench backs are pierced with tracery patterns. Tottington, before it became part of the Stanford Training Area, possessed a fine set of bench ends carved with Perpendicular tracery designs and armrests surmounted by beasts (Pl. LIII). Even these are eclipsed by the benches at Wiggenhall St Mary the Virgin, astonishing in both quality and completeness, and undoubtedly the finest in the county. There are eighteen of them in the nave, all exquisitely carved and pre-Reformation in date; the bench-ends are carved with figures and poppyheads, and the bench backs have traceried open-work. Those on the south side of the nave are less elaborate than those on the north side; six of them contain images of the Virgin at prayer. On the north side, the figures are more finely executed: they represent various saints, each standing within a cusped ogee niche. The details of their costumes suggest an early 16th-century date. It has been argued that those on the south side are earlier, but their (comparatively) inferior execution may be due to different craftsmen and different benefactors: it is significant that the south clerestorey windows are also different from the north ones; the two-light south windows formerly contained scenes from the life of the Virgin, while the three-light north windows contained images of the Twelve Apostles. At Frenze, there are but two medieval bench-ends, along with three 17th-century benches. There are also 17th-century benches at Moulton St Mary and Cockthorpe.

We move on to such miscellaneous items as biers, chests, Commandment Boards, cupboards, doors and font canopies. There are two biers of note, the 17th-century one at Illington and the one from Kempstone dated 1785, now in the St Peter Hungate Museum. A carved-17th century oak chest survives at Shimpling; there are others at West Harling and Thurgarton. The latter church also possesses a 17th-century Commandment Board, as does Moulton St Mary. An unusual survival is the panelled dole cupboard at Wiggenhall St Mary the Virgin, dated to 1639. The same church can also boast a very fine font canopy, dated to 1625, and surmounted by a pelican plucking its flesh. Shimpling and Hales have interesting font canopies too, the latter with an intriguing facial silhouette painted on the underside. Plain medieval doors survive at several churches; the best is that at Morton-on-the-Hill, with its carved panels (Pl. LIV).

Of pews (by which we mean the enclosed private seatings of post-Reformation times), the best example is at Frenze (Pl. LV); 17th-century in date, it is decorated with blind arches and panels of shallow carving, and capped with a dainty balustrade. The pulpit at Frenze is identical in style, no doubt by the same craftsman. Also of the 17th century is the pulpit at Wiggenhall St Mary the Virgin, again with arched panels, and complete with hourglass stand. Of the same period is the pulpit at Shingham, a two-decker, and that at Moulton St Mary, complete with carved back panel and tester (Pl. LVI). Arguably the most elegant pulpit in the county is that designed *c.* 1715 for St George's at Yarmouth (Pl. LXXV), now in the parish church of St Nicholas, with some of its railings now enclosing the lectern, and the tester suspended above the font.

At first glance the gothic-style altar and reredos at West Harling, donated in 1902, seem unexceptional; but set into the reredos are five superbly carved panels, all Flemish and of the 16th century; they depict the Annunication, Nativity, Three Kings with Herod, Christ examined by the High Priests, and the Circumcision. West Harling also has a board of the Royal Arms of Charles II. At Wiggenhall St Mary the Virgin there are the Arms of George III, and the rather faded board at Frenze may be the Arms of James I.

Finally, there are the screens. The best is the late Perpendicular rood-screen at East Ruston, notable for the carved lions at its entrance, and its painted panels (the four Evangelists on the north side, the four Latin doctors on the south). The early 16th-century rood-screen at Wiggenhall St Mary the Virgin also retains eight painted panels (St John the Baptist and seven female saints); a restored screen also surrounds the Kervile tomb. Until 1942 Tottington possessed a fine screen (upper part restored in the 19th century; Pl. LVII). The Perpendicular screen at Corpusty was heavily restored in the 19th century. Pugin's screen at West Tofts is Decorated in style, has a vault, and is surmounted by a rood loft with rood.

Appendix VIII is an attempt to classify the churches in terms of the quality and importance of their contents.

Plate XLII. Crownthorpe, St James: interior in 1941. The church contents are not of high quality, apart from the pulpit which contains three Flemish panels. AA69/2945 copyright Royal Commission on Historical Monuments (England), 1941.

Plate XLIII. Crownthorpe, St James: interior in 1981, a mere shell when stripped of contents. Disused since 1966 and declared redundant in 1974, it has been leased to neighbouring landowners whose use for it remains uncertain.

Plate XLIV (a). Frenze, St Andrew: brass to Ralph Blenerhaysett, d.1475. BB76/5672 copyright Royal Commission on Historical Monuments (England), 1976.

Plate XLIV (b). Frenze, St Andrew: brass to Thomas Hobson, undated. BB76/5675 copyright Royal Commission on Historical Monuments (England), 1976.

Plate XLV (a). West Harling, All Saints: brass of William Berdewell and wife Elizabeth, 1490. AA50/4998 copyright Royal Commission on Historical Monuments (England), 1949.

Plate XLV (b). West Harling, All Saints: brass of William Berdewell and wife Margaret, 1508. AA50/5000 copyright Royal Commission on Historical Monuments (England), 1949.

Plate XLVI. Wiggenhall St Mary the Virgin: brass eagle lectern, dated 1518; one of only eleven in the county.

Plate XLVII. Moulton St Mary: nave south wall, late 14th-century paintings of the Works of Mercy (illustrated here Giving Drink to the Thirsty and Clothing the Naked). AA52/5729 copyright Royal Commission on Historical Monuments (England), 1951.

Plate XLVIII. Moulton, St Mary: Purbeck marble font, 13th century. AA52/5727 copyright Royal Commission on Historical Monuments (England), 1951.

Plate XLIX. Buckenham Ferry, St Nicholas: 15th-century font with carved apostles and saints on both stem and bowl. AA52/5611 copyright Royal Commission on Historical Monuments (England), 1951.

Plate L. North Barningham, St Peter: nave floor. This unusual feature, a flushwork roundel in limestone and terracotta, may be related to the adjacent tomb.

Plate LII. Hockwold, St Peter: monument to Cyrill Wyche, d. 1780, by John Ivory of Norwich.

Plate LI. Moulton St Mary: monument to Edmund Anguishe, d. 1628. AA52/5738 copyright Royal Commission on Historical Monuments (England), 1951.

Plate LIII. Tottington, St Andrew: 15th-century bench-ends in Tottington church in 1923. Since the village was depopulated to make way for the army in 1942, the church has been shut down and the furnishings dispersed. These benches are now in the church of Rockland St Peter. BB60/497 copyright Royal Commission on Historical Monuments (England),1923.

Plate LV. Frenze, St Andrew: 17th-century pew. BB76/5668 copyright Royal Commission on Historical Monuments (England), 1976.

Plate LIV. Morton-on-the-Hill, St Margaret: 15th-century oak door. BB88/1815 copyright Royal Commission on Historical Monuments (England), 1952.

Plate LVI. Moulton St Mary: elegant 17th-century pulpit with back-panel and tester. AA52/5733 copyright Royal Commission on Historical Monuments (England), 1951.

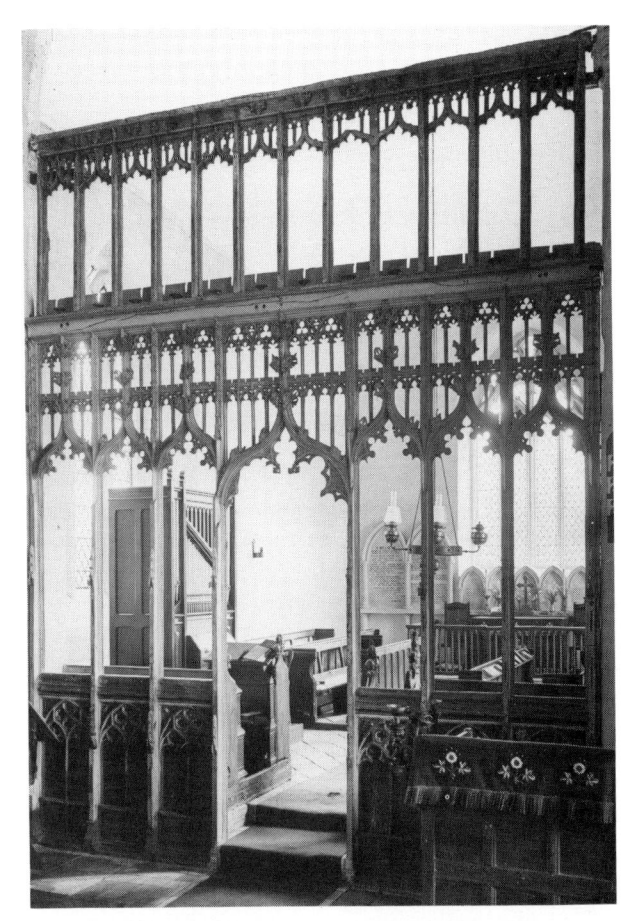

Plate LVII. Tottington, St Andrew: chancel screen in 1923. Like the benches, this has now been installed in the church of Rockland St Peter. BB60/498 copyright Royal Commission on Historical Monuments (England), 1923.

VII. Churchyards
(Plates XVI, LVIII)

The churchyard survives in all Category I sites, most Category II sites, but is rare in Category III, IV, V and VI sites. The vast majority are rectangular in plan, although at Babingley and Barmer part of the boundary wall describes a curve; and at Reepham the boundaries are very irregular (Pl. XVI): Reepham is really three churchyards in one, and there are several other sites with more than one church in the same churchyard (see above). It is comparatively rare to find a churchyard surviving for more than two centuries after the abandonment of the church within it. Boundary walls and headstones were soon removed, unless the churchyard was specifically retained in use after the abandonment of the church (as at Burgh Parva, Fulmodeston, Hindolveston, Hainford, West Beckham; at Weeting All Saints, although the church was abandoned c. 1700, the churchyard continued in use until c. 1900 and was only demolished in the 1950s). It is surprising to find the survival of churchyard boundaries at a number of sites where the church was abandoned two or three hundred years ago (Burnham Sutton, Kirby Bedon, Leziate, Mundham, Rockland St Andrew, Little Ryburgh, Saxlingham Thorpe, Shotesham St Martin, Surlingham, West Wretham).

The oldest surviving headstones are often the finest. There is a particularly good set of 18th-century headstones at Cockthorpe (Pl. LVIII). Quite a good 19th-

Plate LVIII. Cockthorpe, All Saints: 18th-century headstones in the churchyard.

century marble family tomb survives at Burlingham St Peter. But there is, in truth, little in the way of outstanding monuments to report.

There has been a good attempt to tidy up and improve the appearance of the churchyard at Southery.

VIII. Condition of Remains
(Plates I, II, XI, XIV-XXIX, LIX-LXIV, LXXXIII-LXXXVIII)

Unless regularly maintained, all buildings are in a state of deterioration. The continuous effect of the weather tends to set timber rotting, mortar crumbling, brick or stone eroding. On top of this, there are more sudden changes which may affect the stability of the structure, such as subsidence or disaster (fire, flood, lightning). In order to maintain a building in good condition, the weather must be kept out (roofs, rainwater goods, windows and doors intact) and walls kept stable. If not, there begins the downward spiral of decay referred to earlier.

The two main danger areas are collapse of roofs and collapse of towers: Hindolveston best illustrates the latter (Pls I, II); there have also been tower collapses at Barton Bendish, Burlingham St Peter, Feltwell (Pls LIX, LX), Langford, Morton-on-the-Hill (Pls LXI, LXII), Oxwick, Thurgarton, Tivetshall, South Walsham and Whitlingham (as well as the disastrous fall of the crossing tower at King's Lynn St James). The roof at Kempstone collapsed in the 1950s (Pl. LXXXVIII), and threatened to at Oxwick, Panxworth, Sco Ruston, Tivestshall, and Wiggenhall St Peter until removed; it still threatens to fall at Burlingham (Pl. LXXXIII). Further damage occurred at Kempstone when the chancel arch and most of the chancel roof collapsed some time between 1978 and 1983. Once the roof has been removed, the surviving walls need to be capped and kept free of weeds, and the exposed church floors kept clear; this has been successfully achieved at Islington (Pl. XIV) and Great Hautbois (Pls LXXXIV-LXXXVI). If left untended, ivy, saplings and weeds soon take their toll (Pls LXIII, LXIV). Sco Ruston and Tivetshall St Mary have had their walls capped, but the church floors still need to be kept in good condition.

Natural forces of decay are unfortunately sometimes accelerated through vandalism, from the smashing of windows and furnishings at Corpusty and Forncett St Mary to the robbing of jambs and smashing of gravestones at Burlingham St Peter (Pl. LXXXIII) and Tivetshall. Perhaps most devastating of all was the theft of roofing lead from the nave at Islington in 1971 (during this operation the thieves even had the gall to wave at local inhabitants, who assumed they were official restorers); the loss was not realised until heavy rain brought about the collapse of the roof and plaster vault below (Pls XIV-XXIX).

Perhaps the church of St Mary at Southery provides the best example of the changing fortunes of a church fabric. Until 1747 the medieval church (mainly 12th and 15th-century) possessed a square west tower; this fell down, and destroyed part of the nave. The two bells were sold to help pay for repairs, which involved the construction of a new west wall to a reduced nave. With the growth of the village, it became apparent that the church, now considerably smaller, was not big enough; it was therefore widened by a couple of metres to allow for more sittings in 1828. The new work entailed the construction of a new south wall for the nave, the partial rebuilding of the chancel, the heightening of the nave north walls, the remodelling of gable walls, plus a western gallery and a new roof. Ladbrookes's lithograph shows the church as it stood in 1832 (Pl. XI). However, by 1858 St Mary's had been abandoned, replaced by a new church just 200m away. Since this date, the old church has been left to gently dilapidate. A photograph of 1901 shows it windowless and covered by ivy, but with roofs still intact. Most of the roof was dismantled for safety in 1949; the rest caught fire when a bonfire was lit inside the ruins in 1968. The interior of the church was very overgrown until 1986, but in that year the weeds and shrubs were cleared from both church and churchyard, and a grass lawn planted inside the nave.

Appendix IX gives an approximate guide to the condition of all churches with standing remains (except for the most fragmentary). There are thirty which are characterised as being in 'Good Condition', *i.e.* fully repaired and roofed apart from three maintained ruins and one partly de-roofed church. A further twenty are deemed to be in 'Average Condition'; they mostly have roofs, but are not in the pristine state of the previous thirty. Another seventeen could be described as in 'Poor Condition', unroofed ruins with walls either too sound or too low to be considered a danger. Lastly, there are forty-one churches which need to be labelled as in 'Dangerous Condition'; this includes all with any tall uncapped walls, and especially those with unmaintained towers. It should be added that all buildings involve some element of danger, and a ruined building even more so; Appendix IX is intended as a rough guide, not a certification of approval or disapproval by a structural engineer.

Plate LIX.   Feltwell church by Ladbrooke (1823).

Plate LX.   Feltwell, St Nicholas: from the south-east in 1980. Its oddly truncated appearance is due to the demolition of the chancel in 1861 and the collapse of the tower in 1898 while it was being repaired.

Plate LXI.   Morton-on-the-Hill, St Margaret: interior looking west in 1952. AA53/5844 copyright Royal Commission on Historical Monuments (England), 1952.

Plate LXII.   Morton-on-the-Hill, St Margaret: interior looking west in 1978. The tower collapsed in 1959 destroying part of the nave roof. In the care of the Norfolk Churches Trust since 1979, the west end of the nave has now been sealed off and the rest of the church put in good order. BB79/629 copyright Royal Commission on Historical Monuments (England), 1978.

Plate LXIII.   Southwood church by Ladbrooke (1825).

Plate LXIV.   Southwood, St Edmund: from the north-east in 1978. The church was abandoned in 1874 because the majority of parishioners lived nearer to the church of the neighbouring parish.

IX. Recommendations
(Fig. 4)

Responsibilities for preservation up to 1987

Until 1950, the first half of the 16th century had witnessed the greatest number of church abandonments, with a total of seventy-four (Fig. 4). The only half-century likely to approach this total is the second half of the 20th century, whose abandonments so far (December 1987) total fifty medieval churches, three post-medieval churches, plus ten churches or chapels-of-ease founded since 1800, making a total of sixty-three. But although we can draw little comfort from the number of abandonments since 1950, our care in preserving the disused churches compares very favourably with the first half of the 16th century. Of the seventy-four churches abandoned between 1500 and 1550, no less than fifty-five have left no trace of their appearance above ground; eleven are fragmentary ruins; six are substantial ruins and only St Mary-the-Less remains intact since it was made over for use as the French church. Of the fifty medieval churches abandoned between 1950 and 1987, forty-four of them remain fully intact (although some of them have had their furnishings removed), five are largely intact and one survives only as a tower. The three post-medieval churches are all fully intact. The record for churches founded since 1800 has been less successful: two closed but intact, two converted for use as houses, one converted to offices, one partly demolished and four totally demolished (Appendix I).

It must be admitted, therefore, that with a loss of only five, the county has been astonishingly successful in maintaining the fabric of its abandoned churches. The main reason for this is that the responsibility for caring for these churches has been spread among several different bodies. Unless indicated otherwise, these churches have been abandoned since 1950:

Redundant Churches Fund (eighteen churches)
North Barningham (Pl. LXVI)
Barton Bendish, St Mary
Booton
Brandiston (Pl. LXVII)
Buckenham Ferry (Pl. XXVII)
Coston (Pl. XXVI)
Feltwell, St Nicholas (Pl. LX)
Gunton (Pl. XXXVIII)
Hales (Pl. XXIV)
West Harling (Pl. LXIX)
Hockwold (Pl. XXXI)
Islington (Pl. XIV)
Moulton St Mary (Pl. XLVIII)
East Ruston (Pl. XXXII)
Thurgarton
Shimpling
Walpole, St Andrew
Wiggenhall St Mary the Virgin (Pl. LXXII)
(plus West Walton tower, Pl. XXX)

Norwich Historic Churches Trust (fifteen churches)
Norwich All Saints
    St Clement
    St Edmund
    St Etheldreda
    St Gregory
    St James Pockthorpe
    St Margaret
    St Martin at Oak
    St Martin at Palace
    St Mary Coslany
    St Michael Coslany
    St Michael at Pleas
    St Peter Parmentergate
    St Saviour
    St Swithin

Norfolk Churches Trust (ten churches)
Bagthorpe
Barmer
Cockthorpe (Pl. LVIII)
Dunton
Frenze (Pl. LV)
Hargham
Morton-on-the-Hill (Pl. LXII)
Rackheath
West Rudham
Snetterton

Diocesan Board of Finance (six churches)
Crownthorpe (Pl. XLII)
Norwich St Lawrence
Setchey (19th century foundation)
Tivetshall (roofs removed) (Pl. XC)
Tunstall
Burlingham St Peter (abandoned before 1950; Pl. LXXX)

Vested in parishes (four churches)
Forncett St Mary
Panxworth (nave demolished) (Pl. CXIII)
Sco Ruston (roof removed) (Pl. LXXXIX)
South Walsham, St Lawrence (abandoned before 1950)

Vested in Borough Councils (two churches)
South Lynn, St Michael (20th century foundation, largely demolished)
Yarmouth, St George (Pl. LXXIII)

Disposed of by Diocese of Norwich (eight churches)
Babingley, St Felix II (20th century foundation)
Heigham, St Phillip (19th century foundation, demolished, Pl. CXXVI)
Overstrand, Christ Church (19th century foundation, demolished)
Thorpe, St Matthew (19th century foundation, converted to offices, Pl. CXXVIII)
Thorpe, St Leonard (20th century foundation, demolished)
Wymondham, Downham, St Edmund (19th century foundation, converted to house)
Wymondham, Silfield, St Helen (19th century foundation, converted to house)
Yarmouth, St Andrew (19th century foundation, demolished)

Disposed of by Diocese of Ely (one church)
Shingham (leased as private monument Pl. XXXIII)

Friends of Friendless Churches (one church)
Corpusty

Norfolk Museums Service (one church)
Norwich, St Peter Hungate (abandoned before 1950)

The aims of these organisations, and their financial resources, vary considerably. With the Redundant Churches Fund, the church and its contents (if of good quality) are preserved as monuments; the quality of upkeep is exceptionally high. Considering its much more limited resources, the Norfolk Churches Trust have done very well to take on the ten churches leased to them by the diocese of Norwich; again, the quality of upkeep is very high. Should there be further redundancies in the county, the best outcome would be for either of these two bodies to maintain them; but it is uncertain whether either of them will have sufficient resources. The brief given originally to the Norwich Historic Churches Trust unfortunately excluded that of maintaining the church as a monument or in expectation of parochial re-use. Alternative uses have therefore been found for all their churches: it is regrettable that none have been preserved as monuments, and many of the alternative uses found have been rightly criticised as unsympathetic. Most of the churches not cared for by these three bodies have been left to the ingenuity of the Norwich Diocesan Board of Finance. It is hard to find alternative uses for rural churches: Crownthorpe is being converted for use as a craft workshop, but Burlingham St Peter, Forncett St Mary and Setchey remain problematical. Tivetshall St Mary and Sco Ruston have had roofs removed and walls capped, while the nave at Panxworth has been demolished (the latter two now vested in their parishes). Regrettably, neglected churches attract vandalism, and this can reduce the possibility of preservation of the structure as a monument since features and contents of quality are destroyed (Burlingham and Forncett are good examples). Fortunately, two churches have been spared this downward spiral of vandalism and natural decay: St Peter's at Corpusty has been repaired and maintained by the Friends of Friendless Churches since 1981, and St Botolph's at Shingham has been leased to a local landowner as a monument since 1976.

It is often possible to find alternative uses for urban churches, and Norfolk can claim some notable successes here, as well as various less than successful conversions. Re-use by another Christian denomination is eminently sensible: in Norwich, St Mary-the-Less became the French Church as early as the 16th century (but was later transferred to various sects, such as the Swedenborgians, and is now Redundant); St John Maddermarket and St John de Sepulchre in Norwich and St Peter's in Yarmouth are all used as Greek Orthodox churches, and St Mary's in Thetford is Roman Catholic[17]. The church of St Peter Hungate in Norwich was converted for use as an ecclesiastical museum as early as 1932. The following alternative uses have been devised by the Norwich Historic Churches Trust; it is for the reader to decide whether the conversions have been successful or sympathetic: ecumenical centre run by the Mothers' Union (All Saints), prayer and meditation centre (St Clement), planned conversion to offices (St Edmund), sculptor's studio (St Etheldreda), possible use by choral society (St Gregory), puppet theatre (St James Pockthorpe), gymnasium (St Margaret), night shelter (St Martin-at-Oak), planned probation day centre (St Martin-at-Palace), arts and craft centre (St Mary Coslany), sports hall and martial arts centre (St Michael Coslany), exhibition centre (St Michael-at-Pleas), organ builder's workshop (St Peter Parmentergate), badminton Hall (St Saviour), Boy Scouts Association hall (St Simon and St Jude), and Norwich Arts Centre (St Swithin). Of 19th-century churches in Norwich, St Matthew's at Thorpe Hamlet, has been converted into offices (Pl. CXXVIII)[18]. In Wymondham, two chapels-of-ease (St Edmund, Downham and St Helen, Silfield) are now domestic residences. St George's at Yarmouth, a large 18th-century chapel-of-ease, with its wide nave and galleries (Pl. LXXIII), makes a natural theatre and arts centre, as converted by Yarmouth Borough Council; but it is a great shame that its fine original furnishings have been removed, and the interior rather defaced. As with some of the Norwich churches, one feels that St George's would have been an excellent candidate for preservation as a monument with all its contents[19].

Recommendations for the future
Of the churches not formally cared for to date, the author would like to make the following proposals[20]:

1. The future of all Category I churches should be assured. Of the thirty-four in this category, twenty-eight are maintained by the Redundant Churches Fund and the Norfolk Churches Trust. Four of the remaining churches are in the Stanford Training Area (in the care of the Ministry of Defence); one of these, West Tofts, is of such importance nationally, and so near the edge of the Ministry of Defence property, that it should have its furnishings restored and be made open to the general public.

Of the remaining churches, alternative uses have been found for two (Crownthorpe, St James and Yarmouth, St George). One has been declared Redundant as recently as 1987 (Illington), and should be preserved as a monument. Forncett St Mary might have been a candidate for preservation as a monument, but has unfortunately suffered from vandalism and neglect; it should be either fully repaired, or have its roofs removed and walls capped. In equally bad condition is St Peter and St Paul at Runham, but this has yet to be declared Redundant; it is to be hoped that it can be repaired and returned to use. The future of Narford church should be assured; access has been denied by the landowner for the past thirty years.

2. A programme of care should be initiated for the ninety-nine sites with visible remains (Categories II-V). Priority should be given to those of County Importance (section II, Appendix VII). The ruined churches of Bawsey, Castle Rising and North Elmham are Scheduled Ancient Monuments in the care of English Heritage. Similar care should be extended to three ruined churches of exceptional quality: Appleton, Babingley and Wiggenhall St Peter. Because of their quality, these two churches should be cared for in the way the diocese of Norwich is maintaining (de-roofed) churches at Great Hautbois, Sco Ruston and Tivetshall St Mary: walls capped and interior kept clear (the solution at Panxworth was rather less satisfactory, since, although the west tower and churchyard are being maintained, the 19th-century nave and chancel were demolished). It must be emphasized that churches which have their fabric repaired or consolidated in this way should be the subject of thorough archaeological recording, as took place at Panxworth, Sco Ruston and Tivestshall. Without this, the repairs can destroy the archaeological potential of the site. There are a further sixteen churches which are being left to deteriorate, but are of County Importance (Appendix VII). Nine are at present the responsibility of the diocese of Norwich:

Edgefield
Fulmodestone
Hopton
Houghton-on-the-Hill
Kempstone
Roudham
Saxlingham Thorpe
Surlingham St Saviour
Wretham, West

Seven are on private land:
Egmere
Lynn, Kings', St James
Pudding Norton
Snarehill
Walton, East
Wallington
Wolterton

Only five are Scheduled Ancient Monuments (Appleton, Roudham, West Wretham, East Walton and Wolterton). The remaining twelve should be scheduled forthwith.

3. A co-ordinated county 'net' should be established to work towards the preservation of some or all of the monuments designated as Of County Importance. Bearing in mind that the success that Norfolk has achieved to date in caring for its disused churches is largely due to the spreading of the load among a number of bodies, the more groupings able to share the responsibility the better.

The diocese of Norwich (and the diocese of Ely in the south-west part of the county) has an obvious interest and responsibility here. But other bodies have a similar interest, especially those with a responsibility for the environment. English Heritage already has an involvement with scheduled sites such as Bawsey, Castle Rising and North Elmham; such interest could be extended. Norfolk County Council has an equally clear mandate for preserving the environment; ruined churches of County Importance should be within its environmental brief. As a flagship project, together with English Heritage and other interested parties, Norfolk County Council should aim to restore and return to the public the important church of West Tofts; secure the future of the Category I churches of Langford, Stanford and Tottington, all on Ministry of Defence land; preserve the ruined churches of Appleton, Babingley and Wiggenhall St Peter; and, together with the dioceses and local landowners, work out a programme of conservation for the seventeen further Churches Of County Importance listed above. A programme should also be drawn up for the forty-eight sites Of Local Importance (section III, Appendix VII); some responsibility could be devolved to more local bodies (parish councils, P.C.C.s, local landowners etc.).

Of the ruined sites, the following are Scheduled Ancient Monuments:
Appleton
Babingley
Bawsey
Bowthorpe
Buckenham, New, St Mary
Garboldisham, All Saints
Hautbois, St Mary
Ringstead, Great, St Peter
Ringstead, Little
Roudham
Southwood
Walton, East, St Andrew
Wolterton
Wretham, West

To be consistent, the remaining ruined churches should also be scheduled (a total of 77.):
Antingham, St Margaret
Barnham Broom, St Michael
Barwick, Great
Bastwick
Bayfield
Beachamwell, All Saints
Beachamwell, St John
Beckham, East
Beckham, West
Bickerston
Bircham Tofts
Burgh Parva
Burgh St Mary
Burlingham, St Peter
Burnham Sutton
Caister, West
Carlton, East, St Peter
Colveston
Creake, North, St Michael
Croxton, St John
Eccles-by-the-Sea
Edgefield
Egmere
Foulden
Fulmodeston
Gasthorpe
Gillingham, All Saints
Godwick
Hackford, All Saints
Hainford
Heigham, St Bartholomew
Hempton, St Andrew
Hindolveston
Hopton
Houghton-on-the-Hill
Kempstone
Kirby Bedon, St Mary
Letton
Leziate
Lynn, King's, St James
Mannington
Melton, Great, St Mary
Mintlyn
Mundham, St Ethelbert
Oxborough, St Mary Magdalen
Oxwick
Panxworth
Pensthorpe
Pudding Norton
Quarles
Raynham, West

Rockland, St Andrew
Rockland, St Mary, St Margaret
Ryburgh, Little
Saxlingham Thorpe
Sco Ruston
Shotesham, St Botolph
Shotesham, St Martin
Snarehill
Somerton, East
Southery
Stanninghall
Surlingham, St Saviour
Tatterset, St Andrew
Testerton
Thorpe-by-Norwich
Thorpe Parva
Thorpland
Tivetshall, St Mary
Tunstall, St Peter and St Paul
Wallington
Walsham, South, St Lawrence
Walsingham, Great, All Saints
Weeting, All Saints
Whitlingham
Wiggenhall, St Peter
Wood Norton, St Peter

Three Category VI sites are also Scheduled (Caldecote, Sturston, Thetford St John). Should the remaining 122 be scheduled too?

To sum up with reference to Appendices VII and VIII: the churches with architectural features or contents of National Importance are in the care of the Redundant Churches Fund or the Norfolk Churches Trust, with the exception of West Tofts. The same two bodies are responsible for a number of churches categorised as Of County Importance; but in this latter category, there are twenty-one sites for which there is little in the way of consistent preservation of remains:

Appleton
Babingley
Edgefield
Egmere
Forncett, St Mary
Fulmodestone
Hopton
Houghton-on-the-Hill
Kempstone
Lynn, King's, St James
Narford
Pudding Norton
Roudham
Saxlingham Thorpe
Snarehill
Surlingham, St Saviour
Wallington
Walton, East, St Andrew
Wiggenhall, St Peter
Wolterton
Wretham, West

There should be a continuing commitment to the preservation of these sites:
Bawsey
Hautbois, Great
Panxworth
Sco Ruston
Tivetshall St Mary

These constitute a priority for action; although the many sites of Local Interest should not be neglected.

X. Format of Catalogue

A full report has been written for each site, but only thirty-six have been printed in full in the main text. The remaining reports are filed in the microfiche at the back of the volume but a summary for each site can be found in the Catalogue of Sites (pp.50). The catalogue entries are divided into six categories to give an indication of the amount of church fabric still standing at each site. Category I and Category VI are the easiest to differentiate, the former comprising the churches which are fully intact (including roofs), the latter consisting of the churches which have left no trace above ground. Categories II to V are therefore those churches in various degrees of ruination. The six categories are classified as follows:

Category I: Fully Intact (walls fully standing, roofs intact)
Category II: Largely Intact (most of walls standing to full height)
Category III: Substantial Ruin (coherent standing walls)
Category IV: Tower Only (tower forming most substantial part of ruin)
Category V: Fragmentary Remains (very low walling or incoherent remains)
Category VI: Disappeared (no above-ground remains)

There is bound to be a degree of overlap between Categories II and III and Categories III and V, but the classifications remain useful indicators of the amount of church fabric left standing. Some Category IV sites yield more than just a tower, but in all the sites in this Category, the tower stands out as the most substantial part of the ruin.

The sites in Category VI are those with no above-ground remains *in situ*. Several sites have left fragments of carved stone or brick, but if removed from their original location have been recorded under Category VI; further information about sites in this category has been gathered from written sources, drawings, excavations and aerial photographs[21].

The thirty-six site reports in the main text provide six examples from each category. They therefore range from reports on churches which are fully standing and retain all their contents, to reports on sites where there are no visible remains. Whilst they form a representative sample of the whole survey, some have been selected because of the availability of useful illustrations. This is true of the five churches whose fabric was recorded in 1978 (Burlingham St Peter, Kempstone, Panxworth, Sco Ruston, Tivetshall) by Andrew Rogerson and his team from the Norfolk Archaeological Unit (funded by a grant from the Department of the Environment). Of the Category I sites, North Barningham, West Harling and Wiggenhall St Mary the Virgin were selected because of the interest in their contents as well as the quality of their architecture. Brandiston was chosen because of its unusual building sequence, West Tofts because of its situation in the Stanford Training Area and as an example of an important work by one of the 19th century's finest architects, Pugin. St George's at Yarmouth provides an example of an urban church, as well as being that rare thing in Norfolk, a post-medieval foundation. Of the Category II sites, Burlingham, Kempstone, Sco Ruston and Tivetshall chose themselves for the reasons given above; Babingley and Great Hautbois for the intrinsic interest of their sites, with the question of patronage for the former and pilgrimage for the latter. With the exception of West Raynham, the Category III sites have been selected because they shed light on the development of church design in the 11th and 12th centuries; in particular, Snarehill remains unique in the county in terms of design. Amongst the Category IV sites, Hindolveston was chosen for its graphic illustration of structural collapse, and the remaining sites (Egmere, Godwick, Pudding Norton, Wallington) because of their relationship to their deserted villages; Panxworth was recorded by Rogerson's team in 1978. Opportunism accounts for the selection of two of the Category V sites: Weeting, because the outline of the church appeared as parchmarks during the hot summer of 1983, and Burnham Sutton because of the walls revealed by an illegal excavation in 1985. Great Walsingham is of extra interest because of its relationship with important 14th-century churches, Eccles is the only site with any remains after destruction by the sea, Hackford is unique in being one of three churches within the same churchyard, and St James in King's Lynn is of enormous interest because of its reuse after closure in a variety of secular guises and because of the discovery of much carved stone from the site in a house 10km away. Availability of illustrations played an important part in choosing the Category VI sites: there are superbly revealing aerial photographs of Ashby, Holverston, Itteringham and Ormesby. St Giles provided the best drawing of the many Thetford sites, and Fincham has one of the best descriptions prior to demolition.

XI. Format of Reports

One formula has been followed in recording each site:

Identification
a) Eight-figure grid reference (where site is known precisely), which defines a 10m square in the middle of the site.
b) County number, *i.e.* reference number in the Sites and Monuments Record of the Norfolk Archaeological Unit.
c) Diocese (*i.e.* Norwich or Ely).
d) Archdeaconry
e) Deanery
f) Parish, *i.e.* ecclesiastical parish; not post-1950 grouping of parishes.
g) Status: parish church or parochial chapel; disused, ruined or disappeared.
h) Date last in regular use.
i) Ownership and access.

Location and setting
Where to find the church, the context and its environment, its situation within the village, parish, town *etc*.

Architectural description
This is detailed, and proceeds systematically from east to west: chancel (east wall, south wall, north wall, chancel arch, roof); nave (south wall or arcade, north wall or arcade, roof); south aisle; south porch; north aisle; north porch; west tower (outline, tower arch, first storey, second storey, third storey, parapet). See Glossary for architectural vocabulary.

Interpretation and dating
Reconstruction of the phases of construction and an approximate chronology.

Causes of abandonment
Date and probable reasons for abandonment.

Church contents
The contents consist of glass and wall-paintings, as well as monuments and furnishings.

Whereabouts of contents
i.e. those contents removed from the church.

Condition
A brief list of defects, not a surveyor's report.

Churchyard
Shape, boundaries, condition, headstones, date of last burial.

Archaeological Record
Finds from church and churchyard.

Archaeological and architectural assessment
An evaluative summary.

Further references
Includes literature not yet referred to in the report.

Format of plans
Of the thirty-six reports printed in the main text, fifteen are accompanied with detailed measured plans. These plans have been the basis for phase plans in which construction belonging to each new phase is shaded in solid black, with any previous phase stippled.

A disagreeable anomaly in these plans (for which the author, and not the illustrator, is to blame) is the omission of window mullions. The rationale behind this, feeble as it may seem in retrospect, can be found in the difficulty in representing much-renewed mullions in a phase plan without leaving a misleading impression. This difficulty should not have precluded them being drawn on the unphased measured plans.

XII. Historical sources
(Figs. 14, 19; Plates I, LIX-LX, LXIII, XCVII-XCVIII)

The most important sources are the buildings themselves, which will always repay careful study. Even an unpretentious church such as Great Hautbois yields a fascinating historical development, with its extensions to facilitate the access of pilgrims to the image of St Theobald (Fig. 19); other churches may raise interesting questions, for example, whose patronage was responsible for the rebuilding, in three rapid phases, of the church at Babingley (Fig. 14)? To the inquisitive, an examination of the fabric of a church will always generate more questions than answers; and there is a very good chance, especially with the churches in this volume, of noticing something that no-one has observed to date. This survey is not exhaustive and nor does it say the last word on the sites recorded within it.

Second in importance as sources are the drawings of the churches, and, more recently, the photographs. Supreme among the former for artistic quality are those by John Sell Cotman (especially his 'Architectural Etchings of Norfolk' 1838). Whilst generally accurate in their details, Cotman was always able to discover the dramatic or the Romantic in his subject; even to the humble porch at Mintlyn, he imparts a certain grandeur and nobility in decay (Pl. XCVIII). John Ladbrooke's lithographs are more sober and on the whole more trustworthy, if lacking the vision and animation of Cotman. Ladbrooke began his series of Norfolk churches in 1823 and completed it in 1846; the series therefore gives important information about the form of the churches before their mid- or late-Victorian restorations. Some churches have changed dramatically since Ladbrooke's time: in particular, Hindolveston (Pl. I), Southwood (Pl. LXIII) and Feltwell (Pl. LIX, now oddly truncated, Pl. LX, with the loss of both chancel and tower). More recent disasters have been documented by photographs; the archives of the National Monuments Record have furnished a number of photographs of parts of churches that are now gone (*e.g.* the porch and portal at Mintlyn, Pl. XCVII, now destroyed).

Of third importance are the primary written sources, from *Domesday Book* onwards. Medieval valuations of parishes and archdeacon's itineraries are especially useful. Diocesan records are invaluable, particularly the Faculty Bonds (beginning *c.* 1630) which record alterations in church fabric. Parish records can also supply a wide range of information.

Last of all come the writings of historians. Norfolk is fortunate in possessing the 'Essay Towards a Topographical History of the County of Norfolk' by Francis Blomefield, which includes church descriptions gathered by the author from the 1730s to the 1750s (and completed by Parkin from the 1770s) and published initially in five volumes from 1730 to 1775; the edition quoted in this volume was published in eleven volumes from 1805 to 1810. For more recent county-wide church surveys, reference should be made to Bryant, Cautley, Cox, Pevsner and Messent (see Bibliography, p.188). The latter's publications include a slim volume entitled 'The Ruined Churches of Norfolk' (1931), in which he identifies some 240 sites: many of them erroneous (see Appendix IV).

Endnotes

1. These updates, plus print-outs of reports in microfiche from the back of the volume, can be obtained on application to the Unit. It is inevitable that there will be omissions and inaccuracies in a survey of this magnitude. Comments/applications (with A4 SAE) should be addressed to: Ruined Churches, Norfolk Archaeological Unit, Union House, Gressenhall, Dereham, Norfolk.
2. The six demolished are Heigham, St Philip, South Lynn St Michael, Overstrand Christ Church, Lower Sheringham St Peter I, Thorpe Hamlet St Leonard, and Yarmouth St Andrew. The two converted to houses are both in the parish of Wymondham: Downham St Edmund, and Silfield St Helen. St Matthew I at Thorpe Hamlet has been converted to offices. Babingley St Felix II and Setchey St Mary remain intact, but disused.
3. Two were rebuilt in the 17th century: Hoveton St Peter and Santon. Four were rebuilt in the 18th century: Bawdeswell, Gunton, North Runcton, Thorpe Market. Great Yarmouth St George remains the only church to be both founded and built in the 18th-century. Bawdeswell was totally rebuilt again in 1844, and once more in 1950; it now resembles an 18th-century church!
4. Of the 620 medieval foundations still in use, eight were rebuilt in post-medieval times. Of the 308 no longer in use, one (Booton) was rebuilt in the 19th century.
5. By which is meant that part of Norwich within the medieval city walls; parish churches in the suburbs (e.g. Heigham) are included in this survey.
6. There are 254 sites of disused or ruined churches in the county (excluding Norwich); the fact that there are 255 entries in the catalogue is due to the inclusion of the free-standing tower at West Walton: the tower is officially Redundant, but the adjacent church remains in use. The West Walton entry therefore cannot form part of the statistics for churches.
7. The deaneries of Feltwell, Fincham, and Lynn Marshland lie wholly within Norfolk. The deaneries of Wisbech, March and Ely lie mainly in Cambridgeshire, but between them contain six Norfolk parishes. A further anomaly is the parish of Santon near Thetford, in the deanery of Mildenhall: a solitary intrusion of the diocese of St Edmundsbury and Ipswich into Norfolk.
8. Fritton and Hopton are the only Lothingland parishes in Norfolk. Even more oddly, the parish of Knettishall (with an interesting ruined church) in Suffolk belongs to the deanery of Thetford and Rockland in Norfolk. There are only two ruined sites (Flixton and Knettishall) and two demolished sites (Lowestoft St John and St Peter) in the Suffolk part of the diocese of Norwich.
9. Outside King's Lynn proper, the church of West Lynn was destroyed by flood in 1272, that at North Lynn was inundated in the 1680s, and in South Lynn the (short-lived) church of St Michael, built in 1910, was demolished in 1972.
10. *Domesday Book* records the pre-Conquest church of St Benedict, which de Losinga replaced with his new parish church of St Nicholas (Morant, 1872, 227). It is not certain what became of the church at Southtown (presumably not St Benedict's) which was standing in 1254.
11. Stoke Holy Cross is entered in *Domesday* as possessing 1½ churches. Those with two churches in the same entry are: Barton Turf, East Carlton, Carleton Rode, Helmingham, Hempnall, Hoveton, Langham, Rudham, Seething, Shouldham, Tattersett, Tivetshall, Tuddenham, Wheatacre, Worstead and Wroxham. Those with separate entries are Barsham (3), Barton Bendish (2), Burlingham (3), Cressingham (2), Foulsham (2), Hethersett (2), Shotesham (2), Stoke Ferry (2), and Waxham (2).
12. Warner (1986) is wildly inaccurate in listing thirty-eight places in Norfolk with two or more churches in one churchyard.
13. Calendar of Papal Letters, Vol. V, pp. 474-5. I am extremely grateful to Alan Davison for the provision of this reference.
14. 'Ecclesia Sci Martini predicta solvit dicta synodalia pro eo quod parochiani dicte ecclesie Sancti Mathei ruinose percipiunt sacramenta et sacramentalia ibidem et recursum habent ad eandem pestilencie magne contingentis in anno Dni Millesimo CCC mo xl nono'. (Watkin 1947, 26-27).
15. Norwich St Stephen's was finished in 1550; Hoveton St Peter's was rebuilt on the site of the medieval church in 1624; and All Saints at North Runcton was rebuilt on the site of the old church in 1703-13.
16. Babingley formerly possessed a bell made by the same founder (L'Estrange 1874, 87). Intriguingly, three medieval bells from All Saints Barton Bendish, demolished in 1787, have found their way to the belfry of St Michael's at Whitwell.
17. Four churches, Norwich St John Maddermarket and St John de Sepulchre, Thetford St Mary and Yarmouth St Peter have not been included in this survey because they are still in regular use for Christian worship. There is a slight inconsistency here, since they are no longer in use as Church of England places of worship.
18. No doubt alternative uses could also have been found for St Philip's at Heigham, regrettably demolished in 1977.
19. One of Yarmouth's nineteenth century chapels-of-ease, St Andrew's has been demolished.
20. This excludes consideration of the Norwich churches in the care of the Norwich Historic Churches Trust.
21. Bowthorpe, Little Ringstead and Thorpe-by-Norwich are included in Category II because, although only part of the original church survives, the walls mostly stand to full height. Antingham, Burgh Parva, Gasthorpe and Kirby Bedon might have been included in Category IV rather than Category III on account of the relatively good state of preservation of their towers; but they also have substantial remains of chancel and nave. Egmere, on the other hand, has been classified as Category IV despite retaining large portions of its nàve: but there is bound to be an element of overlap between Categories III and IV. Two surprising inclusions in Category IV are Little Snoring and West Walton: both are free-standing towers near to churches which are still in use. In the case of Little Snoring, the tower of *c.* 1100 was evidently the west tower of a church later demolished and rebuilt towards the end of the 12th century on an adjacent site to north. The tower, although still in use, is the surviving remnant of a demolished church. West Walton tower is included because, separate from its church, it was declared Redundant in 1974 and vested in the Redundant Churches Fund.

Chapter 2. Catalogue of Sites; Summary Reports

Paper copies of microfiche reports available from Norfolk Archaeological Unit.

I. Category I

1. **Bagthorpe, St Mary** *TF 7599 3221* Nave, chancel, north vestry; entirely rebuilt 1853. Interesting Norman font. Disused 1970, declared Redundant and leased to Norfolk Churches Trust in 1979. Very small village.
2. **Barmer, All Saints** *TF 8090 3361* Chancel, nave, north aisle, round west tower. Nave and tower late 12th century; north aisle first half 14th century, aisle and chancel rebuilt 1885. Church mentioned in *Domesday*. Disused 1977, declared Redundant and leased to Norfolk Churches Trust in 1978; small village, isolated church (Pl. X).
3. **Barningham, North, St Peter** *TG 1505 3715* See Full Reports, p.56.
4. **Barton Bendish, St Mary** *TF 7097 0544* Chancel, nave, north vestry. Magnificent *c.* 1180 west doorway, moved from All Saints in 1789; chancel *c.* 1340; nave *c.* 1370; tower collapsed *c.* 1710. Medieval wall paintings inside. Church mentioned in *Domesday*. Declared Redundant 1974; St Andrew's more central; vested in Redundant Churches Fund in 1976.
5. **Brandiston, St Nicholas** *TG 1412 2141* See Full Reports, p.60.
6. **Buckenham Ferry, St Nicholas** *TG 3555 0586* Chancel, nave, north vestry, octagonal west tower. Nave first half of 12th century, tower (Pl. XXVII) and north doorway 13th century, chancel *c.* 1300, all thoroughly restored first half of 19th century. Good 15th-century font (Pl. XLIX). Abandoned by 1968, village almost totally depopulated; declared Redundant and vested in Redundant Churches Fund in 1979.
7. **Cockthorpe, All Saints** *TF 9813 4222* Chancel and nave *c.* 1100; tower and south aisle late 13th century; nave heightened and south porch built 15th century; chancel shortened mid-16th century. Calthorp tomb chest and monument. Leased to Norfolk Churches Trust in 1978; very small village.
8. **Corpusty, St Peter** *TG 1150 2940* Chancel and nave in one, tower, south porch; all second half 14th century. Church mentioned in *Domesday*. Abandoned since 1965; isolated location, 1km from village. Leased to Friends of Friendless Churches.
9. **Coston, St Michael** *TG 0621 0620* Chancel, nave and tower all late 13th century; south porch 16th century; chancel shortened eighteenth century (Pl. XXVI). Village almost non-existent; abandoned 1970; vested in the Redundant Churches Fund 1979.
10. **Crownthorpe, St James** *TG 0830 0311* Nave 12th century, chancel and (demolished) north chapel 13th century; south chapel (demolished), south porch and west tower 15th century (Pls XLII, XLIII). Abandoned *c.* 1970; very small village; church at Wicklewood 1.2km south-west; being converted for use as craft workshop.
11. **Dunton, St Peter** *TF 8794 3031* Chancel and nave *c.* 1300; west tower, north wall of nave, south porch, 15th century. Abandoned in 1978, leased to Norfolk Churches Trust; very small village.
12. **Feltwell, St Nicholas** *TL 7123 9089* Round west tower early 12th century (most of it fell down in 1898), also original nave (Pl. LIX); south aisle early 13th century (Pl XXVIII), north aisle 15th century; south porch early 16th century; Flushwork clerestorey; chancel demolished 1861 (Pl. LX). Status reduced to that of mortuary chapel in 1861; vested in Redundant Churches Fund in 1976. Church of St Mary's larger and more central.
13. **Forncett, St Mary** *TM 1662 9383* Church mentioned in *Domesday*. Core of nave 12th/13th century, windows 15th century. Chancel rebuilt in 1869 with adjoining south vestry. West tower built in 1430s. North porch roofless. Interior largely remodelled in 19th century. Poor condition; some of windows vandalised. Abandoned 1979; scattered village, Forncett St Peter church only 1km south.
14. **Frenze, St Andrew** *TM 1352 8043* Chancel and nave in one, 13th century; south porch late 15th century; chancel shortened in 1827. Superb brasses of the Blenerhaysett family (Pl. XLIV a,b); early 17th century pulpit and pew (Pl. LX). Abandoned in 1976, leased to Norfolk Churches Trust 1980; very thinly populated parish.
15. **Gunton, St Andrew** *TG 2290 3413* One of very few churches built by Robert Adam: Doric portico, single nave, west gallery, all 1769 (Pls XXXVIII–XLI). Abandoned 1976, vested in Redundant Churches Fund 1977; very sparsely populated parish.
16. **Hales, St Margaret** *TM 3835 9610* Perhaps the most perfectly preserved Norman parish church in the county: apsidal chancel, nave with two magnificent portals, round west tower, all *c.* 1130 (PLS XXIV, XXV). 15th century wall paintings and font. Abandoned 1967, Vested in Redundant Churches Fund in 1974; isolated site; 1.5km from the village.
17. **Harling, West, All Saints** *TL 9740 8518* See Full Reports, p.65.
18. **Hockwold, St Peter** *TL 7249 8518* South aisle (and arcade), porch and west tower all first half 14th century (Pl. XXXI); chancel and nave first half 16th century. Tower retains original bell-frame. Nave roof early 16th-century (Pl. XXXVII). Some fine 18th century monuments (Pl. LII). Abandoned and vested in the Redundant Churches Fund 1974. Wilton church is more central for the village.
19. **Illington, St Andrew** *TL 9481 8999* Late 11th/12th century nave, with a single-splayed round-headed window in north and south walls. Chancel and west tower 15th century. Former south aisle of two bays, now blocked. South porch. Abandoned and declared Redundant in 1987; tiny village comprising twenty-two people.
20. **Langford, St Andrew** *TL 8375 9654* Nave and square chancel, first half 12th century; west tower collapsed 1764. Fine Norman chancel arch; very good monument to Sir Nicholas Garrod (d. 1727). Abandoned in 1942 to form part of Battle Training Area.
21. **Moulton, St Mary** *TG 4023 0665* Chancel, nave, and round west tower, all *c.* 1300; south porch *c.* 1500 (Pl. IX). 14th century wall paintings (Pl. XLVII); 13th century Purbeck marble font (Pl. XLVIII); Jacobean furnishings (Pl. LVI); alabaster monument to Anguishe family, 1628 (Pl. LI). Abandoned in 1965; village of Moulton over 1km away. Vested in the Redundant Churches Fund in 1980.
22. **Narford, St Mary** *TF 7644 1378* Chancel and nave *c.* 1100 A.D. North and south aisles early 14th century, two-bay arcades. Tower with openwork parapet, Perpendicular in style but rebuilt in the 19th century. Early 16th century south porch. Set in grounds of Narford Hall. Contains good monuments of the Fountaine family. Closed for worship *c.* 1960 by owner of Narford Hall, and access denied to the diocese.
23. **Rackheath, All Saints** *TG 2701 1495* Chancel, vestry, nave, south aisle, south porch, west tower. Nave *c.* 1100, chancel and aisle late 13th century, south porch and west tower 15th century. Monuments to the Pettus family, 17th and 18th century. Isolated site, with village 1km to south-east; abandoned 1948; new church built in centre of village in 1959. All Saints declared Redundant and leased to Norfolk Churches Trust in 1981.
24. **Rudham, West, St Peter** *TF 8195 2764* Chancel, nave, south aisle, west tower. Nave and arcade second half 13th century; tower early 14th century; chancel, nave, north wall, roof and clerestorey *c.* 1430. Excellent 15th century painted glass in nave north windows. Made Redundant and leased to Norfolk Churches Trust in 1979; East Rudham church (1km away) adequate for the needs of both parishes; West Rudham church the more isolated of the two.
25. **Ruston, East, St Mary** *TG 3641 2868* Chancel, nave, south aisle, south porch, west tower. Chancel early 14th century; nave, south aisle and tower mid-14th century (Pl. XXXII); south porch 15th century; north aisle demolished and nave north wall rebuilt 1771. Excellent 15th century painted rood screen; good 15th century font (restored). Isolated site, 2km from village of East Ruston; abandoned in 1975 after deterioration of roof; vested in Redundant Churches Fund in 1981.
26. **Shimpling, St George** *TM 1561 8262* Church mentioned in *Domesday*. Nave *c.* 1100, blocked single-splay window in south

wall. Chancel same width as nave, c. 1300, east window with Intersecting tracery. Round west tower with octagonal belfry and brick stair-turret, all late 14th/15th century. North porch rebuilt 1867. Good arch-braced roof to nave. Superb 15th century font, with lions on stem and Evangelist symbols on bowl. Good painted glass, 14th century canopies in chancel, 15th century angels in nave. Church rather isolated from small village; alternative churches 1.5km and 2km away; vested in the Redundant Churches Fund 1985.

27. **Shingham, St Botolph** *TF 7613 0510* Chancel and nave in one. Nave 12th century, with fine south portal with scallop capitals and geometric motifs (Pl. XXIII). Chancel c. 1340, reticulated tracery in east window (Pl. XXXIII). Good set of medieval benches; fine 17th century two-decker pulpit and altar-rails. Nave roofless and chancel used as mortuary chapel in 1911, subsequently roofed in corrugated iron and brought back into use until 1941; very small, scattered village. Kept in good repair by local landowner.

28. **Snetterton, All Saints** *TL 9940 9100* Chancel, nave, north aisle, north and south porches, west tower. Chancel second half 13th century, remodelled c. 1450; west tower mid-14th century; nave and north aisle c. 1450; porches c. 1501. Abandoned from 1971; church in isolated part of parish, centre of population 1km north; leased to Norfolk Churches Trust in 1978.

29. **Stanford, All Saints** *TL 8576 9471* Chancel, vestry, nave, north and south aisles, south porch, round west tower. Tower c. 1100, belfry 15th century; nave and arcades first half 14th century; chancel, aisles and porch rebuilt 1852-1855. Abandoned in 1942 for Battle Training Area.

30. **Thurgarton, All Saints** *TF 1819 3589* Chancel, nave, south porch, west vestry (formerly tower); chancel and nave first half 14th century; porch 15th century. Interesting carved bench-ends. Fairly isolated site, 1km from centre of population of the village. Vested in Redundant Churches Fund 1982.

31. **Tottington, St Andrew** *TL 8939 9551* Chancel, nave, north and south aisles, south porch, west tower. Chancel and tower first half 14th century; nave and aisles c. 1378-1405; porch 15th century. Originally contained good 15th-century benches (Pl. LIII) and screen (Pl. LVII). Abandoned in 1942 to make way for Battle Training Area.

32. **West Tofts, St Mary** *TL 8360 9289* See Full Reports, p.72.
33. **Wiggenhall, St Mary the Virgin** *TF 5826 1439* See Full Reports, p.76.
34. **Yarmouth, Great, St George** *TG 5261 0734* See Full Reports, p.79.

II. Category II

35. **Appleton, St Mary** *TF 7055 2728* Nave, round west tower, south porch; chancel and south aisle largely destroyed. Nave and tower c. 1100, chancel 13th century, aisle early 14th century (Pl. VIII), south porch 16th century. Church mentioned in *Domesday*. Abandoned late 17th century; small village (ten households in 1428); owned by landlord in 16th century.

36. **Babingley, St Felix** *TF 6662 2610* See Full Reports, p.83.
37. **Bayfield, St Margaret** *TG 1495 4049* Nave c. 1100, chancel 15th century. Abandoned mid-17th century; small village (less than ten households in 1428); had some arable converted to pasture by 1517; site near hall suggestive of emparkment.
38. **Bircham Tofts, St Andrew** *TF 7779 3251* Nave and tower 15th century; chancel demolished in 18th century. Abandoned in late 1940s; small village, church at Great Bircham only 1km away.
39. **Bowthorpe, St Michael** *TG 1773 0910* 14th-century chancel, made into reduced church in 17th century. Excavations in 1985 uncovered a c. 1100 nave and round west tower. Abandoned in 1792 because of lack of parishioners (only one house). New church built adjoining in 1986.
40. **Burlingham, St Peter** *TG 3684 1005* See Full Reports, p.88.
41. **Croxton, St John the Baptist** *TF 9839 3095* Church mentioned in *Domesday*. Nave and chancel in one, 11th/12th century; remains of north porch, 15th century. Nave extended to west in 17th century. Abandoned in 1880; an inconvenient distance from the centre of population; new church built in centre of Fulmodeston 0.9km to east.
42. **Fulmodestone, St Mary** *TF 9930 3005* Church mentioned in *Domesday*. Chancel and nave in one, 12th/13th century; east window with intersecting tracery; west tower c. 1450, good west doorway and sound-holes. Abandoned in 1882, when new church built in centre of village; continued for a time as a mortuary chapel.

43. **Hargham, All Saints** *TM 0199 9135* Chancel and east end of nave intact; most of nave demolished; west tower ruinous; all 14th-15th century. Abandoned and leased to Norfolk Churches Trust, 1979; village deserted by 18th century, wholly owned by landlord.
44. **Hautbois, Great, St Mary** *TG 2617 2043* See Full Reports, p.94.
45. **Hopton, St Margaret** *TM 5300 9996* Chancel and north chapel, nave and north aisle, first half 14th century, west tower and north porch 15th century. Church caught fire in 1865; a new church was built on a different site in 1866.
46. **Houghton-on-the-Hill, St Mary** *TF 8691 0538* Nave 11th century; west tower 15th century; chancel 18th century. Abandoned c. 1945; isolated site, village deserted.
47. **Islington, St Mary** *TF 5709 1689* Nave 12th century, chancel and transepts late 13th century (Pl. XXIX), west tower and north porch late 15th century. Church mentioned in *Domesday*. Abandoned in 1950s, lead from roof stolen in 1970, roof removed in 1972, vested in Redundant Churches Fund in 1973; very small village (Pl. XIV).
48. **Kempstone, St Paul** *TF 8862 1604* See Full Reports, p.97.
49. **Mannington** *TG 1416 3187* Fragments of square chancel, nave almost fully standing, all c. 1100 in essence. Abandoned mid-18th century, village long deserted.
50. **Morton-on-the-Hill, St Margaret** *TG 1263 1587* Nave and round west tower 11th century, chancel c. 1300, north chapel and south porch 15th century including good door (Pl. LIV). Tower collapsed in 1959, partly destroying nave (Pl. LXI, LXII); church abandoned, parish very sparsely populated. Leased to Norfolk Church Trust in 1980.
51. **Oxwick, All Saints** *TF 9101 2532* Chancel and nave in one, and south porch c. 1300; original chancel demolished in 17th century; tower reduced to single storey in 18th century. Abandoned in 1940; village depopulated.
52. **Ringstead, Little, St Andrew** *TF 6836 3994* Single cell, 13th century, possibly the chancel of a larger church. Abandoned probably in second half 14th century; continued as chapel until 16th century; converted to barn in 17th century; small village, depopulated by plague in 1349.
53. **Roudham, St Andrew** *TF 9581 8715* Nave and south tower, c. 1340; chancel c. 1400. Abandoned in 1734, after catching fire (Pl. XIII). Village greatly depopulated.
54. **Sco Ruston, St Michael** *TG 2840 2181* See Full Reports, p.101.
55. **Shotesham, St Martin** *TM 2378 9867* Nave and chancel in one, west tower. Chancel and nave late 15th/early 16th century, nave earlier. Abandoned in 17th century; only 100m from St Mary's, and one of four Shotesham churches.
56. **Somerton, East, St Mary** *TG 4809 1971* Chancel gone, but nave and tower substantially intact; all 15th century. Abandoned by 17th century; chapel of ease to Winterton, only 0.7km east of West Somerton church.
57. **Southery, St Mary** *TL 6227 9469* Chancel and nave. Much 12th century stonework reused in walls; north walls of nave and chancel 15th century; nave west wall 1747; chancel and nave south walls 1828 (Pl.XI). New church built 200m away in 1858; old church abandoned.
58. **Southwood, St Edmund** *TG 3910 9531* Chancel and nave in one, west tower. Chancel 13th century; nave earlier; tower 13th-15th century (Pls LXIII, LXIV). Isolated site, abandoned in 1881, since the parishioners of Southwood lived nearer to Limpenhoe church.
59. **Thorpe-by-Norwich, St Andrew** *TG 2608 2645* South wall of nave, south tower; 16th century. Reduced to a 'picturesque' ruin in 1881; a new church had been built to north in 1866 because the old church was too small for the congregation of this expanding Norwich suburb.
60. **Tivetshall, St Mary** *TM 1663 8581* See Full Reports, p.108. Two churches mentioned in *Domesday* (the other presumably Tivetshall, St Margaret).
61. **Tunstall, St Peter and St Paul** *TM 4170 0801* Chancel, roofless nave and tower, all second half 14th century. Church mentioned in *Domesday*. Nave roof collapsed in 1704, but chancel repaired and remained in use until declared Redundant in 1980; small village; 15th century traceried font.
62. **Walsham, South, St Laurence** *TG 3659 1328* Chancel and most of nave, repaired after fire in 1827; original work 15th century; rubble from tower (collapsed 1971). Remained in use as a parish church until 1890, and as a Sunday School until 1946; two churches in one churchyard.
63. **Wiggenhall, St Peter** *TF 6042 1326* Chancel, nave, west tower; all of one build, c. 1421 (Frontispiece; Pl. XXXIV). Abandoned in 1929; small village; site liable to flooding; St German's church only 1km away.

64. **Wretham, West, St Lawrence** *TL 8999 9148* Chancel, nave, south porch, west tower. Nave 14th century, chancel and tower 15th century. Abandoned in 1793, being too near the newly-built Wretham Hall; villagers also moved away and rehoused.

III. Category III

65. **Antingham, St Margaret** *TG 2526 3278* Ivy covered ruin in same churchyard as St Mary. Nave *c.* 1100, tower first half 14th century, chancel 14th/15th century. Abandoned late 17th century, village too small to support two churches (Pl. XVII).
66. **Bawsey, St James** *TF 6625 2079* See Full Reports, p.114.
67. **Beachamwell, All Saints** *TF 7493 0462* West end of nave survives, *c.* 1100. Abandoned 1688, after collapse of roof; insufficient villagers to repair it; St Mary's only 0.6km away. (N.B. The surviving wall collapsed in July 1989).
68. **Bickerston, St Andrew** *TG 0861 0871* North and south walls of chancel, possibly Norman. Abandoned by 1633, village deserted.
69. **Buckenham, New, St Mary** *TM 0851 9031* Nave of mid-12th century chapel, which served the town until the parish church of St Martin was built in the 1240s; it continued as a castle chapel until abandoned after the Dissolution, mid-16th century.
70. **Burgh Parva, St Mary** *TG 0435 3355* Fragmentary remains of nave and chancel, fully intact west tower; nave *c.* 1100, tower early 16th century. Abandoned *c.* 1665, depopulation; Melton Constable church only 1.5km away.
71. **Castle Rising** *TF 6655 2455* In castle enclosure: apsidal chancel, axial tower, nave; late 11th century, abandoned during construction of castle *c.* 1150 (Pl. VII); new parish church of St Lawrence built at this date.
72. **Elmham, North, I** *TF 988 216* Remains of cathedral of *c.* 1050 within 14th century ruined manor; became the parish church when the see was moved to Thetford in 1071; abandoned as parish church when Bishop de Losinga built a new one to south in early 12th century.
73. **Gasthorpe, St Nicholas** *TL 9820 8120* Chancel 13th century, nave possibly older, both very fragmentary; more survives of west tower, 15th century. Abandoned *c.* 1700; village depopulated.
74. **Kirby Bedon, St Mary** *TG 2793 0541* Fragments of chancel east and south walls; most of chancel and nave north walls, and round west tower survive. Nave 12th century, chancel and west tower 13th century, belfry stage 15th century. Abandoned *c.* 1700; two churches in one village; two churches mentioned in *Domesday*. Parish church of St Andrew just 100m away.
75. **Mintlyn, St Michael** *TF 6571 1928* See Full Reports, p.116.
76. **Mundham, St Ethelbert** *TM 3317 9776* Remains of chancel; most of east wall and some of north and south walls; 13th/14th century. Abandoned in 1749; two churches in one village, cost of upkeep of both too great.
77. **Oxborough, St Mary Magdalen** *TF 7373 0050* North wall of nave survives, *c.* 1100, east wall rebuilt *c.* 1400. Abandoned late 14th century, when new church of St John built in centre of village.
78. **Raynham, West, St Margaret** *TF 8724 2542* See Full Reports, p.119.
79. **Ryburgh, Little, All Saints** *TF 9678 2765* Most of nave west wall stands, along with stretches of south wall; the rest fragmentary. Oldest parts date to *c.* 1100, chancel 15th century. Church mentioned in *Domesday*. Abandoned in 1750, when consolidated with Great Ryburgh (whose church is only 0.8km away).
80. **Saxlingham Thorpe, St Mary** *TM 2308 9660* See Full Report, p.123.
81. **Snarehill, Great** *TL 8915 8351* See Full Reports, p.127.
82. **Stanninghall** *TG 2555 1745* West half of tower and north wall of nave survive, 14th and 15th century. Abandoned second half 16th century; Catholic lord and patron; village deserted.
83. **Surlingham, St Saviour** *TG 3080 0674* See Full Reports, p.131.
84. **Walton, East, St Andrew** *TF 7428 1619* Nave and blocked south arcade. Nave late 11th century, arcade late 13th century. Abandoned 15th or 16th century; two churches in one village, only 150m apart; being used as a mill in 1803.
85. **Whitlingham, St Andrew** *TG 2740 0785* Some of chancel walls and fragments of nave walls survive; 12th century round tower collapsed in 1940; nave of *c.* 1100; chancel 15th century. Church mentioned in *Domesday*. Abandoned *c.* 1650; possibility of structural failure; small village.
86. **Wood Norton, St Peter** *TG 0135 2732* Nave, now a barn; 15th century. Abandoned first half 16th century; two churches in one village.

IV. Category IV

87. **Bastwick, St Peter** *TG 4265 1822* 15th century tower used to house cats. Abandoned early 17th century; combined with Repps; depopulation?
88. **Beachamwell, St John** *TF 7434 0576* Fragments of nave north and south walls, as well as tower; nave 14th century, tower 15th century. In use in 1535, abandoned by 1552; two other churches in the village, St John's being the most isolated.
89. **Burgh, St Mary** *TG 4548 1411* Round tower *c.* 1100, later octagonal belfry; fragments of nave *c.* 1100. Abandoned mid-16th century, two churches in one village; had been used as a barn.
90. **Caister, West, St Edmund** *TG 5086 1172* Only the north-west corner and north wall survive; 14th century. Abandoned in 16th century; two churches in one village; had been used as a barn.
91. **Edgefield, SS Peter and Paul** *TG 0863 3430* Octagonal west tower, early 13th century; nave late 11th century; remains of west end south aisle, 14th century; north and south porches, 15th century. Abandoned in 1883, when new church built nearer the centre of population; much of fabric (including arcade) built into new church.
92. **Egmere, St Edmund** *TF 8968 3739* See Full Reports, p.134.
93. **Garboldisham, All Saints** *TM 0043 8188* West half of 15th century tower. Rest of church demolished in 1736; village unable to support two churches; St John's only 200m away.
94. **Gillingham, All Saints** *TM 4112 9231* Fifteenth century tower, rest of church demolished 1748. Small village, St Mary's only 50m to south.
95. **Godwick, All Saints** *TF 9091 2198* See Full Reports, p.136.
96. **Hainford, All Saints** *TG 2295 1964* Fifteenth century tower. Church demolished 1839, new church built in centre of village 1km away; mortuary chapel added to tower 1840.
97. **Heigham, St Bartholomew** *TG 2165 0974* Fifteenth century tower. Rest of church destroyed by bombs in 1942 (Pl. VI).
98. **Hindolveston, St George** *TG 0281 2915* See Full Reports, p.138. Church mentioned in *Domesday*.
99. **Melton, Great, St Mary** *TG 1404 0612* Fifteenth century tower in same churchyard as parish church of All Saints; the latter was in ruins from the early 18th century. Rather strangely, St Mary's was pulled down (apart from the tower) in 1883 and the ruined All Saints rebuilt (Pl. XVIII).
100. **Panxworth, All Saints** *TG 3473 1358* See Full Reports, p.140. Church mentioned in *Domesday*.
101. **Pudding Norton, St Margaret** *TF 9223 2774* See Full Reports, p.142. Church mentioned in *Domesday*.
102. **Ringstead, Great, St Peter** *TF 7049 4016* Round tower, late 11th century. Rest of church demolished in 1772; too expensive to maintain two churches in one village.
103. **Rockland, St Andrew** *TL 9964 9571* Thirteenth century tower, only 200m from parish church of All Saints. Abandoned *c.* 1700; three churches in one village.
104. **Snoring, Little, tower** *TF 9530 3255* Church mentioned in *Domesday*. Freestanding round tower, second half 11th century; tower arch now blocked with small doorway. Blocked triangular-headed opening above arch. West wall and gable of adjoining nave still *in situ*. Present church of St Andrew only a few metres to north. Two possibilities: either there were two churches next to each other in the same churchyard, of which only the north one survives in full; or the church to which the tower belongs suffered collapse, and was rebuilt on a new site to north, incorporating bits from the old church.
105. **Testerton, St Remigius** *TF 9379 3684* Western part of west tower, late 14th or 15th century. Abandoned *c.* 1680; village deserted.
106. **Thorpe Parva, St Mary** *TM 1609 7902* Western half of round west tower, 14th or 15th century. Abandoned and demolished *c.* 1540, but tower kept on as dovehouse; village deserted.
107. **Wallington, St Margaret** *TF 6282 0768* See Full Reports, p.144. Church mentioned in *Domesday*.
108. **Walton, West, tower** *TF 4711 1335* A free-standing tower, whose parish church of St Mary remains in use. However, the tower was declared redundant and vested in the Redundant Churches Fund in 1974. An outstanding example of Early English design, of the 1240s (Pl. XXX).
109. **Wolterton, St Margaret** *TG 1634 3205* Round tower, *c.* 1390 (Pl. XXXV). Church mentioned in *Domesday*. Abandoned *c.* 1740 to ensure privacy for the Walpoles at Wolterton Hall (only 200m away).

V. Category V

110. **Barnham Broom, St Michael** *TG 0823 0781* Low walling north of parish church of St Peter and St Paul. Abandoned probably in 14th century; two churches in one churchyard.
111. **Barwick, St Mary** *TF 8045 3521* Very low remains located in a wood. Church mentioned in *Domesday*. Abandoned in 16th century; village deserted; a significant amount of land converted from arable to pasture by 1517.
112. **Beckham, East, St Helen** *TG 1550 3984* Churchyard a jungle; only masonry remains 100m away, used to fill ditch. Church mentioned in *Domesday*. Abandoned *c.* 1700; distant from population; West Beckham church nearer.
113. **Beckham, West, All Saints** *TG 1466 3915* Churchyard still in use; outline of church traceable (none of walls more than 1m high): chancel, nave, south porch. Abandoned and demolished in 1890; some of materials used to build new church in village centre 300m to north-west.
114. **Burnham Sutton, St Ethelbert** *TF 8364 4176* See Full Reports, p.146.
115. **Carlton, East, St Peter** *TF 1801 0205* Fragment of west wall of nave, 50m from parish church of St Mary. Abandoned *c.* 1550; the smaller of two churches in one churchyard. Two churches mentioned in *Domesday*.
116. **Colveston, St Mary** *TL 7920 9574* Line of nave north wall visible. Abandoned *c.* 1676; small village (less than ten householders in 1428); deserted by 18th century.
117. **Creake, North, St Michael** *TF 8549 3789* Fragments of round tower. Abandoned in first half of 16th century; roof lead stolen by vicar's brother; very close to parish church of St Mary.
118. **Eccles, St Mary** *TG 4141 2883* See Full Reports, p.148.
119. **Foulden, St Edmund** *TL 7548 9882* Some short stretches of overturned flint masonry remain. Abandoned by 16th century; two churches in one village, St Edmund's the more isolated site.
120. **Hackford, All Saints** *TG 1011 2283* See Full Reports, p.149. Church mentioned in *Domesday*.
121. **Hempton, St Andrew** *TF 9066 2944* L-shaped fragment of mortared flint. Church mentioned in *Domesday*. Abandoned second half of 16th century; village depopulated.
122. **Letton, All Saints** *TF 9756 1545/3* Low fragments of mortared flint in grounds of Letton Hall. Church mentioned in *Domesday*. Abandoned mid-16th century; village depopulated.
123. **Leziate, All Saints** *TF 6950 1993* Bumps in a paddock; trench cutting across mortared flint walls. Chancel demolished in late 16th century, nave demolished in 18th century; village depopulated.
124. **Lynn, King's, St James** *TF 6215 1978* See Full Reports, p.149.
125. **Pensthorpe** *TF 9475 2908* West wall of nave now forming part of cafeteria, formerly cowshed. Abandoned in 16th century; village depopulated.
126. **Quarles** *TF 8842 3841* Fragments of the west end of the nave, 12th or 13th century (Pl. IV). Abandoned by 1571; village depopulated.
127. **Rockland, St Mary, St Margaret** *TG 3120 0399* Low length of flint walling with angle buttress, 4m east of parish church of St Mary. Abandoned by 16th century; two churches in one churchyard.
128. **Shotesham, St Botolph** *TM 2396 9932* A low stretch of walling is all that remains, probably the west wall of a west tower; *c.* 1400. Demolished in first half 16th century; a reduction from four parish churches to three.
129. **Tattersett, St Andrew** *TF 8535 2885* One of two churches mentioned in *Domesday Book*. Simple rectangular outline; walls mainly grass-covered mounds, with coursed flint showing through in places. Carved limestone coffin lid at corner. Abandoned first half of 16th century. All Saints church only 300m to north.
130. **Thorpland, St Thomas** *TF 9365 3218* Parts of south and west walls of nave, 14th or 15th century. Abandoned in 16th century, and used as a barn by 1611. Village deserted, probably in part due to landlord opposition.
131. **Walsingham, Great, All Saints** *TF 9395 3785* See Full Reports, p.152.
132. **Weeting, All Saints** *TL 7756 8869* See Full Reports, p.154.

VI. Category VI

133. **Alethorpe, All Saints** *TF 9491 3133* Abandoned in second half of 16th century, then used as a barn; small village depopulated by landlord oppression in 16th century.
134. **Algarsthorpe, St Mary Magdalen** *TG 1341 0867* Church mentioned in will shortly before 1066. Abandoned first half 16th century; village deserted.
135. **Alpington/Apton, St Martin** *TG 2924 0019* or *TG 3069 0098* Church mentioned in will shortly before 1066. Abandoned second half 16th century, demoted to chapel 14th century; depopulation, proximity to other churches.
136. **Ashby, St Mary** *TG 4229 1522* See Full Reports, p.156.
137. **Barton Bendish, All Saints** *TF 7118 0559* Excavated in 1980 and 1981: seven phases, from *c.* 1100 to the 18th century; demolished in 1789; two other churches in the village.
138. **Barton Turf** *TG 3523* Two churches mentioned in *Domesday*; one must have gone in 12th or 13th century.
139. **Bedingham, St Mary** *TM 2850 9340* Stood in same churchyard as parish church of St Andrew. Abandoned by 16th century; village unable to support two churches.
140. **Beeston, St Andrew** *TG 251 146* Abandoned first half 16th century, small village (less than ten householders in 1428); now deserted. Church mentioned in *Domesday*.
141. **Bittering, Great, St Nicholas** *TF 9592 1736* Abandoned in first half 16th century; very small village.
142. **Blo Norton, St Margaret** *TM 0121 7968* Stood in same churchyard as parish church of St Andrew. Abandoned in 1394; decay of fabric and closeness of neighbouring church.
143. **Bracondale, St Nicholas** *TG 2307* Church mentioned in *Domesday*; still in use in 1428; abandoned at the Dissolution.
144. **Bradcar, St Andrew** *TL 9827 9260* Excavated 1950. Abandoned first half 16th century; Shropham church only 250m away.
145. **Breccles, Little** *TL 967 937* Abandoned before Edward III's time; village totally depopulated.
146. **Broomsthorpe** *TF 850 282* Abandoned first half 16th century; village depopulated.
147. **Brundall, St Clement** *TG 3301 0805* Suppressed as a chapel in 1547; ruins demolished in 1820.
148. **Buckenham, Old, St Andrew** *TM 0731 9130* Served by the monks of the priory, it was abandoned at the Dissolution in 1536; became a barn, then stables. Two churches in one village.
149. **Buckenham Tofts, St Andrew** *TL 8385 9496* Abandoned in the 16th century, only ten communicants in 1603 (who then went to Stanford).
150. **Burnham St Andrew** *TF 8367 4229* Abandoned *c.* 1421; four other churches within 0.5km.
151. **Burnham, St Edmund** *TF 8330 4220* Abandoned mid-14th century; two other churches within 300m.
152. **Burnham Thorpe, St Peter** *TF 8470 4174* Abandoned after 1364; 500m from parish church of All Saints; presumably village unable to support two churches.
153. **Caldecote, St Mary** *TF 7445 0347* Abandoned early 16th century; village had only ten householders in 1428.
154. **Cantelose, All Saints** *TG 1813 0453* Parish church until 1397; combined as chapel to Hethersett until *c.* 1540. Probably one of two churches in Hethersett mentioned in *Domesday*.
155. **Carleton Rode B** *TM 1192* Two churches mentioned in *Domesday*; one must have gone in 12th century.
156. **Carbrooke, Little** *TF 9361 0185* Demolished in 1424 after consolidation with Great Carbrooke; village deserted.
157. **Carrow, St James** *TG 2407* In use in 1520, but gone by mid-16th century.
158. **Choseley** *TF 7541 4091* Abandoned probably in 16th century; village deserted by enclosure of arable land before 1517.
159. **Clenchwarton, South** *TF 5840 1860* Destroyed by the sea, *c.* 1360.
160. **Cockley Cley, St Peter** *TF 8039 0434* Accidentally burnt down second half 16th century; not rebuilt presumably because All Saints, 1km to west, was sufficient to serve the parish.
161. **Congham, All Saints** *TF 7171 2340* Abandoned *c.* 1550; two other churches in village.
162. **Congham, St Mary** *TF 710 237* or *TF 7145 2346* Abandoned late 16th century; one church sufficient for the village.
163. **Cressingham, Great, St George** *TF 8561 0031* Church with nave and apsidal chancel revealed by aerial photographs; abandoned first half 16th century; two churches in one village.
164. **Dereham, West, St Peter** *TF 6669 0213* Stood west of St Andrew's, in same churchyard. Abandoned by first half 16th century.

165. **Doughton** *TF 882 292* Abandoned probably in 14th century. Village deserted.
166. **Dunham, Great, St Mary** *TF 8731 1471* Carved stone, with shafts etc. going back to the 12th century, scattered *ex situ* in garden. Abandoned mid-16th century; parish church of St Andrew only 100m north-east.
167. **Dykebeck (nr Wymondham)** *TG 095 012* Church and village mentioned in *Domesday*; former probably went in 12th century.
168. **Fincham, St Michael** *TF 6857 0635* See Full Reports, p.157.
169. **Foston, St Peter** *TF 655 089* Abandoned *c*. 1540; village depopulated; church at Shouldham Thorpe only 1km away.
170. **Gowthorpe, St James** *TG 2106 0215* Abandoned *c*. 1590; village deserted.
171. **Guist Thorpe, All Saints** *TG 0049 2648* Abandoned in 1547; two churches (St Andrew's 1km away) both in decay, so materials from All Saints used to repair St Andrew's.
172. **Hardwick** *TF 636 185* A deserted village which was served by a parochial chapel of Runcton in 1290; still in use in 1368; abandoned by first half of 16th century.
173. **Harleston** *TM 2451 8329* Chapel-of-ease to Redenhall, demolished 1873; new church built on different site; old church too small, and site too cramped.
174. **Harling, Middle, St Andrew** *TL 9798 8516* Part of churchyard excavated 1981. Church dismantled 1543; very small village; West Harling church only 500m away.
175. **Hautbois, Little, St Mary** *TG 2513 2178* Abandoned second half 16th century; village deserted.
176. **Helmingham, St Mary** *TG 1256 1665* Perhaps already abandoned by 13th century; two churches in one parish (cf Morton-on-the-Hill); two churches mentioned in *Domesday*.
177. **Hempnall, St Andrew** *TM 2131 9509* Abandoned by 16th century; two churches in one parish; two churches mentioned in *Domesday*.
178. **Herringby, St Ethelbert** *TG 4462 1037* Abandoned mid-16th century and pulled down 1610; village deserted.
179. **Hockham, Little, St Mary** *TL 9488 9090* Abandoned probably in 15th century; village deserted.
180. **Holm, St Andrew** *TF 9106 0706* Abandoned late 15th century; village deserted.
181. **Holverston, St Mary** *TG 3041 0309* See Full Reports, p.158.
182. **Irmingland, St Andrew** *TG 123 294* Abandoned second half 16th century; small village (less than ten householders in 1428); deserted by 18th century.
183. **Itteringham, St Nicholas** *TG 154 303* See Full Reports, p.159.
184. **Kenningham** *TM 204 996* Abandoned mid-15th century; village deserted.
185. **Kenwick, St Thomas** *TF 574 195* Chapel-of-ease to Tilney 13th to 15th century.
186. **Kerdiston, St Mary** *TG 0845 2390* Church mentioned in *Domesday*. Abandoned by 14th century; village depopulated.
187. **Keswick, St Clement** *TG 3512 3335* Washed away by the sea after 1382.
188. **Langhale, St Christopher** *'M 2953 9669* Consolidated with Kirstead in 1421. Demolished in reign of James I. Village deserted. Church mentioned in *Domesday*.
189. **Langham Parva, St Mary** *TG 0042 4136* Abandoned in 16th century; church of Langham Magna only 300m away.
190. **Lynford** *TL 8184 9358* Abandoned as a parish church from 1467; the village being deserted; served by a monk of the Thetford Priory until the Dissolution.
191. **Lynn, North, St Edmund** *TF 6135 2115* Destroyed by incursion of sea in second half of 17th century.
192. **Marham, St Andrew** *TF 7097 0961* Some carved fragments in garden of Grove House, but not *in situ*: abandoned in first half of 16th century; two churches in one village.
193. **Markshall, St Edmund** *TG 2280 0480* Abandoned first half 16th century; village depopulated. Church mentioned in *Domesday*.
194. **Massingham, Great, All Saints** *TF 797 230* Abandoned in 16th century; two churches in one village.
195. **Methwold Hythe** *TL 7155 9511* Abandoned by 13th century.
196. **Moulton, Little, All Saints** *TM 1713 8885* Abandoned mid-16th century; village deserted.
197. **Nelonde, St Peter** *TM 1487 9836* Church mentioned in will shortly before 1066. Abandoned first half of 16th century; village deserted.
198. **Oby** *TG 415 144* Abandoned second half 16th century; some fragments built into barn; village depopulated.
199. **Ormesby, St Andrew** *TG 4935 1506* Abandoned late 16th century; four churches in one village.
200. **Ormesby, St Peter** *TG 4913 1468* See Full Reports, p.160.
201. **Overstrand, St Martin (I)** *TG 24 41* Washed away by the sea late 14th century.
202. **Palgrave, Little** *TF 8328 1346* Abandoned by 16th century.
203. **Pattesley, St John the Baptist** *TF 8995 2400* Abandoned in 16th century; village depopulated. Fragments built into Pattesley House, but none apparently *in situ*.
204. **Pickenham, South, St Andrew** *TF 8504* Standing in 13th century; abandoned by 16th century; two churches in one village.
205. **Poringland, West, St Michael** *TG 2628 0101* Abandoned before 1540; village depopulated.
206. **Rackheath, Little, Holy Trinity** *TG 28 13* Abandoned by 16th century; village deserted.
207. **Roxham, St Michael** *TL 640 998* Abandoned by 16th century; no village.
208. **Saxthorpe, St Dunstan** *TG 1165 3020* A parochial chapel, only 0.5km from the parish church; was also a chantry; therefore dissolved in 1547.
209. **Scratby, All Saints** *TG 5079 1540* Demolished in 1548, consolidated with the four Ormesby churches; church mentioned in *Domesday*.
210. **Seething B** *TM 3182 9847* Two churches mentioned in *Domesday*.
211. **Setchey** *TF 635 136* Parochial chapel to North Runcton. Abandoned *c*. 1550.
212. **Shipden** *TG 220 425* Washed away by the sea *c*. 1400.
213. **Shouldham, St Margaret** *TF 6830 0857* Abandoned in 16th century; two churches in one village; two churches mentioned in *Domesday*.
214. **Sidestrand, St Michael** *TG 2623 4005* Owing to its location perilously near the cliff edge, the whole church was carefully dismantled (apart from the tower) in 1880 and rebuilt 0.5km further inland; this turned out to be a wise decision, since the old churchyard and tower collapsed into the sea in 1916.
215. **Snetterton, St Andrew** *TL 9943 9120* Abandoned first half 16th century; two churches in one village.
216. **Stiffkey, St John the Baptist/St Mary** *TF 9751 4299* Abandoned *c*. 1559; two churches in one churchyard.
217. **Stoke Holy Cross B** *Possibly TG 252 017* Two churches mentioned in *Domesday*; one probably abandoned in 12th century; possibly near site of Blackford Hall, which incorporates Norman fragments.
218. **Stratton, St Peter** *TM 2062 9356* Abandoned early 16th century; consolidated to Stratton St Michael in 1449, which is only 150m away.
219. **Sturston, Holy Cross** *TL 8752 9489* Although in a poor state, the church was still standing in 1738; but it disappeared soon after. The village was deserted through landlord oppression second half 16th century.
220. **Summerfield, All Saints** *TF 7479 3850* Abandoned mid-16th century; village deserted.
221. **Swainsthorpe, St Mary** *TG 2255 0045* Abandoned first half 16th century; two churches in one village.
222. **Thetford, All Saints** *TL 8720 8227* Abandoned second half 14th century.
223. **Thetford, St Andrew** *TL 8701 8331* Demolished 1546.
224. **Thetford, St Benet** *TL 870 825* Could be the church excavated in St Michael's Close (see below). Abandoned 13th or early 14th century.
225. **Thetford, St Edmund** *TL 86 82* Abandoned in 15th century.
226. **Thetford, St Etheldreda** *TL 8694 8269* Abandoned first half 16th century.
227. **Thetford, St George** *TL 873 823* A pre-Conquest church which remained as a parish church until *c*. 1160, when it was rebuilt as the conventual church to the Nunnery.
228. **Thetford, St Giles** *TL 8705 8310* See Full Reports, p.161.
229. **Thetford, St Helen** *TL 8394 8735* Mentioned in *Domesday*; apsidal church excavated 1961-2; abandoned by 14th century.
230. **Thetford, Holy Trinity** *TL 8675 8302* Founded *c*. 1072, abandoned 1547.
231. **Thetford, St John** *TL 8630 8305 or TL 8640 8295* A pre-Conquest foundation mentioned in *Domesday*, converted to use as a leper chapel before *c*. 1307.
232. **Thetford, St Lawrence** *TL 8630 8305 or TL 8607 8306* Abandoned *c*. 1400.
233. **Thetford, St Margaret** *TL 8637 8251* Pre-Conquest foundation mentioned in *Domesday*, converted to chapel of leper hospital before 1304.
234. **Thetford, St Martin** *TL 86 82* Pre-conquest foundation mentioned in *Domesday*, abandoned perhaps 12th century.
235. **Thetford, Great St Mary** *TL 8675 8306* Pre-Conquest parish church mentioned in *Domesday*, raised to cathedral status from 1072 to 1094, then used as the church of the Cluniac priory until

1114, and occupied by a Dominican friary from 1335 to 1538.
236. **Thetford, St Michael** *TL 86 82* Abandoned by end of 15th century.
237. **Thetford, St Nicholas** *TL 8685 8322* Abandoned in 16th century, tower survived until 19th century.
238. **Thetford, Church at Red Castle Site** *TL 8607 8306* Excavated in 1957-8: the rectangular chancel (and north-east corner of nave) of a church identified, perhaps erroneously, by the excavation as St Martin's; dated by them to mid-11th century; possibility of earlier wooden structure.
239. **Thetford, Church on site of Gas Works, Bury Road** *TL 8695 8240* Very briefly excavated in 1957; part of the west tower of a church, probably 11th century; identified by some as St Edmund's, but this remains uncertain.
240. **Thetford, Church on site of St Michael's Close** *TL 8705 8232* Excavated 1969-70, identified as St Michael's (certainly in error; it might be St Benet's): a wooden church of the second quarter of 11th century, replaced by a masonry church *c.* 1100; abandoned towards end of 12th century.
241. **Thorpe-by-Norwich, Old Thorpe Church** *TG 2671 0902* Excavated by R.R. Clarke in 1951: 11th century burial ground, single-cell apsidal church added in early 12th century, rectangular chancel later added, systematically destroyed in the 16th century; church probably moved to new site of Thorpe St Andrew (see above, site 59).
242. **Thorpeland, St Thomas** *TF 6168 0827* Abandoned soon after 1488; church mentioned in *Domesday*; village deserted.
243. **Thurketeliart (nr Aldeby)** *TM 4493* Church and village mentioned in *Domesday*; both now disappeared, perhaps in 12th century.

244. **Topcroft, St Giles** *TM 2692* Abandoned in first half of 16th century.
245. **Wacton, Little, St Mary** *TM 1739 9165* Abandoned *c.* 1520; isolated site; only 0.6km from Great Wacton church.
246. **Warham, St Mary the Virgin** *TF 9481 4162* Abandoned second half 16th century; three churches in one village: two churches mentioned in *Domesday*.
247. **Waxham, Little, St Margaret** *TG 4450 2650* Abandoned soon after 1383; village deserted.
248. **Weasenham, St Paul** *TF 8522* Abandoned after 1368.
249. **Wicklewood, St Andrew** *TG 0698 0234* Abandoned soon after 1367; two churches in one churchyard.
250. **Windle, St Andrew** *TM 426 932* Abandoned *c.* 1440; village deserted.
251. **Winston, St Andrew** *TM 4009 9317* Abandoned after 1440; village deserted.
252. **Worstead, St Andrew** *TG 3034 2596* Abandoned mid-16th century; two churches in one village; two churches mentioned in *Domesday*.
253. **Wreningham, Little, St Mary** *c. TM 163 988* Abandoned soon after 1406; village so completely disappeared, even its site unknown.
254. **Yarmouth, Great, St Benedict** *site unknown* Owned by Bishop Aelmer before 1066; abandoned in favour of de Losinga's new church *c.* 1100.
255. **Yarmouth, Southtown, St Nicholas** *TG 5206* Listed in 1254; money given for fabric in 1379; united with Gorleston in 1511; tower still used as a sea-mark in 16th century.

Chapter 3. Category I

I. Barningham, North: St Peter

Identification TG 1505 3715. *County No.*6639.
Diocese: Norwich. *Archdeaconry*: Norwich. *Deanery*: Repps. *Parish*: North Barningham. *Status*: parish church, now vested in Redundant Churches Fund. *Date last in regular use*: 1976.
Ownership and access: Redundant Churches Fund, right of way to churchyard.

Location and Setting
(Fig.1, No.3)
In isolation just east of a small road from Matlaske to Sheringham (some 6km further north). There is a farm 400m to west, and the ruins of North Barningham Hall (early 17th century) 500m further down the track to east.

Architectural Description
(Fig. 6; Pl. LXV)
Chancel, nave, north aisle, north porch and west tower; constructed largely of flint. Porch and nave roofs are tiled, the rest are covered with slates.

Chancel. The chancel is built of coursed flint with limestone quoins. The east wall is pierced by a three-light Perpendicular window with four-centred head; the supermullioned tracery has an ogee archlet to the middle light. The hood-mould has a deep concave profile. Just below the middle light are two chamfered stones forming the base of a single-light window (presumably a lancet). At the same level, but 1.5m to south, is part of the chamfered sill of a similar window; there are some pieces of brown conglomerate in this area, suggesting a blocked opening. It looks as if the east wall originally had three separate lancet windows. There are no remains of the northerly window, but the wall is very patched around the area where it would be expected. The masonry of the upper part of the east wall differs from lower down, with smooth flint pebble replacing cut flint. Inside, there is a thick stone stringcourse, of round section, at sill level.

The masonry of the chancel south wall is like that of the east wall, except the uppermost 0.5m is recessed slightly and capped with a dentil frieze of 18th century brick. In one or two places the flint coursing has a herringbone appearance. There are two windows, both two-light with square heads and hood-moulds. The eastern is the smaller of the two, and appears to be mainly 19th century restoration. The other window is taller and has four upper lights, but this upper part looks restored too. Both have segmental rear-arches. Within, below the eastern window, is an ornate double piscina and sill-sedilia. The arch over the sedilia has gone, but that over the piscina remains intact: a big ogee arch with large cinquefoil cusps (the lower ones themselves sub-cusped); these cusps have been encrusted with a dark grey mortar to give a monochrome flushwork effect. The arch is flanked by pinnacles encrusted with this dark mortar to form a two-light tracery pattern. The only fully surviving pinnacle is the westernmost, which rises from a stone corbel carved as a bearded head. At the back of the sedilia arch is a central rib springing from an animal head corbel, and abutting the sedilia arch at its apex. The extrados of the arch is surmounted by crockets. Both arches spring from round half-shafts with moulded capitals and bases. The piscina basins differ, the eastern one with trefoil lobes, the western one a quatrefoil.

The chancel north wall has the same features as the south wall, but has no windows. However, there is evidence of a window-sized blocking half-way along the wall, filled with flint pebble and 17th-century brick. On the inside at this point is the large monument to Margaret Pope (d. 1624).

There is no chancel arch, just a step down to the nave. A slight vertical set-off marks the junction of chancel and nave on the interior north side, but outside the nave and chancel walls are flush. Both chancel and nave have arch-braced roofs, mainly 19th-century but incorporating earlier elements. An angel bearing a shield forms the wooden corbel at the junction of chancel and nave roofs.

Nave. A buttress with two set-offs marks the division of chancel and nave south wall on the outside. The buttress is made of flint, faced with 17th-century brick framing panels of knapped flint and set on a wide flint plinth. There are two identical buttresses further west, spaced evenly; but this buttress marks some rebuilding probably made necessary by the removal of the rood stair; a tall niche within is all that remains of the latter.

This eastern part of the nave south wall is on alignment with, and of similar construction to, the chancel south wall. It contains a two-light Perpendicular window identical to its neighbour in the chancel. West of this window there is a clear vertical masonry break, formed by the quoins of the south-east corner of the first masonry nave. The quoins are made of large blocks of conglome-

Plate LXV. North Barningham church by Ladbrooke (c. 1830). The view is essentially the same today; there is no longer a shed at the west end of the aisle.

NORTH BARNINGHAM

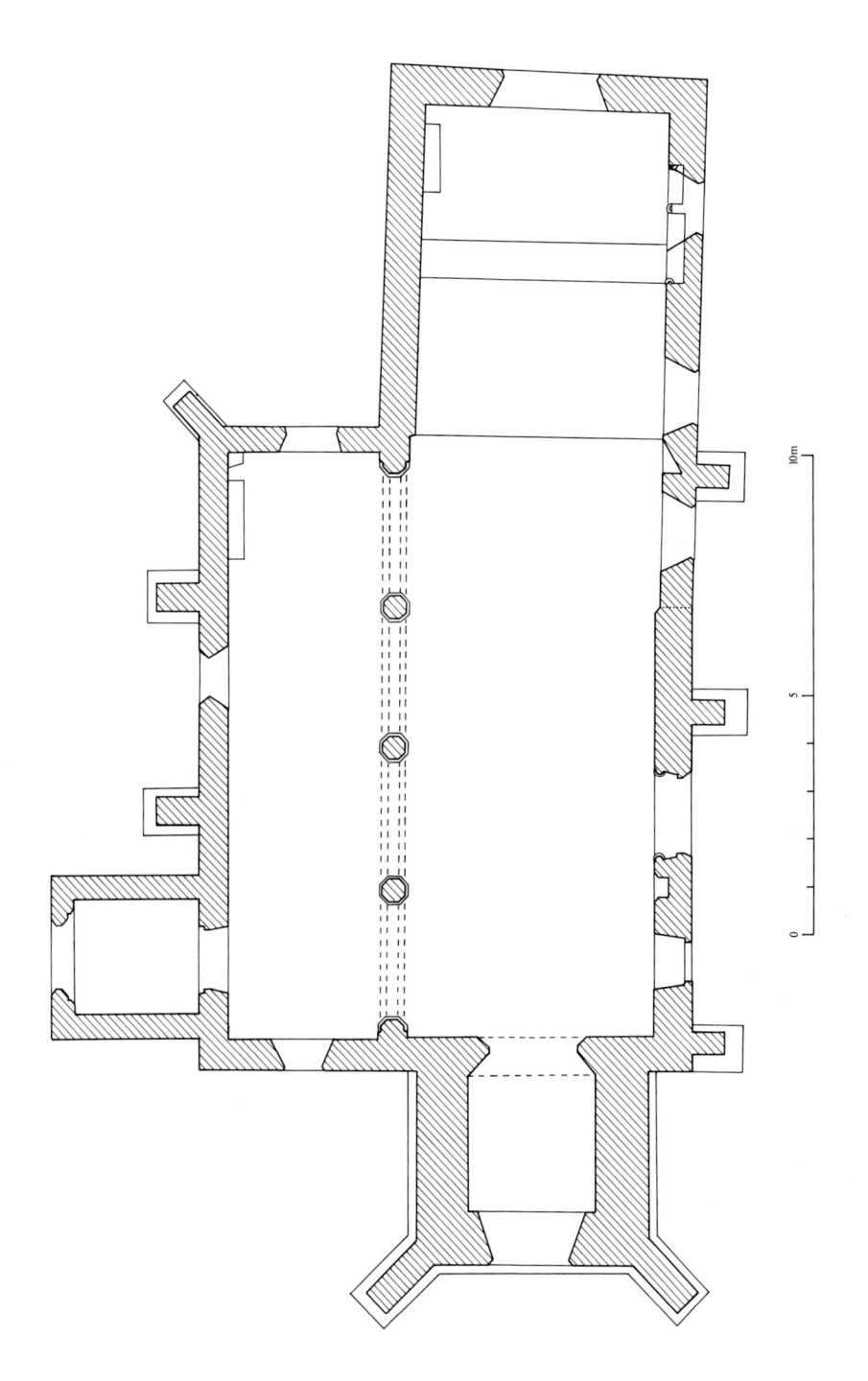

Figure 6. North Barningham, St Peter: plan. Scale 1:150. Note building break in south wall of nave.

rate, carefully squared, interspersed with Roman bricks (13 in all). On the inside, there is a vertical set-off at this point. West of the quoins, the masonry consists of flint with occasional pieces of conglomerate, in clear courses with wide mortar joints. This masonry stands to about 4.5m high, above which is a 1.5m heightening of (later) flint pebble masonry.

A large three-light Decorated window pierces both the fabric of the first nave wall and its heightening. It has intersecting ogee tracery, forming latticed shapes above the main lights. All tracery and mullions are rounded with sunken quadrant mouldings. The hood-mould has scroll terminals. On the inside, the rear-arch has round half-shafts with moulded bases, capitals, and a concave arch. Immediately west of this is a niche, 2m from the ground, with segmental head and hood-mould. Further west is the small pointed south doorway, simply chamfered on the outside, and with a hood-mould. The southwest corner of the nave has large conglomerate quoins like those of the original south-east corner (Pl. LXVI).

The original north-west corner of the nave can be seen in the west wall, just north of the tower, again in squared conglomerate with occasional Roman bricks.

The nave is divided form the north aisle by a four-bay arcade. The piers are octagonal, with moulded bases and capitals of an attenuated Perpendicular type.

Aisle. The outer walls of the north aisle are built of coursed flint, with a diagonal buttress with two set-offs at the eastern corner, and simple limestone quoins at the western corner. In the east wall is a two-light Perpendicular window with square head and four batement lights, identical to the two in the south wall. The internal corners each have a square statue corbel; below the south-east one is a piscina on an octagonal shaft.

Behind the Palgrave monument in the east bay of the aisle (see below), the north wall has been rebuilt in flint pebble, with a slight set-off near the eaves. Two sloping buttresses, in 18th century brick, support the wall. Between them is a plain Y-tracery window. Further west, the north doorway has a continuous external wave-moulding; its hood-mould, with fillet, springs from carved corbels, the one to east adorned with oak leaves, that to west a coil motif. Just east of the door, on the inside, is some painted black medieval lettering.

The west wall of the aisle differs from the other walls: it is built of flint pebble, and pierced by a 19th century Y-tracery window.

Porch. The north porch has no windows. It is built of galleted flint. The outer doorway has a plain chamfered four-centred arch with no responds. The hood-mould is surmounted by voussoirs of alternating limestone and flint. Above is a small stone statue niche with segmental head (restored, but based on an original).

Tower. The masonry of the west tower is of flint, but, unlike the nave, the coursing is less clearly stratified. The plinth continues round the diagonal western buttresses. In the lowest storey of the west wall there is a large three-light Perpendicular window with transom. In the middle storey there is a small cusped window in north and west walls. Above a stone stringcourse is the belfry stage, each wall pierced by a two-light window with rectilinear oculus. The crenellated parapet is lined with brick and stone. Inside the church, the tower arch has polygonal responds, wave moulded to east; the capitals are concave polygons, supporting chamfered arches.

Interpretation and Dating
(Fig.7)

The oldest part of the church is the west and most of the south wall of the nave. It is characterised by its wide flint coursing, and the use of large conglomerate quoins with

Plate LXVI. North Barningham, St Peter, from the south-west. The quoins of the Phase 1 nave can be made out; notice also that the nave has been first lengthened, then heightened.

NORTH BARNINGHAM

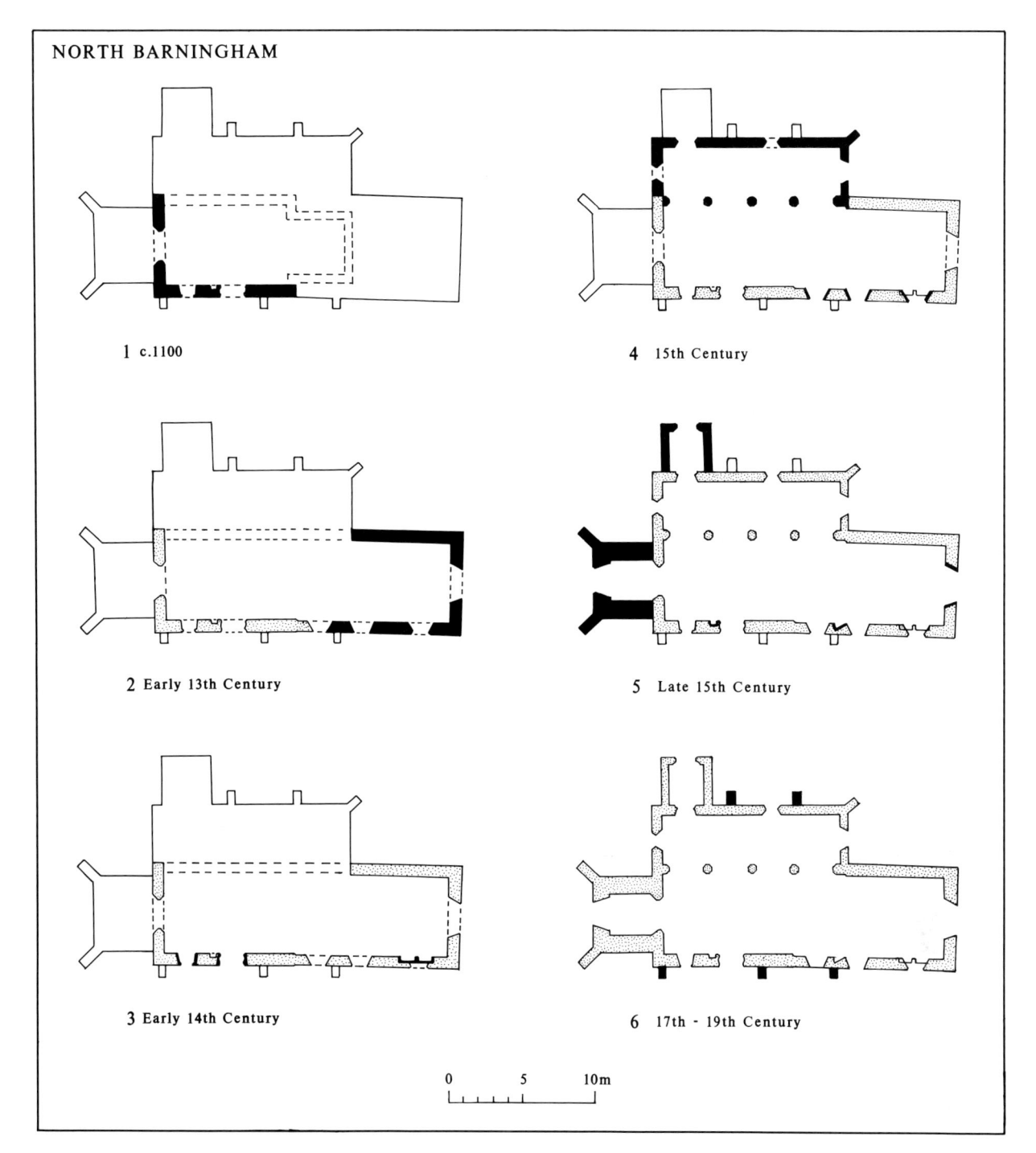

1 c.1100

2 Early 13th Century

3 Early 14th Century

4 15th Century

5 Late 15th Century

6 17th - 19th Century

0 5 10m

Figure 7. North Barningham, St Peter: phase plan. Scale 1:400.

occasional Roman bricks. No specifically dateable features survive, but in Norfolk this type of masonry is typical of the 11th and early 12th centuries.

The next phase involved a new chancel and extension of the nave to east. A dating clue is provided by the fragmentary remains of two of the three original east windows of the chancel. An early 13th-century date is likely.

Early 14th-century alterations did not much affect the plan, but transformed the appearance of the church, with the heightened nave, the sumptuous nave south window and the piscina and sedilia in the chancel.

The nave arcade belongs to the 15th century. A bequest of 20s to the body of the church in 1448 could relate to this work (Cattermole and Cotton 1983, 238). It would seem sensible to assume that the outer walls of the aisle belong to this phase. Certainly the east window conforms with this, although the presence of two Y-tracery windows suggests an earlier date. It is clear that the west window is 19th-century. The north window has either been re-used, or it is contemporary with the aisle and presupposes an earlier arcade before the present one was built.

The tower and the porch appear to be the last of the main phases. Their details suggest a late 15th-century date.

Finally, the south buttresses were built in the 17th century (see above), those to the north in the 18th century, judging from the brickwork. The church was thoroughly restored in the 1890s.

Causes of Abandonment
For over two centuries the users of the church struggled to keep it open. In 1745, there were only two inhabitants in the parish (NRO, FCB2, 92), and the church was in poor repair. It actually went out of use in 1886 because of its bad state, but was re-opened in 1891 and re-roofed in 1894. The parish population today may be greater than in 1745, but not by much. The church at Winter Barningham, only 1.5km to south, remains in use, and the churches at Matlaske, Bessingham and Plumstead are not far away. By the early 1960s, St Peter's was only being used once a year. It was finally declared Redundant, and vested in the Redundant Churches Fund in 1976.

Church Contents

Ceramic. The chancel floor is covered with Victorian tiles, mainly red and black, with some fleur-de-lys motifs around the altar area. The rest of the church is pammented. There is, however, an exceptional area of tiling and stone inlay in the middle of the nave (Pl. L). It looks like a rose window, about 1.5m in diameter, set into the floor and filled with brick and terracotta rather than glass. Eight stone 'spokes' from the eight main 'lights' terminate in trefoil cusping; between the main lights and the outer perimeter, oval and rounded 'tracery' holes are filled with terracotta. A clue to its identity may be provided by the trapezoidal black stone sepulchral slab adjoining the roundel to east. It is inset with a small brass inscription to Robert Bakon (d. 1472). It seems likely that the stone and terracotta roundel functions as an unusual and elaborate cross to mark this grave. The use of terracotta in funerary monuments is not unknown in the late 15th century, but is unlikely to be earlier.

Metal. Equally important are the magnificent brasses at the end of the north aisle to Henry and Anne Palgrave (d. 1516). He wears armour ('robust and swagger' according to Pevsner) while she is in contemporary dress. Beneath him is another brass with their five sons, beneath her their seven daughters. The four shields at the corners are reproductions, the originals were stolen in the 1960s.

Stone. Next to these brasses is another grave slab whose inset brass inscription has now gone. It was that of James Bacon (d. 1531). The only other floor memorial is the large slab, carved with an heraldic device, of Sir Augustine Palgrave (d. 1710). This is just north of the altar and next to the large marble monument, set into the chancel north wall, to John Palgrave (d. 1611). The black marble tomb chest displays five shields. These are 19th-century restorations; the surviving original pieces are lying by the south door. Above are three figures (all defaced): a woman with sword and scales (Justice), a man with a spade (Toil), and a woman with an olive branch (Peace). Over the figures is an elaborate pink and white alabaster architectural framework, with heraldic shields, decorative fruit, and strapwork.

Just west of this monument, and set high in the wall, is the astonishing alabaster monument to John Palgrave's daughter, Margaret Pope (d. 1624). Her cloaked effigy can be seen kneeling in prayer, with lectern and open bible, within a baldachino whose curtains are pulled aside by two angels. An elaborate coat-of-arms fills the curved pediment above.

Perhaps the grandest of the three monuments is that in the north aisle to Elizabeth (d. 1633) and Sir Austin Palgrave (d. 1639). Two big Doric columns in grey marble rise from the tomb-chest and support a semi-circular split pediment, containing a large painted coat-of-arms. Beneath this, two oval niches contain the marble busts of Sir Austin and Elizabeth, both very fine portraits.

The font is plain, octagonal and 19th century, as is the small font cover.

Wood. In the nave, eight of the benches have medieval bench-ends with poppyheads. The rest of the furnishings, including the choir-stalls and wooden lectern, were provided in 1894. The fine 17th century oak chancel rails with turned balusters were brought recently from St Mary Coslany, Norwich.

Other fittings include a modern oak altar table, a harmonium, two very plain doors, and a piece of 17th century panelling at the west end of the nave. There is no electricity or lighting of any kind.

Whereabouts of Contents
Pulpit with canopy dated 1629, at Sustead church.
    17th century table at Letheringsett church.
    19th century altar rails at Matlaske church.
    19th century lectern at Erpingham church.

Condition
Very good. All the rainwater goods have recently been replaced in plastic, the chancel roof has been retiled, and a wide dry trench dug around the church. Inside, there is a certain amount of peeling plaster, and a scar by the tower arch marks the line of an old boiler flue.

Churchyard
The rectangular churchyard is hedged all round. The grass has been kept low. Access is from a track running outside the south boundary of the churchyard. The gravestones are all of the 19th and 20th centuries.

Archaeological and Architectural Assessment
The church has an 11th or 12th-century core. The 14th-century sedilia and piscina are unusually fine, and there is a good window with intersecting tracery and a four-bay Perpendicular arcade.

However, the most lasting impression is provided by the three magnificent early 17th-century monuments of the Palgraves; also the splendid early 16th-century brass. The 'rose-window' floor motif is unique.

It seems likely that some below-ground evidence will have been lost through the recent excavation of the wide dry-trench around the church.

Further References
Blomefield, 1805-10, VIII, 92.
Bryant, 1900a, 17.
Cattermole and Cotton, 1983, 238.
Cox, 1911, I, 165.
Gunn, 1884b, 333.
Pevsner, 1962a, 200.

II. Brandiston, St Nicholas

Identification TG 1412 2141. *County No.*7473.
Diocese: Norwich. *Archdeaconry*: Norwich. *Deanery*: Sparham. *Parish*: Brandiston. *Status*: parish church, now Redundant. *Date last in regular use*: 1971.

Ownership and access: Redundant Churches Fund

Location and Setting
(Fig. 1, No. 5)
Brandiston is not so much a village as a scattering of houses around some minor roads, 2km south of Cawston and 3km west of the B1149 Norwich-Holt road. The church is just beyond the northern edge of a disused Second World War airfield. A pretty tree-lined track leads north to the churchyard, and originally continued for a further 200m to the 17th century hall. The old rectory stands immediately west of the churchyard, but the remaining houses which form Brandiston are mostly scattered about 1km further west.

Architectural Description
(PL. LXVII)
Nave and chancel (in one), south porch, north aisle, and round tower against the west wall of the aisle (Fig. 8). Constructed mainly of flint.

Chancel. Viewed from the south, the only sign of differentiation between chancel and nave is that the chancel roof is leaded and of fractionally shallower pitch than the pantiled nave roof. In fact the original chancel was demolished and the last bay of the nave turned into the present chancel in the 18th century. It is clear that the east wall is a blocking, constructed of a fairly random fill of flint with occasional bricks and pieces of limestone. The gable is built regularly in brick, a stone gable cross above. The wall is pierced by a large three-light window, Perpendicular in style but 19th century in date, and based on the south window of the chancel (see below). Its rear-arch has a double hollow chamfer but no hood-mould. Either side of the window, externally, is a bulky buttress with three set-offs, built of brick. All brick used in this east wall appears, by size and character, to be of the 18th century; the blocking must therefore date to this period. Extending the wall to north and south are similar buttresses with three set-offs. The one to north is of brick, like the other two; but that to south is of flint with stone facings (although the upper part is brick) and belongs to an earlier phase.

The south wall of the chancel originally continued further east, as the eastern termination of the wall is rough and broken-off. The wall is constructed of mortared flints in fairly neat courses. Just west of the southeast buttress there is the outline of a small blocked priest's door. The arch head is built of alternating brick and flint, part of one of the stone jambs survives. Further west, there is a large three-light window surmounted by a hood-mould, with tracery of four upper lights set between super millions.

The chancel north wall is intriguing. It clearly incorporates a blocking, but probably not of the same period as the east wall. It is built of small coursed flints, without the pieces of limestone and brick so evident in the east wall. From within, this can be seen to be the blocking of a large arch which formed the first bay of a four-bay nave arcade. On the outside, two large stone corbels above the line of the arch, with rebates to contain a wall beam (or wall posts), mark the line of the former aisle roof. The window set within the blocked arch was presumably re-located. It is of three lights with a plain hood-mould, and a transom forming a lower register of lights; above the upper register is a supertransom supporting four batement lights. The whole window is set within a segmental rear-arch.

The present chancel has the most interesting roof in the church. It is of two bays, with arched braces springing from two simple stone corbels.

Plate LXVII. Brandiston, St Nicholas, from the south-west. The nave windows display tracery of two different designs but belonging to the same building phase, illustrating the overlap of Decorated and Perpendicular forms current in the second half of the 14th century.

BRANDISTON

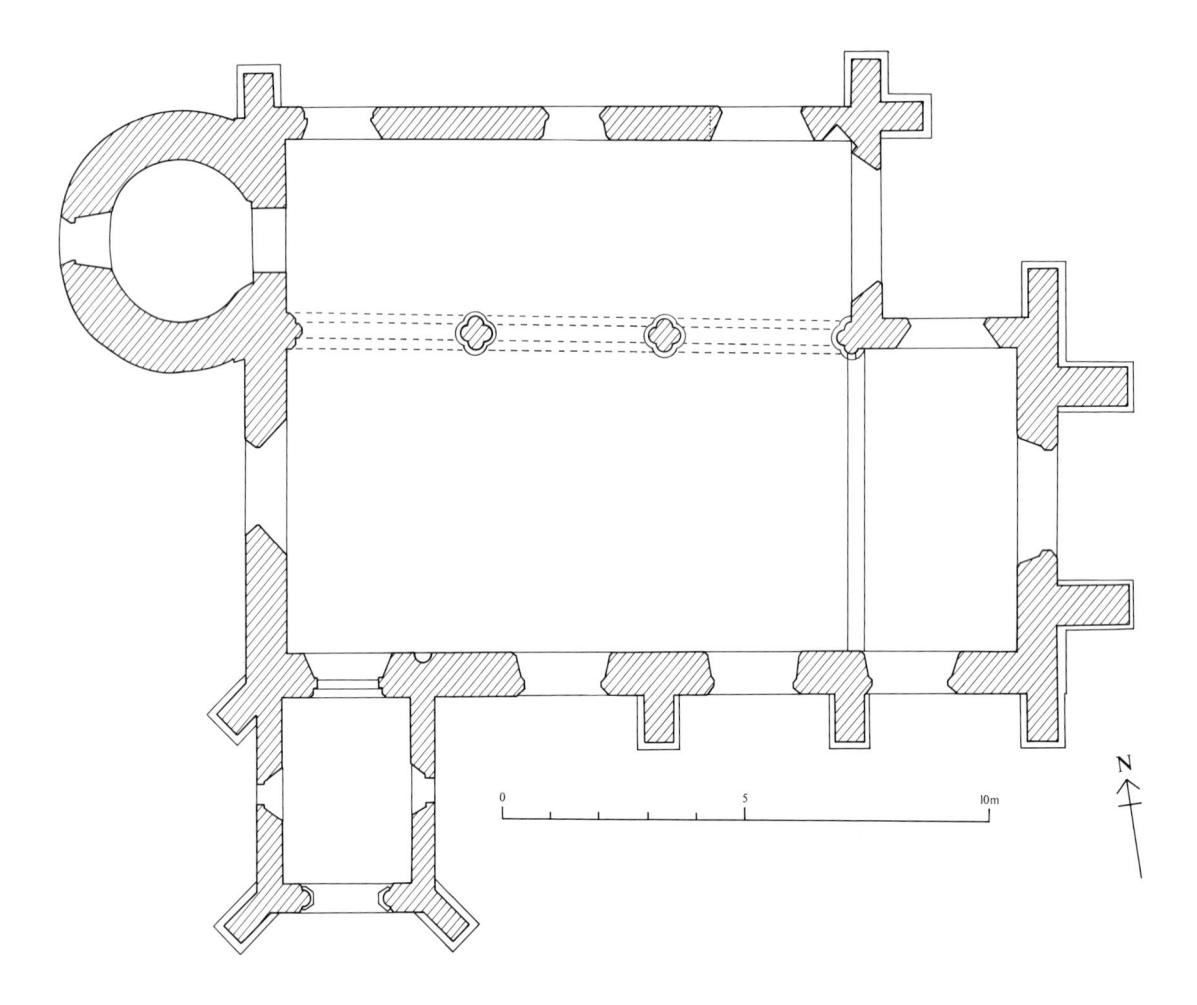

Figure 8. Brandiston, St Nicholas: plan. Scale 1:150. The north aisle, with a round tower to west, formed the original nave.

Nave. As has been established, the present chancel is in reality the eastern bay of a four-bay nave. There is no window in the last bay of the south wall because of the porch. The two nave windows are identical in size to the one already described in the chancel south wall; the western of the two windows has identical tracery. Between these two, the head of the remaining window has tracery of a five-petal type, radiating from the supermullion rising from the archlet of the middle light (Pl. LXVII). On the inside, the arrises of the reveals and rear-arches of all three windows are lined with a double convex chamfer; they all have a plain hood-mould on the outside. Above the hoods, all of the windows have arches of alternating flint and limestone (occasionally brick). Between each window is a buttress of brick and flint with three set-offs and a moulded stone plinth. The south wall itself is composed of small coursed flints, with occasional stretches of brick patching. Several putlog holes are visible, some remaining unblocked. At the eaves there is a shallow brick cornice. At the western end of the wall there is a plain south door: on the outside, there is a wide double-convex chamfer and hood mould; on the inside, the rear-arch is segmental, with a double-convex chamfer.

A diagonal buttress with three set-offs stands at the south-west corner. The nave west wall is of the same construction as the south, and contains an identical three-light Decorated window. The upper gable of this wall appears to have been rebuilt, in flint.

A three-bay arcade divides nave from north aisle. The piers are quatrefoil in plan, with moulded base and capital. This arcade formerly continued into the present chancel bay; the easternmost pier has become a respond, and it is possible to observe the way in which its capital is partly hidden by the blocking of the chancel north wall. All the arcade arches are double-chamfered. The west respond is polygonal, including its capital. The ceiling is plastered; there is a single tie-beam, halfway along.

Porch. The south porch is quite substantial. It has diagonal buttresses with two set-offs, and limestone facings and plinth. It originally had a shallow-pitched roof, clearly marked by masonry of small flints; a higher, steeper roof with larger flints was added, probably in the 17th century to judge from the brick coping. Masonry benches flank the internal walls of the porch, and east and west walls are pierced by a single cusped window with rectangular hood-mould. The porch arch has half-round responds, with octagonal moulded capitals supporting a chamfered arch; the whole has a chamfered outer arch and hood-mould. A cusped niche surmounts the apex of the arch, filled with a 20th-century statue of St Nicholas.

Aisle. The north aisle is the most complex part of the church to interpret. Terminated to west by a round tower, the aisle looks as if it formed the original nave, to which the new nave to the south was added. At the north-west corner, there is a buttress of flint with limestone facings and two set-offs. East of the buttress, the aisle wall is built of large, neatly-coursed flints. This masonry continues for 9m; at which point there is a clear vertical break. Flints and thin Roman bricks form the quoins of the north-east corner of the wall which terminates at this break. Flint masonry continues east of this break, and the present north-east corner of the aisle has an angle buttress in flint and limestone with two set-offs. The whole wall is capped by a narrow brick cornice, like the nave.

Of the openings in the aisle, only the north door, near the north-west buttress, is similar in construction to work in the nave. Its limestone jambs are the same as the south door, and the door arch is formed of alternating flint and brick voussoirs, as in the nave.

None of the window arches in the aisle are built in this way; indeed, all three of its windows differ in style, and have no counterparts in the rest of the church. The window in the east wall is most spectacular, wide, three-light and reticulated. The reticulations have ogee cusps, as do the three main lights; the eyelet is divided into two mouchettes by a supermullion. There is a hood-mould on the outside, but no mouldings of any sort inside. The window has the appearance of having been reset, as must be the case since the aisle formerly extended further east by a bay.

The eastern window of the aisle north wall is very different. It is still of three lights with a plain external hood-mould. But its design is much more sober, with a supertransom and two batement lights. It is set within a wider rear-arch. Its closest counterpart is the chancel north window. There is an arched recess at the internal north-east angle of the aisle: the entrance to a rood-stair? The remaining aisle window, set half-way along the north wall, has only two lights. Its head comprises four daggers radiating from a saltire cross. The external hood-mould is thicker than that of its neighbour to east. Internally, the rear arch has a double convex chamfer with nice spherical stops at the bottom.

Like the nave, the roof is plastered, with principal rafters showing through.

Tower. The round tower adjoins the west wall of the aisle. It has suffered considerable rebuilding in the 19th century. The flints of its walls are conspicuously large. In plan, the tower has the appearance of abutting a pre-existing wall, since it has a flattened east face rising above the west wall of the aisle. The upper stage is octagonal, with limestone facings, but no windows. Below this stage, two-light windows face north, west and south; they are Perpendicular in style but 19th century in date. An identical window, facing west, lights the ground floor. A small fill of masonry, rectangular in section, occupies the re-entrant angle between tower and nave/aisle west wall. Just south of the tower, some large flints are possibly quoins of the former nave.

Interpretation and Dating
(Fig.9)
The oldest part of the church appears to be the western part of the north aisle. With a round tower at its western extremity, this was evidently the nave of an earlier church. The surviving north-east quoins give the size of the church, but there are no other features. The round west tower is probably an early addition, for reasons given below. It is impossible to be precise, but we are probably dealing with a church of 11th or 12th-century date. There are no visible remains of its chancel.

The western of the two windows in the north wall was probably added while it still served as a nave; its 'four-petal' tracery has clear parallels with the south walk of the cloister of Norwich cathedral, of the 1330s. The reticulated east window of the aisle must share a similar date; the wall it is set into must date between the late 14th century and the 18th century, for reasons given below. The window may have been the east window of the chancel which replaced that of the first phase (but before the new nave and chancel were built south of this church). It might have stood a bay further east, to be later left as the east window of the aisle of the enlarged church.

This modest structure was massively enlarged in the second half of the 14th century. A large new nave was built south of the old one, reducing the latter with its chancel, to the status of an aisle. Two of the nave windows are of unequivocally early Perpendicular type, the other two are more characteristically Late Decorated but they are undoubtedly of the same building programme and date, a good example of 'overlap'. Alas, the chancel which belonged to this phase was demolished without trace probably in the early 18th century, to judge from the brick used in the blocking of the nave. Indeed, the nave extended further east than at present, but probably not by much. Tom Martin, towards the middle of the 18th century, drew a plan of the church showing the original extent of the chancel and noting 'This part of the chancell down & the east end built here' (Martin 1771, 1).

At some stage, the east bay of the north aisle was demolished. The blocked nave arcade shows that it existed at least to the late 14th century. Equally clearly, it must already have disappeared before the 18th-century blockings took place, since the wall filling the eastern bay of the arcade predates the 18th-century buttress against it. This bay is pierced by a window of 15th-century type, so possibly it was then that this alteration took place. Another 15th century window was inserted at the east end of the north wall of the aisle.

Later restorations include the blocking between nave and chancel, dateable to the early 1700s; the re-roofing of the nave, after selling the bells, in 1772 (NRO, FCB3, 4, 198). A further restoration took place in 1850. In 1890 the tower was largely rebuilt and made into a vestry.

Causes of Abandonment
The church was closed in 1971 because of the danger caused by lumps of plaster falling from the ceiling. This appears to have been the final straw for a church in a very small and scattered village. It was vested in the Redundant Churches Fund in 1981.

Church Contents

Ceramic. Pamments form the flooring throughout most

BRANDISTON

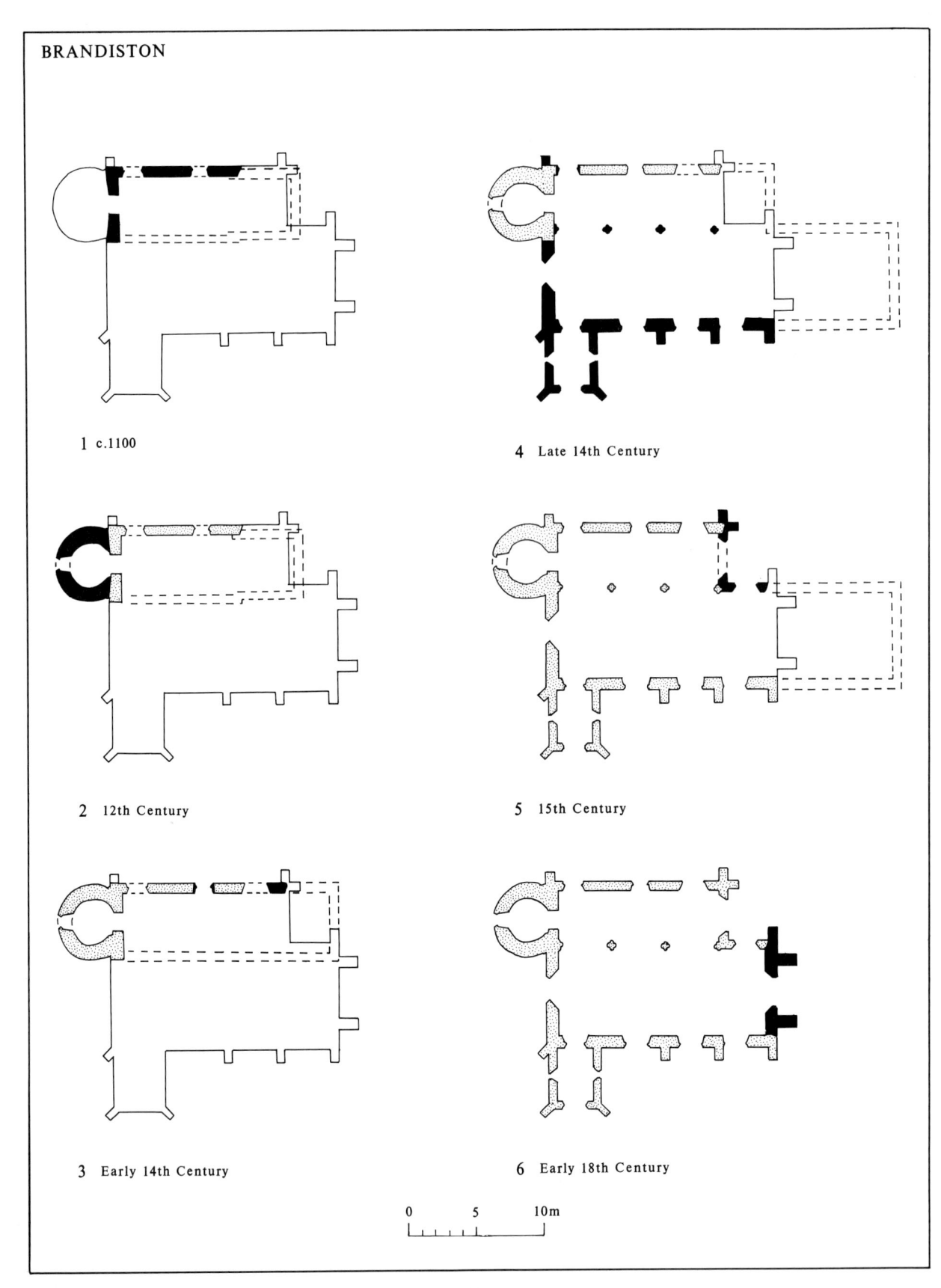

1 c.1100

2 12th Century

3 Early 14th Century

4 Late 14th Century

5 15th Century

6 Early 18th Century

0   5   10m

Figure 9.   Brandiston, St Nicholas: phase plan. Scale 1:400.

of the church; wooden parquet flooring covers the chancel and tower.

Glass. There are a few fragments of painted glass. The south window of the chancel contains some old glass in its upper lights in brown and blue, with some yellow fleur-de-lys. The chancel north window also contains some old fragments, with black engraved lines. In the north aisle, the middle window contains a good quality painting of St John and St Nicholas, dated to 1921.

Metal. Two brass inscriptions, near chancel steps, 1845, 1852. Nave south wall: brass inscription, Harry Atthill (d. 1879). Two iron and one brass lamp brackets, brass incense burner.

Paint. Painting of Crucifixion, west end of nave.

Stone. At the east end of the nave are floor slabs to the Atthill family (1758, 1778, 1788); there are two more near the font (1810, 1816, the former set in brass). Several more floor slabs flank the font (one to John Durrant d. 1756); there are four further slabs in the floor of the porch. At the east end of the north aisle is a trapezoidal tomb slab, evidently medieval.

There are several wall monuments. South of the east window of the chancel there is a 'gothick' affair in buff stone, inset with a slate inscription to William Atthill (d. 1847); north of the window a small white marble tablet with black outline, to Sarah Bircham (d. 1837; made by J.Freeman of Aylsham). On the nave south wall: grey and white marble, Mary Rackham (d. 1822); white marble, black surround, Edward Atthill (d. 1845; made by J.Stanley, St Stephen's, Norwich). West wall of nave: white marble, black surround, Anthony Atthill (d. 1876; made by H.Parfitt, Stalham); white marble, black surround, John Wilder (d. 1884). North aisle: white and grey marble Anthony Enright (d. 1917).

The font is plain, octagonal, of 1892. There is a stone water stoup just east of the south door.

Wood. The wooden altar and reredos, in gothic style, dates to 1918; two large plain candlesticks stand nearby. The nave contains 24 benches with poppyheads, all 19th century. Reading desk, pulpit and organ belong to the early 20th century. Small (19th-century) statue of St Nicholas at the junction of arcade with chancel.

Condition
The church is in fairly good condition. There are some very minor roof leaks in places, but the floor is good and window glass is in place. Most of the plaster is intact, but flaking in places. The problem of falling plaster seems to have been solved. On the outside, rainwater goods are in good condition, and walls have been kept free of creeper.

Churchyard
The churchyard forms a rectangle around the church with a recent extension at the south-east corner. Hedging and shrubs form the boundary, with entrances at the south-west and north-west corners. There are many 18th and 19th-century headstones; the latest burial dates to 1976 (flowers still kept there). Near the south-west entrance to the churchyard is a stone pillar capped with a bronze sundial (with rotating dial; 'W.B. FECIT'). All paths are well kept, and most of the churchyard is covered with long grass. At the northern edge there are some large trees, beech, poplar and horse-chestnut.

The path from the north-west entrance runs north towards Brandiston Hall (200m to north; 17th-century, greatly enlarged in 19th-century).

Archaeological and Architectural Assessment
As it stands, the church is a very interesting example of 14th-century Decorated/Perpendicular overlap. The quality of the arcade and window tracery is very high. Also, there is the interesting development of the church site, from a modest 11th/12th-century structure with round tower, now forming the north aisle to a much larger church.

There are three points which archaeological excavation would clear up. All three concern chancels. The first chancel must lie beneath the east bay of the aisle; it must have been extended further east on at least one occasion; and the late 14th-century chancel, east of the present nave, lies completely underground.

Further References
Blomefield, 1805-10, VIII, 195.
Cox, 1911, I, 188.
Martin, 1771, 1.
Pevsner, 1962a, 101.

III. West Harling, All Saints
Identification TL 9740 8518. *County No.*6051.
Diocese: Norwich. *Archdeaconry:* Norfolk. *Deanery*: Thetford and Rockland. *Parish*: Harling, East with Harling, West. *Status*: Parish church, now redundant. *Date last in regular use*: 1976.
Access and ownership: Redundant Churches Fund, access across field (public footpath).

Location and Setting
(Fig. 1, No. 17; Pl. LXIX)
The village of East Harling is south of the A11, some 12km east of Thetford. A small road south-west of the village leads, after 1km, to the hamlet of Middle Harling, whence a track leads to the site of the church. By continuing along the track from the site of Middle Harling church for another 500m, a big wood is reached. Almost immediately, a field opens out into the coniferous woodland; the church, with surrounding churchyard, stands in picturesque isolation at the far end of the field (Pl. LXIX). The churchyard is fenced off from the field, and entered through a wide wooden gate. There is no village at West Harling, only a few isolated farms and cottages.

Architectural Description
(Figs 10, 11; Pl. LXIX)
Chancel, nave, west tower, south porch, and north vestry off the chancel (Fig. 10). Constructed mainly of flint, with tiled roofs.

Chancel. The chancel east wall is built of small coursed flints with limestone quoins. The large three-light east window (uncovered from behind blocking masonry in 1884) is of cusped intersecting form (Decorated). There are delicately carved label-stops; the head of a man to north, a woman to south. The masonry of the gable, with its stone coping and gable cross, seems to belong to the 1884 restoration, as does the strange stone roundel above the apex of the window.

The masonry of the south wall is the same as that of the east. Below the coping of the gable wall is a delightful carved kneeler depicting the head of a man and a Disney-like dog. Near the south-east corner, in the upper part of the wall, the outline of a window opening can be made out, blocked in flint. On the inside there is a double piscina, set within a modern square recess; only one piece of stone forms the remnant of the mullion which originally divided the two piscinas. Immediately west is the shallow-arched recess of the sedilia, looking rather new (possibly the 1902 restoration), but with a fragment of old painting on its back wall: a red lattice with black dots, framing black fleur-de-lys. Further west is the priest-door, with a plain chamfer on the outside, and then a tall Y-tracery window. Both of these are constructed of buff-orange stone, unlike the greyish stone elsewhere, and belong to the restoration of 1902, when priest-door, piscinas and sedilia were discovered.

At eaves level there is a carved corbel at the east end of the north wall depicting the head of a hooded woman. The masonry of the chancel north wall is the same as the rest of the chancel; unusually, the lowest quoin of the north-east corner is a large upright slab. Near to the east corner is the north wall's only window, a deeply splayed lancet with chamfer and rebate on the outside. The rest of the wall is masked externally by the vestry. On the interior, there is a rectangular aumbry near to the east wall (uncovered, like the lancet, in 1902). Further west are two 19th-century openings, a doorway into the vestry and a large arch into the organ loft.

The chancel arch is disappointingly small and plain: two orders with hollow chamfers, and no capitals. The lower stones of the responds are rather damaged, the limestone a pinkish hue showing it has suffered fire damage. Absence of damage higher up suggests the arch may have been rebuilt. The wall above has a stone coping on the exterior and is surmounted by a gable cross. Just north of the chancel arch is a plain hood-moulded niche. The barrel roof dates to 1902.

Vestry. On the outside, the west wall of the vestry masks the junction of nave and chancel since it abuts the quoins of the north-east corner of the nave. Masonry is of flint, but more carelessly coursed than the nave. It has a flattish lean-to roof, the walls having either brick or stone coping. There is a plain pointed window in north and west walls, and a west doorway; the jambs of the west window are set in concrete, the others in stone. Ladbrooke's drawing (1820s) shows the 'vestry' in existence, but with no openings, and a roof extending unbroken from the chancel. It had to be re-roofed in 1844, when a dormer window (cusped, two-light) was inserted in the north wall of the chancel above the vestry, to illuminate the organ loft. Since the 18th century the whole structure had been a burial vault for the Croftes family; in 1844 it was converted to a vestry and lobby to the organ loft.

Nave. The south wall of the nave displays a complex history, (Pl. LXIX). The south-east corner with the last 2.5m of the south wall, can be dated to the restoration of 1902: neat flint masonry with orange-buff machine-cut quoins. There is no buttress at this corner, but the east wall of the nave has been thickened almost up to eaves level. The 1902 work goes up to, and continues above, a remarkable two-light plate tracery window: the tympanum above the two lancets is pierced by a quatrefoil.

The lancets have an external rebate, like the one in the north wall of the chancel - they also have chamfered leading edges. Below this window, the wall is a blocking of random brick and flint (Fig. 11).

West of the window, for 0.5m, there is a vertical patch of coursed 18th-century brick. Coursed flint masonry continues west for nearly 2m. At this point there is a vertical scar of masonry, with a stone chamfered plinth course. Thus a wall, about 0.5m thick, ran south at this point. Probing in the ground immediately south of this feature established that the wall continued south for well over 1m, and therefore belonged to the chapel described by Blomefield (see below).

The existence of a chapel adjoining the south-eastern part of the nave is corroborated by evidence inside the church. There is a change in wall thickness just east of the point where the south-running wall of the chapel joined the nave outside; east of here the wall is some 10cm thicker. The plate-tracery window has broken-off stone jambs which originally formed a narrower internal splay than that presently enveloping the window; the window has clearly been transferred here from another location. Its present rear-arch is Decorated, a very shallow pointed arch, with multiple mouldings; the label-stops had carved heads (now defaced). On the east side, the convex-chamfered arris of the rear-arch rests on the shaft and capitals of a delightful angle piscina with cusped ogee head. To the west, the chamfered arris extends down to the ground, suggesting that it originally formed an entrance, rather than a rear-arch to a window. The stonework shows signs of fire damage.

West of the patching associated with the south chapel, the flint masonry is clearly coursed and undisturbed. The wall is pierced by a two light Perpendicular window (supermullioned). The stops of the hood-mould are carved lion heads, and the arch is turned in alternating brick and flint. Further west, the south door is plain, with a double-convex moulding on the outer face and signs of fire damage. The south-west corner of the nave has plain limestone quoins.

The north wall of the nave is similar in construction to the south (apart from the disturbed masonry on the south chapel site). In fact the north wall is notably undisturbed, and apparently all of one (Perpendicular) phase. There are two supermullioned windows of identical style and construction to the one in the south wall, including lion-headed label-stops which are also found on

Plate LXVIII. West Harling church by Ladbrooke (c. 1838).

WEST HARLING

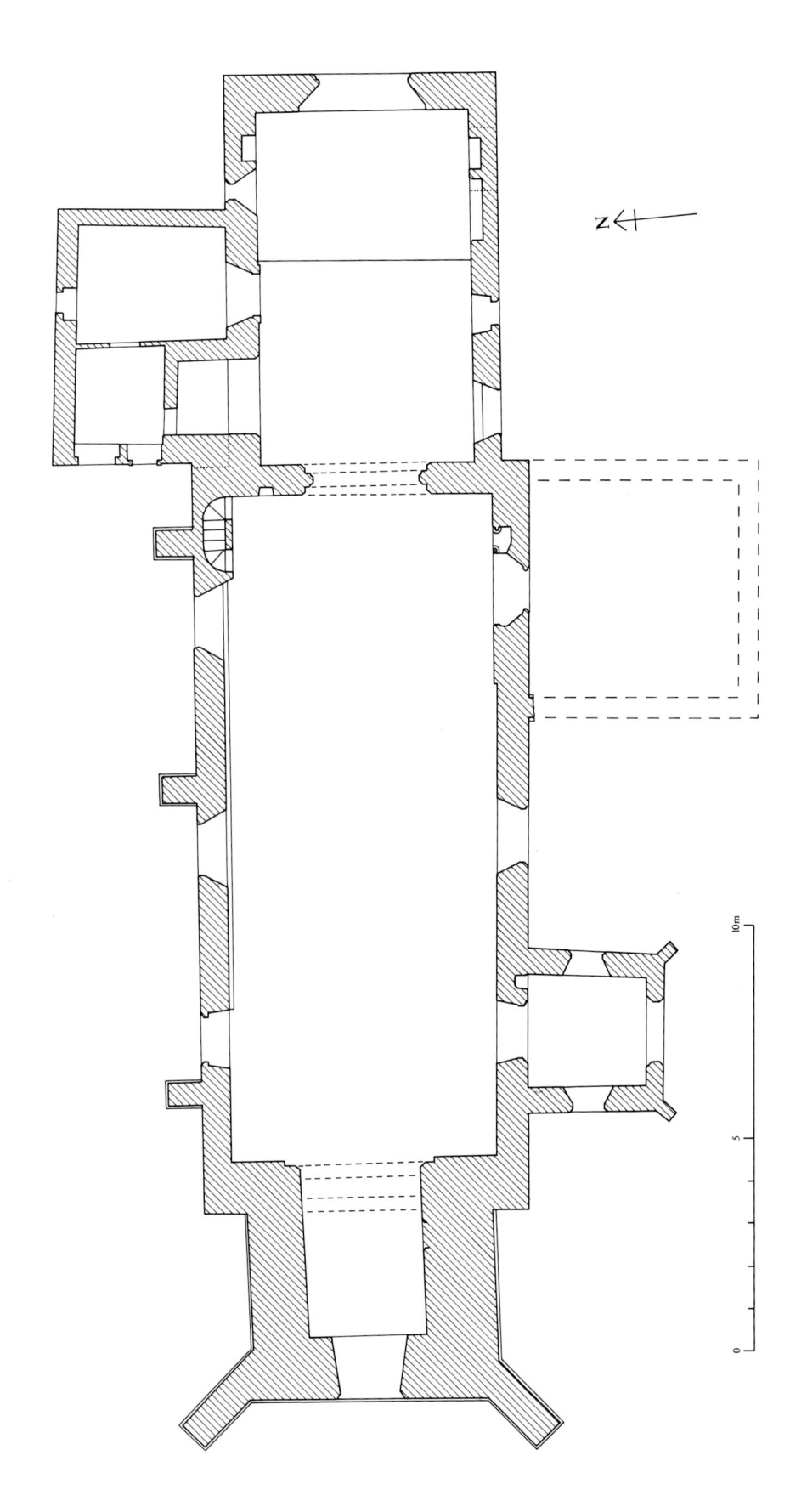

Figure 10. West Harling, All Saints: plan. Scale 1:150. The outline of the Berdewell chapel at the south-east corner of the nave was discovered by probing.

WEST HARLING

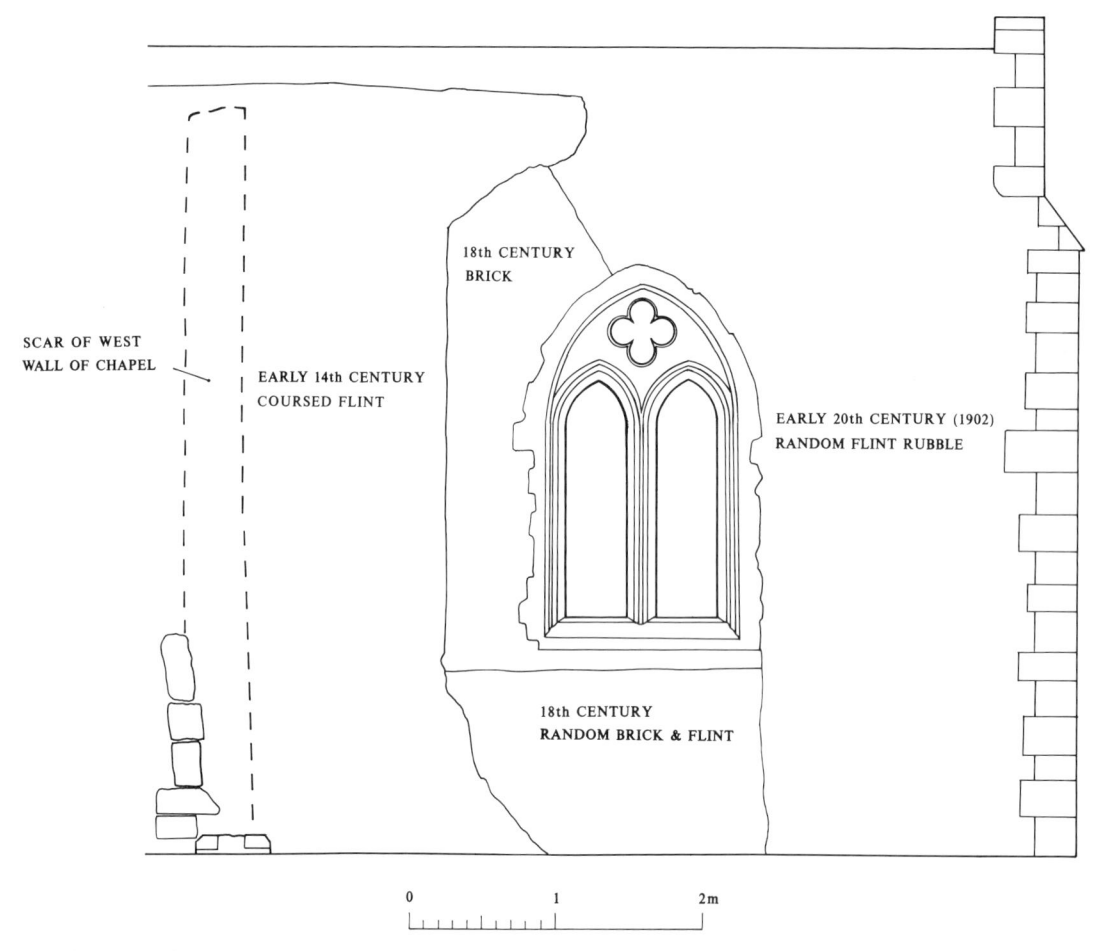

Figure 11. West Harling, All Saints: elevation of south-east corner of nave, showing 13th-century window re-set in nave wall. Scale 1:50.

the hood-mould of the north door. Three identical buttresses (flint with limestone edging and two set-offs) support the wall. Behind the eastern buttress, on the inside, is a fully preserved rood-stair; through a low four-centred arch, nine steps lead to a chamfered brick opening above. The hammerbeam roof dates to 1902.

Porch. The south porch is built of coursed flint, with stone edgings to its diagonal buttresses. East and west walls are each pierced by a cusped two-light window, set within a square hood-mould on the outside. The outer doorway has a continuous double wall moulding, but no capitals. Brick alternating with flint surmounts the hood-mould, whose stops are superbly carved: a woman's head on the east side, a bishop's head (with mitre) on the west. Above the arch is a rectangular stone-lined recess (for a statue) and above that a flat rectangular piece of stone, perhaps originally a sun-dial.

Tower. The west tower is very stately. Its diagonal west buttresses are so angled as to make the tower appear tall and narrow on north and south sides but broad and sturdy to west. There is a base course filled with flint and stone chequerboard pattern (diagonal chequerboard on east face, rectilinear on north and south). The chequerboard continues on the leading faces of the buttresses. The eastern side of the tower is supported by buttresses at right-angles to the wall. The flint masonry of the tower is better coursed than elsewhere. In the lower storey, there is a two-light west window, with 19th-century (Perpendicular) tracery. Its hood-mould is original, with lively carved label stops depicting a man and a woman. The arch is four-centred and stilted. On the south face at this level there is a cusped niche with ogee head and hood-mould adorned with crockets and finial, no doubt for a statue. The presence of a stairway in the south-east corner is revealed by a tiny window, with triangular head, slightly higher up.

Small ogee windows to north, south and west, light the first-floor of the tower; the one to west has a rectangular hood. The belfry stage has a very plain paired lancet in each face, set within a brick and stone relieving arch. On the north, there are remains of the east jamb of an opening immediately below the belfry windows; this could belong to an earlier belfry window, later blocked and replaced. There is evidence of blocking in the west face too. Indeed, the present belfry windows belong to the repairs of 1756, when a faculty was sought to sell four of the five bells and demolish the tower and spire, then much decayed (NRO, FCB/2/3/54). The spire was taken down, and the tower partly demolished; in consequence, the belfry stage has been rebuilt, and a new crenellated parapet in brick added. On the interior, the tower arch is double chamfered, with no responds. There is a small doorway to the stair turret in the south wall.

Interpretation and Dating
(Fig.12)
First of all it is necessary to deal with the form of the south chapel. This was demolished in 1733, after it had been damaged while workmen were rebuilding the nave roof. We learn that it measured 20ft by 20ft (6.1m x 6.1m), that its roof was attached to the nave roof, and that it was built of brick and stone and covered in tiles; and that 'the lord of the manor used to sit in the aisle, but the late lord converted it into a vestry' (NRO, FCB 1, 1, 619). Blomefield, writing in 1736, states that

> 'on the south side of the church was a chapel dedicated to St Mary the Virgin, called Berdewell's chapel, not, as I imagine, because that family was buried in it, (for I meet with none), but because it belonged to Beaufo's manor, which came early to the Berdewell's. This in all probability was founded by Nicholas de Beaufo (d. 1326); but whoever was its founder, he was interred, or rather immured, in its south wall, for it falling to decay very lately, a faculty was obtained to take it down, and in so doing, the body of the founder appeared to be laid in a stone coffin, enclosed in the south wall, which (by the present patron's order, was presented as it was found, and being carved with bricks, now lies undisturbed, in the nature of an altar tomb. I am told there was a small silver thing like a candlestick in the coffin, but rather think it to have been a crucifix.' (Blomefield, 1805-10, I, 297).

He adds 'Most of the Gaudy's were buried in this chapel. The founder's tomb appeared on the outside of the south wall; it had an arch turned over it, and the gravestone or lid of the coffin was about two feet from the ground.'

We can thus reconstruct the chapel almost precisely. We know the position of the west wall of the chapel, and the position and size of the entrance from the nave. If the entrance is symmetrical about the axis of the chapel, then the east wall of the chapel lay 5.15m from the west wall. If we allow for a wall 45cm thick (like the west wall), the east wall joined the nave precisely at its south-east corner, a very convenient point. This gives an internal width of 5.45m, externally 6.25m: close enough to the 20ft (6.1m) mentioned by the 1733 faculty.

If Blomefield's hypothesis is correct, then the chapel was built in the first half of the 13th century, with the tomb of the founder, Nicholas de Beaufo (d. 1236) built into a recess on the outside of the south wall. The plate tracery window re-set into the blocked chapel entrance appears to confirm this date, as the window may have come from an outer wall of the chapel. There are, however, three areas of doubt. Firstly, it may be that the plate tracery window (itself clearly dating to the first half of the 13th century) comes from another part of the church. Could it be the 'double lancet' mentioned in the parochial notes (framed at the west end of the church) found during the 1902 restoration? Secondly, the (blocked) entrance to the chapel is early 14th-century in date; this does not prove that the chapel cannot be earlier, but it is the only dateable element of the chapel *in situ*. Thirdly, Blomefield does not appear to have firm evidence for attributing the chapel to Nicholas de Beaufo; it could be an early 14th-century foundation. The sarcophagus described by Blomefield is now inside the church; a trapezoid shape, but not precisely dateable.

We move on to the phasing and dating of the church. The earliest phase of the present building is the chancel. The lancet in the north wall, and the plate tracery uncovered (as I take it) in the south wall in 1902, place it no later than the first half of the 13th century.

Plate LXIX. West Harling, All Saints, from the south. The scar left by the Berdewell chapel can be seen to the west of the (re-set) plate-tracery window.

WEST HARLING

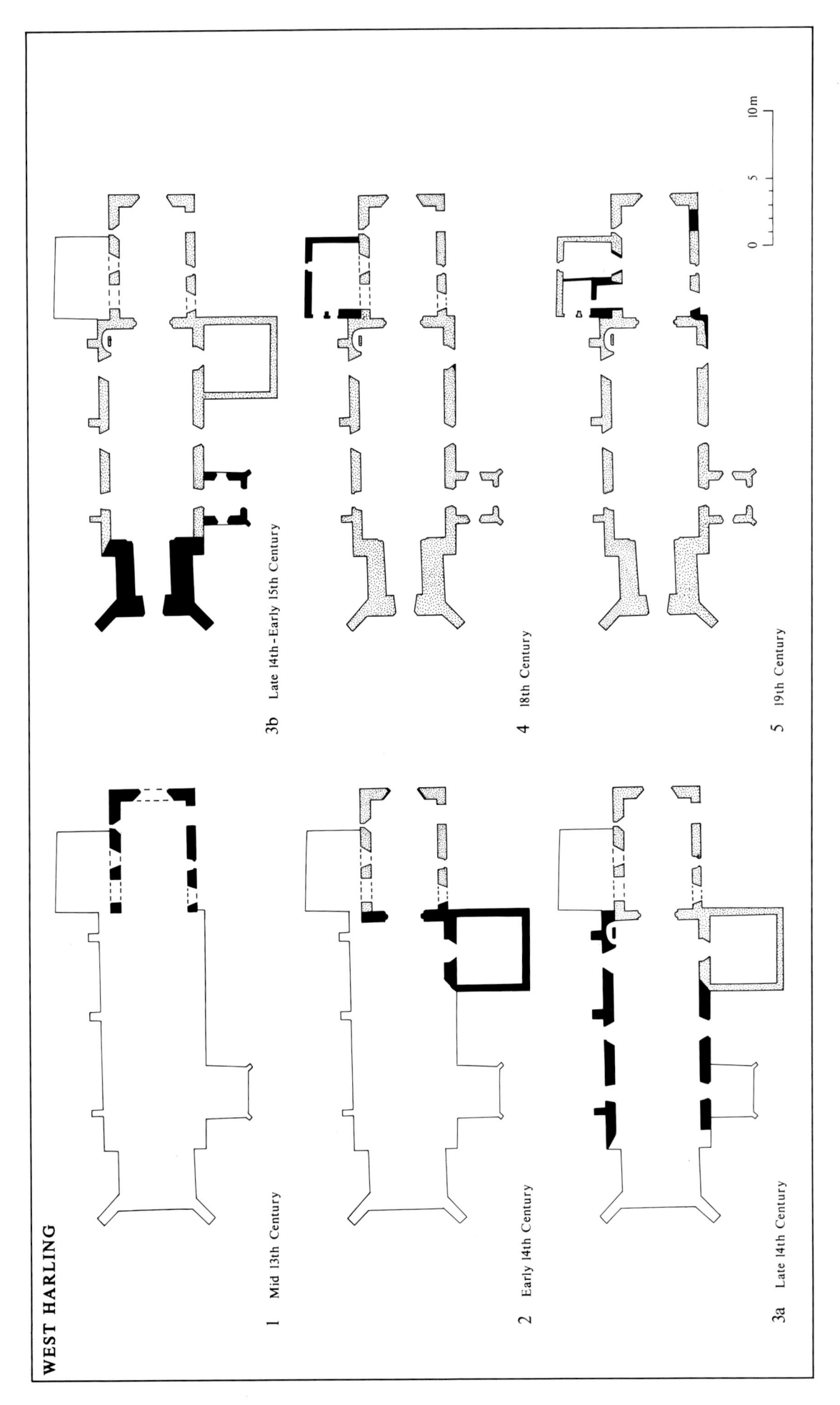

1 Mid 13th Century

2 Early 14th Century

3a Late 14th Century

3b Late 14th–Early 15th Century

4 18th Century

5 19th Century

Figure 12. West Harling, All Saints: phase plan. Scale 1:400.

The second phase belongs to the first half of the 14th century. There must have been a remodelling of the chancel (east window, chancel arch). It is probable that the south chapel belongs to this phase, unless the entrance to it was merely remodelled.

Both chancel arch and south chapel entrance show signs of damage by fire. They are the only parts of the nave not rebuilt in the late 14th century, so it may be that most of the nave was destroyed by fire at this date. In particular, the north wall of the nave has the air of being planned afresh (rather than having windows and other features inserted in an older wall). The supermullioned tracery points to the late 14th century.

Tower and porch are certainly no earlier than, and possibly slightly later than this phase. The drop-tracery of the tower west window is unlikely before the late 14th century, and is probably 15th-century. The belfry stage was rebuilt *c*. 1756.

The only remaining part of the fabric to date is the north vestry. It was the burial vault of the Croftes family in the second half of the 18th century. The south chapel had been used as manorial pew and burial vault for the Berdewells and then the Gawdys up to 1723; it was then turned into a vestry, until pulled down in 1733. William Croftes became lord of the manor in the 1740s, so it seems probable that he was responsible for erecting a new burial vault for the new manorial family. In 1844, this was converted into the vestry we see today.

During the 1844 restoration, the west window was opened out; presumably some of the tracery was still *in situ*. In 1890, the church was re-furnished, and in 1902 more re-furnishing and a complete restoration took place (including replacing the roofs). The effect has been to give a late Victorian/Edwardian feel to the interior of the church.

Causes of Abandonment
The church is isolated, and there is no village: common enough causes for abandonments in the 20th century. The causes go back earlier, however. It seems that, over a long period of time, lands and settlements had been acquired by the manorial family. By the middle of the 18th century, the original settlements had mostly disappeared, and the parish had been made into an estate (Davison, 1980, 303). The church became, in effect, an adjunct to the estate, a manorial chapel. Ironically, West Harling Hall was demolished in 1931, but the church survives. It was vested in the Redundant Churches Fund in 1977.

Church Contents

Glass. Fragments of old painted glass can be found in the upper lights of the Perpendicular window in the south wall of the nave, and in those of the north wall; the eastern one contains the figures of an angel and a saint, probably 16th century. There are some panels of the 19th-century glass in the east window of the chancel; scenes of the Crucifixion, Evangelists, etc. The west window, in the tower, contains the scene 'I am the Resurrection and the Life', dated 1850.

Metal. Most spectacular among the monuments are the three brasses along the centre of the nave. Two are to the Berdewells, and may have come from the south chapel originally. One is to William Berdewell (d. 1490) and his wife Elisabeth (Pl. XLVa). The second is to William Berdewell (d. 1508) and his wife Margaret (Pl. XLVIb).

The third shows a priest, Radulphus Fuloflove (d. 1479); Blomefield describes this brass being in the chancel, so it must have been moved.

Inside the vestry there are three pewter plaques to the Croftes family: William Croftes (d. 1770), Mary Crofts (d. 1772) and Richard Croftes (d. 1785).

The brass eagle lectern and the eight tubular bells in the tower were installed in 1890.

Other fittings (mostly 19th century) include, in the chancel: a brass chancel rail (telescopic), two small brass candlesticks, and a large brass chandelier; a harmonium in the organ loft; 6 brass wall-brackets (for candles) and 2 brass chandeliers. There is a brass First World War plaque.

Stone. The 15th-century stone font is octagonal. It has a traceried panelled shaft, surmounted by a carved head at each corner. The panels of the bowl are alternately carved with shields and rosettes.

The stone coffin found in the south chapel in 1733 was brought into the church in 1834, and stands west of the south door.

There is a very fine marble bust, set into the south wall of the chancel, to Richard Gipps; it was carved, *c*.1780, by Joseph Wilton. There are also three black floor slabs in the chancel, to Henry Cressemer (d. 1719), James Smythe (d. 1759) and Richard Deane (d. 1825).

In the nave are the following wall tablets: marble Nicholas Colborne (d. 1846; made by Temouth, S.C., of Pimlico); 10 brass plaques to the Nugent family (last one in 1922) next to the family pew, dated 1893; marble, Lord Colborne (d. 1854; made by T.Gaffin, London); marble, Charles Ridley (d. 1854; by Ruddock, Lopham). On the floor, there is an indent, some illegible floor slabs, and one to Emma Boky (d. 1824) and Robert Boky (d. 1828).

Wood. To the restoration of 1890 belong the oak benches and pulpit; In 1902 Sir Edmund Nugent donated the altar table and reredos. Set into this reredos are 5 wooden panels of magnificent Flemish 16th-century workmanship; they depict the Annunciation, Nativity, Three Kings with Herod, Christ examined by the High Priests, and the Circumcision. Their provenance is not known.

There is also a large early 19th-century table, a large oak chest with iron straps, a panel of the Lord's Prayer and the Creed, and a Charles II coat of arms.

North and south doors are both medieval.

Condition
The church is in first-class condition throughout.

Churchyard
The churchyard is quite well maintained. Saplings and trees are concealing the gravestones in the north-east corner. There are remains of a brick enclosing wall at north and east boundaries; south and west, there is a post and wire fence. Most of the headstones are 19th-century.

Archaeological Record
Just 100m east of the church is the site of Berdewell Hall: a moated stone building, pulled down and replaced by a new West Harling Hall, *c*.1725-37, which in its turn was demolished in 1931. The house platform remains. The site of the village was probably north of the church, where building materials have been found from time to time. Roman pottery and coins have been found within 200m to north and west of the church.

Archaeological and Architectural Assessment

The church contains good quality work of 13th to 16th-century date; plate tracery is particularly rare in parish churches. It has an interesting sequence of building, including an early 14th-century remodelling, and a fire followed by rebuilding in the late 14th-century. There is also the intriguing problem of the Berdewell chapel, located at the east end of the nave, and now below ground. Inside, the monuments, especially brasses, are very fine.

Further References
Blomefield, 1805-10, I, 297.
Bryant, 1901b, 52.
Cox, 1911, II, 204.
Davison, 1980.
Pevsner, 1962b, 375.

IV. West Tofts, St Mary

Identification
TL 8360 9289. *County No.*5156.
Diocese: Norwich. *Archdeaconry:* Norfolk. *Deanery:* Thetford and Rockland. *Parish:* West Tofts with Buckenham Parva. *Status:* parish church, now disused. *Date last in regular use:* 1942.
Ownership and access: strictly private access, Ministry of Defence.

Location and Setting
(Fig. 1, No. 32)
The church of West Tofts stands within the Stanford Battle Area, and cannot be visited by the general public. It is situated 4km east of Mundford, approached from a very straight forest lane. The church is only 500m from the entrance to the Battle Area; close by stand derelict cottages, rectory and pub, all forming the nucleus of the village which was evacuated in 1942. The churchyard itself is surrounded by wire fencing capped with barbed wire. A large notice makes it clear that it is out of bounds to H.M.Forces.

Architectural Description
(Pl. LXX)
The church consists of chancel, nave, north aisle, west tower, south porch, and off the chancel a south chapel and a north vestry. It is constructed of flint.

Apart from the nave arcade and the west tower, the church was completely, and magnificently, rebuilt by A.W.N.Pugin from 1849. Because so much belongs to the rebuilding, the character of the masonry can be dealt with from the outset. It is of knapped flint, neatly faced, giving an exceptionally dark (grey or black) surface; random pieces of uncut flint with a brownish patina speckle and enliven this sombre surface. All dressings are in limestone, some of which has weathered to an orange-brown hue. The masonry of the west tower is similar, but not as uniform or precise as the 19th-century work. Pugin was clearly trying to tone-in his work to the masonry of the tower.

Chancel. The chancel is taller than the nave, with a steep tiled roof (Pl. LXX). It has clasping buttresses with two set-offs and gable copings at the east end. A stone base course continues round all external walls. The superb five-light east window is Decorated in style, based on Norfolk three-petal and five-petal designs of the 1340s, but, being Pugin, never merely copying. It is comparable to the five-light east window designed by him in the early 1840s for St Giles's, Cheadle. There are fine carved heads on the labels. The three south windows are two-light but in the same style, and separated by a buttress. There are two windows of this type on the north side. On the inside, fabulous carved leaves form the springing of the rear arches to these windows, again with hood moulds and carved stops.

Sutton Chapel. Visible only from the interior, the church has a crossing intervening between chancel and nave. Its east arch has nook shafts with fillets and a moulded arch (capitals obscured by screen). The west arch has octagonal responds and capitals. It is surmounted on the outside by a bell-cote containing two bells. The north wall of the crossing is pierced by a two-light window and to south is the Sutton Chantry. This chapel extends south of the chancel wall by 1.5m, with diagonal buttresses at the corners. The arch leading into the chantry springs from above a lancet window on the east side (a blocked lancet to west); on the outside, this window is recessed behind the line of the chancel south wall, opened up through a squint: surely a 'jeu d'esprit' by Pugin. The three-light south window with intersecting tracery is Decorated in style but more Geometrical than in the chancel. Beneath it, set into the base course, is a pointed segmental arch, forming a tomb recess in the exterior wall (hidden underneath it is the memorial to Sir Richard Sutton, d. 1855). The chantry has an elaborate tierceron vault on the inside, with delicately carved bosses (figure of Christ in the centre). The vault springs from four green marble shafts with foliate capitals, which in turn rest on corbels carved with the Evangelist symbols.

Vestry. If the Sutton Chantry is fantastic in a serious way, the vestry north of the chancel is fantastic in a light-hearted way. An arch high up in the north wall of the chancel forms the opening of the organ loft (now removed). Below the opening, a doorway with flat lintel and cusped corbels opens into the vestry. Inside is a panelled room, with three cusped lancets against the east wall and a late 13th-century style fireplace against the south wall (the chimney protrudes above the chancel roof). To north is a spiral staircase leading to the organ loft, to west is a door. The complexities of this structure are revealed in its exterior masses and varying roofs. Most remarkable are the wall surfaces themselves. There is a stone base course, with walls built of knapped flint up to 3m from the ground. Above this line the stair-turret and passage to the organ loft are of half-timber construction, the turret itself capped with a conical roof.

The scale of the vestry and stair-turret is altogether less grand than the church, almost domestic and no doubt more fitting to its function. Indeed, the vestry complex is very reminiscent of the late medieval houses of Rouen, and it is no surprise that in 1836 Pugin had published 'Details of antient houses of the 15th and 16th centuries selected from those existing at Rouen and Caen and Beauvais and Gisors and Abbeville and Strasbourgh and etc.'

Nave. The nave is less impressive than the chancel. It has lower walls and roof-line, and no buttresses. Even the base course is plainer. Simple Y-tracery fills the three windows, and a horizontal stringcourse connects the springing of the hood-moulds. The rear arches are moulded, and a stringcourse connects the interior hood-moulds too. A scar above the south doorway indicates that it replaces a taller opening, no doubt an earlier window or doorway. There is a cusped piscina in the north-east corner.

The four-bay north arcade is original (*i.e.* not Pugin), of early Decorated type: quatrefoil piers of four clustered shafts, with moulded bases and capitals, and double hollow-chamfered arches.

Porch. The south porch is enveloped by the same stone base-course as the nave wall. The outer doorway has polygonal responds with fillets, wave-moulded arch and continuous outer order; the hood-mould with leaf terminals is continued by a stringcourse, broken by a single cusped ogee window in east and west wall. Above the arch is a stone panel depicting a figure with a scroll. The doorway into the nave has nook-shafts on pedestal bases, with foliate capitals and carved heads on the label-stops.

Aisle. Instead of the lean-to roof one would expect in Norfolk, the north aisle has its own gabled roof. The outer walls were built by Pugin. Unlike the nave, it has the more elaborate stepped base course which we find on the chancel. The buttresses are different, though: all with two set-offs, diagonal at the two corners, the three along the north side simply at right-angles to the wall. All four north windows are identical, with convex chamfers, hood-moulds, stops with carved heads, and two-light Decorated tracery with mouchettes in the single reticulation.

The west window in the west wall is identical, but taller. In the east wall, the window is three-light with cusped reticulations. The rear arches of all these windows are pointed but rather flat. A stringcourse continues round the whole aisle just below window level on the inside. Below the east window of the north wall, on the inside there is an arched tomb recess with cusped and crocketed canopy. A stone corbel carved with an angel forms a statue base in the south-west corner.

Tower. The west tower has at each corner a large diagonal buttress with three set-offs. Round the bottom is a magnificent stone base frieze with a running inscription recording the names of the donors: All the (on buttress): begyners at the werk: Andro Hewke: John Rolff; John Olyver and Amy hys wyfe: Wyliam Olyver: Wyliam Rolff: John Rolff: John Hewke (on buttress): Robert Rolff (on buttress): Sir John Vyse, Parson (on buttress, higher up). The two panels of the frieze in the middle of the west wall were placed there by Pugin when he blocked the doorway here. The originals had been removed in the early 19th century, when the doorway was inserted; they were later incorporated into the village school, and were recovered for safe-keeping when the school was demolished in 1977.

There are signs of patching in the flint walling of the west tower immediately above the renewed frieze stones, indicating the presence of a blocked doorway. Above the frieze this wall has a two-light Perpendicular window with supermullioned drop-tracery. The four-centred arch, with stringcourse, is turned in double

Plate LXX. West Tofts, St Mary, from the south-east. Apart from the 15th-century tower, this shows Pugin's work of 1849-56. The church, which is in Ministry of Defence property, has had its windows boarded and most of its contents removed since its forced abandonment in 1942.

courses of alternating brick and flint. A small rectangular window is all that lights the second storey. Belfry windows are constructed in identical fashion to the ground-floor west window, but with simple cusped Y-tracery. The tower is crowned by a crenellated flint parapet (with stone copings) and a small stone pinnacle at each corner. On the north face of the tower, a stair-turret protrudes slightly, next to the north-west buttress. There are no inscribed frieze stones on this face, but on the south side are some panels which read: 'IHS: MR: O: P: NO: BIS' (Jesu, Mary ora pro nobis). On the inside, the tower arch has no responds, but the chamfered inner arch springs from corbels carved with angels.

Interpretation and Dating
(Pl. LXXI)
The oldest part of the church is the nave arcade, of c. 1290-1300. Evidence of a blocked opening above the south doorway suggests that the south wall may be remodelled rather than rebuilt, and this is confirmed by Ladbrooke's lithograph of the 1830s: four windows, each with Y-tracery and stringcourse linking the labels.

We are fortunate in having an accurate date for the tower. John Vyse, Parson, whose name appears on the south-west buttress as one of the 'begyners at the werk', was rector from 1451 to 1486. John Olyver left money to the tower in 1482, Andrew Hewke in 1484, and William Olyver in 1518: all names appear in the frieze also. Thus the tower was in building in the 1480s, and not finished until the early 16th century.

Before moving on to Pugin's work of the mid 19th-century, it is worth considering the form of the church in the late Middle Ages, and the changes which took place up to Pugin's time. In Blomefield's day (c. 1740) the church was about the same size as it is today. It had west tower, nave and north aisle, and the chancel measured about 33ft by 18ft: not quite as long as Pugin's chancel. There was also a door on the north side leading (according to Blomefield) into a vestry. Chancel and nave were thatched, but the north aisle was tiled (Blomefield, 1805-10, II, 256). It appears that the church, by the late medieval period, was quite sizeable, and had survived intact until the 18th century. It was then that a period of decay set in. In 1756 a high wind blew part of the roof off, and damaged the church to the extent that two of the bells had to be sold to pay for repairs (NRO, FCB/2, 3, 54).

Worse was to befall the church. In 1786, because the chancel and aisle were 'ruinous and decayed' and the village small (only 74 inhabitants), a Faculty was granted to

> 'take down and dilapidate the said chancel and also the said North Isle and instead thereof to erect a new gable of stone two feet and three inches thick within the arch at the east end of the said church and to build up the four archways between the pillars on the north side of the said church with stone walls fourteen inches thick, to put the present East Window of the chancel into the new East Gable of the church and the other (2) chancel windows on the north side of the church between the two arches nearest the West End'. (NRO, FCB/3, 5, 316).

The church was thus reduced to tower and nave. A new, but very small, chancel may have been added at this time, or it may belong to the repairs undertaken by Sir Richard Sutton in the late 1820s. This was its state by the time Ladbrooke sketched it (Pl. LXXI), and up to the time Pugin began work.

Pugin's work began in 1846 with the addition of a mausoleum (the Sutton Chantry) to the south side of the existing chancel for the family of Sir Richard Sutton. This must have been remodelled a few years later, when the larger chancel was built.

With the arrival of Augustus Sutton as Rector of West Tofts in 1849, a new and ambitious rebuilding was embarked on. In fact, although it involved much rebuilding, it was more a question of restoring the church to its pristine state before the 18th-century dilapidations. The Faculty bond of 1849 expressly mentions the desire to build a new aisle and south porch on the foundations of the old: 'it is proposed to erect the said north aisle and the said south porch on the old foundation' (NRO, FCB/7, 11, 119). It was also intended to build a screen at the east end of the aisle for a burial place for John Sutton and his family, and to build a larger chancel and a spire on the tower. It was to be financed by John Sutton, at a cost of £1,320 starting with the north aisle and funding the rest when possible. Pugin's plans for the whole church (with all its fittings) were complete by 1850, and when he died in 1852 it had not been finished. The aisle had been built by 1850, nave restored and south porch built in 1851. Work began again in 1855, when the spire was erected (it was removed in 1929) and the new chancel begun. This work, along with the Sutton Chantry, was completed in 1856. All fittings had been installed by 1857, when the new chancel was dedicated.

West Tofts is one of Pugin's best achievements, a blend of asymmetrical masses and forms combined high-quality craftsmanship and meticulous design. Despite the scale of rebuilding, however, it should be emphasised that what Pugin achieved was essentially a restoration. It seems he deliberately set out to restore the form of the church as it would have been at the end of the Middle Ages. He was most particular in preserving the form of the nave south wall, and in following the outline of the porch and north aisle. He knew of the larger chancel which existed before 1786, and possibly also the north vestry beyond; both chancel and vestry have been retained. Details of window tracery relate very well to early 14th-century work in Norfolk. (There are one or two inaccuracies. Single aisles from Norfolk churches almost always have lean-to roofs, and not separate gables; in basing the masonry on that of the tower, he disregards the fact that tower masonry was usually better finished than that of other walls; base-courses all the way round a church are very unusual in the 14th century.) His finished work is both convincing and full of conviction.

Causes of Abandonment
The church was in regular use until 1942, when the whole village was evacuated to make way for the Battle Training Area.

Church Contents
Apart from a few monuments, all the interior decor was designed by Pugin. Much has been removed to other churches.

Ceramic. The chancel floor tiles (Minton) are blue with fleur-de-lys at the east end, elsewhere alternating green and yellow with incised crosses. In the Sutton Chantry, the design is in blues, red, yellow and white. Red and yellow tiles form the floors of vestry and crossing. In the middle of the latter is a large marble tomb slab to Bernard Howard (d. 1745). The nave is paved with red and black tiles.

Glass. Most of the painted glass has been removed from the chancel windows, although the upper lights remain. The three windows of the nave contain painted glass depicting St John the Baptist, St John the Evangelist, St Andrew, St James, St Lawrence and St Stephen. The north aisle also contains painted glass (blocked). Dismantled painted glass from the rest of the church, and other Battle Area churches, lies heaped in a corner.

Metal. A fine iron grill of cusped pointed arches and leaves marks the entrance to the Sutton Chantry.

Stone. Against the east wall is a superb stone reredos, with nine carved and painted figures, and diaper tiling below. The Sutton Chantry is especially richly adorned. The south wall has a stone dado with quatrefoils, the rest with wooden linenfold panelling. Colour is also an important element in the Sutton tomb itself (to Mary Elizabeth Sutton, d. 1842). The tomb-chest has quatrefoils enclosing enamelled shields; the black marble top is inset with coloured stones, and capped with a brass foliate cross. Six marble columns, with spurred bases and curled-leaf capitals, support a canopy of cusped arches with crockets and finials, and interior vault: all painted.

In the nave, there are four large ledger slabs, to John and Thomas Jermyn (first half 17th century), Benjamin Barwick (d. 1669), Robert Partridge (d. 1710), James Brown (d. 1778). Between the windows are marble wall monuments: white, with grey capitals: Henry Partridge (d. 1733); white, with urn and cartouche: Henry Partridge (d. 1754); white with coloured background: Martha Partridge (d. 1750).

The stone font stands near the west wall of the north aisle. It is octagonal, with quatrefoil panels around the bowl, supported by four leaning angels; it was made in 1857, copying the one at Mundford.

Wood. The chancel is sumptuously furnished. It has a painted waggon roof, with carved bosses. Below the stringcourse at window-sill level, the eastern part of the chancel is painted with geometric designs and angels in quatrefoils; the western part is panelled in wood up to this level, backing the choir stalls which return round the east side of the chancel screen (the stalls are decorated with Perpendicular tracery, and stand on a stone base). The screen is Decorated in style, with a lovely cusped ogee doorway, and rood loft with vaulted coving supporting a rood with crucifix. High up in the north wall is the organ loft (although the organ case has been removed), a wooden balcony painted with angels. The eastern bay of the aisle was Sir John Sutton's chapel. It is divided off from aisle and nave by a painted wooden screen, Perpendicular in style; this bay also has a painted waggon ceiling, like the chancel, to emphasise its importance.

Whereabouts of other furnishings
Many of the furnishings were removed in 1950. Their whereabouts in 1968 were located by A. Hunt of the Norwich Diocesan Registry:
  Colchester Garrison Church: pews, choirstalls, pulpit.
  Hilborough church: altar, 2 tables, prayer desk, statue of St Mary, chair, book-case, processional cross head, altar frontals.
  South Pickenham church: organ, with painted case.
  South Creake church: crucifix and 6 candlesticks.
  Scoulton church: prayer desk.
  Southery church: vestments, carpets, curtains.
  Kirby Bedon church: 2 brass candelabra.
  Shotesham All Saints: chalice and paten.
  Norwich St Giles: 2 brass candlesticks, 1 brass candelabra.
  Norwich St Margaret: articles of plate.
  Norwich St Martin-at-Palace: harmonium and stool.
  Norwich Museums: 2 chalices and some glass.
  8 bells stored in the church, stolen recently.

Condition
The condition of the church is very sound with good roof, rainwater goods, walls *etc*.

One window in the chancel and one in the crossing are blocked with corrugated iron. The west window in the tower is boarded up.

Churchyard
The churchyard forms a rectangle around the church. Its tall boundary fence is made of strong wire, capped with barbed wire. The gate is padlocked.

There are many 19th-century gravestones, some in the form of medieval stone coffins. The churchyard is well tended and not overgrown. There are some yew trees south of the church.

Archaeological Record
Scheduled D.M.V. site immediately north of the churchyard with lots of earthworks.

Plate LXXI. West Tofts church by Ladbrooke (1832). The chancel and north aisle had been removed in 1786 and a squat new chancel added. This shows its appearance prior to Pugin's rebuilding.

Site of Caston Hall 100m east, a moated 14th-century hall, rebuilt in 1776 and used as a rectory; only ruins of its outbuildings remain.

Archaeological and Architectural Assessment
West Tofts, even disused and deprived of may of its furnishings, is a magnificent church. The medieval parts (the arcade and west tower) are very fine, the latter of particular interest on account of its frieze of donor plaques. The rest of the church, by Pugin, is simply superb. Pugin was one of the greatest 19th-century architects, and Stanton, who has written the best monograph on his work, describes his achievement at West Tofts as 'brilliant: The rebuilding of St Mary's and its adornment was one of Pugin's finest accomplishments'. (Stanton, 1971, 138-9). In its local context, there are no 19th-century churches in Norfolk of higher quality than this.

Recommendations
It is clearly outrageous that a magnificent and important church like this should be locked away from public gaze (visits only allowed with authorised pass, available certain days a year).

This suggestion has been made many times before, but since the church is only 500m from the outer edge of the Battle Area, and at its main access, it should be possible to create a small enclave to exclude the church from the Battle Area. It could be returned to use as a place of worship, or maintained as an important building in its own right. Concomitantly, it would be appropriate to try to return its original furnishings, now dispersed, in order to restore the splendour of Pugin's work.

Further References
Blomefield, 1805-10, II, 256.
Cox, 1911, II, 74.
Pevsner, 1962b, 378.
Pugin, 1836.
Stanton, 1971, 138-9.
Tricker, 1981.

V. Wiggenhall, St Mary the Virgin

Identification
TF 5826 1439. *County No.*2252.
Diocese: Ely. Archdeaconry; Wisbech. *Deanery:* Lynn Marshland. *Parish:* Wiggenhall St Mary the Virgin with Islington. *Status:* parish church, now in RCF. *Date last in regular use:* 1981.
Ownership and access: Redundant Churches Fund; right of way to church across private land.

Location and Setting
(Fig. 1, No. 33)
There are altogether four Wiggenhall parishes, two on either side of the Great Ouse, in the flat fenland 6km south of King's Lynn. The village of Wiggenhall St Germans straddles the river, and has the only bridge crossing before the Lynn ring road. Its church is on the east bank, whereas the church of St Mary the Virgin is 1.3km further west. There are very few houses within the parish of St Mary the Virgin, and no village centre at all. The church is at the end of a no-through road running north from the St Germans-Tilney Lane. It is approached through the drive of the 19th-century rectory. The churchyard is flanked by garden to north, south and east, and there is a large cornfield to west. At the time of writing (August 1983), the church was being restored for the RCF. A larger number of bats appear to reside inside the church, particularly around the roodstair.

Architectural Description
(Pl. LXXII)
The church consists of chancel, nave, north and south aisles, west tower, and south porch. It is surprisingly uniform in style. Apart from the tower, every wall is covered in concrete rendering (Pl. LXXII). Very little masonry is visible, but where it can be seen, it tends to be a great mixture of carstone (both brown and sandy), limestone, brick and flint. Roofing material consists of slate for chancel and nave, lead for aisles and porch.

Chancel. The east wall of the chancel had just finished receiving a new coat of concrete rendering when visited (August 1983). Fortunately, E. Rose had been able to observe it after the wall had been stripped prior to re-rendering, and noticed that it was composed of flint containing large amounts of medieval brick and some erratic stone; it also had a stone-edged and brick-edged putlog hole (N.A.U. file). The corners have angle buttresses with two set-offs and limestone facings. The four-light east window is supermullioned with cusped Y-tracery in the reticulations. The south wall has Perpendicular tracery of the same type, but its two windows have only two lights. All of the windows have external hood-moulds and hollow-chamfered rear arches. A buttress with two set-offs forms the midpoint of both north and south walls. East of that, in the south wall, is a small pointed priest's door, with hollow chamfer and hood. The north wall has a single two-light window (identical to those in the south wall) west of the buttress. The interior is very plain. Below the south-east window is a sedilia bench with cusped angle piscina. The chancel arch has round responds, bases and capitals, supporting an arch with chamfered inner order and a continuous outer order of two convex chamfers. The chancel roof consists of plain braced collars.

Nave. On the nave side, a rood stair runs south behind the chancel arch, forming a bulge to east (and on the exterior at junction of chancel and south aisle), and opens above in the angle between nave and chancel. The nave is of five bays. Each pier is quatrefoil in plan, with fillets in the re-entrant angles. Unlike the chancel ach, the bases and capitals are polygonal, the arches double chamfered. Above the apex of each arch is a clerestorey window, the south ones different from the north. Each south window is two-light, supermullioned, with four panels in the head, set within a very flat segmental rear arch; on the outside, the hood-mould is square; the masonry of the south clerestorey has recently been rendered (1983). On the north side, each window is three-light, with cusped intersecting tracery; the profile of the window arch is four-centred (without hood-mould) on the outside, pointed segmental on the inside.

The roof has polygonal crown-posts resting on embattled tie-beams, which are supported by wall-posts with arched braces, all encompassed within a canted ceiling.

South Aisle. The south aisle has angle buttresses at either corner with two set-offs, and an additional buttress at the junction with the chancel, beneath the bulge of the rood-stair. East and west walls have identical windows: three-light with through-mullions, two panel lights divided by the supermullion rising from the centre-light, and taller cusped side-lights.

The south wall has four windows, two either side of a buttress. Each is two-light with cusped segmental archlets supporting two upper lights framed by supermullions. The rear arches of all aisle windows have convex chamfered leading edges and internal hoods. The windows rise from a continuous stringcourse at sill-level on the inside. Externally, the hood-moulds all have carved terminals, the head of a man to the right, a lion to the left. There is a piscina at the eastern end of the south wall, with the outline of a consecration cross above.

The south doorway is sumptuously Early English: two orders of nook-shafts with bell capitals and waterholding bases, the free-standing shafts interposed with keeled and filleted mouldings, all supporting an arch of seven deeply-undercut orders; the hood-mould has carved terminals, a crowned king to west, a mitred bishop to east; the rear arch is segmental.

Porch. Absence of rendering of the south porch west wall reveals its construction in medieval brick, like the upper part of the tower. It has a Perpendicular window in east and west walls, two-light with a quatrefoil in the reticulation. The exterior base-moulding continues round the small corner buttresses too; these are at right-angles to the wall, and set back slightly from the corner to leave space for a canopy (presumably for statue) across the outer corners. The outer doorway has polygonal responds (no capitals) and a double-convex chamfered continuous moulding. Above the arch is a square stone sundial, inscribed 'Joseph Rockley, Esq., Churchwarden 1742. *Tempus Fugit.*' Inside, the porch has a stone barrel vault supported by transverse ribs.

North Aisle. The north aisle is identical to the south-aisle. Only the doorway is different: still Early English, but simpler, with two hollow chamfered orders to the arch, and leaf terminals to the hood-mould. Roofing of both aisles consists of a simple lean-to, of 19th or 20th-century date.

Tower. The west tower is the only totally unrendered part of the fabric. It has a polygonal stair-turret in both of its western corners (access to north-western stair beginning at belfry stage only), reinforced with clasping buttresses. The belfry stage is built mainly of brick; lower down the wall is composed of buff-orange carrstone, interspersed with pieces of limestone, boulder-erratics, and lava fragments (presumably from querns). Particularly in the lower parts, there is much re-used limestone, including pieces with chamfers, quirks and rolls (could be 12th-century). The west window of the lower storey is two-light and supermullioned, with carved heads terminating its hood-mould. Inside, the tower arch is double chamfered, and has no responds; in the south-west corner the doorway to the stair-turret has a wave-moulded continuous chamfer. Above this level, there is an external set-off, with above a small rectangular opening on each outer side; to east, a large blocked opening led into the roof-space. The two-light windows of the belfry stage are identical to the lower storey window. This stage is capped with a stone concave cornice and a large gargoyle at each corner. The brick crenellated parapet (continuing the polygonal outline of western stair-turrets) is capped with stone copings.

Interpretation and Dating

North and south doorways are both of the 13th century, and are probably re-inserted. The rest of the church is remarkably uniform in style, all 15th-century Perpendicular. It may be that the differences in window type between north and south clerestoreys are due to the programme of painted glass which they formerly displayed. On the south side, the windows contained scenes from the life of the Virgin, whilst on the north side the twelve Apostles were depicted; with four windows to each clerestorey, each window on the north side had to consist of three lights. Blomefield was able to record personally this glass in 1730 (1805-10, IX, 179-182). Of course, it could be that the north clerestorey was rebuilt, perhaps early in the 16th century, to contain the new theme in painted glass.

Causes of Abandonment

The relative remoteness of the church from its community, and the proximity of St German's (1.3km east), have led to Redundancy. There is no centre to Wiggenhall St Mary the Virgin; the local community centres on St Germans. The church was vested in the Redundant Churches Fund in 1981.

Church Contents
(Pl. XLVI)

Ceramic. At the end of the north and south aisles are some medieval floor tiles; a few have diagonal incisions.

Glass. Fragments of medieval painted glass can still be seen. In the south aisle, the upper lights of the windows contain armorial glass of the Keriviles, Howards, Thorpes, Morleys, Werehams etc. There are similar fragments in the north aisle too, and in the north window of the chancel. A figure of an apostle survives in the north clerestorey.

Metal. At the east end of the south aisle is a heart brass with jar scrolls (two have gone); it used to read: 'Orate p. aia Dni Roberti - Kervile Militis de Wygenhale - Filii Edmunid Kervile de - Wygenhale, cujus cor. hic humatur'; Robert Kervile died abroad *c.* 1450, and his heart is buried here.

Six bells are in the tower: two of 1638, one of 1765, the rest 1873. There is a superb brass eagle lectern (Pl. XLVI). It contains the inscription: 'Orate p. aia fratis Robti Barnard, gardiani Walsingham Anno Domini 1518'. Therefore it is the latest of the three dated examples in the county (Oxborough 1489, St Gregory's Norwich 1496; there are eleven altogether in the county). On the altar table are two brass candlesticks and a brass cross.

Stone. At the east end of the south aisle is the magnificent alabaster monument to Sir Henry Kervile (d. 1624) and his wife Mary. The two life-size figures are recumbent on a panelled chest, he in armour resting on a helm, she resting on a cushion. The central panel of the chest contains the figures of their two children, a baby and a little girl. The other panels contain heraldic shields. Against the wall, and behind the recumbant figures, is a black marble inscription surrounded by an architectural framework of paired Corinthian columns and arched entablature; surmounting the pediment is the figure of a deer.

South of the tower arch is the marble monument to Edmund Harwick (d. 1759), surmounted by an escutcheon with deer, its architectural framework containing flaming urn. On the north aisle wall is a small marble tablet to Richard Thomas Powell (d. 1832).

There are many floor monuments. Next to the heart brass is the ledger slab to Grace Berners (d. 1680) and Katherine Berners (d. 1682).

In the chancel are the slabs to Gregory Berners (d. 1715), John Daville (d. 1800), William Berners (d. 1725), Hatton Berners (d. 1713), Bridget Berners (d. 1704), Hatton Berners (d. 1693), and William Money (d. 1835). In the nave there is a brass, and ledger slabs to William Robinson (d. 1665), Etheldreda Harwicke (d. 1765), John Cary (d. 1807), Edmund Harwick (d. 1816), Ann Harwick (d. 1782), Edmund Harwick (d. 1759), Thomas Harwick (d. 1700), and Thomas Harwick (d. 1705). In the south aisle: Elizabeth Cary (d. 1815), Mary Harwicke (d. 1686). In the north aisle: Eleonor Crisp (d. 1801), and Ann Stond (d. 1805).

Where there are no ledger slabs, the floor is of pamments; but the chancel has (comparatively recent) stone paving.

The stone font is set against the western pier of the north arcade. It is surrounded by a concentric platform of two steps. The font step is octagonal, with moulded base and capital; the bowl is very plain.

Wood. The benches are quite outstanding. There is a set of eighteen of them in the nave, all sumptuously carved and all pre-Reformation in date. The bench backs have openwork tracery, some with the letters VRA (presumably standing for '*Virgo Regina Ave*'). The bench-ends all have poppy-heads, with a single carved figure on either side. Those on the south side of the nave are less elaborate than those to north. The flanking figures are standing on the south side, seated on the north side. The bench ends contain recessed niches; six of those on the south side contain images of the Virgin in prayer, with the letters VB (no doubt '*Virgo Beata*'); two of them have two standing figures; one has an escutcheon with the letters VB. On the north side, the figures are much more finely executed; they stand on pedestals, within a cusped ogee niche; they represent various saints with their respective identifying items, such as chairs, scroll etc.. In the aisles, the bench-ends do not have canopied figures, but do have poppy-heads flanked by seated figures or animals. To judge from the detailed costume of the figures on the north side of the nave, these benches must date to the early 16th century. Those on the south side may be earlier; but it may be that they are cruder owing to different benefactors; it is worth remembering that north and south clerestoreys differ in style too; and the Virgin Mary theme of south benches was reflected in the painted glass of the south clerestorey whilst benches and glass on the north side followed the theme of saints and apostles. Could it be that different bene-

Plate LXXII.   Wiggenhall St Mary the Virgin, from the south-east.

factors were responsible for different halves of the nave, and that the benefactors of the north side of the nave were wealthier than those on the south side? It is interesting that a theme in painted glass above should be echoed in the furnishings below.

The font is surmounted by an elaborate wooden canopy, consisting of four columns supporting either arches (by means of pendants), and an octagonal pyramid roof capped by a pelican plucking its flesh; it is dated to 1625, and it is conceivable that the font is contemporary.

The lower part of the wooden rood-screen survives. There are eight painted panels, seven of them female saints (Saints Mary Magdalen, Dorothy, Margaret, Scholastica, Catherine, Barbara, Mary the Virgin) and St John the Baptist. There are also some names of donors below: Thomas Lucy, Omphrey Karvyle, Mathu Clerke. The style of the figures' costumes suggests an early 16th-century date.

Both aisles have parclose screens in the last bay, Perpendicular in style. The one in the north aisle is 19th-century, and most of the upper parts of the one in the south aisle is 19th-century restoration, with original lower parts.

The pulpit is 17th-century, with arched panels, and an iron hour-glass stand. It had been temporarily moved out of place when visited to make way for a new sounding board and tester.

At the west end of the nave is a fine wooden dole-cupboard, dated to 1639. The panels forming the screened vestry look old, possibly 17th-century.

Above the chancel arch is a panel containing the Royal Arms of George III, inscribed 'J.SUTTERBY 1791'.

There is a two-manual organ at the east end of the north aisle.

The reredos and oak panelling in the chancel date to 1930. There are also some 19th-century choir-stalls and reading desk in the chancel. The chancel rails are quite modern.

In the nave is a wooden 19th-century reading desk, with a 17th-century chair. On the reading desk is a large illustrated bible of 1717.

Condition
The church is in the process of being restored (August 1983). So far, this has involved the rendering of chancel east wall and nave clerestorey south wall. Also, a dry trench has been dug around the whole exterior of the church. Lead roofs of porch and aisles are being restored.

Churchyard
The boundaries of the rectangular churchyard are hedged and treed. There is a large Douglas fir and several yew trees south of the church, lime and ash trees to north. Most of the headstones are 19th and 20th-century, but there are some 18th-century ones just south of the church. The grass is kept down, and there are several well-tended graves.

Archaeological Record
Dry area cut around church about 25cm deep, not reaching below topsoil: some medieval brick and glazed tiles found in the trench. The tiles have been identified as medieval Flemish, three with green glaze, two with dark-green glaze, and one with brown glaze (tiles now in NCM).

St Mary's Hall 200m north-east: a mid 16th-century hall, demolished in 1800 except gateway and stables, hall rebuilt in 1864.

Archaeological and Architectural Assessment
The architectural highlights of the church are probably the sumptuous south doorway and the austere but grand west tower. The rest of the church is not without interest, but remains somewhat bland in its uniformity. However, this blandness is put to flight by the quality and elegance of its furnishing, fittings and monuments. The quality and completeness of the early 16th-century benches are not bettered anywhere in the county. Combined with screens and brass lectern, the interior of the church must convey to an almost unique degree what the interior of a pre-Reformation church looked like.

External rendering may have concealed evidence vital for a complete and accurate phasing of the fabric. It is a shame that no fabric recording took place after the stripping of plaster from chancel east wall and south clerestorey.

Further References
Blomefield, 1805-10, IX, 179-182.
Bullmore, 1917.
Cotton and Tricker, 1983.
Pevsner, 1962b.

VI. Great Yarmouth, St George

Identification
TG 5261 0735. *County No.*4336.
Diocese: Norwich. Archdeaconry; Norwich. *Deanery:* Flegg. *Parish:* Great Yarmouth, St Nicholas. *Status:* Parochial chapel, now disused and redundant. *Date last in regular use:* 1959.

Ownership and access: Yarmouth Borough Council.

Location and Setting
(Fig.1, No.34)
A surprising fact about Great Yarmouth is that it formed a single parish from its foundation in the 11th century, and until the 18th century was served by a single parish church, St Nicholas's (which replaced the pre-/conquest church of St Benedict, see site no. 254). This is the largest parish church in England, it is claimed, and no doubt it served the largest parish in the country in terms of population. As the town grew, its population extended southwards, but it was only in 1714 that work began on a new church nearer the centre of population: St George's, the finest church of this period in Norfolk, yet only a chapel-of-ease to St Nicholas's. It stands about 600m south of St Nicholas's on a paved pedestrianized island at the intersection of some busy streets, and remains living proof that the men of Yarmouth of old had heard of Sir Christopher Wren. Now used as an Arts Centre, its intimate atmosphere is a good setting for theatrical productions.

Architectural Description
(Pls LXXIII, LXXIV)
The church consists of chancel, galleried nave and narthex surmounted by a tower. Without the latter, it

would be difficult to know which end is which, such is the symmetry of design: the wide four-bay nave is flanked by aisles with quadrant-shaped terminations to east and west; a further quandrant delineates an elliptical chancel to east and narthex to west (Pl. LXXIII). Masonry is of brick, with pale limestone for pilasters, quoins, doors and windows. The Mansard roofing is of copper with lead edgings.

Chancel. A proscenium arch now marks the entrance to the chancel, and a stage fills the chancel space itself. The east end is in the form of an elliptical apse, with a shallow rectangular projection to east. On the outside, giant flat pilasters with richly carved Corinthian capitals support a broken pediment, which formerly framed a large round-headed east window. This window has been blocked with bricks identical in type to those used in the rest of the church; a doorway must have been inserted below the window at the same time, since its semi-circular lunette extends into the blocked opening. The stone base-course (which runs round the whole building) has been cut into to receive the door, which is preceded by four stone steps.

The elliptical part of the chancel is articulated on the outside by means of a vertical panel of fine ashlar pierced by two windows, one for the ground-floor with a three-centred head, the taller gallery window with ordinary round head. The keystone and imposts of these windows stand proud. Above the gallery window, a flat stone stringcourse continues round the whole building, marking the beginning of the brick parapet above. On the inside, the elliptical chancel is plain, with only a dentil cornice to break the wall surface.

The chancel has a further bay west of the elliptical apse, although this also forms the east termination of aisles and galleries. It has a curved external wall, articulated in the same way as the apse, with its stone panel on the outside. On the inside the aisles and galleries begin to curve in but do not traverse the chancel; two square wooden Doric piers support the gallery ends (on either side), and these are surmounted at gallery level by two fluted Corinthian columns. Formerly, these columns supported a plaster barrel vault which performed the function of a deep chancel arch. Within the gallery, the east wall, next to the fluted columns, is decorated on either side with an ornate wooden niche, round-headed and set within a rectangular frame, decorated with rich foliate pilasters.

Nave. The nave consists of four bays with aisles and galleries (Pl. LXXIV). The straight external walls project slightly beyond the curvilinear chancel and narthex. Corners are formed of ashlar blocks alternating with four courses of brick. Giant Doric pilasters articulate each bay on the outside, pale stone contrasting with brickwork. The pilaster capitals, at the level of the springing of the gallery windows, are surmounted by entablatures with single triglyph friezes, to parapet level. Projecting stone panels form a continuation of the pilaster into the parapet. The windows are the same shape as those of the chancel, but in brick rather than stone (although stone is used for keystones, imposts and sill). Gallery windows are divided into twenty-four

Plate LXXIII. Great Yarmouth, St George, from the south-west. Unlike the interior, the exterior has not suffered too much since becoming redundant in 1972.

Plate LXXIV.   Great Yarmouth, St George, interior looking west in 1959. Since then, all furnishings have been removed and plaster ceilings taken down. BB59/150 copyright Royal Commission on Historical Monuments (England), 1959.

panels, smaller aisle windows have just sixteen, and all are sash opening.

On the inside, only the north aisle retains its wooden piers, square in section resting on small stone plinths; they support a Doric wooden entablature and parapet for the gallery. On the south side, the piers have been removed and replaced by a modern block wall. Both galleries survive, however, with Doric columns rising from pedestals. Plaster arches originally sprung from the columns, but these have been removed revealing plain wooden uprights. The nave used to be covered by a plaster barrel-vault, but this has been taken down, now exposing the roof structure. In essence the roof is simply a series of collars with through purlins supported by the gallery uprights, with suspended arched braces to support the plaster ceiling.

Narthex and Tower. With its curvilinear plan, the narthex keeps symmetry with the chancel. It retains the same system of articulation as the chancel, with stone panels, but doorways set into the north-west and south-west corners to allow access to the aisles. The doorways are thus set into convex curving walls, and are surmounted by a pediment rising from carved consoles. At the south-west corner above the gallery window there is a painted sundial.

A western projection marks the west face of the tower, with the main doorway in the west face. The doorway is the same as those of the aisle, but flanked by giant Doric pilasters to support another pediment higher up; the architrave of this pediment is broken by a large round-headed sash window. The tower rises in three more storeys above the parapet level. The next storey has a round-headed window flanked by pilasters opening to north and south, with a balustrade above; then comes an essentially octagonal belfry containing a large bell, with paired Doric columns at the four diagonals; and finally a small octagonal stage with lead cupola, surmounted by an elaborate iron weathercock with openwork dragons.

On the inside, curved wooden staircases lead up to the gallery level. The western gallery itself is supported by two wooden Doric columns, and originally housed an organ. The eastern face of the tower can be seen from inside.

Interpretation and Dating

The documentation is unequivocal. In 1714, the John Prices (both elder and younger) of Wandsworth were given the contract to build a church in the same manner as St Clement Dane's in the Strand. The church would cost £6,300 and permission was given to re-use material from the ruined west aisle of St Nicholas's. (NRO, FCB/1, 503). St George's was consecrated in 1715, but not fully furnished until 1720; the large east window was blocked in 1732 (Ecclestone, 1974).

Causes of Abandonment
From having too few churches up to the 18th century, Yarmouth has found itself with too many in the 20th century. The southern part of the town is now served by two Victorian churches (St John's 600m south-east, and St James's 1km south of St George's), while the northern part is served by St Nicholas's (600m to north) and a couple of modern district churches.

Since the Second World War, the congregation of St George's has declined, and the last service was held in 1959. It was united with St Nicholas's in 1964. Until 1966 it was being considered for re-used as a maritime museum. Finally, St George's was declared redundant in 1971, to become an Art, Music and Drama Centre under the control of Yarmouth Borough Council. A thorough restoration of roof and external walls has taken place, funded by the RCF and the Department of the Environment.

Whereabouts of Furnishings
Tragically, the superb early 18th-century furnishings (Pl. LXXIV) have all been removed. Excellent early 18th century pulpit and pews removed to St Nicholas's; tester placed above font. Royal Arms and some panelling also at St Nicholas's.

Organ at St John's, Smith Square, London.

Font with R.C.Community at Waltham Abbey.

Condition
All plaster ceilings have been removed, but the roof is in sound condition.

External masonry is good; some of the stones of the south-west doorway are slightly out of place.

Interior sound apart from the galleries; south arcade recently replaced by a block wall.

Churchyard
There are no visible monuments, but the churchyard north of the church is grassed and part of the stone boundary wall survives. Part of the ground north of the church was given up to improve the traffic junction. South of the church, new gardens and car-parking space have replaced the churchyard.

Archaeological and Architectural Assessment
Most of the beauty of the church interior has been destroyed through the removal of ceilings and furnishings, leaving a bare shell. The exterior remains very attractive, an important monument and part of the Yarmouth townscape. Summerson (1983, 311) is perhaps a little unfair in calling it 'a crude imitation' of St Clement Danes. Pevsner (1962a, 146) is nearer the mark when he describes it as 'a naive, unlearned design more lovable than admirable.' Both are a bit harsh in their judgements, probably as a result of the comparison with Wren's city churches, which leaves St George's wanting. Nonetheless, St George's remains an important outlying example of the new ecclesiastical architecture of the metropolis, and one of several churches built by Price (he also built St George's, Southwark). Within the context of Norfolk, it is of very great significance, as the greater of only two churches built in the county in this period (i.e. first half of the 18th century); North Runcton is the other church. It would be hard to estimate its value within the context of Norfolk and East Anglia as a whole.

Further References
Ecclestone, 1971.
Pevsner, 1962a, 146.
Summerson, 1983, 311.

Chapter 4. Category II

I. Babingley, St Felix

Identification TF 6662 2610. *County No.*3257.
Diocese: Norwich. *Archdeaconry*: Lynn. *Deanery*: Heacham and Rising. *Parish*: Wolferton and Babingley. *Status*: parish church, now disused and ruined. *Date last in regular use*: 1895.
Ownership and access: Diocese of Norwich; private access.

Location and Setting
(Fig.1, No.36; Pls LXXV, LXXVI)
The site of Babingley village can be found 1km north of Castle Rising, just north of the Babingley river. The marshes which extend to west were formerly part of an estuary of the Wash. Rising was a port in the 12th century, as was Babingley no doubt until the estuary silted up. Rising Haven, as it was called, ceased to be tidal by the end of the 17th century.

The church is an attractive ruin, set in its overgrown churchyard in the middle of flat arable fields (Pl. LXXV, LXXVI). It is roofless, but its walls stand to almost full height. Access is difficult. A track leads west off the A149 Lynn-Hunstanton road, past the picturesque iron church built by the Prince of Wales in 1894-5 (Babingley is part of the Royal Estate of Sandringham); continuing west for 1km, past Hall Farm, the church can be seen 300m to south, with no track leading to it. A legend, going back at least to the 17th century, claims that the church here was built by Felix of Burgundy, after landing here to evangelize the East Angles in A.D. 631.

Architectural Description
(Fig. 13; Pl. LXXVII, LXXVIII)
The roofless church consists of chancel, nave, south aisle, west tower and south porch (Fig. 13). If the legend of

Plate LXXV. Babingley church by Ladbrooke (1825). The nave was still in use but the chancel had been in ruins for over a century.

Plate LXXVI. Babingley, St Felix, from the southwest: a church rebuilt on a much larger scale in the first half of the 14th century, then reduced in size in the 17th century.

St.Felix is true, there is no evidence for his church in the surviving fabric. Masonry consists of coursed flint.

Chancel. The chancel is unusually large. It is built mainly of grey Sandringham stone, roughly squared, with some pieces of brown carstone; more carstone is used in the east wall. There are no buttresses, but limestone quoins at the corners.

The east wall has an external chamfered stringcourse, in limestone, at about 2m from the ground. It forms the sill for the very large east window, which has chamfered limestone jambs, concave arch moulding, and hood-mould; fragments of tracery survive, indicating a three-light window with flowing tracery. Above the apex of the window is a small opening, an ogee arch piercing a rectangular limestone block. The east gable remains remarkably intact despite being part of an unroofed chancel for the last four hundred years.

At the east end of the chancel south wall, the remains of a piscina and triple sedilia can be made out. They have continuous moulded arches with squared-off spandrels, and label stops carved with hardly decipherable heads. Above is a window, but the tracery has gone. Further west, near the chancel arch, is a very tall window open-

BABINGLEY

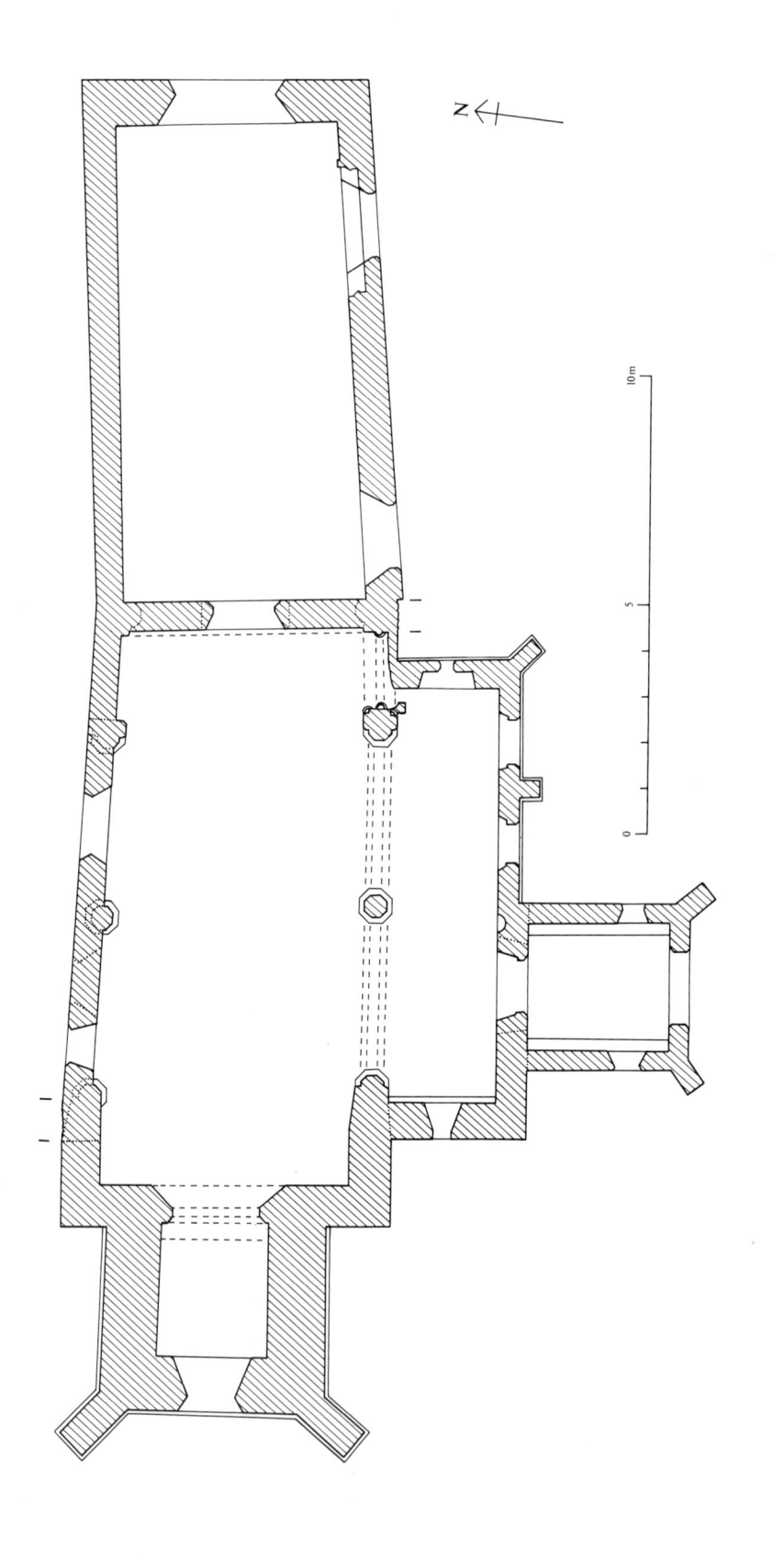

Figure 13. Babingley, St Felix: plan. Scale 1:150.

ing. The stringcourse, continuing round from the east wall, descends below the sill of this window.

There are no features of any sort in the chancel north wall. At its west end, there is a clear vertical break with the nave.

The chancel arch has been blocked. The half-octagonal responds of the arch are just visible beside the blocking. The fill consists of coursed clunch with occasional pieces of reused worked limestone; Sandringham stone is more common higher up. This wall is pierced by a two-light reticulated window with segmental head (clearly reused — could it have come from the east window in the chancel south wall, being exactly the right size?)

It is set within a rear-arch lined with 18th-century brick and headed with a wooden lintel. This in turn has been set within an earlier, slightly wider opening lined with thinner bricks (5cm), probably of the late 16th or early 17th-century. This window, clearly contemporary with the blocking, was also taller and headed with a wooden lintel.

Nave. The nave has two distinct types of masonry. The west wall extending either side of the tower, and the westernmost 2m of north and south walls, are built of flattish pieces of carstone in neat courses. The western quoins are limestone. Further east is the two bay arcade (blocked on the north side) (Pl. LXXVII). The masonry above the arches consists of lumpy grey Sandringham stone, poorly coursed, with large beds of mortar. Furthermore, the arcade wall is some 30cm thinner than that of the western 2m of the nave; evidently, the two types of walling are not of the same phase. Patching in medieval brick is evident in the angled surface where the thicker wall begins.

The two-bay arcades are quite wide, with double chamfered stone arches springing from octagonal moulded capitals and octagonal piers. East of the eastern responds there is another arch, much lower than the main arcades: a single tomb recess, communicating with the aisles on either side of the nave near the chancel arch (Pl. LXXVIII). The arches of the two tomb recesses are more complex than the nave arcade, with a series of convex mouldings and heavy cusping (mostly broken away) underneath. The arch is surmounted by a gablet; on the north side, traces of a crowning finial can be made out (the gablet on this side has been restored with ferro-concrete).

The outer order of the arch was originally supported by nook-shafts, on both nave and aisle side (walled up in

Plate LXXVII. Babingley, St Felix, nave looking east in 1947. The north arcade and the chancel arch were blocked in the 17th century; the Decorated east window probably came from the south wall of the chancel. The roof has now gone. AA47/9209 copyright Royal Commission on Historical Monuments (England), 1947.

Plate LXXVIII. Babingley, St Felix, tomb recess at east end of the south arcade looking south, 1947. There is a similar tomb on the north side. Both were an integral part of the building programme of the first half of the 14th century, suggesting an important patron. AA47/9214 copyright Royal Commission on Historical Monuments (England), 1947.

the case of the tomb to north), and an inner octagonal respond supporting an inner order. The north tomb recess was completely blocked when the north aisle was demolished. On the south side the tomb is partly blocked by the east wall of the south aisle, and partly by early 17th-century brick. Beneath this tomb recess, set into the floor, is a medieval stone sarcophagus with shaped head-piece to west. The blocked north arcade has been inset with two two-light windows, and a pointed doorway, probably reused from the aisle. The west wall of the south aisle does not bond into the nave wall. The masonry of this wall contains some very large boulders in the lower part; a set-off 1.5m from the ground marks the use of varied carstone above; it is pierced by a lancet window.

Aisle. There are two types of masonry to the aisle south wall. West of the porch, it is of the same rough build as the west wall. East of the porch, the masonry consists of thin slate-like carstone, carefully coursed. The diagonal buttress at the south-east corner, and the buttress half-way between porch and corner, are edged with deep-red bricks (5cm thick, early 17th-century type). Either side of the mid-wall buttress is a window opening with stone jambs, but the tracery has not survived; they each had two lights. A single light window, with tracery above, pierces the aisle east wall. East of this wall, on the outside, the scar of an earlier east wall can be seen at the junction of nave and chancel. The south door is pointed, with a pointed segmental rear-arch; a vertical building break either side of the door shows it is a late insert. There is a niche for a water-stoup east of the door.

Porch. The south porch belongs to the same building programme as the eastern part of the south aisle. It is built of deep-red brick, of early 17th-century type; the northern 1.5m of the east wall is built of carstone on the outside, and courses in with the aisle. The porch has diagonal buttresses, and a single window in east and west walls. The outer archway has brick imposts and a hollow-chamfered hood-mould. Inside, the porch has a pointed barrel vault, again in brick.

Tower. The west tower is contemporary with the nave west wall. The neat carstone masonry courses through perfectly. Neat limestone forms a facing to the diagonal west buttresses. The west wall is pierced by a fine two-light Decorated window with eyelet and mouchettes in the reticulation; the window is surmounted by a prominent hood-mould. At first floor level, the masonry is predominantly of rough lumps of grey Sandringham stone, reminiscent of the nave walls above the arcade. This stage is pierced by a thin lancet window in north, west and south faces, and a larger square opening in the east face below the roof-line (there is a lower roof-line with shallower pitch below it). Above a stone string-course, the belfry stage reverts to neat carstone masonry. It is pierced by a large Y-tracery window in each face. The crumbling crenellated parapet is capped with stone.

BABINGLEY

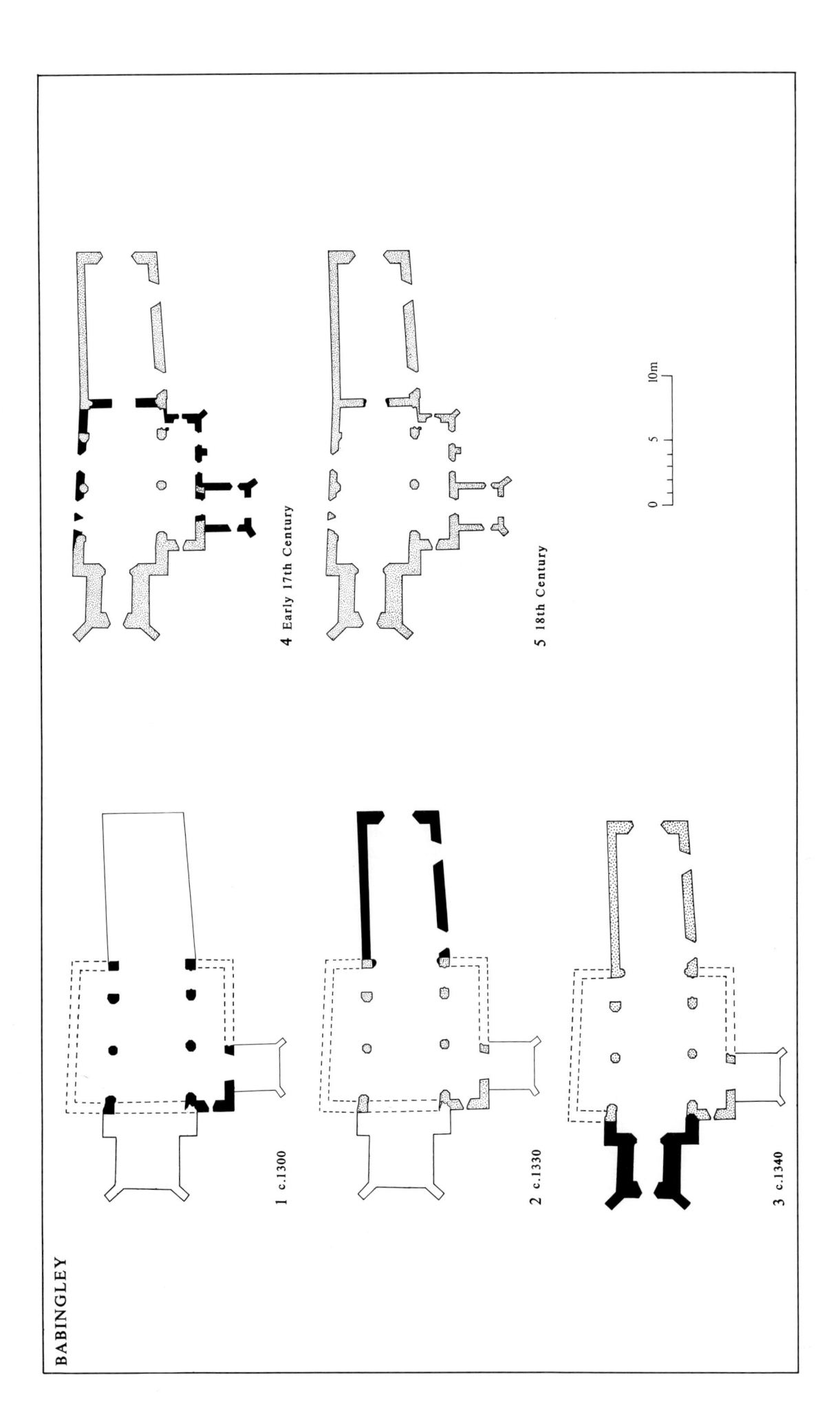

1 c.1300

2 c.1330

3 c.1340

4 Early 17th Century

5 18th Century

Figure 14. Babingley, St Felix: phase plan. Scale 1:400.

Interpretation and Dating
(Fig. 14)
There are three distinct phases to the main fabric of the church. The first consists of the arcade and aisles, added to a pre-existing nave whose west wall probably aligned with the west walls of the aisles; this phase makes use of much Sandringham stone, and is poorly coursed. Secondly, the chancel was added to the nave; the masonry here is similar to the nave, but uses more carstone higher up. The third phase involved the extension of the nave to west and the addition of the west tower; there is still scarring where the original west wall was pulled down. Carstone is greatly used, particularly in the lower part of the tower.

The odd thing about these three clear and evident phases is that they were all built within a short space of time. All belong to the first half of the 14th century. The nave arcade is early 14th-century in style, possibly as early as *c*. 1300. The east window of the chancel (Phase 2) cannot be much later: the tracery is of flowing Decorated type, probably of *c*.1330. To complete the Decorated rebuilding came the tower (Phase 3), whose west window has tracery comparable to Great Walsingham and Beeston-next-Mileham; Fawcett (1980, 293) has dated these between *c*. 1330 and *c*. 1350.

It is likely that we are dealing with a single, co-ordinated building programme, divided into three distinct building campaigns. No doubt this was done to enable the church to continue in use during the rebuilding: thus the pre-existing chancel could remain in use during Phase 1 while the old nave had aisles added; after that, the chancel could be demolished and replaced by a new one; lastly came the addition of the tower.

Why such a lavish building programme around the middle of the 14th century? Maybe the cult of St Felix was achieving some prominence at this time; the tradition of Felix building the first church here could well be as old as this. But it seems that personal benefaction was promoting the reconstruction; the two canopied tombs at the ends of the aisle are an integral part of the building programme. Quite possibly, the patron was none other than Robert de Ufford, Earl of Suffolk, who held the advowson at this time and had a manor in the parish; it was a later Earl of Suffolk, Michael de la Pole, who rebuilt Cawston church on a grand scale in the early 15th century. The quality of the work at Babingley suggests a major patron.

By 1602, however, the church had fallen into great decay.

'Babinglie The Church there greatlie decaied, and scarce anie Ornaments fitt for devine service. The Inhabitants (being verie few) are pore men, and the lande for the most part in the occupac'on of Mr William Cobb, esquier, Lord and Patron of the Manor & Church there, by whose default the said church is decaied.' (Tymms, 1866, 225).

Probably soon after this inventory of ruined and decayed churches had been written (and possibly because of it), the church was put into repair. It appears that the chancel was left as a ruin, the north aisle demolished and north arcade blocked, and the south porch along with the south aisle east of it built anew. The deep-red bricks (5cm thick) belonging to this phase are of early 17th-century type. Certainly by 1671, the chancel had no roof or windows (NRO, ANW, 4, 19), and the north aisle was in decay in 1682 (NRO, ANW, 4, 57).

Finally, in the 18th century the window in the chancel arch blocking was removed and replaced by a 14th-century Decorated window, no doubt removed from the derelict chancel.

Causes of Abandonment
By the early 17th century, the population of the parish was very small: only 8 communicants in 1603. So large a church could not be maintained, and so the chancel and north aisle were abandoned. This 'reduced' church continued in use until 1895, when a new iron church was built 1km north-east next to the Lynn-Hunstanton road. The building of this church was financed by the Prince of Wales for the inhabitants of this part of his Sandringham estate. The church of St Felix, in its isolation, was left as a ruin.

Condition
The church is roofless, but most of its walls stand to full height. Floors are completely overgrown with trees and saplings (except the porch, which has its vault intact).

Churchyard
There are no actual boundaries surviving, but the churchyard remains fully intact and surrounded by arable fields. The southern edge is curved, but it is not circular in plan (as Messent remarks). The churchyard is very overgrown. There are some 18th-century headstones, but most are of the 19th century.

Archaeological Record
Flint flakes, some Romano-British sherds, Ipswich Ware, Thetford, Grimston, Stamford and other wares found around churchyard, but no deserted medieval village earthworks visible; also a scatter of medieval brick and oyster shells nearby; flint hand-axe found inside the churchyard.

Archaeological and Architectural Assessment
There has been a settlement at Babingley since at least Middle Saxon times, but there is no evidence to corroborate the legendary landing of St Felix in 631. What is certain is that the village is of considerable antiquity, but no houses were standing by 1588 (according to the map made in that year; Moralee, 1588, 7).

The church is unusually fine, both in scale and quality. The stonework is particularly well carved. It is not often that we come across so extensive a scheme of rebuilding, all achieved within about 40 years and with three distinct phases, from about 1300 to 1340 . It would be interesting to know more about the benefactors, which an excavation of the nave tomb recesses might elucidate.

Both church and site are of outstanding interest.

Further References
Blomefield, 1805-10, VIII, 347.
Cox, 1911, II, 134.
Fawcett, 1980, 293.
Messent, 1931, 12.
Moralee, 1988, 7.
Pevsner, 1962, b , 80.
Tymms, 1866, 225.

II. Burlingham, St Peter

Identification TG 3684 1005. *County No.* 8524

Plate LXXIX. Burlingham, St Peter, from south, 1978.

Diocese: Norwich. *Archdeaconry:* Norwich. *Deanery*: Blofield. *Parish*: Burlingham St Andrew with St Peter. *Status*: parish church, now disused. *Date last in regular use*: 1935.
Ownership and access: Diocese of Norwich.

Location and Setting
(Pl. LXXIX)
The village of North Burlingham lies just to the north of the A47 Norwich to Yarmouth road, 3km west of Acle. It is a small village with a population of 108 (in 1978), and yet possesses two parish churches; St Andrew's at the western end of the village, and St Peter's 400m further east. The latter has been left to decay for several decades now, and retains a dangerously dilapidated roof (Pl. LXXIX). Access is from the old Norwich road (the village is now by-passed), through a gap in the hedge and across a small square field (originally part of the churchyard).

Architectural Description
(Figs 15, 16; Pl. LXXXII)
The church consists of chancel, vestry, nave, north and south porches, and round west tower (collapsed) (Fig.15). Masonry is mostly coursed flint.

Chancel. There is evidence of two phases of construction in the east wall. The lower part, with its diagonal buttresses (the north-east one has been repaired with 17th-century brick), is original medieval masonry; but the upper wall, along with the east window, belongs to the 19th-century restoration; the masonry of the latter is neater, with squared cut flints. There are obvious cracks between the original walling and the inserted window. Of three lights, this window is Perpendicular in style, with supermullions. On either side on the interior there is a small rectangular niche surrounded by a 19th-century canopy.

The south wall is similar in character to the east, comprising medieval flint masonry pierced by 19th-century features: two windows and a priest-door. Both windows are two-light and Decorated in style with a multi-cusped quatrefoil reticulation (Fig.16, No.3); they belong with the 19th-century restoration, but are probably based on the originals (*cf*. Ladbroke's lithograph of 1822, Pl.LXXX); indeed, the medieval sill of the western window seems to be there still . There is a quatrefoil vent-hole (19th century) near the ground.

There are no windows in the north wall of the chancel owing to the presence of the vestry on the outside. The interior wall is scarred with the remains of five 19th century memorials. There are two openings: a doorway into the vestry, and a rectangular opening to the boiler (formerly housed in the vestry); brick patching above this opening indicates a probable blocked window

Plate LXXX. Burlingham, St Peter by Ladbrooke (1822).

BURLINGHAM ST PETER

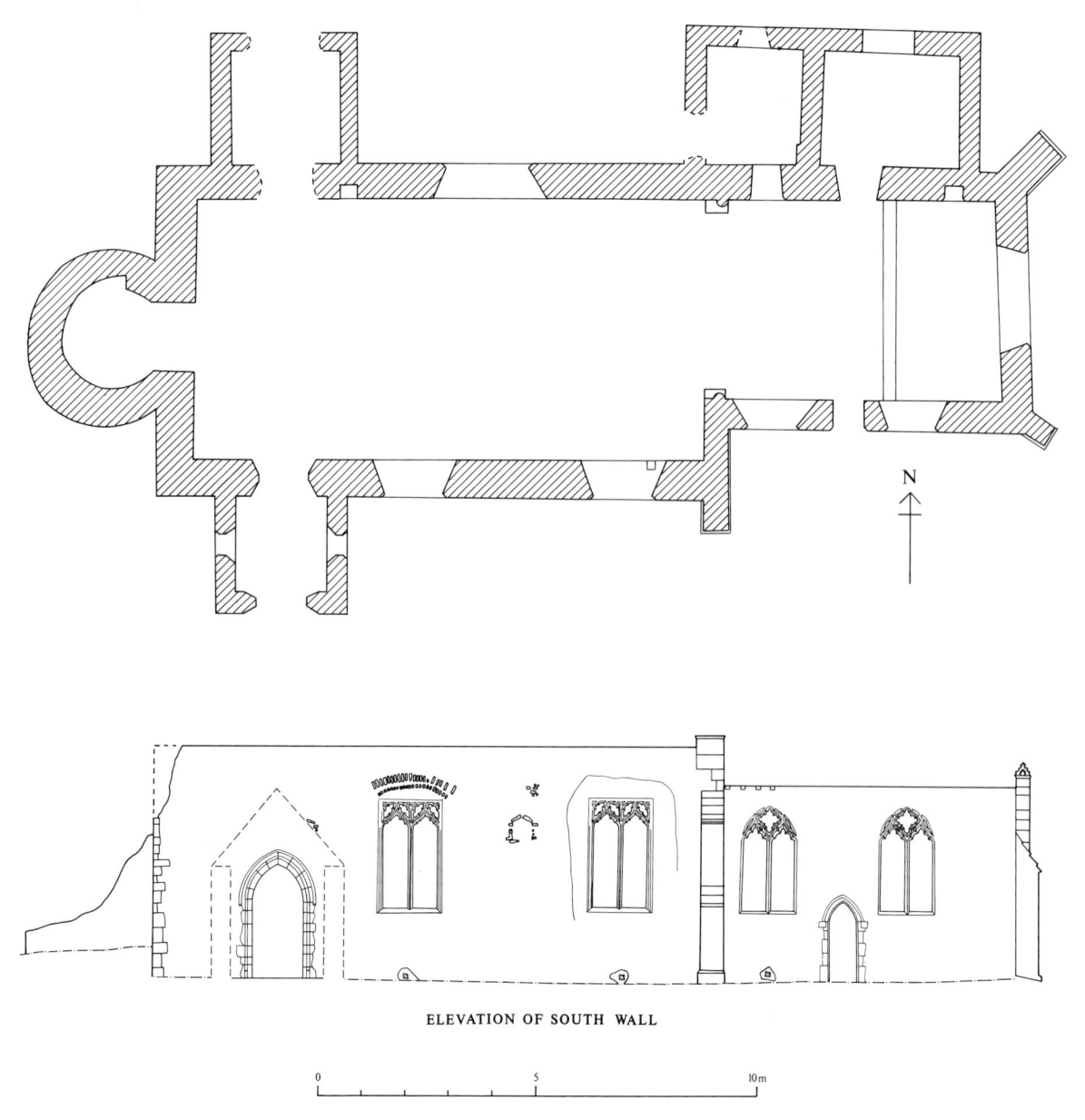

Figure 15. Burlingham, St Peter: plan and south elevation. Scale 1:150.

(directly opposite the western one in the south wall).

The chancel arch and arch-braced roof are both 19th-century.

Vestry. The vestry is a 19th-century addition to the north wall of the chancel. It is flint-faced, and has a double-pitched roof; in the south wall there are two small windows, one single-light and one two-light; the west wall is pierced by a doorway. On the inside, the vestry is reinforced with brick, and the western part has had a concrete ceiling inserted for use as a boiler-house.

Nave. The nave south wall was originally unbuttressed. It is constructed of flint in irregular courses, peppered with medieval brick, occasional fragments of limestone, and the odd lava quern. The wall is pierced by two-light Perpendicular windows of identical design: ogee main lights rising to the square window head (Fig.16, No.2).

There is a small cusped piscina on the inside of the eastern window. The western window appears to be original, the other a 19th-century copy; the former is surmounted by a segmental relieving arch of two courses of brick. Halfway between the two windows is a blocked niche, 0.3m high and about 3.5m from the ground; the niche is lined in medieval brick, and has a triangular head. A similar niche, at the same level, is partly blocked by the 19th-century porch west of the windows (Fig. 15). The niches mark a change in masonry: above them, the flint is much more neatly coursed.

It seems likely that the niches mark the position of large tie-beams belonging to the previous roof (as, for example, in the church at Frenze) and kept in position for structural reasons after a new higher roof had been erected. This new roof (which in Ladbrooke's day appears to have been leaded) would have been erected at the same time as the large Perpendicular window, since the latter

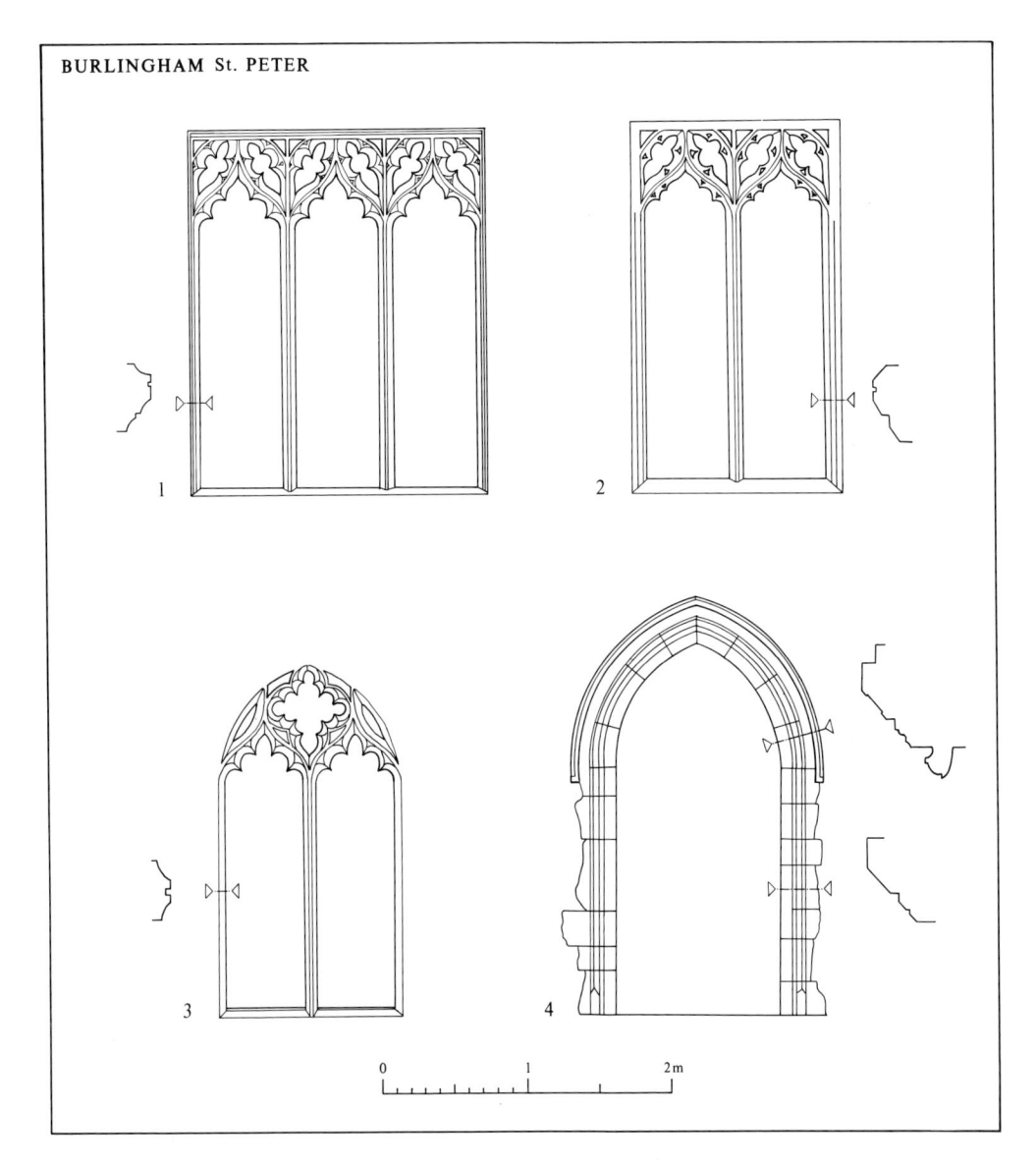

Figure 16. Burlingham, St Peter: 1. Nave north window. 2. Nave south window. 3. Chancel south window. 4. South porch doorway. Scale 1:50.

rises above the level of the niches; the present roof is later still, belonging to the 19th-century restoration. To this same restoration belong the small quatrefoil ventilation holes just above ground level; also the east buttress, in fact the whole east wall of the nave, constructed in neat cut flint similar in character to the east gable of the chancel. The moulded south doorway has also been largely restored, but retains some original jambs.

The north wall of the nave has a single Perpendicular three-light window set within a square head, and identical in design to the two-light windows in the south wall (Fig.16, No.1); the label-stops have well-preserved female faces. The rear-arch is partly rebuilt with new limestone and 19th-century brick. West of the window, the masonry is of the same character as the south wall; but east of the window, the wall has been rebuilt or refaced in flint and 18th-century brick. The north door remains merely as an opening, all the stonework having been robbed. On the inside there is a large scar caused by the removal of the wooden gallery. Near the window there are further scars where two wall memorials have been scraped off (Pl. LXXXII); this has revealed some old plaster behind one of the memorials, with remnants of painting (leaves, branches and lettering) in grey outline, perhaps 16th-century in date.

Plaster stripping by the Norfolk Archaeological Unit in 1978 revealed a vertical masonry break in the west wall of the nave, south of the tower. The masonry north of the break is of different character to that south of it; there is no such break on the north side of the tower. All western quoins have been robbed. Most of the west wall was destroyed by the collapse of the tower.

South porch. Constructed of neatly squared flint, with a moulded doorway in stone, this porch is a 19th-century addition (Fig.16, No.4).

North porch. Here the coursed flint walls, with the occasional medieval brick, resemble the nave walls. Its quoins and jambs have been largely robbed.

Tower. The round west tower collapsed in 1906, and today its maximum height is a mere 3.15m. It is constructed of flints of moderate size, while the low tower arch (head collapsed) is of medieval brick with a little flint, and seems to be of one build with the tower. Before its collapse, there was an octagonal belfry stage.

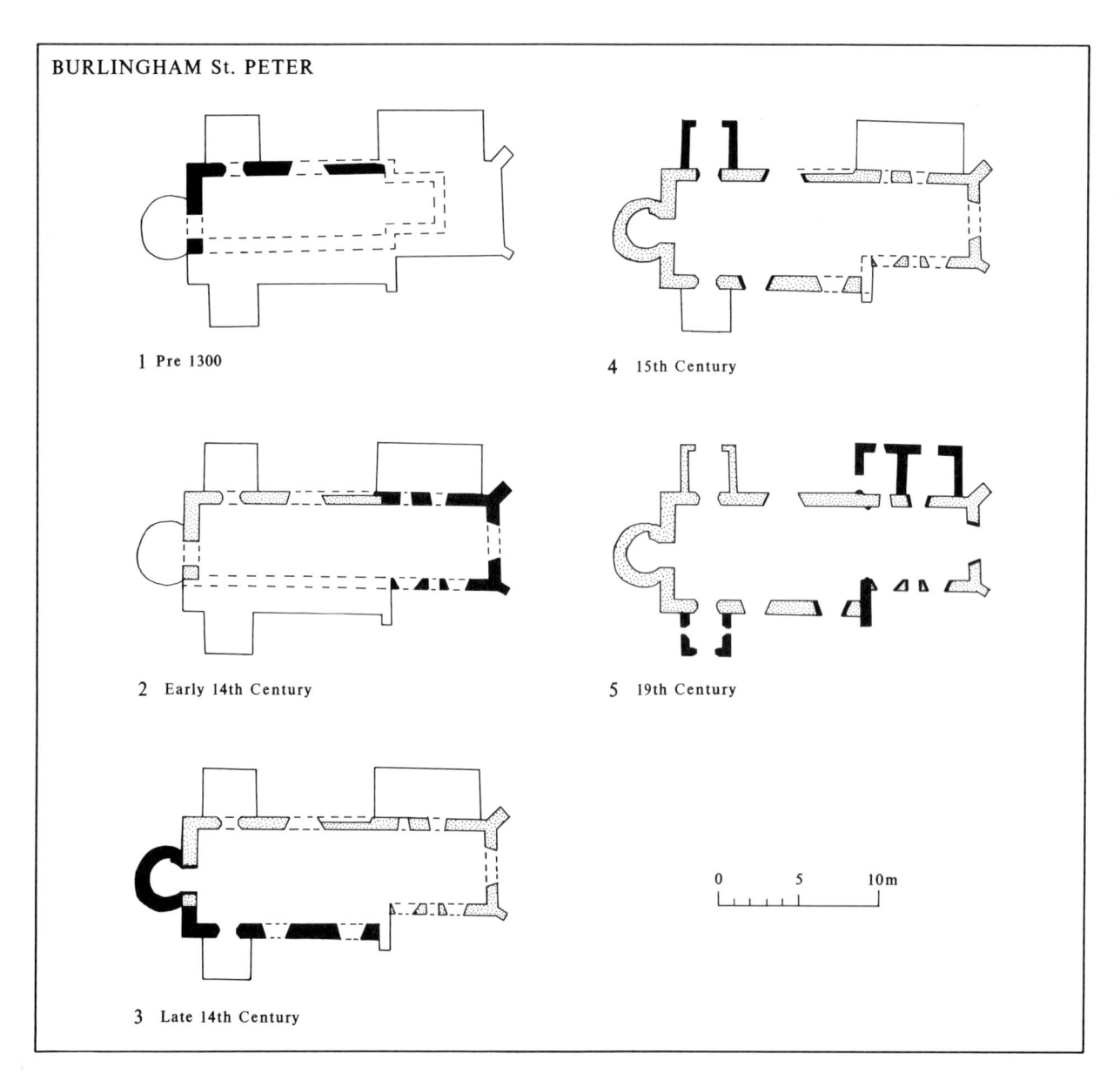

Figure 17. Burlingham, St Peter: phase plan. Scale 1:400.

Interpretation and Dating
(Fig. 17; Pl LXXX, LXXXI)
The correct phasing of this church hinges on the interpretation of the building break in the west wall of the nave (see above). It seems most likely that the break represents the southern termination of the original west wall, i.e. the nave used to be narrower, with its south wall linking up with the vertical break. This explanation has the additional merit of shedding light on an anomaly in the layout of the church: why is it that the north wall of the chancel is in alignment with the north wall of the nave, whereas the south wall of the nave juts out some 1.5m south of the chancel south wall (Pl. LXXXI)? This apparent lack of alignment is most noticeable when viewing the chancel from inside the nave, with the chancel and chancel arch a very long way off the axis of the nave. However, if a narrower nave is posited, with its south-west corner marked by the building-break noted above, the resultant nave would be the same width and on the same axis as the chancel. We end up with a relative chronology for the church as follows:

Phase 1: nave, narrower than today, whose south wall aligned with the present chancel; there may have been a narrower chancel originally. All that survives of this phase is the north wall and part of the west wall of the nave.
Phase 2: the present chancel replacing the Phase 1 chancel.
Phase 3: nave widened to south (present nave south wall); round west tower added on axis of newly widened nave.
Phase 4: nave heightened, large Perpendicular windows and north porch added.
Phase 5: 19th-century restoration, including addition of vestry and south porch.

The absolute chronology for this sequence is less secure. All that can be said of Phase 1 is that it must antedate Phase 2. Phase 2, the present chancel, probably belongs to the first half of the 14th century; its south windows are Decorated in style, and although the actual tracery dates to the 19th-century restoration, comparison with the lithograph of 1822 (Pl. LXXX) indicates that the restorers were faithfully copying the originals. Phase 3, noticeable for its use of brick, may be tentatively slotted into the second half of the 14th century. Then Phase 4,

Plate LXXXI. Burlingham, St Peter: interior looking east, 1945. AA46/4563 copyright Royal Commission on Historical Monuments (England),1945.

with its large Perpendicular windows, will fit comfortably onto a 15th-century date bracket.

Phase 5 is securely dated as the restoration of 1873-4. This work was very thorough, involving: the addition of vestry and south porch, the re-roofing of the entire building (selling the lead and replacing with Welsh green slate), rebuilding the chancel arch and the wall above it, restoring all quoins and window tracery, replastering the interior and laying a new floor with Minton's tiles.

Causes of Abandonment
It is ironic that, after so thorough a restoration as that of 1873-4, the church was only to last another 60 years. The great blow came in 1906, when the tower collapsed 'with a deafening roar and a cloud of dust' (Hill, 1939, 56), together with the gallery, clock and three bells. Most of the west wall of the nave had also been demolished; but, despite the catastrophe, the noble congregation bravely tried to soldier on with the church. The gaping hole in the west wall was boarded up, but we learn that conditions were difficult, for 'when the wind is to the west, this boarding creaks with a dismal monotony, to the terror of the Sunday school children and the annoyance of the priest.' (ibid.) . With the neighbouring church of St Andrew only 400m away (to which St. Peter's had been united as early as 1872; NRO, FCB/8, 12, 170), the number of services held in St Peter's decreased, and it was finally closed in 1935. Most of the furnishings were then sold to other churches by the vicar (ibid.).

Whereabouts of Furnishings
In the church of Burlingham St Andrew: monuments to the Mileham family (1615), Ann Horth (1797), James Birkin Burroughes; a 15th-century wooden screen (across the tower arch); some carved poppy-heads.

In the church of Blofield St Andrew and St Peter: 22 carved benches (including angels holding musical instruments).

In the church of Earlham St Anne: chancel chairs, vestry cupboard and table, chalice, paten and flagon (1715).

In the church of Lingwood St Peter: reading desk.

In St Peter Hungate, Norwich: three 15th-century bells.

Condition
Drastic contrast between 1945 (Pl. LXXXI) and 1978 (Pl. LXXXII). Great danger of roof collapse; west wall and all windows and openings open to the weather; large crack in chancel arch and wall above; considerable damage by vandalism: stones robbed, graves smashed, tiles stolen.

Churchyard
The churchyard forms a rectangle to north, west and east of the church; not to south. It is very overgrown. The headstones are mainly of the 19th century. There is an exceptional monument in the north-east corner: in marble, and Gothic in style, it is dedicated to the Burroughes family, with inscriptions from the 1840s to the 1880s.

Plate LXXXII. Burlingham, St Peter: interior looking east, 1978.

Archaeological and Architectural Assessment
Behind the vandalised appearance, and the thoroughness of the 1873-4 restoration, lies a fabric of the 14th and 15th centuries (and perhaps earlier). The old chancel (Phase 1) and nave south wall have probably left remnants below ground.

Further References
Blomefield, 1805-10, VII, 224.
Bryant, 1907.
Cautley, 1949, 182.
Cox, 1911, II, 4.
Hill, 1939
Messent, 1936, 49.
Pevsner, 1962,a, 107.

III. Great Hautbois, St Mary

Identification TG 2617 2043. *County No.*7677.
Diocese: Norwich. *Archdeaconry;* Norwich. *Deanery*: Ingworth. *Parish*: Coltishall with Great Hautbois. *Status*: parish church, now disused. *Date last in regular use*: 1863. *Ownership and access*: Diocese of Norwich; right of way to churchyard along track from road.

Location and Setting
The church stands on its own, about 1km north-west of Coltishall. There is no village as such, just a few houses on the road to Coltishall, all a long way from the church. St Mary's stands on rising ground 200m north of the River Bure. From the Lammas-Coltishall road, a track leads south, past a field to the clump of trees which surround the churchyard. A new church (Holy Trinity) was built 400m to east in 1864, leaving St Mary's unroofed except the chancel. Nave and aisle are pleasantly grassed.

Architectural Description
(Fig. 18; Pls LXXXIII-V)
The church consists of chancel, nave, south aisle, round west tower and south porch (Fig. 18, Pl. LXXXIII). Masonry consists of coursed flint.

Chancel. The chancel alone is roofed (Pl. LXXXIV); the chancel arch was blocked with a flint wall in 1864, when the new church of Holy Trinity was built and the chancel of St Mary's was spared to remain as a mortuary chapel. The east wall has angle buttresses, those facing east being original to the fabric of the chancel, the other two largely

Plate LXXXIII. Great Hautbois church by Ladbrooke (1822).

rebuilt in brick in the 18th century. The wall is pierced by a three-light Perpendicular window, its four-centred head inserted within a higher two-centred arch; it has drop-tracery with supermullions. Below the window, on the inside, runs a stone stringcourse of scroll section. The stringcourse continues along the eastern half of the north wall, until it meets a vertical offset where the western half of the wall is thicker. There is a lancet window rising from this stringcourse to north, now blocked with pieces of re-used limestone; this blocked area contrast with the flint walling of the rest of the chancel. A buttress faced in 18th-century brick, marks the line of the interior offset. Another window, further west, is blocked in flint. On the south side, the south aisle overlaps the western half of the chancel. East of the aisle, a single lancet window, with limestone dressings, pierces the chancel south wall. West of this a large pointed arch, with chamfered limestone jambs, opened into the aisle; it is now blocked with flint. The chancel arch does not survive, and a small pointed doorway pierces the flint blocking.

Nave. The nave is slightly wider than the chancel. It is built of small, uncut flints, roughly coursed; Roman bricks (3-3.5cm thick) are interspersed occasionally. At the north-east and north-west corners, the quoins survive; they are fairly large blocks of ironbound conglomerate, laid side-alternately. A few identical quoins can be seen south of the tower, marking the junction of nave and south aisle.

In the north wall, the north doorway has chamfered limestone jambs and a pointed arch in chamfered medieval brick. Further east is a large window opening with segmental head; it has no stone dressings, lined in flint. It is possible that this opening was created in the 18th century after the removal of an earlier window; the space exactly fits the Perpendicular three-light window in the chancel (which is inserted in an earlier arch), so this might be its original location. An iron railing now bars the opening. The south wall is opened up by an arcade of two bays. The octagonal pier and responds have moulded bases and capitals, all in limestone (Pl. LXXXV); whereas the two chamfered orders of the arches are made of brick (outer order medieval; inner order remade in brick in 18th or early 19th century). The east respond has a niche carved in it, perhaps for a statue.

Aisle. The south aisle overlaps the chancel by a bay. Its flint walls are capped with slates. Quoins are made of small limestone blocks. All windows are lancets, of two different types. The window in the east wall, and the eastern of the two in the south wall, are faced with limestone at inner and outer edges of its splay, and are of identical size with pointed segmental rear arches. The lancet in the west wall, and the western of the south windows, are both equally narrower, faced in limestone on the outer face, but with brick segmental rear arches. We are probably dealing with two phases, although this is not revealed in the masonry. There is a blocking, probably of a piscina, at the end of the south wall. The south doorway is partly robbed, but has a brick pointed segmental rear arch.

Porch. The south porch is an addition to the aisle. It has limestone quoins at the corners. The outer arch has a hollow chamfer and hood-mould, with responds, bases and capitals. Above, the arch is turned with brick alternating with knapped flint. North and south walls have a

GREAT HAUTBOIS

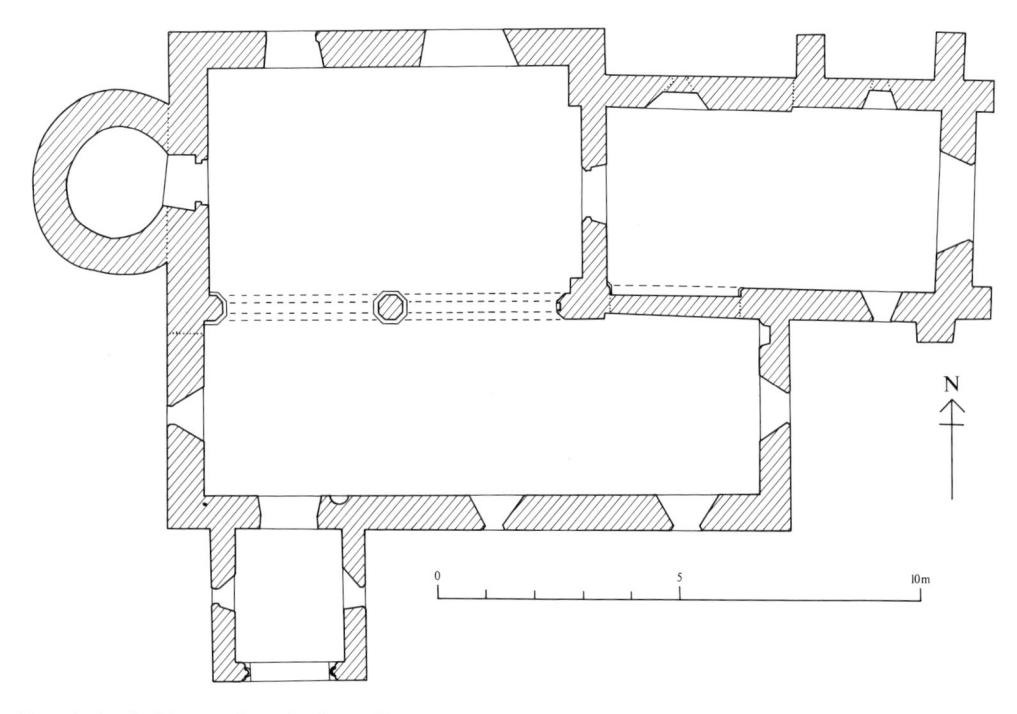

Figure 18. Great Hautbois, St Mary: plan. Scale 1:150.

single cusped window set within a rectangular frame.

Tower. The round west tower is certainly of different phase from the nave; the clean vertical joint is clearly visible on the north side. Masonry technique is similar to the nave, but the flints tend to be larger. The tower itself is extraordinarily tall and thin, and with its distinct batter is rather reminiscent of a light-house. There is a rectangular west opening at ground-floor level, with flint jambs and a brick lintel; above it, a similar opening has an arched lintel, made of conglomerate. There are single belfry openings to north, south, east and west; these have flint jambs and non-radial flint voussoirs forming an elliptical, almost triangular, arch. The present tower arch is small, merely a pointed doorway, with limestone arch and chamfered brick jambs (interspersed with some limestone). However, there are remains of two earlier doorways, one with its apex 1m higher than the present door, but of the same width; the other 1m higher still, and slightly narrower. Roman bricks, not set radially (they

Plate LXXXIV. Great Hautbois, St Mary, from the south; only the chancel is roofed.

Plate LXXXV. Great Hautbois, St Mary; arcade from the south-west. The door leads into the chancel.

leave a triangular gap at the apex) are used for voussoirs. Just south of the tower arch is a piece of carved limestone set into the wall; it is an arcade spandrel with dog-toothed ornament, presumably *ex situ*.

Interpretation and Dating
(Fig.19)
The nave is the earliest part of the church. It is defined by the three sets of conglomerate quoins, and probably also a very tall round-headed west door (the lower arch cuts into it, so it could not have been a lower opening with window above). It is probably 11th century in date, but it is not possible to be more precise. The western part of the chancel north wall probably belongs to this phase too.

At a later date, the round west tower was added, and a slightly lower doorway inserted; this probably belongs to the early 12th century.

In the 13th century the chancel was extended to east, and a chapel added to south. The arch into this chapel exists, and the walls and windows of the east end of the aisle may belong to this phase. It is quite possible that this chapel housed the famous image of St Theobald; it was supposed to have miraculous powers, and pilgrimages were made to it, *viz.* the will of Agnes Parker of Keswick in 1507: 'Item I owe a pilgrimage to Canterbury, another to St Tebbald of Hobbies, and another to St Albert at Cringleford' (Blomefield, 1805-10, V, 297). The fragment of dog-tooth ornament re-set in the west wall of the nave suggests that the detailing of this phase was sumptuous. It may be that the unusually sited niche in the east wall of the aisle actually housed the image of the saint.

The next phase is more difficult to disentangle. To it belongs the two-bay arcade, clearly of 14th-century type. The aisle, however, contains lancet windows which one would not expect beyond the end of the 13th century. The two eastern ones can be explained as part of the south chapel, to which the aisle was appended. Perhaps the pressure of pilgrims wishing to approach the image of St Theobald resulted in the chapel being opened up to west in this way. The western two windows must have either been re-used (from the nave, or the chapel west wall perhaps), or belonged to a 13th-century aisle which was rebuilt in the 14th century. These windows were re-set at the same time as the arcade was built, as shown by the use of brick for their rear-arches (the eastern windows use stone). It seems that this phase (Phase 4) followed some sort of damage to the earlier fabric, possibly a fire: the west wall of the nave seems to have been affected, with a new tower arch being built, a piece of 13th-century carving inserted in the wall, and the north door either partly or wholly rebuilt. Perhaps the devastation which necessitated this phase was responsible for the burial of the Norman font, dug up by Repton in 1805.

In the 15th century, the porch was added, and the three-light east window produced; the latter may originally have belonged to the north wall of the nave (see above).

Later work involved the repairing of the chancel with added buttresses, in the 18th century. This same restoration may be responsible for the rebuilding of the inner order of the nave arcade. Finally, nave, aisle and porch roofs were removed in 1864, and walls capped.

Causes of Abandonment
The church is now in a very isolated position. The 1863 Faculty for building a new church describes St Mary's as 'inconveniently situated with a bad approach to it, and distant from any inhabited houses or dwellings of any kind'. Also it was 'wholly incapable of being advantageously enlarged'. The church was already in a dilapidated state, and divine service had 'long since' been discontinued (NRO, FCB/7, 11, 340). Lead from the roof was sold to help pay for the new church, dedicated to the Holy Trinity in 1864 (by Thomas Jekyll). Fortunately, the walls of the old church were capped and maintained, and the chancel fitted as a mortuary chapel.

Church Contents
Two ledger slabs in the chancel, dated 1778 and 1790. Two tombs were dug into the aisle after 1864, dated 1894 and 1907. Pammented floor in chancel. The exceptional Norman font, discovered in 1805, was moved to Holy Trinity in 1864.

Condition
Only the chancel is roofed; it leaks in places. Most of the window glass has gone; much of the plaster is flaking. Gutters and downpipes are intact.

The interior woodwork of the tower is very decayed. All other walls are capped and in surprisingly good condition.

Churchyard
The churchyard is large and irregular in shape, ringed with trees all the way round. There is a steep slope to south, towards the river. Gravestones are 19th and 20th-century; one is in the form of a broken column. The churchyard is very well kept. The latest grave is dated 1960.

Archaeological Record
Roman bricks in nave and tower. 13th-century spandrel set into west wall.

Medieval sherds and tiles found within churchyard.

Archaeological and Architectural Assessment
The church fabric is of some antiquity, probably going back to the 11th century. It is a small building, even with its 14th-century aisle. Sc   interest centres on the pil-

GREAT HAUTBOIS

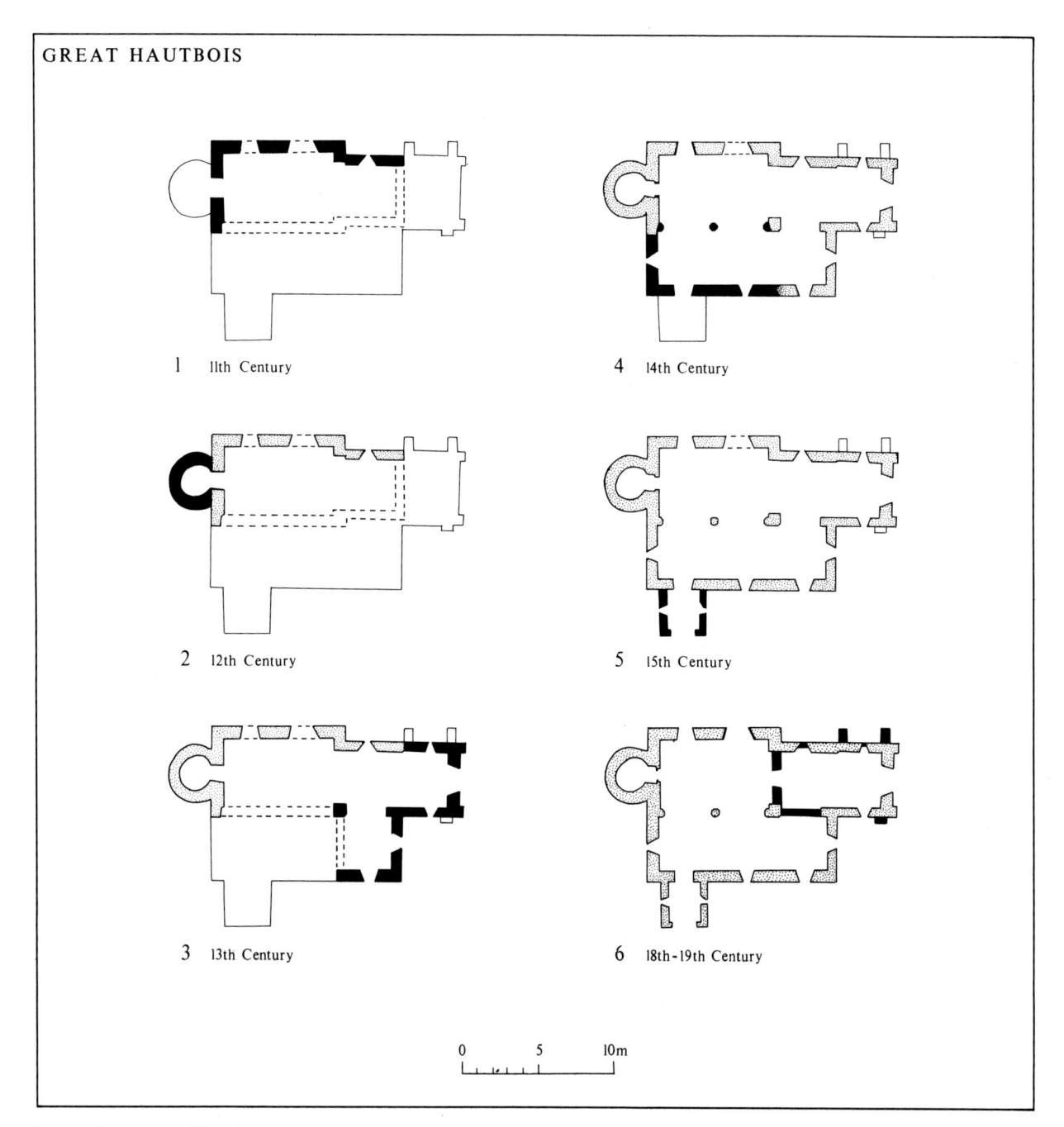

1 11th Century

2 12th Century

3 13th Century

4 14th Century

5 15th Century

6 18th-19th Century

0   5   10m

Figure 19. Great Hautbois, St Mary: phase plan. Scale 1:400.

grimage function of the church. It seems likely that the renowned image of St Theobald was located in the chapel constructed south of the chancel in the 13th century. The niche in the east wall of this chapel may have housed the image. This chapel was opened into a new south aisle in the 14th century. The reason for the modest size of the church, despite its evident fame, may be explained by the fact of it being appropriated to Coxford Priory in 1199, and from 1245 all proceeds of the church were devoted to the work of hospitality carried out by the priory.

The close proximity of medieval castle (with causeway) and hospital (200m south of the church), and finds of sherds in the churchyard, makes Great Hautbois an important medieval site. Unfortunately, it looks as if the south aisle has been dug into by post-1864 graves. The magnificent Norman font was dug up in the nave in 1805; there may be other finds of similar interest below ground.

Further References
Cox, 1911, I, 153.

Messent, 1931, 20.
Pevsner, 1962, a, 160.
Purdy, 1906.

IV. Kempstone St Paul

Identification TF 8862 1604. *County No.*4092.
Diocese: Norwich. *Archdeaconry*; Lynn. *Deanery*: Brisley and Elmham. *Parish*: Litcham with Kempstone and East and West Lexham. *Status*: parish church, now disused and ruined. *Date last in regular use*: c.1901.

Ownership and access: Diocese of Norwich; access probably private.

Location and Setting
(Pl. LXXVI)
All that survives of the village of Kempstone is a farm and Kempstone Lodge, a grand 18th-century house. The church stands just south-west of the Lodge. The site is 1.5km south of Litcham, and can be reached by a track

Plate LXXXVI. Kempstone church by Ladbrooke, c. 1830.

off the lane to Great Dunham. The church was in good condition when drawn by Ladbrooke in *c.* 1830 (Pl. LXXXVI); it is now in a very sorry state. The ditch-lined churchyard survives, but has become a copse and trees stand right up to the walls of the church. A large beech tree adjacent to the chancel is actually growing into the north wall. The collapsed and collapsing masonry of the church are a considerable danger. When visited in 1978, the chancel arch was cracked and deformed; by 1983, it had fallen in.

Architectural Description
(Figs 20-22; Pls LXXXVII, XXI)
The church consists of chancel, nave and west tower (Fig. 20). Recording of the fabric was difficult owing to collapsed masonry and roofing, and trees and creeper obscuring surviving walls. Masonry is principally of coursed flint, roofing (where it survives) of pantiles.

Chancel. The chancel is built of small flints in neat mortared courses. The walls are rendered internally. In 1978, most of the roof survived, but the western half has fallen in since the collapse of the chancel arch. The three-light east window is the finest in the church, with its reticulated tracery reminiscent of nearby Beeston; some plain glass still survives in it, but most has been pushed through by encroaching ivy. The eastern corners have diagonal buttresses.

The south wall of the chancel stands to full height. At its eastern corner there is the robbed cavity of a piscina; it was removed in 1978. West of it is a two-light Perpendicular window with square head and hoodmould, set within a segmental rear-arch lined with 17th-century brick (Fig. 21, No. 1); there is a sedilia. The internal splay of another window is visible further west, but this has been blocked by an 18th-century or early 19th-century fireplace; its brick flue proceeds through the window opening and into a chimney built at the junction of nave and chancel. The iron grate and surround survived until 1978.

The chancel north wall has a two-light Perpendicular window identical to that in the south wall (and opposite it), but with a more pointed rear-arch. The north wall itself was rebuilt in the 19th century, as the vertical chains of brick in the wall show. The doorway at the west end of the wall is pointed and framed in wood, and is approached by steps from the outside.

In 1978 the subsiding chancel arch was still intact; already four-centred, the apex of the arch has assumed an even lower profile (Pl. LXXXVII). By 1983 it had gone, except for the lowest voussoirs. It was double chamfered; the limestone polygonal responds, moulded capitals and bases survive, but are out of alignment in places. Before its collapse, the gable wall above was built of 18th-century brick. North and south of the arch are substantial buttresses, faced in 18th-century brick on the north side, of flint and limestone, but largely refaced with 18th-century brick on the south side.

Nave. The south wall of the nave is built of coursed flint, with most of the internal rendering still intact. There is a slight change of alignment two-thirds of the way along, from the west, where the wall veers slightly to south. In this eastern portion, there is a two light Perpendicular window with square head; the leading edges of internal splay are stone and original, but the window tracery and brick segmental rear-arch are 19th-century reworkings

KEMPSTONE

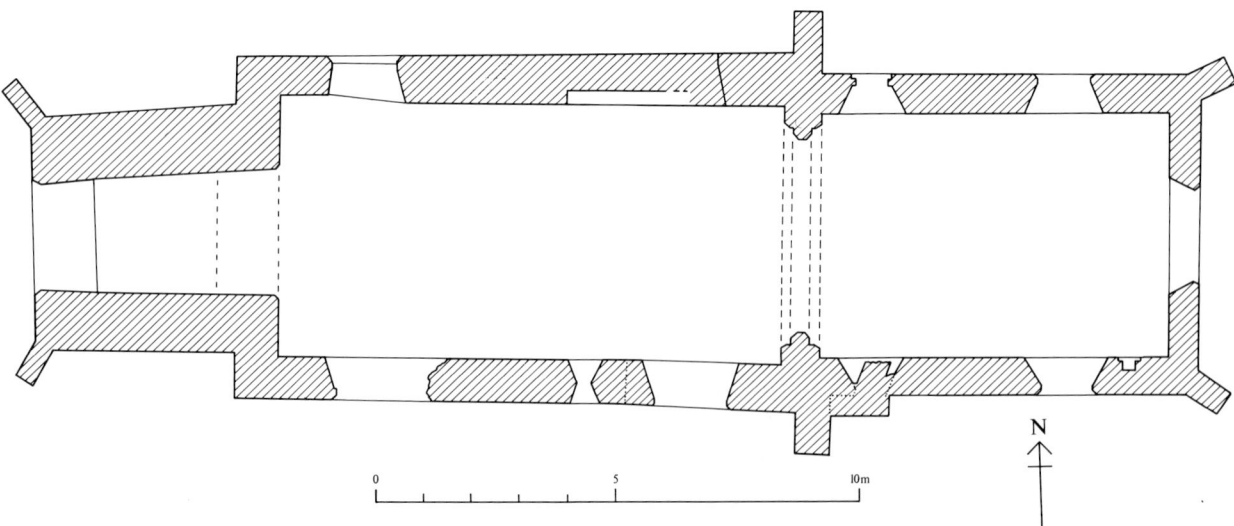

Figure 20. Kempstone, St Paul: plan. Scale 1:150. Note the building break and change of alignment in the nave south wall.

KEMPSTONE

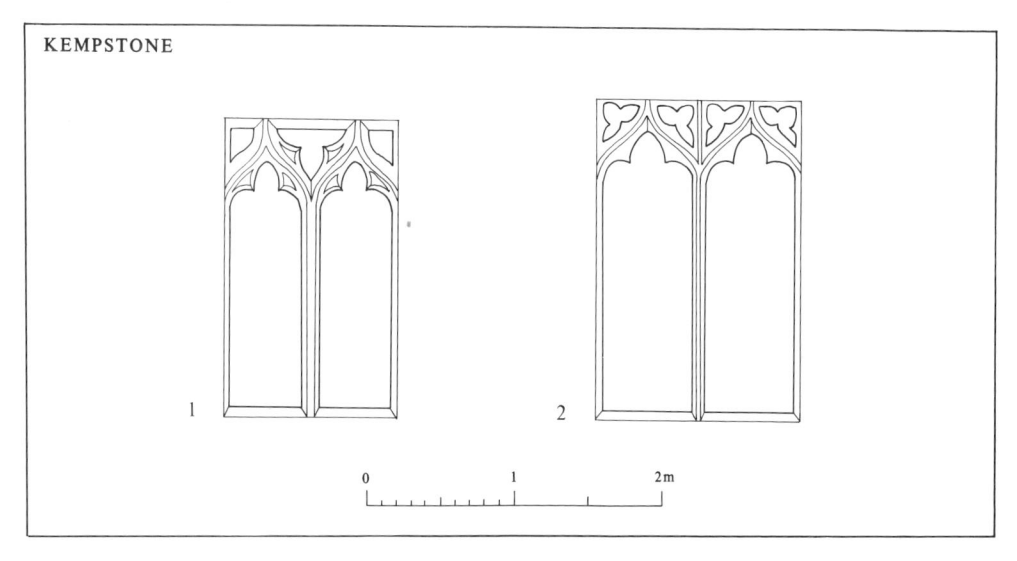

Figure 21. Kempstone, St Paul: 1. Chancel south window. 2. Nave south window. Scale 1:50.

(Fig. 21, No. 2). Just west of the change in alignment is a round-headed double-splayed window (Fig. 22, Pl. XXI). It was blocked until recently (Bryant in 1903 noted traces of a blocked round-headed window), and after removal of the blocking, Rogerson was able to record the window for the first time:

'The external arch is framed of large flints with a particularly large one acting as an off-centre keystone. The inner surfaces are plastered over a mortar skim, except the lower external surface which is roughly finished with mortar. In the centre at the meeting of the splays a roughly rectangular groove survives around the soffit of the arch but is missing from the damaged jambs. This is presumably a window or a shutter rebate. On the surface of the mortar skim the internal and external splays of the arches carry impressions of radially set timbers. These timbers must have acted as shuttering during construction. Much of the facing of the wall on the interior around the window has collapsed, and the lower western corner of the interior has been pierced by a horizontal hole containing timber and packed with chalky boulder clay. The eastern external jamb contains a fragment of Rhineland lava quern. The window has been blocked with loosely packed mortared flints'.

(Rogerson, N.A.U. File 4092).

West of this window, the south wall has collapsed as far as the south door. Only the west jambs of the doorway survive. The unbuttressed west corners of the nave survive, but it was impossible to determine their form due to the thick encrustation of ivy.

Most of the nave north wall has collapsed, with the pantiled nave roof on top of it (making recording of the fabric problematical). Where visible, the flint masonry is not as neatly coursed on the south wall. Its only window was near the chancel; only the east jamb survives, in white Georgian brick, like the Lodge; (this window was blocked when observed by Bryant in 1903). West of this, the wall has collapsed; in 1978 a recess in this part of the wall could be seen, 27 cm deep and rendered like the remaining internal walls. Further west is the pointed north doorway, its bottom half blocked with flint to leave the upper part as a window. The wooden intersecting tracery of this window survived until 1978. The wall of the nave is thicker east of the doorway than west of it.

Tower. It is difficult to make out the features of the west tower because of the abundant ivy. Its masonry is of flint in reasonably straight courses. The west corners have diagonal buttresses. At ground level, there is a big three-light Perpendicular west window with supermullions. The tower arch is triple chamfered, with no responds. The belfry windows are no longer visible beneath the ivy, but were each a single light with cinquefoil cusped head.

Interpretation and Dating
(Fig.23)
A proper phasing of the church has been made very difficult through collapse of walls and covering of ivy.

Plate LXXXVII. Kempstone, St Paul, interior looking east, 1978. The chancel arch had collapsed by 1983.

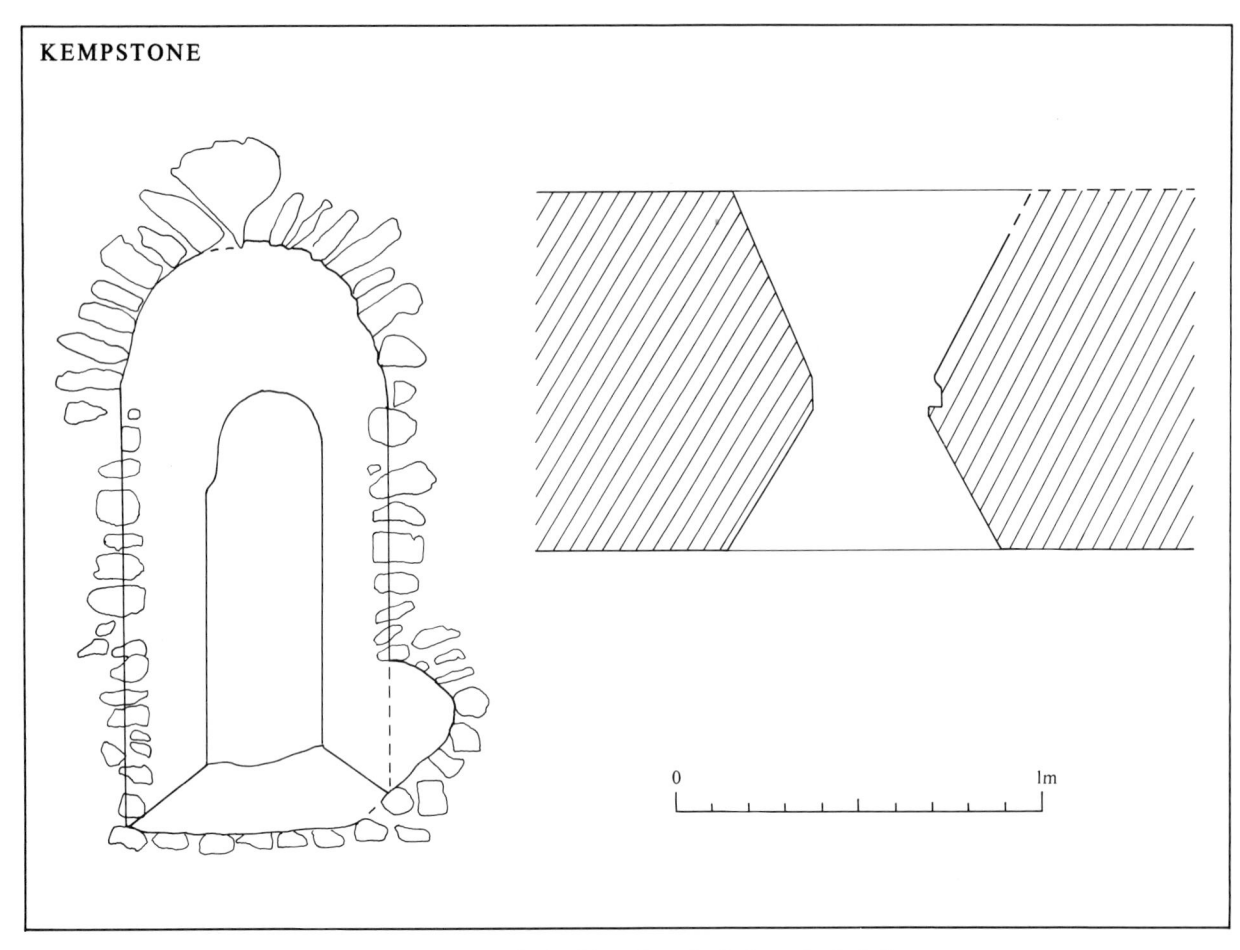

Figure 22. Kempstone, St Paul: nave south wall, double-splayed window. Scale 1:20.

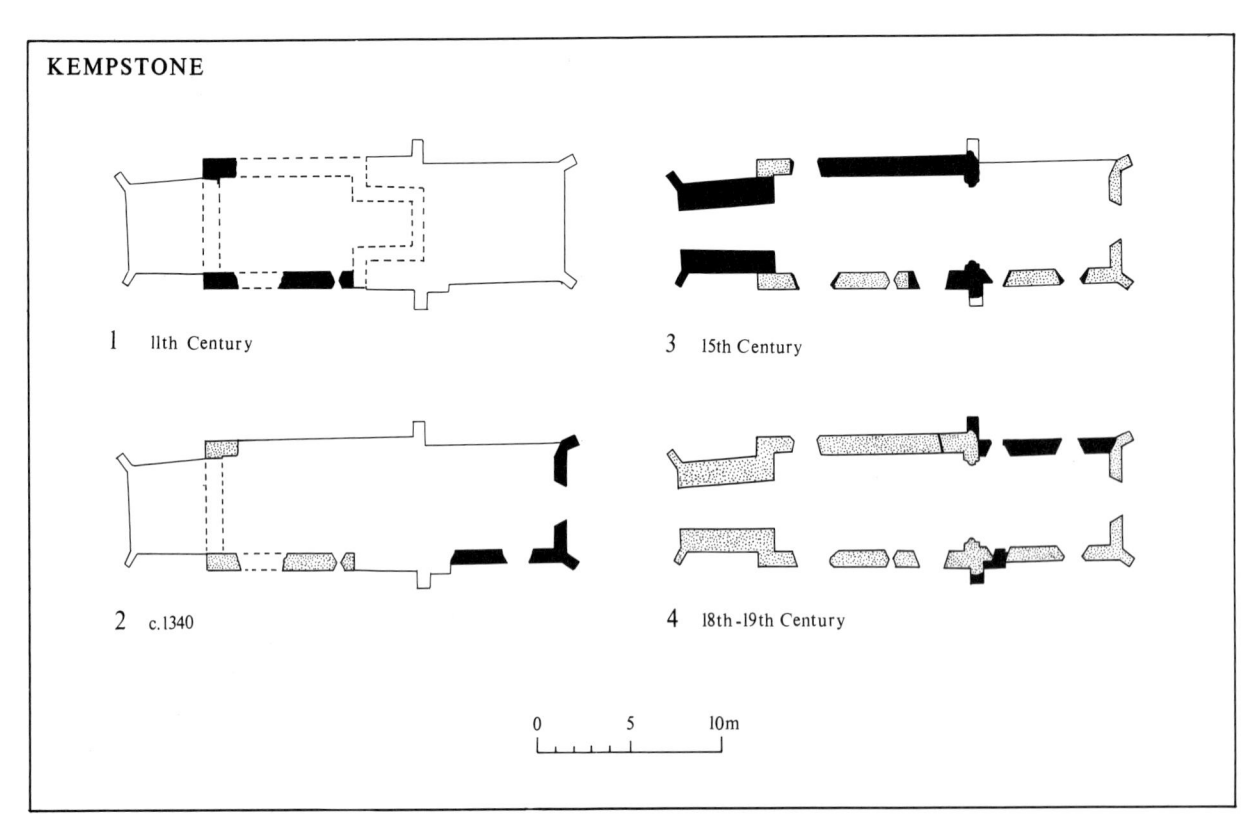

Figure 23. Kempstone, St Paul: phase plan. Scale 1:400.

The earliest dateable feature is the double-splayed window in the nave south wall. These usually belong to the 11th century, either side of the Conquest of 1066. The western two-thirds of the nave south wall belong to this phase; the south-west quoins may also belong, but it was impossible to see them. Possibly the north-west quoins are likewise 11th-century; this wall continues up to the north door, from which a thicker wall proceeds (maybe the offset noted in the north wall further east picks up the original wall again).

The earliest feature of the chancel is the Decorated east window, dateable like nearby Beeston to the 1340s. Chancel arch and additional windows in nave and chancel are Perpendicular. The west tower, to judge from its ground-floor window, is Perpendicular also.

There are several 18th-century additions, including the nave north window, and buttresses north and south of the chancel arch. 19th-century work includes the rebuilding of the chancel north wall. The open fireplace and flue built into the chancel south window are probably early 19th-century. The nave roof was retiled as late as 1904.

Causes of Abandonment
From the 19th century, the scattered population of the village has been declining. The site of the deserted medieval village lies south and west of the church. Only Kempstone Lodge and a few farms remain within the parish.

By the end of the 19th century the church had been abandoned and was partly ruined. Bryant, writing in 1903 recorded that 'the Church is so much decayed that no services are how held in it; the inhabitants attend at Beeston.' (Bryant, 1903, 120). The thatched nave was in ruins at the time. When Cox visited it in 1904, 'the whole was in miserable dilapidation through the devastating influence of unchecked ivy.' No services had been held for about 20 years. By 1904, the nave was roofless, and had shrubs and trees growing in it. In that year the Earl of Leicester paid for a total restoration, involving the repairing and retiling of the chancel roof, restoration of walls, the nave walls were partly rebuilt and a new tiled roof built, and tower and buttresses repaired. The church was then to be used only as a mortuary chapel (NRO, FCB/11, 15, 351). These remedies did not last long. Cautley in the late 1940s described the church as 'derelict' (Cautley, 1949, 213). By the 1950s, the nave roof had collapsed and it was in ruins again. The chancel arch and most of the chancel roof collapsed some time between 1978 and 1983.

Church Contents
None remain. Gone are the marble altar slab, wooden screen with pierced quatrefoils beneath the tower arch, Royal Arms over the chancel arch; gone also are the monuments on the chancel north wall to Charlotte Dungannon (d. 1828), William Fitzroy (d. 1837), George Fitzroy (d. 1827); on the south wall to Catherine Fitzroy (d. 1808), Elizabeth Henry (d. 1839); and on the south wall of the nave, Frederick Fitzroy (d. 1863), listed by Bryant (ibid). Pevsner lists 18th-century box pews and 17th-century bier (Pevsner, 1962, b, 216); Pevsner did not view them, and I cannot confirm their existence.

Other fittings survived until 1978. These include the piscina, wooden box pew against the south wall of the chancel and the iron fire surround belonging to the same.

Whereabouts of Church goods
The octagonal Perpendicular font now serves the church of St Cuthbert's, New Sprowston.

The cusped piscina arch was removed to Priory Farm, Litcham, in 1978.

Church plate (chalice of 1567, undated paten) is now at Litcham church.

Condition
The church is in an appalling and dangerous state. Roof tiles and timbers are scattered all over the floor. Nave walls have collapsed in places. The chancel arch fell in very recently. There is a clear risk of injury to any visiting the site.

Churchyard
No gravestones were visible; some 18th-century ones have been removed to Kempstone Lodge.

The churchyard has become a small wood. Some trees grow right next to the church (one of them obscures the double-splayed window in the south wall). A ditch forms a clear perimeter to the churchyard.

Archaeological Record
In the fields south and west of the church are faint undulations of Kempstone deserted medieval village. There is a moated site south-east of the churchyard; also soil marks of a house north of the churchyard.

In the church, fragments of four glazed medieval floor-tiles were reused in the masonry, two of them triangular.

Pottery remains have been found outside the churchyard: Ipswich Ware, Thetford Ware, glazed Grimston Ware; also 15th-century and post-medieval pottery.

Fabric recording by the Norfolk Archaeological Unit took place in 1978, providing the material for Figs. 21 and 22.

Archaeological and Architectural Assessment
St Paul's is a modest, unspectacular church. The east window is Decorated and comparable to nearby Beeston; the rest is rather ordinary. Most interest centres on the unblocking of the double-splayed window in 1978, confirming a probable 11th century date for the fabric of the nave. The site is also of interest for its relationship with the deserted medieval village of Kempstone.

Further References
Allison, 1955, 151.
Blomefield, 1805-10, IX, 523.
Bryant, 1903, 118.
Cautley, 1949, 213.
Cox, 1911, I, 61.
Pevsner, 1962b, 216.
Wade-Martins, 1980b, 29.

V. Sco Ruston, St Michael
Identification TG 2840 2181. *County No.* 7692.
Diocese: Norwich. *Archdeaconry*: Norwich. *Deanery*: Tunstead. *Parish*: Sco Ruston. *Status*: parish church, disused and made a safe ruin. *Date last in regular use*: *c.*1970. *Ownership and access*: Norwich Diocesan Board of Finance.

Location and Setting
(Pls LXXXVIII, LXXXIX)
The roofless church of Sco Ruston can be found just east

Plate LXXXVIII.   Sco Ruston church by Ladbrooke (c. 1830).

of the B1150 Norwich-North Walsham road, 2.5km north of Coltishall. The overgrown churchyard is approached by a grass track which skirts a solitary house. There is no sign of village, or even hamlet, anywhere near the church (Pl. LXXXVIII, LXXXIX). Much of the exterior of the church is obscured by thick ivy.

Architectural Description
(Figs 24, 25, 26, 27)
The church consists of chancel and nave in one, south porch, and ruined west tower (Fig. 24). When visited in 1977, the church still retained its peg-tiled roof, which had been removed by 1986. The walls are constructed mainly of flint.

Chancel. There is no structural division between chancel and nave; formerly a screen marked the entrance to the chancel. Masonry consists of coursed flint, with occasional pieces of conglomerate (even puddingstone and lava in the east wall), and putlog-holes lined with medieval brick. The east wall is pierced by a three-light window of cusped intersecting tracery (Fig. 27, No. 3). Above the springing-level of the window, the masonry changes: no conglomerate, medieval brick or puddingstone, just smoothly-cut flint of obvious 19th-century workmanship. The gable is capped with limestone slabs; the stone cross which adorned the apex lay smashed on the ground in 1977. The corners of the east wall are formed of limestone quoins. A single sloping buttress protrudes from the wall, near the north-east corner; it is constructed of flint with an eastern face of 18th-century brick.

Moving to the south wall, there is a buttress with three set-offs and a base-course (the year 1860 inscribed in the latter) constructed of flint with limestone edgings, situated next to the eastern quoins; it seems to be of the same phase as the upper part of the east wall. At this point on the interior, there is a simple niche for a piscina. Further west, the wall is pierced by a plain-chamfered Y-tracery window (Fig. 26, No. 5). There are no windows in the north wall; in fact the only feature is the buttress near the east wall, identical to that in the south wall (save the 1860 inscription).

Nave. The masonry of the nave has the same character as the chancel: coursed flint, occasional conglomerate pieces, brick-lined putlog-holes. The uppermost 1m represents a heightening of the wall, and comprises larger, more evenly-coursed flints and more brick.

In the south wall, a buttress with two set-offs marks the division of nave and chancel; it contains some pieces of burnt limestone, and a base-course with carved shield. The buttress projects from a slight bulge in the wall formed by the rood-stair. At this point on the inside, the blocked doorway to the rood-stair can be made out; both jambs and sill are burnt, and most of the arch (probably four-centred) is missing; the blocking consists largely of reused limestone. Further west the wall is pierced by two-light Perpendicular window, with four-centred arch and hood-mould, enclosing cusped ogee main lights and drop tracery (Fig. 26, No. 3). On the inside there is a plain piscina below the eastern edge of this window.

Returning to the exterior, another buttress with two set-offs separates the two nave windows; it contains many post-medieval bricks; a limestone plaque in the base-course is carved with an heraldic device comprising three water wheels (Fig. 25). The window west of the buttress has two-light tracery with a single cusped reticulation (mostly 19th-century restoration), hood mould and concave chamfered rear-arch (Fig. 26, No. 4).

The south doorway is Decorated, with continuous mouldings (including sunken quadrant) and hood-mould; and concave rear-arch (Fig. 27, No. 2); the rear arch is segmental, and there is a water stoup just east of the jamb. West of the doorway there is a clear vertical masonry break, caused by the rebuilding of the west end in the early 18th century (see below). The western quoins are made of reused limestone blocks.

As with the south wall, a buttress with two set-offs marks the junction of chancel and nave on the north side. Much of this buttress has been refaced with 17th-century brick. The two windows in this wall are separated by similar buttresses: to east, the window consists of two

Plate LXXXIX.   Sco Ruston, St Michael, from south-west, 1977. The roof has since been removed.

SCO RUSTON

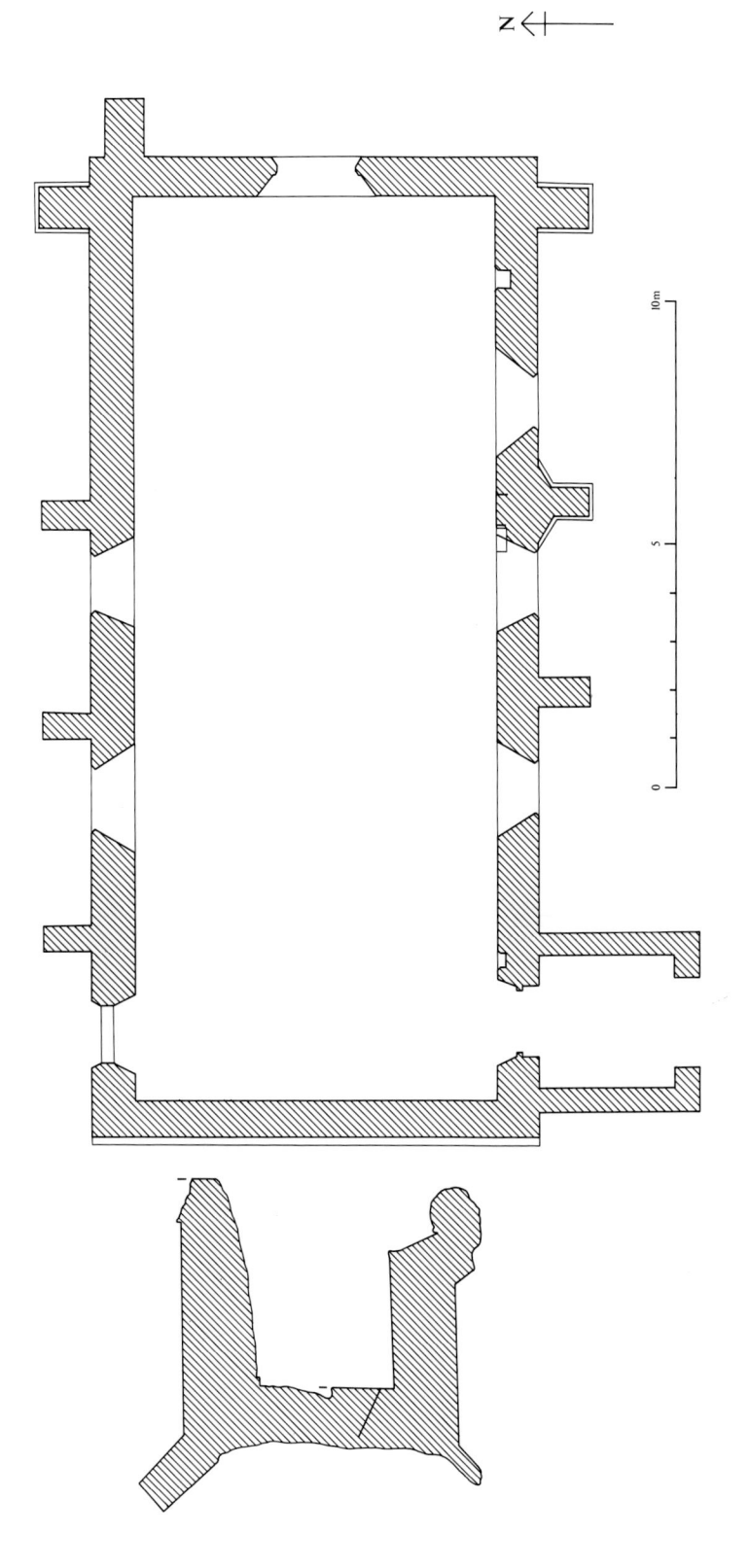

Figure 24. Sco Ruston, St Michael: plan. Scale 1:150.

SCO RUSTON

ELEVATION OF SOUTH WALL

ELEVATION OF NORTH WALL

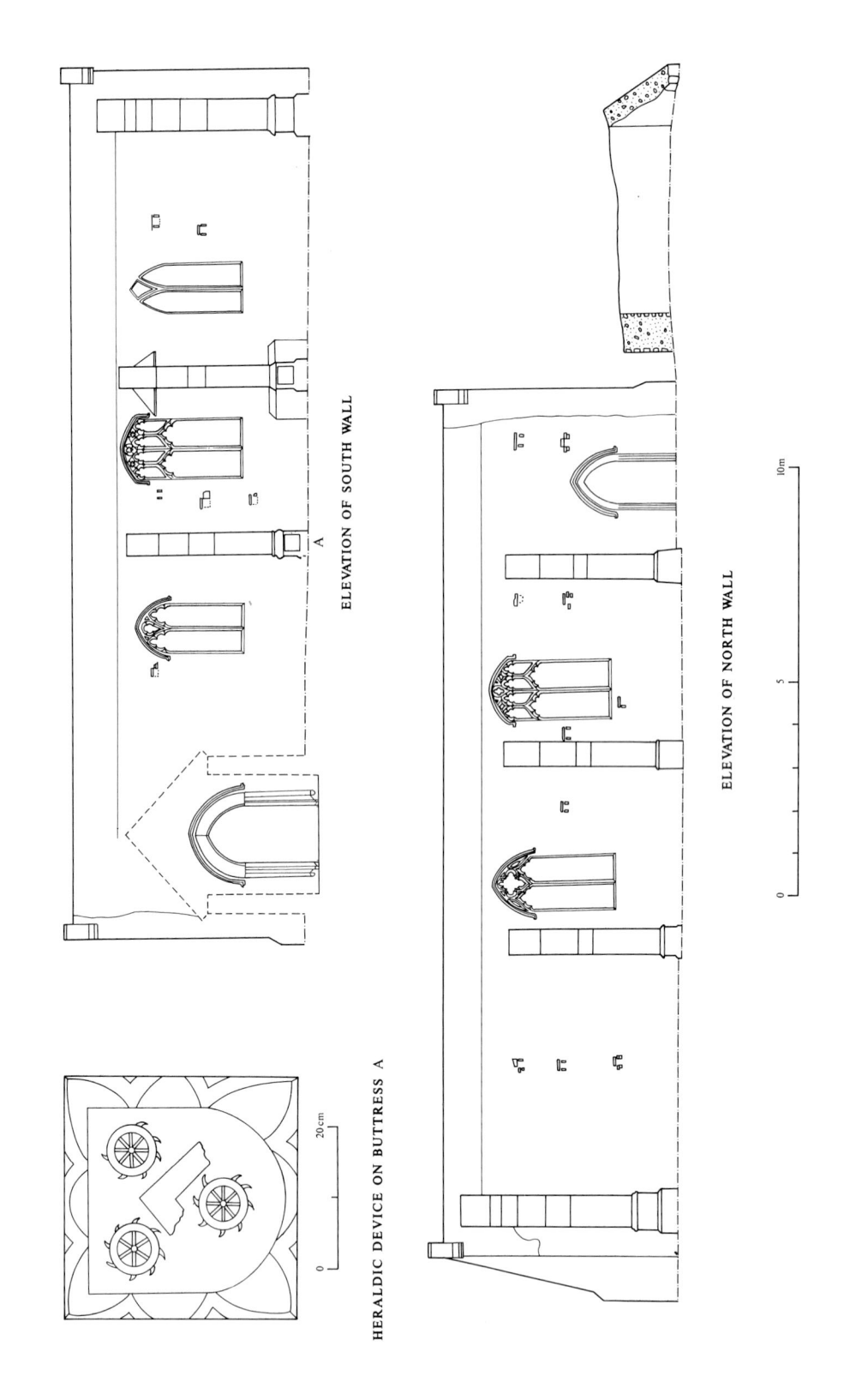

HERALDIC DEVICE ON BUTTRESS A

Figure 25. Sco Ruston, St Michael: elevations of north and south walls. Scale 1:150.

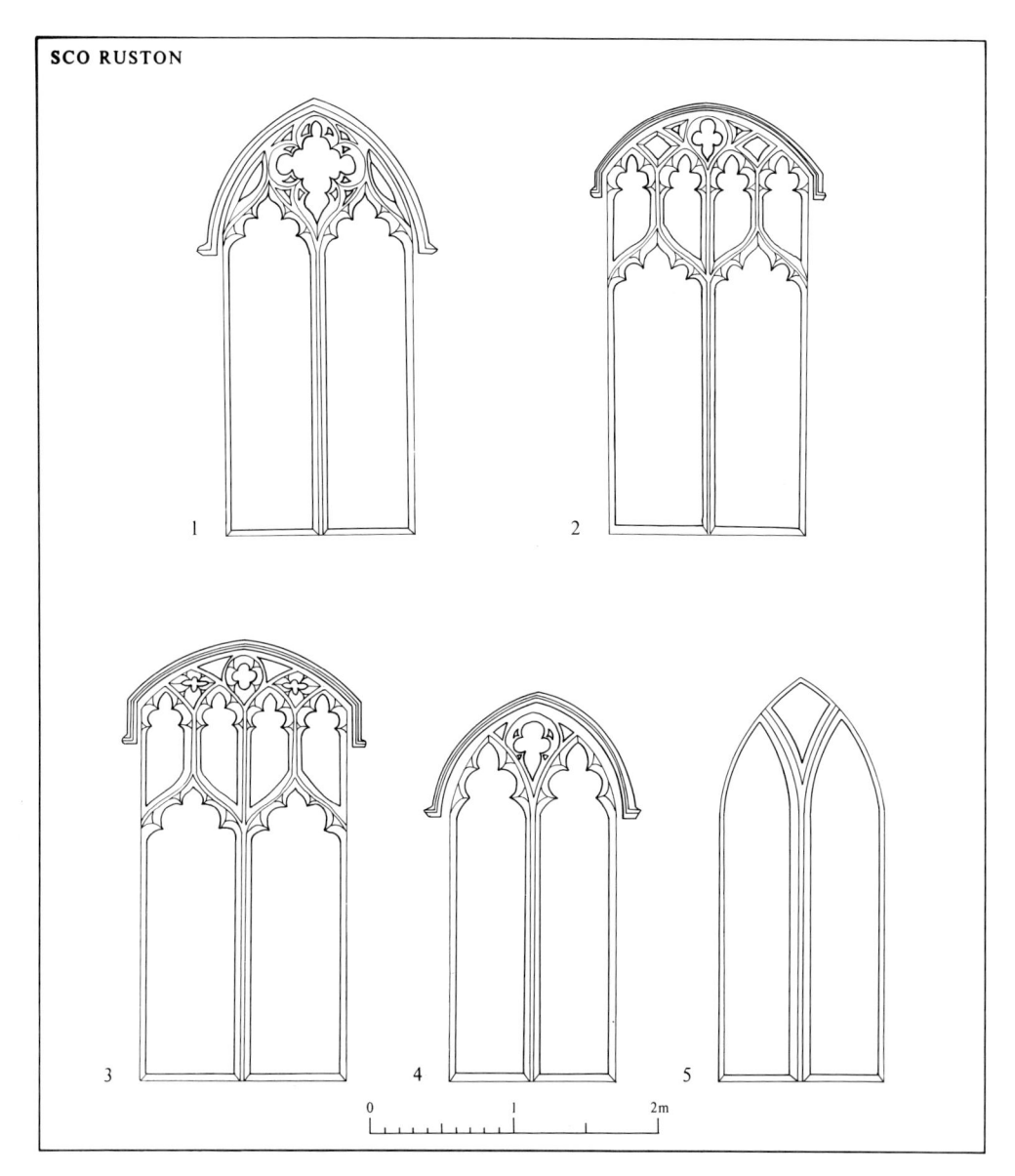

Figure 26. Sco Ruston, St Michael, windows: 1 & 2. Nave north wall, 3 & 4. Nave south wall. 5. Chancel south wall. Scale 1:50.

main lights with cusped ogee heads supporting a sub-cusped reticulation (Fig. 26, No. 1); to west, the two-light Perpendicular window with drop tracery is of the same design as the east window in the south wall (Fig. 26, No. 2). Another brick-repaired buttress intervenes before we come to the north doorway, like its opposite counterpart, but smaller and blocked with 19th-century brick (Fig. 27, No. 1). A vertical break extends from the top of this doorway to the eaves.

The west wall is entirely different in construction to the rest of the church. It consists of flint regularly interspersed with chunks of reused limestone, as well as occasional bricks, both medieval and post-medieval. There is an external base-course with limestone set-off. The wall is capped at the apex with a stone bell-cote, which still retains its bell-wheel.

South Porch. The windowless porch appears to be of the 19th century, certainly judging from the outer doorway: this is Perpendicular in style, with half-shafts and polygonal capitals, in stone as unweathered as other examples of Victorian restoration in the church. However, the flint side walls may be older; and it should be noted that a porch quite like the present one is recorded in Ladbrooke's lithograph of c.1830 (Pl. LXXXVIII). It seems likely that the porch was heavily restored rather than rebuilt.

Tower. In June 1703, the west tower collapsed, destroying part of the nave with it (see below). It was decided to leave the tower in its ruined condition, shorten the nave by some two metres, and build a new west wall using materials from the tower. Today, the south wall survives to a height of 11.75m, while north and west walls nowhere exceed 3m, and the east wall has gone completely. The masonry differs from that of the nave: the external walls of the tower are faced with larger, better cut flints. At the south-east corner, the ruined remains of the base of a stair-turret can be made out; at the south-west corner, part of the masonry fill of a diagonal buttress can be discerned.

In the surviving fragment of the west wall, the south jamb of the lower storey window can still be seen; it contains some medieval brick. There is also a remnant of the north-west diagonal buttress.

Very little of the north wall survives; a scar at the

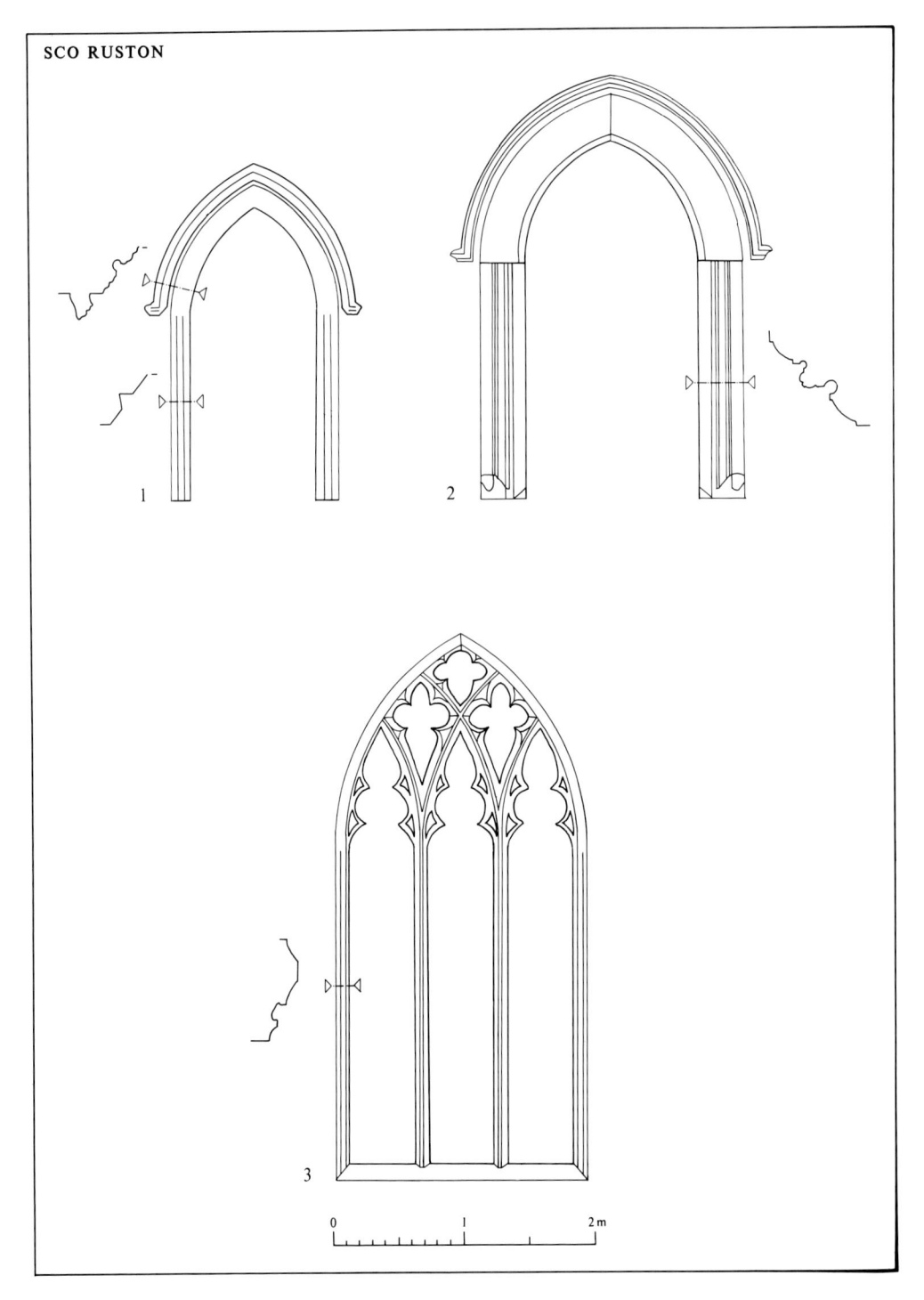

Figure 27. Sco Ruston, St Michael, doorways and window: 1. North doorway. 2. South doorway. 3. East window. Scale 1:50.

east end may indicate the position of the tower east wall.

Interpretation and Dating
(Fig.28)
The earliest dateable features are the two chancel windows (intersecting tracery and Y-tracery), which may be dated to c.1300. Nave and chancel appear to be of one build, and should therefore both be assigned to the very early 14th century. The masonry of the tower is different from the nave and chancel, and may be later; if the restoration of the porch reflects its original form (as indicated by Ladbrooke), and tower and porch are contemporary additions, we may ascribe both to the 15th century. The heightening of nave and chancel may also belong to this phase.

The disaster of 1703 necessitated considerable rebuilding. The Faculty (NRO, FCB/1, 1, 453) records that 'the steeple having been for many years ruinous and out of repair lately fell down, and by the fall thereof part of the roof of the church is broken down.' They therefore proposed to shorten the nave by 6ft, build a new nave west wall and erect a new roof. To help pay for this reconstruction, two of the three bells were sold, and materials from the fallen tower were used in the new west wall. It was probably around this time that the brick buttress was added to the chancel east wall.

Further repairs took place later in the 18th century, when a Faculty of 1777 gave permission for the sale of the

SCO RUSTON

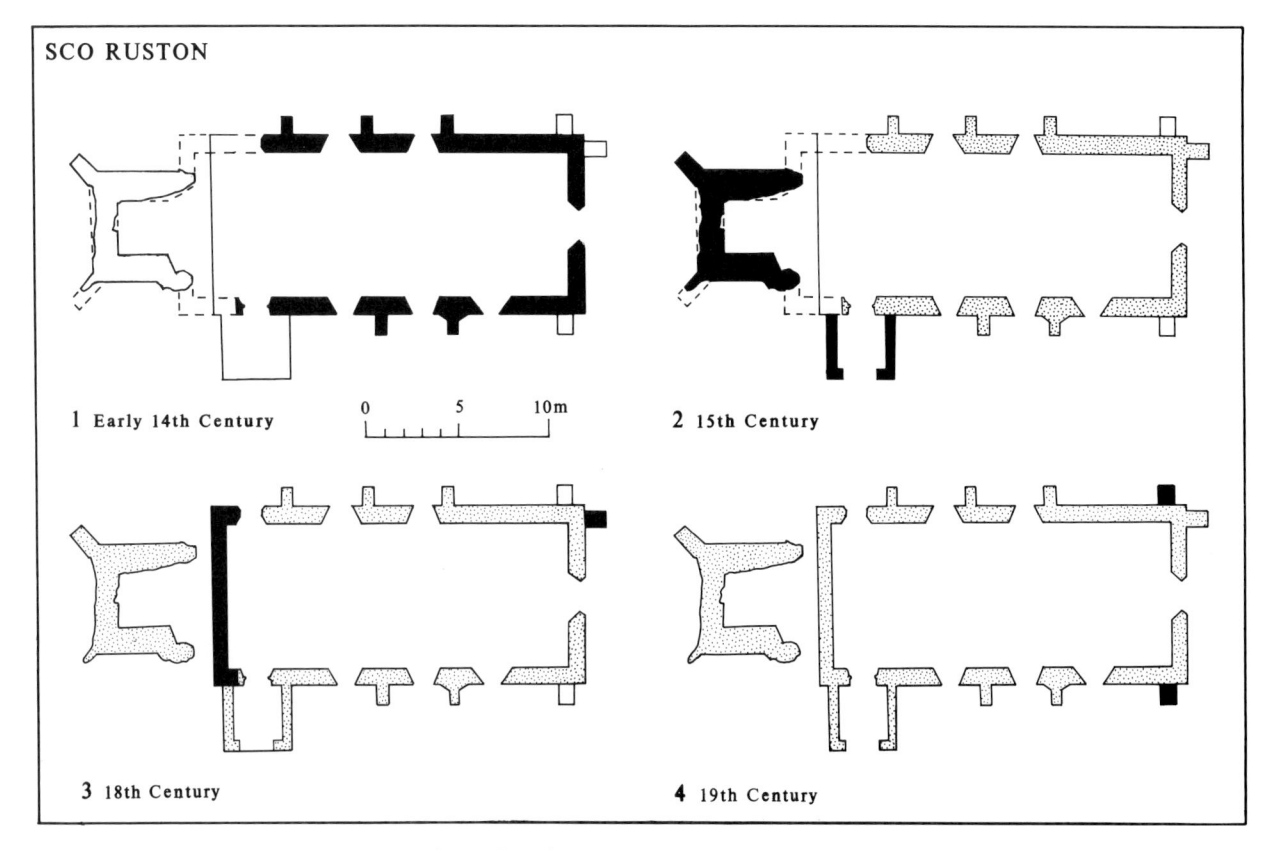

1 Early 14th Century
2 15th Century
3 18th Century
4 19th Century

Figure 28. Sco Ruston, St Michael: phase plan. Scale 1:400.

remaining bell in order to pay for the erection of a bell cupola at the west end (NRO, FCB/3, 5, 112); the cupola is depicted in Ladbrooke's lithograph, c.1830, Pl. LXXXVIII.

A thorough restoration was carried out in 1860 (although, strangely, there is no written record of it). The work involved the rebuilding of the upper part of the east wall, the replacement of the cupola by a stone bell-cote on the west wall, the virtual reconstruction of the porch, and many repairs to doors, buttresses etc., The dating for this work is solely provided by the base-course of the southeast buttress, firmly inscribed '1860'.

Causes of Abandonment
Even in the 18th century, the paucity of parishioners was noticeable (as the two Faculties mentioned above made clear). Today there are no more than three houses in the former parish (now united with Tunstead). By the early 1970s, the church was in poor repair. It was subsequently effectively decommissioned through the removal of its dangerous roof by the Diocesan Board of Finance.

Church Contents
Plain 19th-century floor tiles in chancel and nave; ledger slabs at west end of nave dating to 1690; 1796; 1800.

Whereabouts of Furnishings
As recently as 1962, Pevsner (1962, a, 311) was able to record two medieval benches and an unusual south door; their whereabouts are unknown. Cox (1911, I, 246) described the door thus: 'The special feature of the church is the 15th-century south door of the church, which is remarkable for bearing in the centre outer panel a raised inscription in black-letter text, recording that it was the gift of Stephen Bolte and Eleanor his wife.'

The 19th-century pulpit, font and stove were still in the church (but smashed up) in 1977; they had been removed by 1986.

Condition
When visited in 1977, the church was in quite a dangerous condition: holes in the roof, vandalised windows and floor, thick ivy growing up all external walls. By 1986, the roof had been carefully removed, walls cleared of ivy and generally tidied up; however, weeds were beginning to grow in the nave and on the tops of bare walls, and ivy was starting to recolonise the recently cleared surfaces.

Churchyard
The small churchyard forms a rectangle around the church. A hedge forms its boundary, and there are a few trees. It is mostly overgrown with brambles and nettles, but part of the churchyard north of the church has been kept clear around a recent group of gravestones (latest 1984).

Archaeological Record
Fabric recording by the Norfolk Archaeological Unit took place in 1978, providing the material for Figs. 24–27.

Archaeological and Architectural Assessment
The church is small and modest, mainly of the 14th and 15th centuries but extensively restored in the 18th and 19th centuries and made into a 'safe' ruin in the 20th century. It is really only of local interest; there are no exceptional features.

Further References
Blomefield, 1805-10, XI, 73.
Cautley, 1949, 241.

Cox, 1911. I, 246
Messent, 1931, 31.
Messent, 1936, 209.
Pevsner, 1962a, 311

VI. Tivetshall, St Mary

Identification TM 1663 8581. *County No.* 10971.
Diocese: Norwich. *Archdeaconry*: Norfolk. *Deanery*: Redenhall. *Parish*: Tivetshall. *Status*: parish church, now disused and ruined. *Date last in regular use*: 1947.
Ownership and access: Diocese of Norwich.

Location and Setting
(Pl. C)
The village of Tivetshall is hard to find without a good map. It is located 8km north-east of Diss, and 2km west of the A140 Ipswich-Norwich road. The village has possessed two churches since *Domesday*. St Margaret's has been used as the sole parish church only since 1947, and stands 1.3km north of St Mary's, with most of the village half-way between the two. The roofless ruin of St Mary's is rather isolated, 400m from the nearest houses, and next to the small road to Gissing (Pl. XC). The site has provoked a number of ghost stories: the strange figure of an old man with a black dog is believed to haunt the churchyard.

Architectural Description
(Figs 29, 30; Pl. XCI)
The church consists of chancel, nave, south porch and collapsed west tower (Fig. 29). Building materials are principally coursed flint with limestone dressings.

Chancel. Masonry consists of small flints, mainly covered with buff rendering (and just the tips of the flints protruding).

The eastern corners have angle buttresses (but the northern spur of the north-east buttress has been erased) with two set-offs and faced with squared limestone. A superb four-light cusped intersecting window pierces the

Plate XC. Tivetshall, St Mary, aerial view in 1985. Norfolk Archaeological Unit 1985 TM1685/E/AVF12.

Plate XCI. Tivetshall, St Mary, from the east.

east wall (Pl. XCI); some of the tracery has been renewed. There are some 19th-century bricks in the capping of the gable wall.

Near the east jamb of the south wall there is a medieval piscina; the stone lower jambs are original, but the pointed arch above is constructed in 19th-century brick. To west there is a three-light intersecting tracery window with sill-sedilia, and hollow-chamfered rear-arch. A priest-door provides an entrance half-way along the south wall, flanked to east by a buttress with two set-offs; the doorway has a small roll-moulding within a hollow chamfer. The chancel is unusually long: there are two more windows west of the priest-door, with identical Y-tracery and chamfered rear-arches; both have hood-moulds with stops decorated with carved faces, somewhat weathered (Fig. 30).

The north wall also has two Y-tracery windows, directly opposite those in the south wall, and again with carved label-stops. East of the windows there is a vertical scar indicating the position of a former buttress. The removal of the buttress at the north-east corner has already been noted; it is likely that a vestry formerly flanked this part of the chancel, subsequently demolished along with the buttresses. There is no sign of a doorway, but the wall has been patched in places with reused limestone. There is no chancel arch.

Nave. The nave is wider than the chancel by the thickness of two walls. This can be observed very clearly at the junction of nave and chancel south walls, where the nave wall simply overlaps the exterior of the chancel wall; this overlap has developed into a vertical crack some 10cm wide. A buttress with three set-offs, placed at the junction of nave and chancel, gives the impression of vainly trying

TIVETSHALL ST MARY

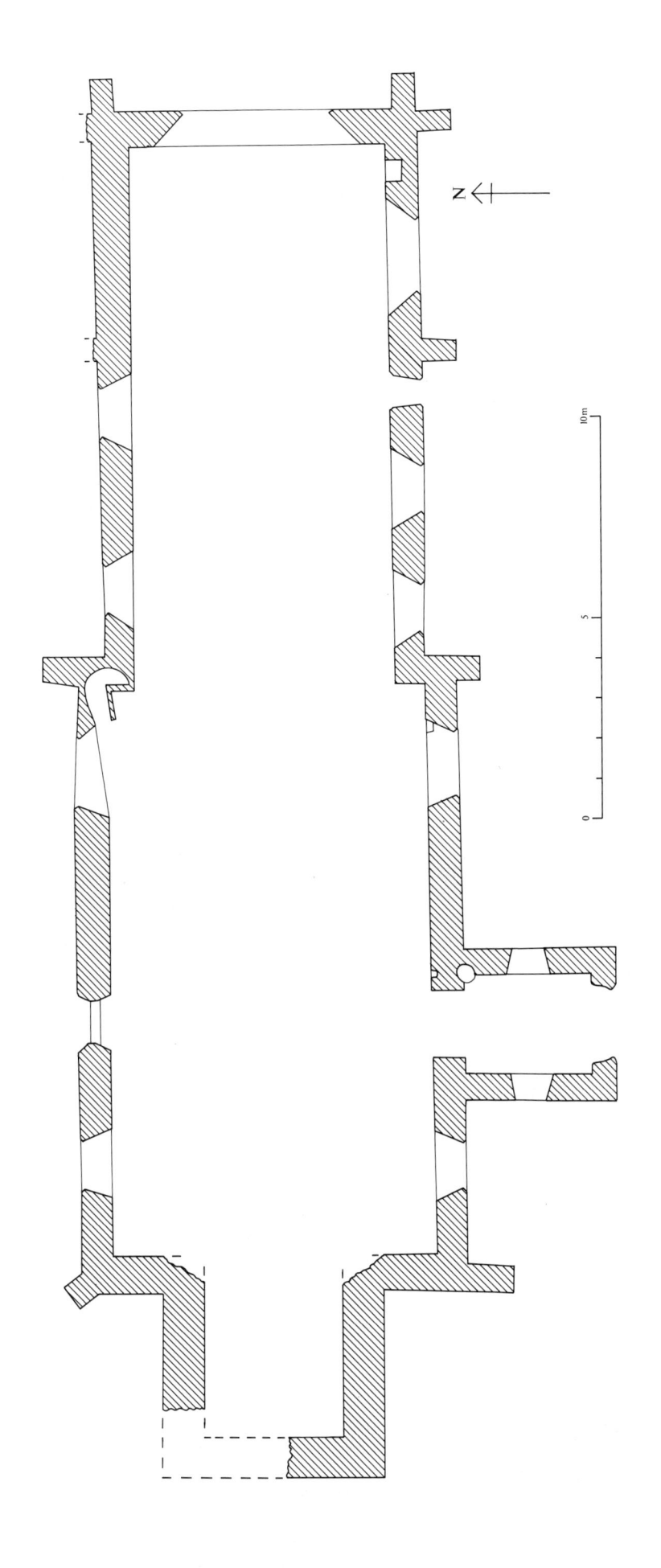

Figure 29. Tivetshall, St Mary: plan. Scale 1:150.

to close this crack; a battle it is clearly losing, given the outward lean of the nave south wall. West of this buttress there is the opening for a large (originally three-light Perpendicular) window; the head and tracery have gone, along with the sill, but some of the lower jambs remain. There follows a long stretch of plain wall, comprising roughly coursed flints with the occasional fragment of lava (also the rim of a limestone mortar was found in 1978 built in the wall). As a result of vandalism (*c.* 1979) the south doorway has had to be largely rebuilt in brick, a plain pointed arch; the segmental pointed rear-arch has survived better, although some of the lower jambs have been rebuilt in brick. There is a rectangular aumbry inside the nave east of the doorway. West of the doorway there is another window; when visited in 1978, it contained Y-tracery, but that has now (1987) gone. The south-west corner is supported by a large sloping buttress in early 19th-century brick.

There used to be a three-light Perpendicular window and rood-stair at the east end of the north wall. Already in 1978, both features had been destroyed, leaving a gap in the wall and a pile of rubble outside. Only the scar of the stair turret is now visible, in medieval brick, and only a single stone jamb of the adjoining window remains. Further west the north doorway has survived reasonably intact; it consists of a continuous double hollow-chamfered arch, plus hood-mould (in 1978 the doorway was found to be blocked with 18th-century brick, subsequently removed). West of the doorway is a Y-tracery window whose tracery has been removed since 1978. Most of the diagonal buttress at the north-west corner of the nave has been destroyed.

The west wall of the nave presents a puzzling sequence. It has, however, been coherently analysed by Andrew Rogerson in the course of fabric recording in 1978 (N.A.U. file 10971):

'Close to the angle between the north wall of the tower and the west wall of the nave evidence on the exterior shows that the lower part of the tower abuts against the nave wall, but coincident with a horizontal change of mortar in the nave wall the tower wall oversails the nave. 90cm north of the angle there is a marked vertical crack. The lower part of the wall stops abruptly with a straight edge and rectangular gaps in the mortar which suggest robbed quoins. The straight edge extends no further upwards than the change in mortar already mentioned. The mortar above the change is similar to that in the whole height of the wall north of the vertical crack. South of the tower the evidence is not clear. A large crack at the point where the tower and nave walls join may be the result of subsidence and not structural phasing. There has also been much repatching internally and externally at this point. To sum up, it is clear that the lower part of the west wall of the nave on the north side is earlier than the tower, and that the upper part is later than the tower'.

Tower. Most of what was once an unbuttressed west tower is now a pile of rubble some 3m high, filling the site of the tower and the area around it, including the west end of the nave. Only the south wall stands much higher than this mound of debris. There is a set-off with stone stringcourse about 5m from the ground on the external face of this surviving wall; the rest is quite featureless. Originally, there were single-light belfry windows. As indicated above, the tower postdates the lower part of the nave west wall, but was certainly built before the upper part of the wall.

South porch. The flint masonry of the porch is similar to, but not necessarily contemporary with, the nave south wall. This structure has been shamefully vandalised since the fabric was recorded in 1978. The single-light windows in medieval brick which pierce the east and west walls have been smashed to pieces, and the heads of the arches broken through. The outer doorway had already undergone extensive repairs in the 19th century; the only medieval survivals are the lower two jambs (in stone), the rest has been rebuilt in 19th-century brick. Inside the porch, there is a holy-water stoup at the north-east corner

Interpretation and Dating
(Fig.31)

There are five distinct medieval phases. The first four phases can be disentangled by careful study of the structural sequence, even before we begin to consider dates. For the reasons outlined above, the earliest part of the church must be the west wall of the nave below the change in mortar; this represents the west wall of a nave much narrower than the present one. Of this (Phase 1) church, nothing remains of the chancel or the nave north and south walls, and very little survives of the west wall. To this nave was added a west tower, since it can be seen that the present tower abuts the Phase 1 west wall; the tower is thus Phase 2. Likewise the north and south walls of the present nave incorporate a heightening of the west wall; and the vertical masonry breaks leave no doubt that this heightening post-dates the tower; the new nave is therefore Phase 3. An equally evident building break separates the nave from the chancel (a wide vertical crack on the south side). Since the two walls overlap one another, it is difficult to be certain which is the earlier. If the chancel predates the nave, then it could, arguably, be part of Phase 2 and contemporary with the tower. It is equally likely that the chancel is later than the nave, and has therefore been tentatively designated as Phase 4. Phase 5 incorporates later medieval additions, such as the eastern windows of the nave, the rood-stair, and the porch.

Transposing from relative to absolute chronology can be a dubious art, especially when there are no real 'absolutes'. In this particular case, it makes more sense to start with the latest phase and move back to the earliest. Phase 5, which includes the large 3-light windows at the end of the nave, will fit comfortably into a 15th-century date. The chancel, which has been assigned to Phase 4, points to a *c.* 1300 dating, with its cusped intersecting east window. As indicated above, it is difficult to be sure whether the chancel came before or after the nave, both being pierced by similar Y-tracery windows. They cannot be very distant from each other in date, so assuming the nave to be the earlier, a date towards the end of the 13th century would be acceptable. We have even less data regarding Phase 2, the tower. No dateable features survive; but Ladbrooke's lithograph (*c.* 1830) indicates that the belfry stage possessed a single opening in each face. This, combined with the absence of buttresses, suggests we are dealing with a tower of typically 13th-century type (*cf.* Rockland). All we can say of Phase 1 is that it is earlier still: pre-1200 is an open but not misleading suggestion.

There were also some post-medieval additions, but of a fairly insignificant order: the south-west buttress seems the most noticeable.

TIVETSHALL ST MARY

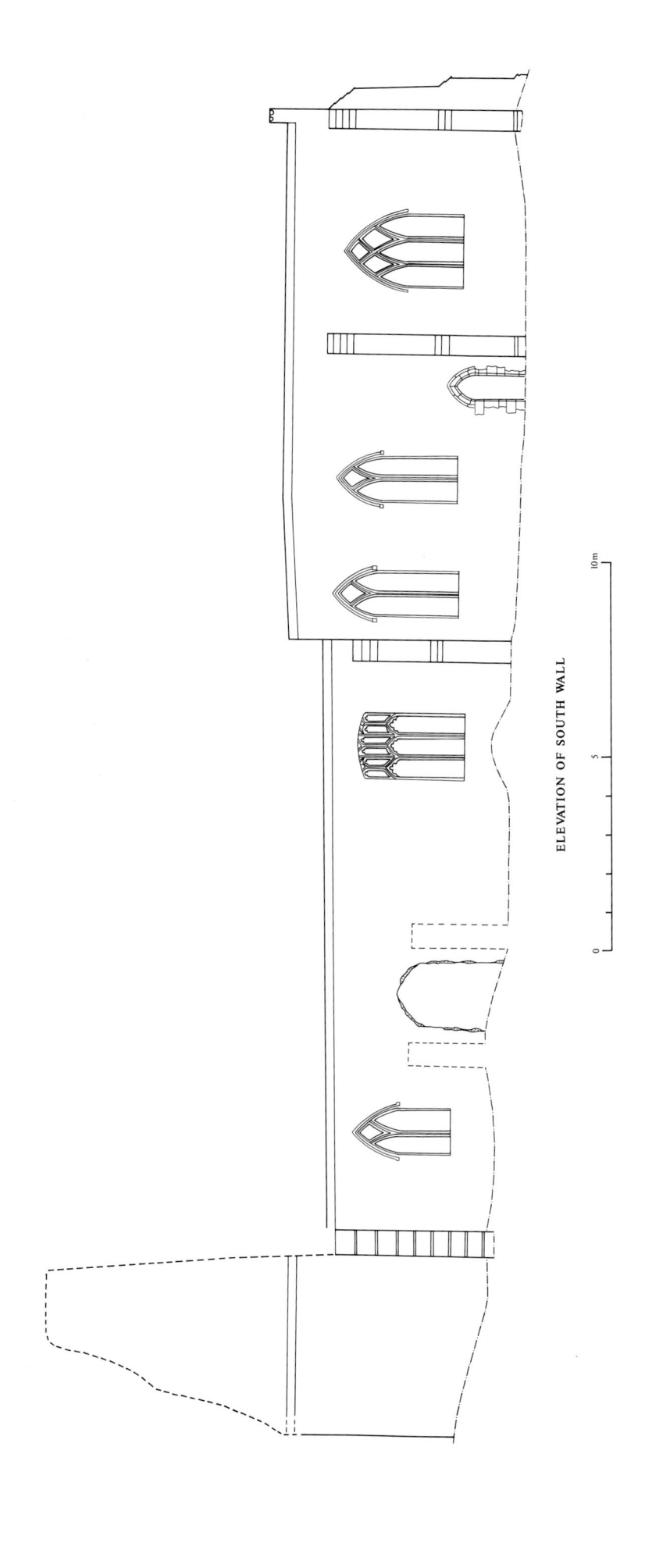

Figure 30. Tivetshall, St Mary: elevation of south wall. Scale 1:150.

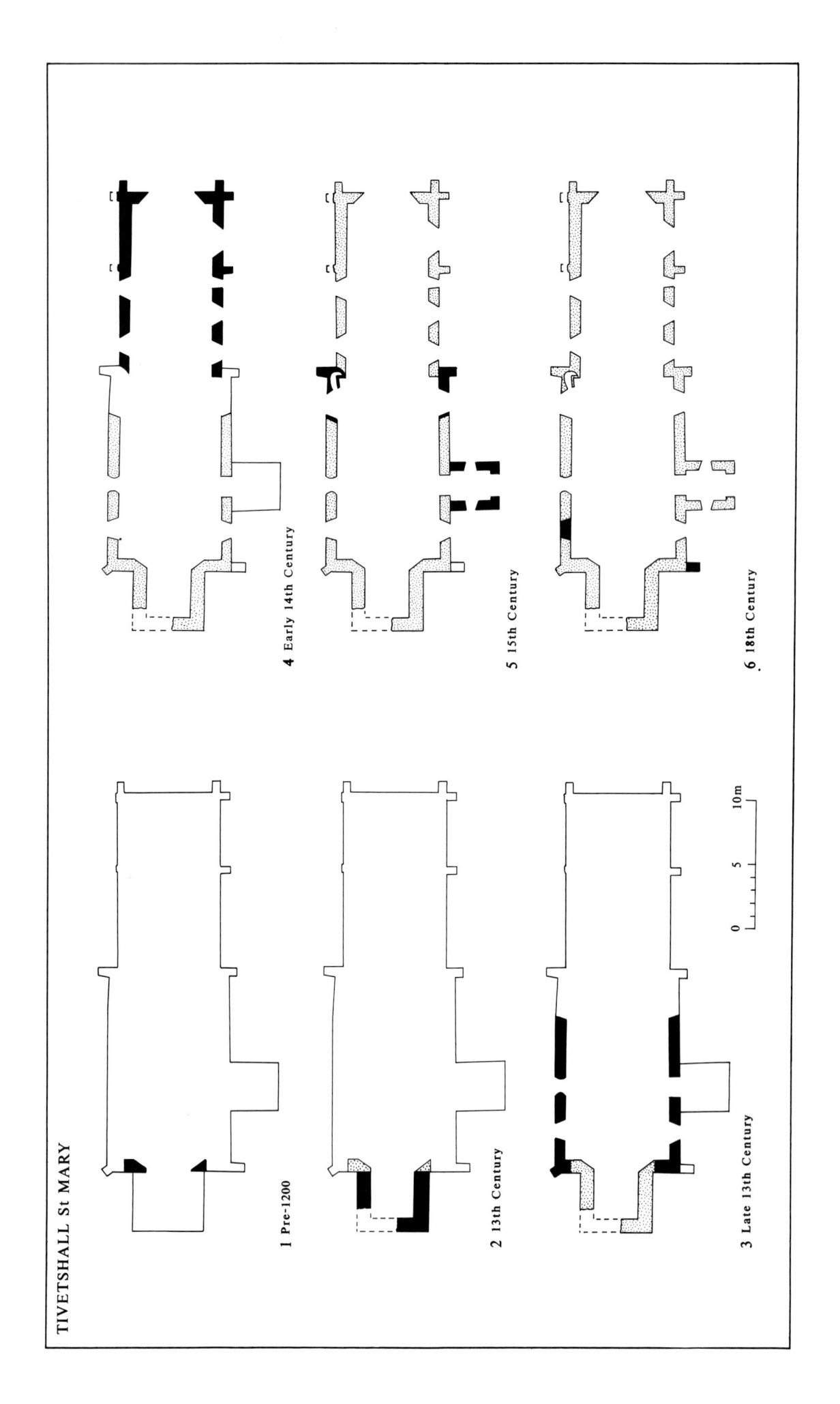

Figure 31. Tivetshall, St Mary: phase plan. Scale 1:400.

Causes of Abandonment

In the end, it became impossible for a moderate-sized village like Tivetshall to support two parish churches. Parishioners were struggling as early as 1702, when we read that the church 'is fallen into very great decay, and the inhabitants are not able to defray the charge of the repairs, and to make it decent and fit for the publique worship of God' and that it is a 'ruinated Church, which is in great danger of falling to the ground.' (NRO,FCB/1,442). They did succeed in repairing the church, but it was always difficult to support two churches within a small village.

Matters came to a head in 1947 when both St Margaret's and St Mary's were in a poor state of repair. The joint Parochial Church Council then held discussions about which of the two churches could be effectively maintained and which would be abandoned. In fact the decision for St Mary's came from above, when a low-flying aeroplane removed part of its tower, causing much of the rest of the tower to collapse onto the nave. St Mary's has remained out of use since, although the churchyard has been kept up.

Church Contents

All that remain are two black ledger slabs in the chancel floor, to John Boys (d. 1661) and his wife Hellen (d. 1669).

Whereabouts of Furnishings

Painted glass from the east window removed to Tivetshall St Margaret's. Whereabouts of 'plain Stuart table and the arms of George IV' (as recorded in Cautley, 1949, 256) unknown.

Condition

The church is a roofless ruin. After the collapse of the tower in the 1940s, it has been left to gradually deteriorate. The chancel roof was finally removed in 1978, and the walls capped. There has been some further deterioration since then, especially at the east end of the nave, where the large Perpendicular windows have collapsed; also some of the walling of the porch has been destroyed, apparently the work of vandals. A large mound of rubble occupies the site of the collapsed tower. There are a few brambles and shrubs growing in the nave.

Churchyard

The churchyard has been fairly well looked after. Most of it has been kept clear, although there are a few areas of brambles, and the odd shrub north of the church. Most of the headstones date to the 19th century, but there are some 18th-century ones (1723 appears to be the earliest). The churchyard has remained in use, and some of the graves were still being tended in 1987. A hedge forms the boundary to east, south and west, including some mature trees. A ditch forms the boundary to north.

Archaeological Record

Fabric recording by the Norfolk Archaeological Unit took place in 1978, providing the material for Figs. 29 and 30.

Archaeological and Architectural Assessment

St Mary's at Tivetshall is a good example of a mainly 13th-century Norfolk church. It possess five medieval construction phases, the earliest being pre-1200. The Phase 1 church could even be the one mentioned in *Domesday Book*. Tivetshall is one of a number of Norfolk villages which possessed two churches at *Domesday*; and according to Blomefield (1805-10, I, 205), St Mary's was the mother church. Thus it remains an important site which may retain some below-ground evidence of the 11th-century church.

Further References

Blomefield, 1805-10, I, 205.
Bryant, 1915, 295.
Cautley, 1949, 256.
Cox, 1911, II, 196.
Messent, 1936, 250.
Pevsner, 1962, b, 357.

Chapter 5. Category III

I. Bawsey, St James

Identification TF 6625 2079. *County No.*3328.
Diocese: Norwich. *Archdeaconry; Lynn. Deanery*: Lynn.
Parish: Gaywood with Bawsey and Mintlyn. *Status*: parish church, now disused and ruined. *Date last in regular use*: 1771.
Ownership: English Heritage. *Access*: probably private.

Location and Setting
The crumbling tower and nave of the church forms a notable landmark for motorists glancing eastward from the A149 King's Lynn by-pass. Standing in complete isolation at the very top of a low hill, it rather resembles a ruined castle. The site is 4km due east of the centre of King's Lynn, and only 0.5km east of the by-pass. The village of Bawsey has completely disappeared; the nearest sign of habitation is Church Farm, 400m south of the church. The church is a Scheduled Ancient Monument.

Architectural Description
(Pls XCII-V)
The roofless remains comprise chancel, central tower and nave. The principal building material is coursed flint (cover photograph).

Chancel. Only the south-east corner survives of the rectangular chancel. The rubble masonry contains carstone, flint and grey Sandringham stone. The east jamb of a window in the south wall is visible, with niches for piscina and sedilia on the inside. On the outside, the corner had a diagonal buttress with two set-offs, faced with limestone.

Tower. The central tower, standing to full height in places, looks perilously unsafe (Pl. XCII). The whole of the south-west corner has gone, and the east wall is ominously cracked from top to bottom. The masonry of its thick walls consists mainly of carstone rubble, interspersed with flint. Quoins, jambs and facings are of squared limestone.

The tower east wall is cracked, and slants obliquely to east. The round-headed chancel arch has stone voussoirs with carstone rubble intrados; likewise the arch has stone corner jambs with carstone between. It has a chamfered plinth, and a socket for door or screen. To west, the arch has single nook-shafts with tiny cushion capitals; above the chamfered impost the western arch voussoirs have a roll-moulding. On either side of the arch on the east side, broken-off walling indicates the width of the original (narrower) chancel, (excavations in 1930 revealed an apse; *Antiq.Journal*, 1931, 11, 169). Between the lines of the original chancel walls, and above the chancel arch, the semi-circular scar of a barrel-vault can be made out. Above the scar is an unsplayed opening, with carstone rubble jambs and triangular head, evidently an opening from the tower into the space above the chancel vault. The gable line of a steep roof is visible higher up in the east wall. A second gable line is higher still, with limestone copings cutting across the Norman belfry window.

Plate XCII. Bawsey, St James, looking east. The triangular-headed opening above the chancel arch led into the roof-space above the chancel vault.

Most of the south wall of the tower has collapsed. At the surviving south-east corner, most of the quoins have been robbed; some of the remaining ones are laid upright-and-flat.

By contrast, the north wall survives almost complete. The north-east quoins are mostly robbed, but some are upright-and-flat. The north-west corner has most of its quoins intact; these are all upright-and-flat at first floor-level, but side-alternate above. At ground-floor level, the north wall has a single-splayed window, round-headed, with limestone edgings. Above it is another round-headed window, single-splayed, with limestone outer edgings but rubble inner ones.

Only the northern half of the tower west wall survives above the ground-floor arch. The tower arch is more sumptuous than the chancel arch (Pl. XCIII). On the east face it has single nook-shafts with scallop capitals, chamfered imposts with double quirks, and an arch roll-moulding. The west face has two orders, each with its own nook-shaft, scallop capitals (only one surviving), the inner order with bold chevron decoration, the outer with double roll-moulding. Where masonry survives, the gable-line of the nave roof is visible.

Fragments of all four belfry windows survive. Only one jamb of both south and west belfry windows remain. North and east windows have both jambs, but the arch

Plate XCIII. Bawsey, St James, tower arch looking east, with chancel arch beyond; tower arch shafts, with scallop capitals and arch with chevron decoration.

Plate XCV. Bawsey, St James, tower from south *c.* 1900, showing north belfry opening intact. BB88/1817 copyright Royal Commission on Historical Monuments (England).

Plate XCIV. Bawsey, St James, tower from the south, showing belfry openings.

heads have collapsed (Pl. XCIV). All have limestone edgings to outer and inner arch faces. The form of the belfry windows can best be reconstructed from the surviving details of the south one. The outer arch has a nook shaft and cushion capital. This originally framed two smaller openings supported by a mid-wall shaft, as the photograph of *c.* 1900 shows (Pl. XCV).

Nave. The nave is slightly wider than the tower (about 0.5m either side). There are no surviving windows. The masonry is mainly carstone rubble, with some puddingstone, and more flint used higher up.

There is a large brick and rubble buttress with two set-offs at the junction of the nave south wall and the tower. Towards the west end of the wall there is a doorway. A cushion capital of the east jamb is all the decoration that remains, apart from the chamfered impost (with quirk). Within the jamb is a draw-bar hole over 1m deep.

A gap in the north wall opposite suggests a door here originally. There is a buttress, made of medieval brick, at the junction of the nave wall and the tower.

The nave west wall has no doorway. The western corners have been reinforced with large diagonal buttresses, faced in limestone, with two set-offs.

Interpretation and Dating

There are only two phases. The original church consisted of apsidal chancel (vaulted), central tower and nave with south doorway. At a later date, the nave was reinforced with buttresses and a new larger chancel built; this phase is medieval, probably 14th or 15th-century.

Most of the surviving fabric, the first phase, is mature Norman work, say *c*.1120. Some writers have claimed a pre-Conquest date for the church on account of certain 'Saxon' details, probably the long-and-short quoins of the first floor of the tower and the triangular-headed doorway above the chancel arch. If true, this means that the Normans erased every Saxon feature, replacing windows doorways *etc.*, but oddly omitting the first floor of the tower, which thus remains 'Saxon'; or, more, ludicrously, the ground-floor of the tower was built by Normans, the first-floor by Saxons, the belfry by Normans again. These are unlikely theses. It seems safer to assume that post-Conquest Romanesque architecture retained the use of long-and-short quoins and triangular headed doorways, part of a wide repertoire of techniques.

Ladbrooke's drawing of *c*.1831 reveals some details which no longer survive. The south wall of the tower appears to have had a large opening, no doubt leading to a chapel or transept. Above the west arch of the tower were two round-headed openings, wall-piercings reminiscent of the Norman church at Melton Constable.

Causes of Abandonment

The village of Bawsey was destroyed by enclosures as early as 1517. By the 17th century, the church was beginning to deteriorate. The 1679 Visitation records the tower being out of repair (NRO, ANW/4/51). It seems that the church struggled on until the later 18th century. Baptisms are recorded up to 1771, burials to 1773. By the early 19th century, the church was a roofless ruin, isolated as it is today.

Condition

The church is a roofless ruin, standing in a rough mound of nettles and elder. The walls look rather unsafe, especially with large cracks in the tower.

Churchyard

It is impossible to discern the extent of the churchyard. There are no monuments or boundaries, just a rough mound on which the church stands, surrounded by ploughed land.

Archaeological Record

The original apsidal chancel was excavated in 1930 (*Ant.J.*, 1931, 11, 169).

A late Saxon grave slab with interlace was found in 1960 on the north side of the church, now in Lynn Museum (*Med.Arch.*5, 1961, 309); a small fragment of a similar one was found 10 years before.

In the vicinity of the church, two Iron Age electrum torcs were found, along with Iron Age and Ipswich Ware pottery.

Evidence of the Late Saxon and medieval village surrounding the church is represented by finds of sherds within 100m of the church, to north and south-west.

The octagonal font is in the orchard next to Church Farm, 400m to south, and is used as a flowerpot. The front doorway of Church Farm is a reused Norman one, presumably from the church.

Archaeological and Architectural Assessment

Bawsey church is one of the more important of the county's ruins. It remains a solitary remnant of a deserted village. It is a landmark, one of the most impressive examples of the Norman parish church in the county, with an unusually large central tower. There are still some good architectural details surviving in the arches of the tower.

The extent of the churchyard and adjoining village is not known.

Further References

Allison, 1955, 143.
Antiq. J. 1931, II, 169.
Blomefield, 1805-10, VIII, 340.
Cox, 1911, II, 134.
Med. Arch. 5, 1961, 309.
Messent, 1931, 13.
Pevsner, 1962, b, 84.

II. Mintlyn, St Michael

Identification TF 6571 1928. *County No.*3410.
Diocese: Norwich. *Archdeaconry*: Lynn. Deanery: Lynn.
Parish: Gaywood with Bawsey and Mintlyn. *Status*: parish church, now disused and ruined. *Date last in regular use*: *c.* 1700.
Ownership and access: private.

Location and Setting

The site of the deserted village of Mintlyn is located 4km east of the centre of King's Lynn, and just east of the A149 by-pass. The name survives in 'Mintlyn Farm' (demolished), 'Mintlyn Wood', and since 1981 in 'Mintlyn Crematorium'; but apart from one or two houses and farm buildings, Mintlyn no longer exists as a parish, village or even a hamlet. The old Mintlyn woods have been extended since the First World War with conifer plantations and some natural woodland. The eastern part of this land is destined to be quarried for the extraction of its fine Sandringham sand, excellent for glass-making. The remains of Mintlyn Church are on private land at the western edge of the wood, some 800m south of the B1145 Lynn to Bawdeswell road. It is on one of the highest points in the area, overlooking Lynn and the flat marshlands to west. The ruins, enclosed within an overgrown rectangular churchyard, stand at the corner of an arable field. Just 50m to south is the track of the dismantled Lynn to Fakenham railway (later Midland and Great Northern).

Architectural Description

Almost nothing survives of the chancel, there are fragmentary remains of the nave, and faint indications of a south porch.

Chancel. Clearance of the site might help to reveal the outline of the chancel, but dense undergrowth made it impossible to follow any mounds that may have provided its plan. A minute spur of wall, attached to the nave east wall, indicates the position of the chancel south wall. It appears that the chancel wall was demolished and the resulting scar mended with bricks. The bricks are late medieval in type, with a surprising variation in hue: yellow, orange, red or dark brown. The line of the chancel south wall is suggested by several pieces of limestone projecting east from the brickwork. The limestone pieces are all re-used, and the whole gives the appearance of an intention to continue the wall to east, an option that was evidently not taken up. In other words, it looks as if the chancel was demolished, its wall-scars tidied up to provide an option for rebuilding another chancel there at a later date.

Nave. The south-east corner is, apart from the west end, the only area to retain any standing masonry. This corner is constructed almost entirely of medieval brick, of the same type as described above. A wide buttress, at right-angles to the south wall, continues south of the corner in the same brickwork; the upper part of the buttress has quoins of small limestone blocks. West of the buttress there is a reveal with an externally splayed surface beyond, looking like a reversed window; the brickwork must incorporate the blocking of a splayed window towards the end of the nave south wall.

There is a curious feature on the inside face of the wall, about 30cm from the south-east corner. A vertical slot, square in section (about 10cm x 10cm) is set into the brick masonry; it seems that the bricks have been constructed around a vertical timber (now gone). The purpose of the timber is a mystery: perhaps a support for a rood-loft? Near the ground, and apparently below the timber slot, there is a broken stone niche, possibly a piscina originally.

From the south-east corner, the brick east wall of the nave extends north by 25cm, where it forms a straight north face, perhaps a respond. Separated by a crack, another stretch of wall (in identical brick masonry) blocks at least part of the chancel arch, if indeed the above-mentioned respond formed a chancel arch. This blocking extends north for 1m, but has collapsed beyond this; it may have formed a complete east wall to the nave.

Most of the nave south wall consists of a high mound, of fallen rubble, some 2m higher than the present 'floor' of the nave. The mound is greatly overgrown, but odd pieces of squared or moulded limestone are still visible in places. Fortunately, the western 2m of wall survive to full height. The masonry consists of blocks of brown conglomerate, of ranging size, interspersed with occasional pieces of flint, reused limestone and iron smelting slag. The top three or four courses are of brick. Only the west jamb of a window survives, part of the sill and lower courses of chamfered limestone remaining in place. Chamfered limestone also lines the rear-arch jambs.

Similarly, only the western 1.5m of the nave north wall survives. Again, the west jamb of a window is still in place. East of this point, however, the wall has collapsed and forms a mould of rubble, including some squared limestone.

By contrast, the nave west wall stands virtually to full height. Its masonry is of roughly squared conglomerate blocks, interspersed with flint, smelting slag and some reused limestone. There are also occasional pieces of tile, either from roof or floor. Several putlog holes are evident, lined in medieval brick. At the corners, the quoins are of large, smoothly-cut blocks of limestone. In the middle of the wall there is a large Perpendicular window with depressed two-centred head. Only the uppermost jambs and the arch-head, in limestone, remain. However, the broken-off tracery indicates a two-light window with cusped eyelet. The hood-mould is of chamfered brick. Most of the limestone jambs of the rear-arch are in place, along with its pointed segmented head (in chamfered brick). Curved mouldings in these jambs show that many of the stones are reused. The sill of the window has broken away, and now provides an entrance into the ruins. Above the window, most of the gable is

Plate XCVI. Mintlyn, St Michael, south doorway and south porch looking north, *c.* 1935. A pile of rubble is all that remains today. B37/609 copyright Royal Commission on Historical Monuments (England).

built of late medieval brick, with the gable-line of the roof quite discernible.

South Porch. Low rubble mounds, extending a surprisingly long way south from the nave south wall, indicate the position of the south porch. There are many scattered fragments of limestone on the ground, including the chamfered responds of (presumably) the outer doorway of the porch. The carved Perpendicular base of one of the responds was lying on its side, *ex situ*, when visited. Much of the floor space was taken up with a large trapezoid stone coffin lid, broken off at one end, bearing a raised design (possibly a cross).

Interpretation and Dating
(Pls XCVI-III)
The standing remains indicate two phases of construction. Firstly, the nave (and possibly south porch) was built, in conglomerate masonry with limestone quoins and window jambs. The form of the west window, with its depressed two-centred head and brick hood-mould, suggests a late 15th-century date. This church evidently replaced an earlier one, as witness the pieces of re-used limestone incorporated into the walls.

There was a church here in the first half of the 12th century: an arch of this date formed the south doorway and was still in place some sixty years ago (Pl. XCVI). In view of the lack of surviving fabric today, it is uncertain whether the masonry which surrounded this arch belonged to the 12th century, or whether the doorway was re-set in the 15th-century masonry of the west end of the nave, which is all that survives today. When depicted by Cotman in 1838 (Pl. XCVII) the arch, with its cushion

Plate XCVII. Mintlyn, St Michael, by Cotman (1838), showing the south doorway of the already ruined church.

Plate XCVIII. Mintlyn, St Michael: part of tympanum and chevron voussoir of south doorway (*cf.* Pl.XCVI and XCVII), deposited in King's Lynn Museum in 1984.

capitals and chevron moulding, contained a carved tympanum; part of this was found lying on the ground by the author (Pl. XCVIII), and was deposited in the King's Lynn Museum in 1984.

A further reconstruction took place later, probably during the 16th century. The south-east corner of the nave was rebuilt in brick, blocking a window towards the east end of the south wall. It seems that a rebuilding of the chancel was projected, but probably not carried out. This change of plan is suggested by the fact that the chancel arch must have been blocked very soon after the construction of chancel arch responds, and that the projected chancel south wall has been sealed with brick of identical type to the responds. It is not certain whether the brick gable of the nave west wall belongs to this (16th-century phase) or the late 15th-century phase.

Causes of Abandonment
If the interpretation given above is correct, then the chancel was bricked off and abandoned from the 16th century. The 17th century saw a period of further decline. In 1603 the church was served by a curate, with only fourteen communicants (Jessopp 1888, 29). By the later 17th century, the church fabric was evidently in decay. The Visitations record a steady deterioration: 'The roof wants tiling of ye church' in 1673 (NRO ANW/4/29); and in 1682 'The bell is riven ye clapper of it broken & ye rope wanting' in 1679 (NRO ANW/4/51); 'There is noe font but they make use of a bason to baptize with. The church is very much darkened by reason of the elder & ivy grow there & hinder the light & the ivy grow through the roofe into the church.' (NRO ANW/4/57). The church must have been abandoned not long after this last entry.

Of the village of Mintlyn, a map of 1690 shows about five cottages near the site of Mintlyn Farm, 600m to west. Perhaps the proximity of King's Lynn (4km to west) is partly responsible for the depopulation of Mintlyn, Bawsey and Leziate.

Condition
(Pl. XCIX)
Most of the walls are now mounds of rubble. The surviving masonry at the west end of the nave is in surprisingly good condition, but the tops of the walls are loose in places. The interior is overgrown, with pieces of worked stone and rubble lying around.

Although in decline for a long time, there has been a considerable deterioration this century: the photograph taken *c.* 1920 (Pl. XCIX) shows not only the 12th-century south doorway surviving, but also the south wall of the porch; the wall has now gone, and fragments of the porch doorway lie scattered on the ground.

Churchyard
Unlike neighbouring Bawsey, the churchyard has not been encroached by neighbouring fields. Hedgerows still line the rectangular boundary. There are no visible churchyard monuments; the whole is overgrown with bracken, nettles and elder.

Archaeological Record
Traces of at least three iron bloomeries in field north of church, with remains, of ore, slag and 2nd-century Roman pottery; medieval sherds in same field. Some smelting slag built into church.

South of the churchyard, finds of two fragments of hypocaust tile, one samian ware sherd and several Roman coarse ware sherds.

Plain limestone circular bowl of font lay inside church in 1981, now (1984) used as flowerpot at Whitehouse Farm (600m south-west).

Norman tympanum (western half) and one voussoir of chevron moulding found on ground inside church and removed to King's Lynn Museum, 1984.

Medieval stone coffin in south porch.

Archaeological and Architectural Assessment
Below the present remains, there is an early 12th-century church, some of whose materials were incorporated into

Plate XCIX. Mintlyn, St Michael: view from the south, c. 1935; the porch and south doorway have since collapsed. B37/608 copyright Royal Commission on Historical Monuments (England).

the 15th-century rebuilding. Nothing is yet known of the form of the chancel.

Much more of the 15th-century masonry is probably standing beneath the rubble of collapsed upper walls. A mass of squared and moulded freestone lies scattered around the ruins. The church appears to be little altered since the 17th century.

The site of the deserted village (mentioned in *Domesday*) is not known precisely.

Further References
Cox, 1911, II, 146.
Jessop, 1888, 29.
Messent 1931, 26.
Pevsner 1962, b, 84.

III. West Raynham, St Margaret

Identification TF 8724 2542. *County No.*2380.
Diocese: Norwich. *Archdeaconry:* Lynn. *Deanery*: Brisley and Elmham. *Parish*: East Raynham St Mary with West Raynham St Margaret. *Status*: parish church, now disused and ruined. *Date last in regular use*: 1733.
Ownership and access: Diocese of Norwich.

Location and Setting
Of the three Raynhams (East, West and South), West Raynham is the most populous. Yet East and South Raynham both retain their churches, while St Margaret's stands in ruins. The Raynhams are a group of villages along the Upper Wensum valley, 6km south-west of Fakenham. East Raynham is noted for its Hall, begun in 1638 in the Inigo Jones style. Close to the Wensum, East Raynham church stands in the grounds of the Hall, isolated but well looked after. On the other side of the river, a mere 600m to west, lies the village of West Raynham. The ruined church is at the north end of the village, next to a public house. A gate leads into the churchyard, a bit overgrown but still in use until recently, and the ivy-clad remains of St Margaret's can be found at its northern edge.

Architectural Description
(Fig. 32; Pls C, CI)
The remains indicate that the church consisted of chancel, north chapel, nave, north aisle and west tower (Fig.32). Most of the masonry is of mortared flint.

Chancel and North Chapel. The east wall has collapsed, leaving no trace of a window. Both corners had clasping buttresses, set back from the corners; the internal and external corners of the buttresses are lined with late medieval brick. The buttress of the north-east corner is leaning and collapse appears likely. There are many mounds of fallen masonry.

The eastern part of the south wall does not survive above the heaps of fallen rubble, but the rest stands to full height (about 6m). It begins by a collapsed window whose western reveal is still intact along with the springing of the window arch; the limestone outer jamb is still in place, whose original reveal is marked by a refacing of the internal wall surface with 16th-century brick. Better preserved is the priest-door to west, with chamfered stone jambs and hollow-chamfered hood-mould springing from foliate carved corbels. The rear-arch has a segmental head, and there is a small draw-bar hole next to the western jamb.

West of the priest's door, one finds a complexity of building phases. There is a tall, narrow window opening whose interior face has been lined with 16th-century

Plate C.   West Raynham church by Ladbrooke (*c.* 1838). The north arcade can be glimpsed through gaps in the nave south wall.

brickwork; the window jambs have been robbed. Immediately west of this there is a fill of flint masonry, wedge-shaped in plan, which joins chancel to nave. This blocking appears to fill an earlier window opening whose plaster-lined western reveal can be made out behind the blocking. On the inside, the blocking is terminated to north by a respond whose limestone lowest course still exists, a half-octagon with two quirks on a plain chamfered base; (this suggests that it supported a double-chamfered chancel arch). The window west of the priest-door was therefore wider originally, but has been partly filled to accommodate a new chancel arch.

Only very low fragments of the chancel north wall survive. Most of it was presumably knocked through when a north chapel was added, in line with the north aisle. Again, there are only fragmentary remains of the flint north wall of this chapel, and its eastern termination cannot be defined with certainty.

Nave. The internal angle of the nave south-east corner is occupied by a projecting polygonal base, in stone, for supporting a pulpit. Resting on this, in the angle of the corner, is an octagonal stone respond with moulded base and capital of Decorated type; it is possibly *ex situ*, and no doubt was used to provide the support for an outer order to the chancel arch. On its west side is a plastered respond, in chamfered medieval brick, supporting a wall arch going west. Within the wall arch there are remains of a window; only the stone east jamb remains in place, with sunken quadrant moulding. Fragments of tracery lying on the ground bear the same sunken quadrant moulding; none of the pieces have any cusping, and it would appear to be possible to reconstruct a Decorated window with intersecting tracery. Looking at the west reveal of the window, it can be seen that the nave wall has been thickened by the addition of the wall arch, and that the west respond of this arch protrudes slightly into the window splay.

There are no further wall arches, but the rest of the nave wall seems to have been thickened on the inner face; the coursing of the flint masonry on this side is conspicuously poor. On the outside, there is a buttress mid-way along the wall, with all edgings gone. A second window pierced the wall west of the buttress; fragments of tracery survive in the arch-head, with characteristic sunken quadrant mouldings. It looks as if it was a two-light window with Y-tracery. Collapse of the masonry west of here has meant that the form of the nave south-west corner cannot be determined.

North Aisle. The north arcade has entirely gone, apart from the springing of the westernmost arch, visible in the west wall of the aisle; it can be seen that the limestone arches were double-chamfered. Piers and arches were still in place in the 1830s (Pl. C), but none remain so today. However, remains of a pier can still be seen, lying on the ground near the west end of the church (Pl. CI). It had octagonal stone drums, and Decorated moulded capital and base. The stone of the capital has been hollowed out, and a hole drilled through it to suggest a piece was converted to use as a font; remains of a brick soakaway in the floor of the church nearby tend to confirm this.

Not much of the aisle north wall survives; in places it stands to a height of 3.5m. The only remnant of a window is that at its junction with the north chapel, and is merely the eastern splayed reveal. Two unevenly spaced buttresses support the north wall, both with robbed edgings. The north-west corner apparently had limestone quoins, but those too have gone. More of the west wall survives, with neat masonry of knapped flint interspersed with occasional bricks.

Tower. Only the north wall and part of the west wall are still standing. The masonry is of knapped flint with occasional bricks, as in the west wall of the aisle. It appears that the tower itself was pierced with doorways, although of course only the north one survives. This pointed doorway retains its limestone jambs, with a continuous chamfer on its outer face, with a convex and concave moulded outer order, surrounded by a hood-mould. On the inside, the rear-arch is higher and has a pointed segmental head. Whilst the tower north wall must stand to almost full height, its mantle of ivy obscures any openings higher up.

Plate CI.   West Raynham, St Margaret: interior looking north-west, showing springing of west arch of north arcade.

WEST RAYNHAM

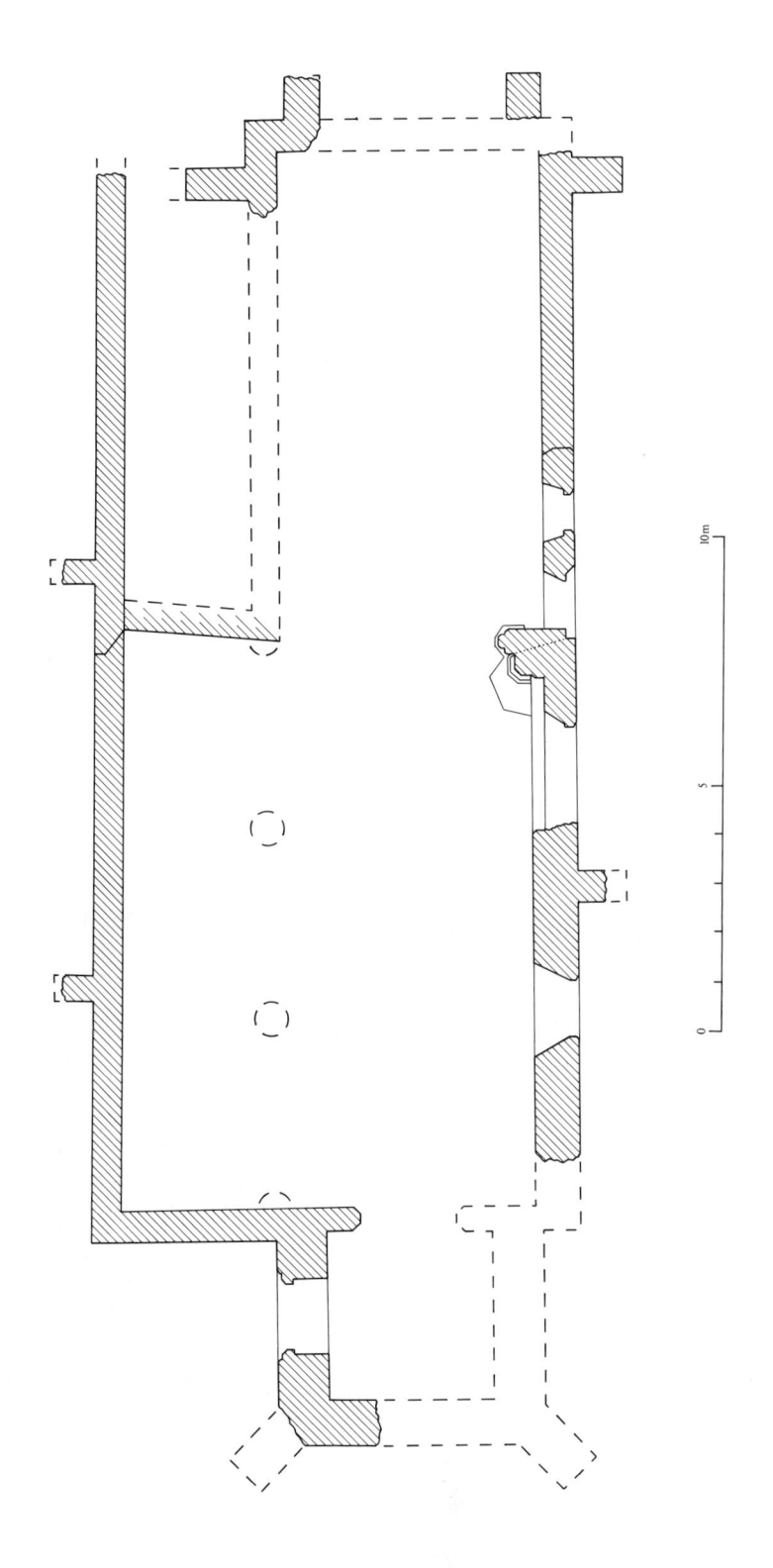

Figure 32. West Raynham, St Margaret: plan. Scale 1:150.

WEST RAYNHAM

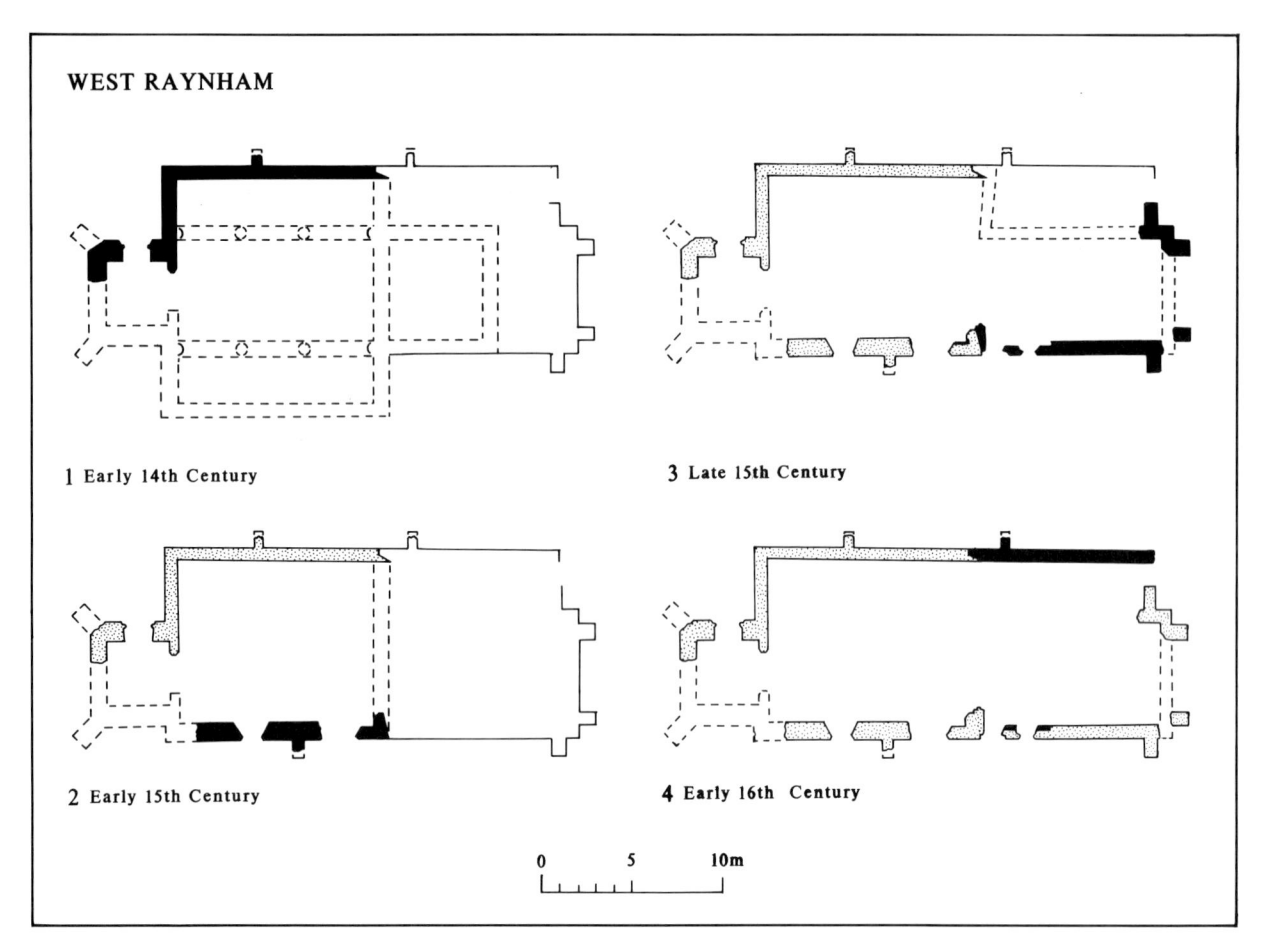

1 Early 14th Century

2 Early 15th Century

3 Late 15th Century

4 Early 16th Century

0 5 10m

Figure 33. West Raynham, St Margaret: phase plan. Scale 1:400.

It looks as if it had a diagonal buttress at the corner, but only a broken-off scar of masonry remains today.

Interpretation and Dating
(Fig.33)
This is a frustratingly difficult building to interpret. It has undergone many alterations and much destruction; and those walls which survive are largely obscured by encompassing vegetation. The following interpretation must therefore be regarded as somewhat tentative.

The earliest features consist of the nave windows and the aisle piers, all clearly Decorated in style. One of the nave windows appears to have been of two-light Y-tracery, the other of three-light intersecting tracery, suggesting a date of c.1310. It is possible that the tower and the aisle walls belong to this phase too. None of the piers remain in place, but it is likely that the arcade possessed three bays.

Several factors indicate that there was originally a south aisle too. Firstly, the masonry of the nave south wall (external surface) is not as neat as tower or aisle wall, and does not use such carefully cut flints interspersed with brick. Secondly, the two windows in the south wall do not represent a balanced composition: one two-light window, and a larger three-light window. Thirdly, some extra piers need to be accounted for. It seems that a pier was converted to use as a font (see above); this must have taken place before the church went out of use, and therefore before the north arcade had gone (it was still standing in the 1820s). If the pier, reused as a font, cannot have come from the north arcade, where did it come from? Another pier seems to have been built into the south-east corner of the nave, perhaps to be used as a respond; the same question applies. If, however, the existence of a south aisle is accepted, then these questions are easily answered. Lastly, a south aisle would eliminate the curious asymmetry of the church; clearly, it is not unusual for a single aisle to be added to a pre-existing nave, but it would be rarer to find nave, tower and single aisle to be planned as such from the outset.

These factors argue in favour of a church with nave, two aisles and west tower, built around 1310. It would seem that the south aisle disappeared at a relatively early stage, certainly before the end of the 15th century (see below). Perhaps this occurred early in the 15th century; two of the south aisle windows would then have been built into the new south wall of the nave; and the two redundant piers could also be reused, one as a font, the other as a respond. Perhaps the new south wall was badly built; it needed strengthening at the end of the 15th century by thickening the masonry and providing a brick wall arch around the eastern window of the nave. The chancel was probably rebuilt, or at least its east end remodelled, at about the same time.

A final phase appears to have involved the rebuilding of the chancel arch (partly blocking one of the chancel windows.) This probably took place in the early 16th century. A north chapel may have been added to the chancel around this time.

Causes of Abandonment
St Margaret's remained in use up to the early 18th century. Parkin records that it had a nave and north aisle covered with lead, and a chancel roofed with tiles; it also

had a painted rood-screen (Blomefield, 1805-10, VII, 150). By the end of the 17th century, it was beginning to need some major repairs, and was becoming expensive to keep up. In 1681, the churchwardens asked if they could take down part of the north aisle and sell the lead to finance necessary repairs (NRO, ANW/4/54). In 1733, they petitioned for the sale of two of the three bells to enable them to repair the tower 'which otherwise may fall' (NRO, FCB/1, 624). Whether or not permission was granted, the parishioners evidently felt safer going to St Mary's church at East Raynham (only 600m away) and St Margaret's was abandoned from that time. The 1765 Faculty records that St Mary's had been refurnished about 30 years ago, and that parishioners from both St Margaret's and St Mary's had pews there:

> 'from that time service has been discontinued in the church of Rainham St Margaret which being now in a ruinous condition and the Church of Rainham St Mary wanting much repair in lead and wood work you the said petitioners desire our License or faculty for applying the materials of the said ruinous Church towards repairing the church of Rainham St Mary.' (NRO, FCB/3, 4, 6).

The two parishes had already been consolidated in 1723. (NRO, FCB/1, 566).

Condition
The tower had already mostly fallen by the time Ladbrooke sketched it in the 1830s. Since then, the north arcade has collapsed, and the eastern part of the chancel has gone. The remaining walls do not seem too stable, and further encumbered by a mass of ivy. The interior is overgrown with nettles and elder.

Churchyard
The rectangular churchyard has remained in use until recently. The church stands at its northern edge. A flint wall, in good condition, forms the boundary to west and south, the rest is fenced, and the entrance is through a wooden gate at the south-west corner. There are some 18th-century head-stones near the church and some 19th-century monuments surrounded with iron railings. Most of the churchyard has been kept from becoming a wilderness. The latest grave dates from 1922.

Archaeological Record
Within the church, and just outside it, there are many pieces of brick, chamfered and plain, and worked limestone from windows, chancel arch *etc*. Two ledger slabs remain in the north aisle, Peter Stringer (d. 1662) and Jamima Hensby (d. 1744).

The field east of the church contains some low earthworks. Post-medieval material was ploughed up 300m to north. 400m north-east is the site of Raynham Old Hall.

Archaeological and Architectural Assessment
The church built in the 1320s was splendid in scale and execution. Its subsequent history is complex, consisting mainly of alterations and repairs. Many features, such as windows, could be reconstructed from collapsed remains. Excavation could reveal a great deal, and help to decipher its complicated building history. The site does not seem to have been interfered with much since its abandonment.

Further References
Blomefield, 1805-10, VII, 150.
Bryant, 1900, 97.
Cox, 1911, I, 201.
Messent, 1931, 30.
Pevsner, 1962 b, 377.

IV. Saxlingham Thorpe, St Mary

Identification TM 2308 9660. *County No.*10115.
Diocese: Norwich. *Archdeaconry:* Norfolk. *Deanery*: Depwade. *Parish*: Saxlingham Nethergate with Saxlingham Thorpe. *Status*: parish church, now disused and ruined.
*Date last in regular use: c.*1640.
Ownership and access: access public footpath, ownership uncertain (presumed diocese of Norwich).

Location and Setting
The attractive village of Saxlingham Nethergate lies 1.5km east of the A140, 10km south of Norwich. From the River Tas, which forms its western boundary, the parish spans 5km to Saxlingham Green. The ruined church of Saxlingham Thorpe is located between the settlements of Saxlingham Green and Nethergate. At a sharp bend in the Hempnall road, just 500m south of Saxlingham Nethergate church, an unmettalled track leads west towards a small wood, reached after 300m. Within the western part of the wood stands the remains of St Mary's church.

Architectural Description
(Fig. 34; Pls CII, CIII)
The church consists of chancel, nave and west tower (Fig.34). Some of the walls stand to full height, but there are many gaps. The masonry is mainly coursed flint.

Chancel. The very wide east window has collapsed, leaving two flanking pillars of masonry. The smooth splay of the window finishes 60cm from the ground, forming a sill. Only fragments of masonry survive of the wall below the window. The walls are built of mortared flint, but the quoins at the east corner (presumably freestone originally) have all been robbed. There are occasional pieces of smooth brown boulder; erractics such as these are plentiful in neighbouring fields.

The chancel south wall has two big gaps caused by collapsed windows. There is a small rectangular recess at the east side of the eastern opening, suggesting a piscina. On the west side of the opening the window splay can be made out. The flint masonry west of this opening is more neatly coursed than that east of it. In the masonry west of this opening, a (large) opening blocked with flint can be distinguished. It is difficult to make out the form of the window; it may be round-headed or gently pointed. From the outside, the window blocking has been rendered, but it can be seen that the window's external form is tall and narrow. To west, another gap represents a collapsed window; the jambs of this window descended to form a sill sedilia.

The change of masonry noted above is even more evident in the north wall. The eastern third has dense and less clearly coursed masonry, largely covered with external rendering; the masonry of the western part has larger mortar beds giving clearer courses. Separating the two masonry types is a vertical column of large flints, evidently forming the north-east corner of the original chancel. East of this break, near the north-east corner of the present chancel, the wall is punctured near the

SAXLINGHAM THORPE

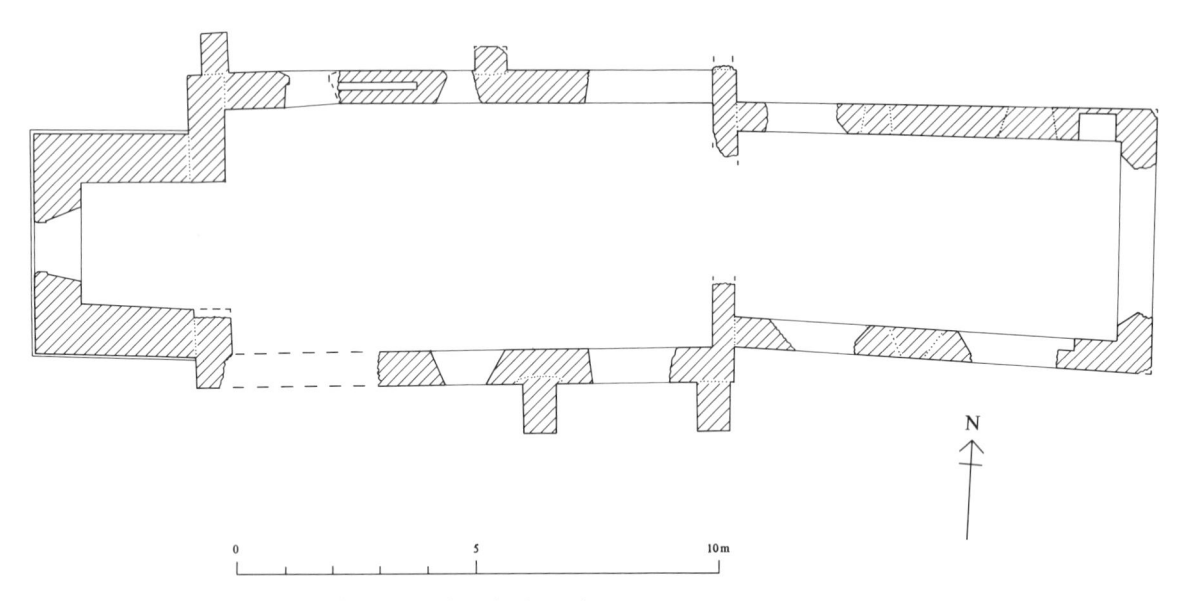

Figure 34. Saxlingham Thorpe, St Mary: plan. Scale 1:150.

ground by a hole some 70cm high; on close inspection it can be seen that this is a rectangular recess (probably an aumbry) whose external wall has collapsed. A limestone corbel, perhaps reused, can be seen high up in the wall near the north-east corner. West of the aumbry, the east and west splays of a window, now blocked with flint, can just be made out. A hole in the wall further west appears to be the result of masonry collapse, and does not represent the site of a door or other feature.

Slightly further west, and higher up, a flint-blocked round-headed window can be seen (Pl. CII). Some of the blocking has come away to reveal the plastered inner splay of the window; the head of the arch is constructed of radially-laid flints. On the outside, enough of the outline of the window can be discerned to show that it has a single splay. Further west, a large window has collapsed, leaving a shallow splay on one side.

Both north and south walls of the chancel terminate with a clean western face, with larger flints and erratics strengthening the corners. The chancel clearly butts onto an earlier nave. There is no sign of a chancel arch, but a profusion of 15th-century bricks on the ground around here might have belonged to such an arch.

Nave. The nave east wall is only 70cm high (*i.e.* above present ground-level) at the point where it adjoins the north and south walls of the chancel, and disappears completely in the middle where one would expect a chancel arch. Continuing to the south-east corner, there are quoins of large flints and boulder erratics. The rest of the wall is built of medium-sized flints in fairly neat courses. At the north-east corner the nave wall has collapsed completely.

Next to the south-east corner is a buttress, going south. It survives to a height of 1.2m. It has been added to the nave, since there is a large crack separating it, and it is of entirely different masonry: knapped flint with galleting, and large medieval bricks. An opening is all that remains of a window just west of the buttress; its western splay is quite clear, that to east somewhat fainter. Then

Plate CII. Saxlingham Thorpe, St Mary: chancel north wall, internal splay of a (blocked) single-splayed round-headed window.

the nave south wall continues for a short stretch at what must be nearly full height (over 4m). There is another buttress at this point, an addition to the wall but actually built into it, necessitating a certain amount of rebuilding of the nave wall where the buttress joins it; the buttress is built of flint (unknapped) and medieval brick, with occasional pieces of reused limestone. Brick and flint blocking the inner nave wall near the buttress may indicate the presence of a small window. West of the buttress there is another collapsed window, leaving no trace but its splay; then a large beech tree occupies the site of the wall.

Only low fragments survive of the easternmost 2m of the nave north wall. Collapsed rubble suggests the site of a buttress matching the one on the south wall. The western splay of a window also reflects a certain symmetry with the south wall. From there to its western corner the north wall proceeds at almost full height, with occasional putlog holes visible. Half-way along there is a brick and flint buttress with robbed external corners. Immediately west of the buttress is a full window opening, lined in medieval brick and flint, but its precise outline has been lost.

Near the west end is the north doorway, the most complete feature of the church. The west jamb of the doorway is intact, constructed of deep-red medieval brick, as is part of the arch above; the arch uses moulded brick in the form of a quadrant chamfer, with a similar hood-mould above. The brick lining has gone from the eastern side of the doorway, but the large draw-bar hole survives. Below ground, the wooden door-sill survives, giving the doorway a height of 1.8m. Above the doorway the wall is of different construction to that of the nave, clearly rebuilt along with the doorway using flint and deep-red brick. However, the last 1.5m of north wall belongs to the original nave. Near the doorway is an angled niche which may have supported a roof-timber.

The quoins of the north-west corner are constructed of large flints. North from the corner is an added buttress of brick and knapped flint, similar to that at the nave south-east corner. Fragments of the nave west wall survive, to which the west tower has been abutted. Nothing above ground remains of the nave south-west corner.

Tower. (Pl. CIII) It is clear that the west tower smoothly abuts the nave west wall. Most of the latter wall has collapsed, removing any tower arch with it. There is therefore no east face to the tower, which must have rested upon the pre-existing nave west wall. Apart from the loss of this wall, most of the rest of the tower stands to full height. Owing to ivy on the outside and heavy rendering on the inside, it is difficult to make out materials and features. However, it can be seen that it is built of mortared flint with medieval bricks of a pale hue forming quoins and edgings.

There is an external base course at ground level, simply capped in brick. The rear-arch of the west window is lined in brick, a pointed arch. Surviving window jambs are of chamfered brick, suggesting the tracery (now gone) was brick too. Higher up, an internal set-off leads to the middle storey, pierced by a small brick-lined rectangular opening in the west face. Most of the belfry stage is intact (apart from the east-face), but no details are visible beneath luxuriant ivy. Ladbrooke's drawing shows the thick tracery of a two-light window with quatrefoil head; from its crudeness the tracery would appear to be of brick.

Plate CIII. Saxlingham Thorpe, St Mary: interior looking west.

Interpretation and Dating
(Fig.35)

The masonry of nave and western part of the chancel are very similar in appearance, and may therefore be reasonably close in date. However, it is evident that nave pre-dates chancel; the latter cleanly abuts the nave east wall. Unfortunately there are no original features such as windows or doors by which we may date the nave; but the rubble quoins and large mortar courses are characteristic of 11th and 12th-century work. Although the nave east wall has a gap in the middle (for chancel arch) there is no sign of broken-off masonry on its east face to receive a contemporary chancel.

There are three possible interpretations: either a chancel belonging to Phase 1 was very narrow, and so its abutment with the nave has not survived a later widening of the chancel arch; or the church was a single cell with no chancel; or thirdly, a masonry nave was added to a wooden chancel which would not have marked the nave east wall. A single-cell church would have been unusual, if not unheard of, in the 11th or 12th century. One may happily contemplate a small wooden structure extended by a masonry nave which retained the wooden church as a chancel, but the grounds for this conjecture are purely circumstantial.

Whatever the form of (or absence of) chancel in Phase 1, it was soon found necessary to build a new one in solid flint and mortar. The masonry of this, Phase 2, is not very different from that employed in the nave, and the rubble quoins are similar too (only north-east ones visible). A further feature survives from this phase, namely the window (now blocked) in the chancel north wall. This is of round-headed, single-splayed form with rubble head of which there are innumerable examples

SAXLINGHAM THORPE

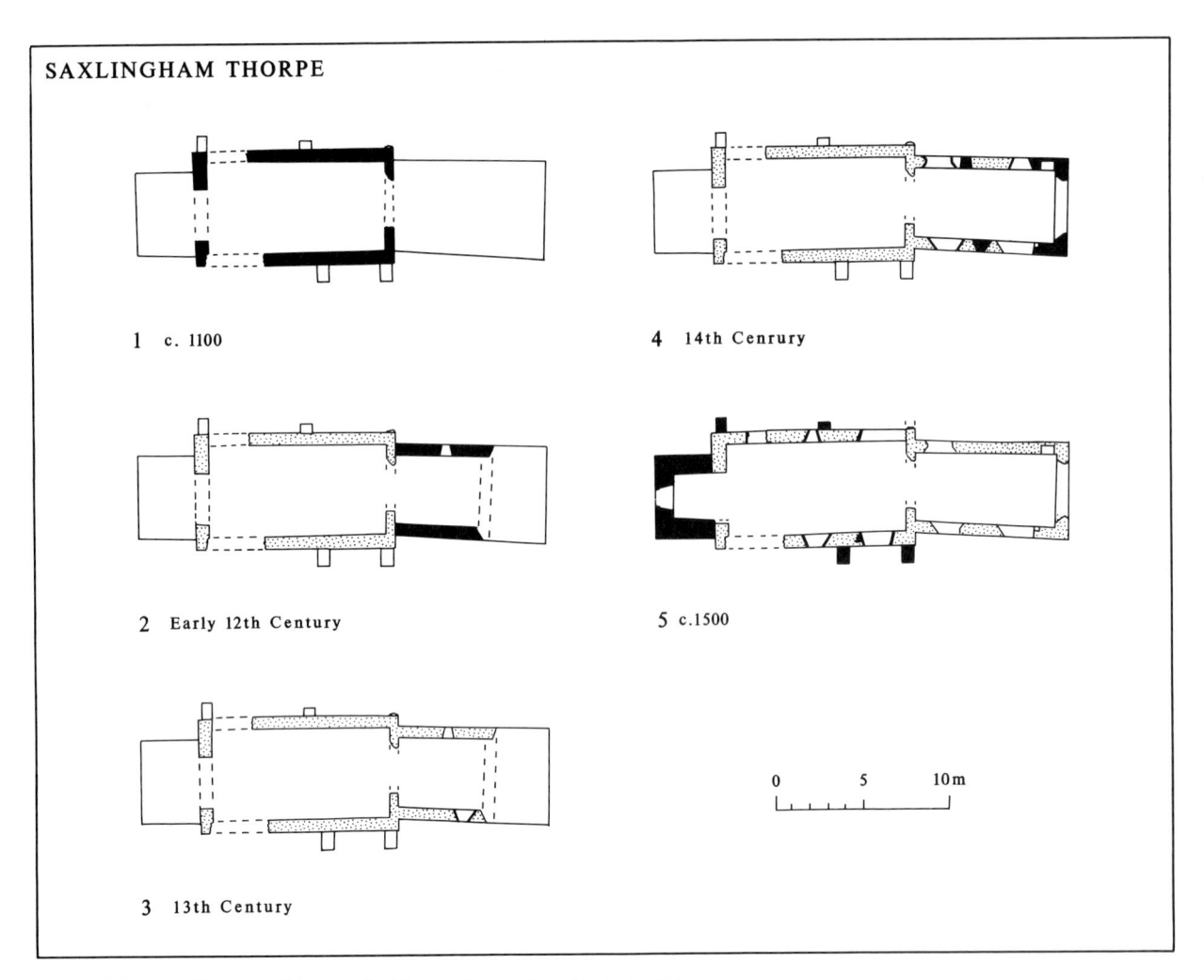

1 c. 1100

2 Early 12th Century

3 13th Century

4 14th Cenrury

5 c.1500

0   5   10m

Figure 35. Saxlingham Thorpe, St Mary: phase plan. Scale 1:400.

from c.1050 to c.1150. Thus Phase 2 has tentatively been assigned a date of c.1100, but this is a crude approximation. In consequence an 11th-century date is suggested for the nave, Phase 1. It is noticeable from the plan that the alignment of the chancel is different from the nave; it 'weeps' to the south.

A single window inserted in the south wall of the chancel is all that represents Phase 3. This window, now blocked, has a very wide internal splay, but is quite tall and narrow on its outer face: it is very different in form from the Phase 2 window in the north wall. Rendering covers the external face of this window, so its precise shape is concealed; in its general form, however, it appears to be a lancet of a type common in the 13th century. Bryant's observation that the chancel east window is Early English of one light is a ludicrous misinterpretation of Ladbrooke's drawing.

The next phase consisted of a major extension to the chancel, combined with the insertion of new windows and blocking of old ones. It is difficult to date this phase with certainty, but the size of the window openings suggest a date after the 13th century, and the absence of brick may mean it predates the 15th-century phases. A 14th-century date is therefore acceptable (rather than certain) for Phase 4.

Phase 5 consists of late 15th-century (or even early 16th-century) work. There are several sub-phases, but it is difficult to organise them into chronological sequence. The most important piece of construction of this phase is the west tower, with its brick edgings and tracery. The buttresses half-way along the nave employ bricks similar to the tower, so the two may be grouped together. In this context, it is interesting that a glazed Flemish tile, dateable to the 15th or early 16th-century, was discovered in 1984 built into the nave south buttress. This gives an approximate *terminus post quem* for the buttress (and therefore the tower), made later rather than earlier by the probability that the tile has been reused. A late 15th or early 16th-century date must also be assigned to the north doorway, with its use of elaborately moulded bricks. Buttresses at north-west and south-east corners also appear to belong to this phase. It is uncertain which of the window openings belong to this phase; certainly the middle window of the nave north wall employs deep red bricks like those of the north doorway. Other windows in the nave might be 14th or 15th-century, but there is insufficient evidence.

Messent (1937, 258) records that there may have been a south porch and a north rood-stair, but nothing survives above ground to confirm this.

Causes of Abandonment

It would appear that the settlement adjacent to the church of Saxlingham Thorpe, thriving as it had been from the Middle Saxon to early medieval period, had been abandoned by late medieval times (information supplied by M.Muir). The church continued in use, but after 1362 it was normal for the rector of Saxlingham Nethergate to hold Saxlingham Thorpe too. By 1617 the rectory adjacent to the church had also been abandoned. Very few marriages were held in the church from that date until the registers end in 1640. It is possible that all services had stopped by this date. Two years earlier, the owners of West Wood (evidently in the parish of Saxlingham Thorpe) had been given licence to attend church at Saxlingham Nethergate rather than Saxlingham Thorpe (NRO, FCB/1, 5).

The process of ruination had begun by the 1660s, since the Faculty of 1687 which allowed the church to be officially abandoned states 'that the church of Saxlingham Thorpe ... is altogether ruined and hath been for the space of 20 years last and upwards' (NRO, FCB/1, 178). We also learn that one of the churchwardens had illegally sold the brass bells of the church for £5 in 1685 (ibid. 179). An estimate was made for the repair of the church in that year, which came to £400, a very considerable sum. The Faculty of 1688 therefore allowed the proceeds from the sale of the three bells to be given to the poor and for the repair of Saxlingham Nethergate church (ibid. 191).

Permission was also given for the disposing of any of the church materials for the upkeep of Nethergate church. King suggests that the superb roundels of 13th century glass in the chancel of Saxlingham Nethergate may have come from Saxlingham Thorpe at this time (King, 1974, 25).

The pattern is a fairly familiar one. The parish population declines (or even disappears), the church struggles on for a while; it is then abandoned, neglected and gradually becomes a ruin. Finally, the building materials are robbed.

Condition
The church is a total ruin, with collapsed stretches of wall. Many walls stand to original height, however, including most of the tower. Apart from the tower, most of the walls are free of encroaching vegetation. The interior of the church has been kept fairly clear in recent years. It is not a safe ruin, and damage to surrounding trees has further endangered the remaining walls.

Churchyard
Low fragments of flint walling form the north, east and west boundaries of the churchyard. No monuments survive, and the site has become a wood of some maturity, full of oak, hawthorn, beech, horse chestnut, sycamore and ash.

Archaeological Record
On the site of the church, fragments of 14th-century painted glass, and early 17th-century plain glass, have been found. Fragments of two glazed Flemish tiles (15th to early 16th-century) have been discovered, one incorporated into the nave south buttress originally (NCM).

Part of the font and an old door from the church have turned up in houses at Saxlingham Green (information M.Muir). Part of a carved font was recovered from the porch in 1990.

The rectory (abandoned by 1617) stood immediately south of the churchyard. Part of its brick enclosing wall survives, and medieval glazed greyware has been gathered from the surrounding field (information M.Muir).

The main settlement of Saxlingham Thorpe appears to have occupied the field north of the churchyard. This has yielded an abundance of Ipswich Ware, Thetford Ware and early medieval ware, but hardly anything of the late medieval period. This suggests that the village, in existence from Middle Saxon times, reached its peak in the 10th and 11th centuries, whence it gradually declined (information M.Muir).

Archaeological and Architectural Assessment
Of particular interest is the single-cell nave of Phase 1, and its possible relationship to an earlier (wooden?) chancel. Apart from a few recent diggings, the site appears to be hardly touched since the 17th century. A thorough archaeological investigation is likely to be very rewarding. It is an important site in relation to its abandoned settlement, as well as in its own right.

Further References
Blomefield, 1805-10, V, 501.
Bryant, 1901, 73.
Cox, 1911, II, 48.
King, 1974, 25.
Messent, 1931, 30.
Messent 1937, 258.
Pevsner, 1962, b, 302.

V. Snarehill

Identification TL 8915 8351. *County No.*5962.
Diocese: Norwich. *Archdeaconry:* Norfolk. *Deanery*: Thetford and Rockland. *Parish*: Brettenham. *Status*: parish church, now disused and made into garage and stables. *Date last in regular use*: Mid-16th century.
Ownership and access: private.

Location and Setting
According to *Domesday* survey, there were two distinct settlements called 'Snareshill', the greater belonging to Thurstin of Thetford in Edward the Confessor's time (Doubleday and Page, 1906, 2, 101). Neither settlements survive, although there is still a Snarehill Hall and Snarehill Farm east of Thetford. The former parish occupied the peninsula of land bounded to north by the River Thet and to south by the Little Ouse; to west the rivers join, in the middle of Thetford. Roger Bigot held Thurstin's land after the Conquest, and gave it to Thetford Priory at its foundation; according to Blomefield the church at Snarehill was appropriated to the priory at an early date; it stood near Snarehill House (Blomefield, 1805-10, I, 294).

Snarehill Hall dates to the 18th century (incorporating older parts), and is located 2km east of the centre of Thetford, 700m north of the A1066 road to Diss. Northwest of the Hall there are some old stables, part of which is used as a garage. On close inspection it can be seen that the stables have been built into the remains of a church.

Architectural Description
(Fig. 36; Pls CIV-CVI)
The remains are difficult to interpret, but it would appear that we are dealing with a nave and some sort of axial tower to east (Fig.36). The chancel has gone, its site occupied by a house (19th-century, but possibly with earlier parts) which abuts the east wall of the axial tower. There is no west tower, and the whole nave west wall has been engulfed by the end wall of a magnificent timber barn (16th or 17th-century) which extends west from the church. Thus the ecclesiastical remains are 'sandwiched' between a house and a barn.

SNARE HILL

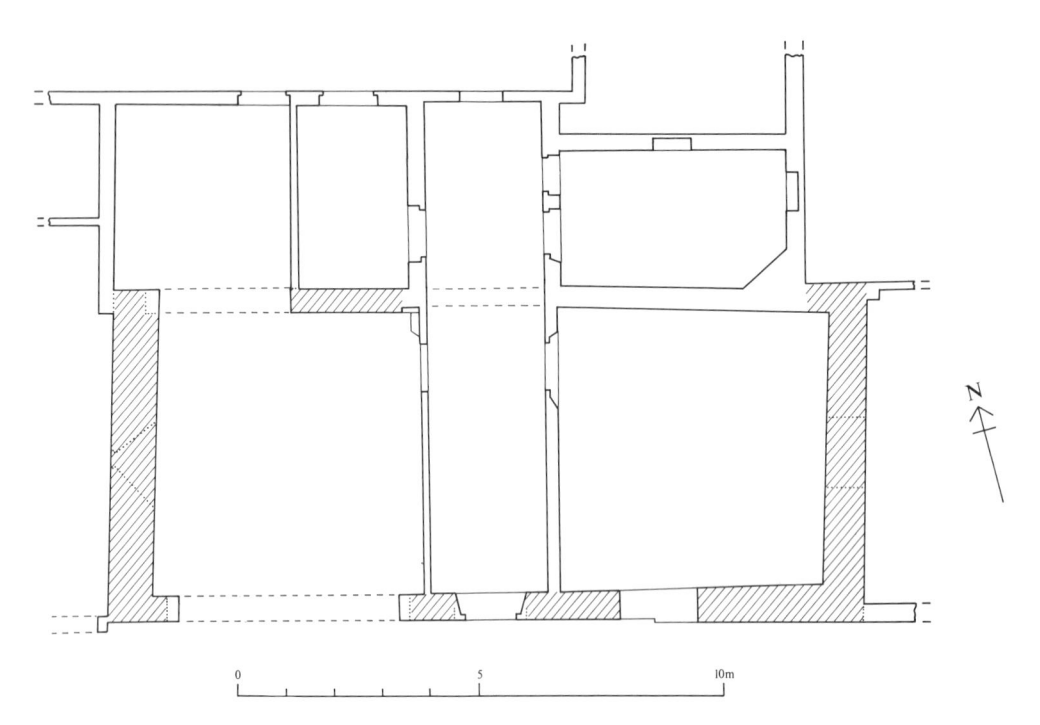

Figure 36. Snarehill: plan. Scale 1:150.

Plate CIV. Snarehill: formerly a church, later on stables, now a garage whose double doors occupy the western half of the nave south wall.

From the 18th century (and perhaps before) the nave has been used as stables. A narrow brick passageway has been built in a north-south direction across the middle of the nave, dividing it into two separate stables; some 17th-century brick is used in the passageway walls. The eastern part is still used as a stable, but the western part was converted to use as a garage this century and provided with bright green sliding doors (Pl. CIV).

Chancel. The chancel itself must have been destroyed by the construction of a house abutting the east wall of the axial tower. However, close investigation revealed the outline of the chancel arch beneath the plastered wall on the stable side. It is only 1.3m wide but extremely tall; the head of the arch no longer exists, so it is impossible to ascertain its precise size. The jambs are of limestone and do not appear to possess any mouldings.

Axial Tower. A word of caution needs to be registered here, since the presence of an axial tower at the east end of the nave is an interpretation of the evidence: one is not obviously aware of the presence of a tower when viewing the remains. Only the east and south walls of this 'tower' survive, the latter to a height of only 1.6m. That it was a tower can be inferred, since its 85cm thick walls are much thicker than the nave north and south walls, and it is a salient feature, *i.e.* it projects forward to the nave walls by some 6cm. There is quoining of its south-east corner, consisting of large limestone blocks, roughly squared, set side-alternately in a 'late Saxon' fashion. 4.5m further west there are the identical quoins of the tower south-west corner (Pl. CV). The intervening masonry consists of flint set in clear horizontal courses interspersed with a few pieces of limestone. This masonry is terminated 1.5m from the ground, and the upper half of the wall has been rebuilt in squared chalk, no later than the 18th century, to judge from the window contained within it.

Nave. Where it joins with the axial tower, the nave south wall is set back some 6cm from the tower south wall. Its masonry is similar, of coursed flint, but there is more interspersed limestone and a number of post-medieval bricks have been thrown in, giving a very patchy appearance. Overall, the wall is about 50cm thick, but various remodellings and repairs have affected it. Again, the upper part of the wall has been rebuilt in squared chalk. A post-medieval doorway leads into the passage which divides the nave; most of the wall west of here has been removed to make way for the sliding doors of the double garage which occupies the western part of the nave. It is possible that there is a single fragmentary piece of the north nave wall surviving the many alterations. The north-west quoins may also survive, but could not be seen. Fortunately the south-west quoins are clearly visible: two of the three lowest quoins are large, somewhat irregular limestone slabs; above these, the quoins are smaller and more regular. Some of the quoins bear faint traces of diagonal tooling.

Only the nave west wall stands entire. Half-way along, with its sill 1.5m from the ground, a partly blocked pointed window can be made out. The leading edge is chamfered, in limestone for the upper part; chalk below. Its deep splay narrows to a thin lancet on the outside, with limestone chamfered jambs. Above the hayloft in the barn, the gable of the west wall of the church can be seen (Pl. CVI). Its masonry is of coursed flint, interspersed with occasional bricks.

Interpretation and Dating
(Fig.37)
From the evidence presented, it would appear that the church had an unusual plan. A rectangular nave led into an axial tower of rectangular plan before proceeding through a tall narrow arch into a chancel of undisclosed form. The fact that the 'tower' part has thicker walls than

Plate CV.   Snarehill: west quoins of salient feature in south wall (either tower or transept); note coarse diagonal tooling.

Plate CVI.   Snarehill: gable of west wall of nave, seen from inside barn.

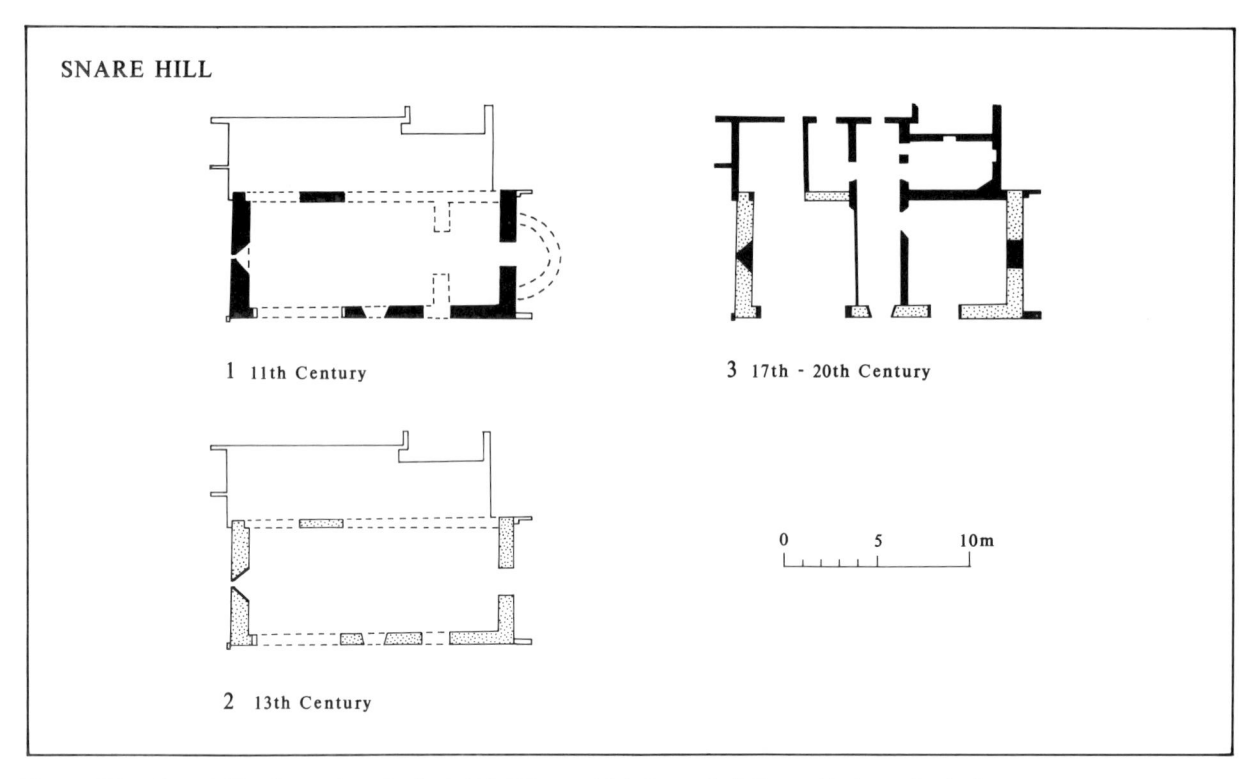

Figure 37. Snarehill: phase plan. Scale 1:400. The apsidal chancel of Phase 1 is hypothetical.

the nave suggests they rose higher than the nave, even though it defined a shape as much a transept as a tower (4.5m east to west, 7m north to south). Rectangular towers are not unknown in an early Norman context (see Surlingham St Saviour in this volume; although its tower possesses buttresses, which Snarehill does not); the early Romanesque towers of Cluny II and Tournus in Burgundy are also rectangular in plan.

There are three features of the church at Snarehill which demand a late Saxon or Saxo-Norman date for the church. Firstly, there are the roughly squared quoins, apparently upright-and-flat at the south-west corner and side-alternate for the tower. Such features occur from the later 10th century until the end of the 11th century, but probably not far beyond. Secondly, there is the tall unadorned chancel arch; such an arch can be found for minor openings well into the 12th century, but there can be very few (if any) used for chancel arches much after the Conquest. Lastly, there is the salient tower. This is feature of several Late Saxon churches: Sherborne Minster (1045-58), Stow (mid 11th century), Norton (late 10th or early 11th century); there may have been the odd survival after the Conquest (Fernie, 1983, 163), but it seems we are dealing with a definite late Saxon design which had been extinguished by the end of the 11th century.

Together, these arguments point to the probability that the church at Snarehill is mid 11th-century in date, late Saxon in type, and constructed before the Norman Conquest. I do not jump to this conclusion lightly but only after a careful weighing of evidence. It is interesting that both the village and church of Snarehill seem to reflect the fortunes of Thetford and its churches, depopulated and largely abandoned by the later Middle Ages. Indeed, Snarehill must have been virtually a suburb of Thetford when the town reached its greatest size in the Late Saxon period. It may be appropriate, therefore, to think of Snarehill church being built during the period when Thetford reached its apogee, *i.e.* the middle of the 11th century. Perhaps the plan of Snarehill represents a type of pre-Conquest parish church common in Thetford (although none have survived). Possibly, and this is more tentative, there is a parallel between the transept-like tower at Snarehill, and the continuous transept of the late Saxon cathedral at North Elmham. Very little is in fact known of the Late Saxon architecture of East Anglia; Snarehill advances our knowledge very considerably.

The only surviving pre-Reformation alteration was the insertion of a lancet window into the nave west wall, no doubt in the 13th century.

Causes of Abandonment
The church was in use in 1254 and 1368 (Allison, 1955, 157). According to Blomefield it cannot have remained in use much longer, since 'it was in ruins in Edward the Third's time' (Blomefield, 1805-10, I, 294). However the Register of Thetford Priory records 11d spent on the church at Snarehill in 1498-9, 2s 6d on thatching the church in 1522-3, and 4s 6d on thatching the chapel in 1525-6 (Harvey, 1975, 507). Either Blomefield's reference is erroneous, or the church was later restored; a third possibility is that either Blomefield's source or the Thetford source refer to a church at Little Snarehill, since only 'Snarehill' is specified. Whatever the case, the church had been abandoned by the middle of the 16th century. The depopulation and disappearance of the village must have been an important factor.

Condition
What survives is in reasonable condition.

Churchyard
There are no visible remains. Bones are dug up from time to time in adjacent gardens.

Archaeological and Architectural Assessment
The unusual design, and the strong probability that this

is a pre-Conquest structure, make the church at Snarehill of exceptional importance for the history of the ecclesiastical architecture of the region.

Further References
Allison, 1955, 157.
Blomefield, 1805-10, I, 294.
Bryant, 1901, 107.
Doubleday and Page, 1906, II, 101.
Fernie, 1983, 163.
Harvey, 1975, 507.
Messent, 1931, 32.

VI. Surlingham, St Saviour

Identification TG 3080 0674. *County No.* 10140.
Diocese: Norwich. *Archdeaconry*: Norfolk. *Deanery*: Loddon. *Parish*: Surlingham St Mary with St Saviour. *Status*: parish church, now disused and ruined. *Date last in regular use*: c. 1705.
Ownership and access: Diocese of Norwich, access by public footpath.

Location and Setting
Surlingham is an attractive Broadland village, just 8km east of Norwich and reached by minor roads from Trowse. The parish occupies a peninsula of land south of a bend in the River Yare; the ferry connection with Brundall, north of the river, used to be an important crossing point, but now only takes foot-passengers. St Mary's, the parish church, has a nave and round west tower of Norman date. A track skirting the north side of the churchyard leads north-east beside marshes, and after 300m a low hill is reached. The wild meadow here makes a splendid picnicking spot, overlooking marshes and the river to north, with the ruins of St Saviour's set within an overgrown churchyard to south.

Architectural Description
The roofless church consists of chancel, nave and vestigial remains of a south porch. The site was very overgrown, and therefore quite difficult to record.

Chancel. Most of the chancel east wall survives; it is built of medium to large cut flints, set in a pebbly buff mortar. The arch to the east window still stands; a minute fragment of tracery in the head of the window shows that it must have had a single mullion. Only the stone head of the arch remains, jambs, sill and surrounding masonry having been robbed away. Fragments of surviving limestone show that the east corners of the chancel had ashlar quoins, now robbed.

Of the rest of the chancel, most of the walling has collapsed leaving humps of rubble. However, the westernmost 4.5m of chancel north and south walls survive to a height of some 3.5m. At the point where both these walls begin, there is a flat external pilaster-buttress projecting a mere 15cm in flint, without dressed stone. There are equivalent buttresses in both north and south walls 3m further west, again in large flints and providing lateral support for the chancel arch. Between the buttresses, the masonry consists of largish flints in clear horizontal courses, and there is a distinct external set-off near the ground. The south wall is pierced by a window opening; the head has collapsed but the splay, particularly to east, shows up clearly. There are no signs of an equivalent window in the north wall, but a curved cavity in the wall by the chancel arch marks the beginning of a spiral staircase.

The chancel arch is faced in medieval brick, interspersed with occasional flints. The pointed archway itself has chamfered leading edges, and is supported by a chamfered brick inner order without responds. It is easy to observe that the chancel arch has been inserted into an earlier flint wall. The vertical joint is very clear on the south side of the arch. Fragments of re-used limestone, including round shafts, have been used to fill the crack between the two different pieces of walling. On the east face of the chancel arch, at springing level, are two square holes which probably held corbels originally, perhaps for a rood beam. A considerable amount of the gable wall above the chancel arch remains intact, swathed in ivy.

Chancel and nave are not in alignment; the chancel 'weeps' noticeably to south.

Nave. There are two large gaps in the nave south wall due to collapsed windows. Like the western part of the chancel, masonry consists of large flints in neat horizontal courses. Towards the west end of the wall, there is a doorway. The walling above it has not collapsed, but all freestone of the doorway itself has been robbed, save a single limestone jamb on the east side at ground level.

Hardly any of the nave north wall survives, other than the spur of masonry attached to the west wall. The west wall itself retains a good deal of its fabric. It had an axial window which once began about 2m from the ground; part of the splay can still be seen. Most of the west quoins remain, consisting of extremely large flints.

South porch. Low fragments of walling either side of the south doorway mark the position of the porch. There is also a buttress-like stub of masonry just east of the south door, a part of the porch east wall.

Interpretation and Dating
(Pl. CVII)
The core of the church is Norman of the late 11th century. The use of large flints in clear horizontal courses, with an absence of freestone for quoins and buttresses, are characteristic of this period. Flat pilaster-buttresses are also common in the post-Conquest era.

The disposition of the four pilaster buttresses is intriguing. They are located either side of the chancel arch and again 3m further east. Between them, the chancel wall is considerably thicker than further east (and also thicker than the nave wall). Combined with a spiral stairway in the north-west corner of the chancel, the evidence points incontrovertibly to the former presence of a tower at this point, *i.e.* occupying the westernmost 3.5m of the present chancel. This axial tower would have had internal dimensions of about 4.4m by 3.3m, making it rectangular in plan. No original doors or windows survived from this church, but pieces of limestone round shafts (filling the crack between the inserted brick chancel arch and earlier wall) are undoubtedly Norman; it is highly probable that they came from the Norman chancel arch contemporary with nave and axial tower.

The east end of the chancel, with its (former) freestone quoins, appears to be an addition to this earlier structure. No building break is visible, owing to the collapse of chancel walls east of the 'tower'. By analogy with other churches, it is probable that the Norman church

Plate CVII. Surlingham, St Saviour, by Ladbrooke (*c.* 1828).

Plate CVIII. Surlingham, St Saviour: view from the west after clearance of vegetation in 1985.

possessed an apse east of the axial tower. It is difficult to date this new chancel, but tracery fragments in the east window may be of the early 14th century. A further alteration took place in the 15th century when the present brick chancel arch replaced an earlier Norman one. This alteration must have necessitated the dismantling of the central tower; or, even more likely, it followed after the collapse of the tower, otherwise it is difficult to explain the reason for replacing a splendid stone Norman arch with a modest brick one. The eastern arch and wall of the tower would have been swept away, the western wall replaced by a new arch and gable wall. This would also explain another oddity, the excessive length of the chancel (it is the same length as the nave).

There appear to have been two additions to the nave: a south porch, and an (enlarged?) west window. Both show up in Ladbrooke's drawing of the ruins as they existed *c.* 1828 (Pl. CVII). The west window had cusped tracery, probably of the early 14th century.

Causes of Abandonment
When there are two churches within one village, it is common for one to be abandoned at some stage. St Mary's stands 300m south-west of St Saviour's, and is in the heart of the old village. St Saviour's is isolated, and this is no doubt a telling factor when it comes to parochial reorganisation.

From the 16th century, the church was served by a curate, but soon after 1705, the service was removed to St Mary's, and the church became dilapidated (Blomefield 1805-10, V, 463). Blomefield actually visited the ruins of St Saviour's in 1726 during a journey up the Yare valley (Linnell, 1951, 69):

'From Blofield I cros'd Surlingham ferry and saw there the ruins of the old parochiall chapell of St Saviour standing all alone on ye side of a hill...This church seems not to have been disused many years. The stepps on which the font stood are left and severall stones in the church overgrown with bushes, briars etc.'

Having sketched the church, he gives approximate dimensions: nave '15 yards long and 6 broad', 'S porch 5 yards long 3 broad', 'chancel is exact as long and as broad as Church'. There is also a sketch of a coffin lid with foliated cross found in the churchyard south of the church.

Condition
(Pl. CVIII)
By the 1830s, the church was a roofless and windowless ruin with vegetation covering the tops of walls. Most walls were still standing to full height apart from the totally ruined porch. Today many walls have collapsed (nearly all of the nave north wall, and most of the chancel). Some walls stand to more-or-less full height, and much of the gable wall remains above the chancel arch. Much of the standing masonry is covered by a thick mantle of ivy. The walls are very crumbly in places. Notices warning of the dangerous state of the ruins have wisely been put up, and the church has been fenced off within the churchyard. Inside, the church is overgrown with nettles, elder and brambles. In October 1985 a Y.T.S. team was able to clear the whole site of vegetation, making it much more accessible (Pl. CVIII).

Churchyard
The outline of the rectangular churchyard is still intact and bounded by mature trees and hedges. Within, it is overgrown with nettles, brambles, briars and saplings, as appears to have been the case in Blomefield's day. There are no visible monuments but Blomefield was able to record a medieval sarcophagus lid and a gravestone of 1683 (1805-10, V, 463). Unfortunately the boundary hedges were destroyed in 1985.

At the western edge of the churchyard there is a length of mortared flint walling lying on its side. This is likely to have been the old boundary wall.

Archaeological Record
Medieval tomb recorded in churchyard by Blomefield (see above).

Fragments of Norman shafts reused near chancel arch.

Roman pottery found 200m south-east.

Archaeological and Architectural Assessment
A point of interest is that St Saviour's, from building technique, appears to have been built at the same time as the earliest parts of St Mary's. It is worth noticing that the two churches display very different planning: St Mary's with a round west tower, St Saviour's with a rectangular central tower. Both appear to be early Norman in date.

The tower of St Saviour's is unusual in possessing an integral spiral stair in its north-west corner. It may be that the remains of its (apsidal?) original chancel lie below ground. Apart from some robbing of materials, the site has remained unchanged since its abandonment in the early 18th century.

Further References
Blomefield, 1805-10, V, 463.
Bryant, 1901, 106.
Linnell, 1951, 69.
Messent 1931, 34.
Pevsner 1962, b, 330.

Chapter 6. Category IV

I. Egmere, St Edmund

Identification TF 8968 3739. *County No.*1955/4.
Diocese: Norwich. *Archdeaconry:* Lynn. *Deanery*: Burnham and Walsingham. *Parish*: Egmere. *Status*: parish church, now disused and ruined. *Date last in regular use*: c.1580.
Ownership and access: private.

Location and Setting
(Pl. CIX)
Egmere is one of the larger deserted medieval village sites in the county. A small road leading to Little Walsingham (4km to east) bisects the former village, marked by its abundance of earthworks. The remains of St Edmund's church stand proudly at the top of a low hill just south of the road. The church site is part of a large meadow, and cattle commonly graze or shelter among the ruins (Pl. CIX). A depressed furrow marks the line of a street adjoining the northern perimeter of the churchyard, and another track flanks its eastern side. The only buildings within sight of the church are a pair of cottages 120m to south-east (now used for holiday accommodation) and a small square stockyard 50m to east.

Architectural Description
(Pl. CX)
The church is notable for its mighty west tower, which stands to almost full height. Sections of nave wall adjoin it to east; hardly anything survives of the chancel. Masonry consists of coursed flint.

Chancel. The chancel has been demolished, but, on the assumption that the masonry east of the rood-stair belongs to the chancel and is not a continuation of the nave, the western 2m of the chancel south wall can be discerned as a low mound of rubble covered with grass. Similar low fragments of masonry can be made out of the north wall. Bumps in the ground suggest that the chancel extended further east by at least 3m.

Nave. The masonry of the nave consists of neatly coursed flint, interspersed occasionally with pieces of reused limestone, conglomerate, brick and tile (both roof-tile and floor tile). There are regularly-spaced putlog holes, usually lined with limestone but sometimes with brick.

The nave south wall is the better preserved of the two. The south-east corner encloses the rood-stair, of which four flint steps survive, the top three capped with limestone. The outer casing of the stairway is a rectangular projection which extends 30cm south of the nave wall. Its corners have limestone quoins, although only one of the stones of the western corner remains *in situ*. Immediately west of this is a collapsed window, whose western splayed reveal survives, along with part of its limestone jamb. Nearly 2m further west there is another window opening; both splayed reveals are there with limestone inner jambs, but the window head has collapsed.

Unfortunately part of the unusual south doorway is missing. From the outside, it can be seen that the external arch has collapsed (presumably constructed of large limestone voussoirs) leaving most of the chamfered stone hood-mould in place, along with a relieving arch turned in flint, medieval brick and small limestone pieces. The doorway must have resembled an Etruscan arch. Most of the jambs have gone too. On the inside, the rear arch remains intact, but is taller than the external arch. The round-headed rear arch is oddly constructed with long curving voussoirs; the jambs remain in place, though there is the strong suspicion that they have been reused. As on the outside, the relieving arch is turned in brick, flint and limestone.

Less survives of the north wall. There are remains of a collapsed window opposite the western of the two in the south wall, with only the west reveal intact. Between the window and the north doorway, there is a small recess on the inner face of the wall which may have contained a water stoup. The north doorway is identical to its south counterpart, but even the hood-mould has gone. However, the lowest stone of the western jamb survives, with its rebate for the door; higher up there is a groove for a bolt, and a deep draw-bar hole which goes back some 1.5m (*i.e.* as far as the east wall of the tower).

The relationship of nave walls to tower is problematical. The inner faces of both nave walls appear to go back into the east face of the tower; the plastered inner surface of these walls continues west into the tower, indicating that the tower has been built onto a pre-existing nave. But to contradict this interpretation, the outer surface of the nave wall appears to be added to the tower: the flint masonry of the nave north wall overlaps the ashlar base-course of the tower. Looking more closely at the internal corners, there appears to be a vertical building break in the nave walls at the point where they adjoin the tower. An explanation will be given below.

Tower. The tower is constructed of neatly coursed flint with dressed limestone edgings. Putlog holes are prominent, lined with limestone and sometimes flint. At each corner there are buttresses with three set-offs, diagonal at the western side, perpendicular to the wall at the eastern side. A limestone plinth with blank frieze on a flint base forms a continuous base-course for the tower external walls.

The base-course does not extend into the church interior. Here, the tower east wall is pierced by an arch of three continuous chamfered orders resting on a polygonal base (all in limestone), with no capitals to form a transition from jamb to (pointed) arch. The tower arch appears small in relation to the tower, but reasonably large in relation to the nave. Above the arch there are two clear roof-lines; one is more steeply pitched, and has a chamfered limestone weathercourse which appears to be contemporary with the tower; the other is shallower and has a has gone. Part of the sill has also gone, leaving an area of eroded masonry beneath.

The middle storey of the tower is singularly unobtrusive. The absence of any stringcourse serves to emphasise the unbroken mass of the tower. Windows at this level are concomitantly small, mere rectangular slits in chamfered stone; but the amount of light from such apertures is maximised by the width of internal splay; the rear arches have pointed segmented heads. Each wall face has a single window; the south window is offset to west to allow for a doorway from the stairway onto the first floor.

The stringcourse between middle storey and belfry stage is again noteable by its absence. While taller than those of the stage below, the windows of the belfry are not especially big. All four retain their jambs, pointed heads and hood-moulds (all in limestone), along with fragments of tracery. Only the north window remains perfect, with mullion and tracery head intact: two cusped lights with quatrefoil reticulation. Masonry above window level is rather crumbly, and any signs of a parapet have gone. On the inside, the newel of the spiral stairway is completed by four small stone ribs which supported a small (largely collapsed) domical vault.

Interpretation and Dating

The surviving remains indicate three phases of building. It appears that the tower is an addition to a pre-existing nave (see above), and that portions of this nave survive, enclosed within the masonry of the east wall of the tower. It is impossible to date this nave from such vestigial remains. However, some of the limestone reused in the later nave could be 12th-century Norman work, and it is possible that the unusual later doorways are a reworking of earlier (and demolished) Norman ones.

Judging from the roof-line (the steep one), this church was not very big. By contrast, the west tower is a massive addition, and a work of excellent quality as well as abundant quantity. The surviving complete belfry window is of simple Decorated type, so a date towards the middle of the 14th century would seem appropriate.

Some time later, the original nave was totally demolished, leaving just a roofline and two scars of masonry against the east face of the tower. A new nave (and chancel) was subsequently built on the lines of the old, with the nave walls built right up against the scar-like stubs of the old nave walls. This new nave incorporates much older work, including worked limestone, late medieval brick, and floor-tiles. Some of them have been identified as Bawsey tiles, presumably of the second half of the 14th century. The round-headed doorways of the nave are post-medieval in appearance, probably of the second half of the 16th century.

The destruction of the first nave must have taken place soon after 1538-9, when the Priory of Walsingham, which held the patronage of the church, was dissolved. Allison (1955, 147) records that 'between 1553 and 1558, the parson, Thomas Halker, complained to the Chancery Court in London that the former parson and the lessee of the rectory had pulled down part of the church and taken lead from the roof; the lead and the greatest bell from the steeple had been sent to the coast for export.' It would appear, from the evidence of the standing remains, that the nave was totally rebuilt following this complaint; most likely during the reign of Mary. Much material from the old nave must have been reused. Despite this, by the end of the 16th century the church was 'profaned and turned into a barn.' (Jessop, 1888, 25).

Plate CIX. Egmere, St Edmund: ruined church with cows.

Plate CX. Egmere, St Edmund: tower arch, looking west, first half of 14th century. The nave was demolished c. 1540 but rebuilt later in the 16th century.

brick weathercourse (Pl. CX). Inside the tower, a doorway (most of the arch head broken away) in the south-east corner leads into a spiral stairway (of limestone) which is contained within the thickness of the wall. In fact, on its east side the wall is desparately thin, and a chunk of masonry has collapsed leaving a section of stairway visible from inside the nave. Apart from this unintentional hole, the stairway is lit by slit windows framed in chamfered limestone.

A large window with elegantly pointed head pierces the west wall of the lower storey. The springing of the arch is slightly set back from the limestone jambs, suggesting that an inner (tracery bearing) order to the arch

Causes of Abandonment
The church was abandoned as a consequence of the depopulation of the village. A village of modest size in the 12th and 13th centuries, with (combined with Quarles) 31 tax-payers in 1334, by 1524 there were only 5 tax-payers (Cushion et al., 1982, 89), and only one household by 1603 (Jessop, 1888, 25). It seems that the church was initially abandoned in 1538-9, but then restored to use, only to be finally abandoned in the later 16th century. In 1602 it is described thus: 'Egmer. — The Church ther and Chauncell decaied and profaned, by Sir Nicholas Bacon, Knight, Lord of the mannor & patron, and his predecessors, and by Mr Thomas Bostock, Clerk, now p'son & Incumbent there, & his predecessors sometymes p'sons & Incumbents there, and is made a barn'. (Tymms, 1886, 225).

Condition
All walls are crumbling at the top, and there is a scatter of fallen flint around. A chunk of wall on the east side of the spiral stairway has fallen. The tower is in a surprisingly good state of preservation, but the remains are not particularly safe.

Churchyard
No boundaries or monuments remain above ground, but the line of the churchyard wall, flanked by a sunken street, can be made out on the north side; another adjoining street probably marks the east boundary.

Archaeological Record
The surrounding DMV is a Scheduled Ancient Monument. Three Roman sherds, one Ipswich Ware sherd, many Thetford Ware and Grimston Ware sherds found. Sherds of late 13th/14th-century green glazed pottery found near church. Deep pits west of church are post-medieval, probably marl pits.

Bawsey tiles found reused in nave walls, fragment also found on ground inside church.

There used to be a medieval corbel built into the wall of the cottage south-east of the church, but no sign today.

Archaeological and Architectural Assessment
The church is important in its own right, and also as a major feature of Egmere DMV. The tower is a good example of mid-14th century work, although out of scale with the rest of the church. It would be interesting to know how much more of the pre 14th-century church might be recoverable both below ground and within the masonry of the tower.

Without doubt the most intriguing aspect of the church is the great probability that the nave, as it remains today, dates to the reign of Mary I (1553-8). Not only is it unusual to find churches built during her reign, which makes Egmere very rare; but it also suggests a policy of renovating and re-opening churches closed during the previous decade or so. The church has good potential for excavation.

Further References
Allison, 1955, 147.
Blomefield, 1805-10, IX, 223.
Bryant, 1898, 31.
Cox, 1911, I, 206.
Cushion, Fenner and Goldsmith, 1982, 84.
Messent, 1931, 18.
Pevsner, 1962b, 154.

II. Godwick, All Saints

Identification TF 9019 2198. *County No.* 1104.
Diocese: Norwich. *Archdeaconry*: Lynn. *Deanery*: Brisley and Elmham. *Parish*: Tittleshall and Godwick. *Status*: parish church, now disused and ruined. *Date last in regular use*: 16th century.
Ownership and access: private.

Location and Setting
The deserted village of Godwick has left many traces of its past in the form of earthworks, a ruined church tower and demolished Hall, and an early 17th-century barn. It is located 8km south of Fakenham, between the villages of Whissonsett and Tittleshall. A farm remains today, 300m east of the church, with the new Hall (19th-century) 200m further north. The site of the church is surrounded by earthworks, preserved beneath sheep pasture. The outline of the churchyard can be made out, with the main east-west street flanking it to north, and a smaller street to west. Slight mounds are evident east of the tower, but the outline of the church cannot be discerned. The tower itself remained almost complete until 1981, when the east face collapsed.

Architectural Description
(Pl. CXI)
Only the tower remains. The following is a description of it as it stood in 1980, with an updating of its state since June 1981.

The masonry of the lower storey consists of medium-to-large flints set in rough courses, interspersed with occasional pieces of reused limestone and brick. It has an external base-course in flint capped with chamfered limestone. The base-course stops 70cm from the east corners of the tower, and scarring is visible in the masonry of north and south walls up to a height of 6m, suggesting the nave west wall adjoined the tower here. The eastern quoins of the tower were evidently applied to these corners after the nave wall had been torn down. These quoins are made of limestone up to 4m from the ground, and brick above. The western quoins are also of limestone up to 4.5m from the ground but have a neater appearance; again, brick is used above. An interesting point to notice is that the rendering (of which a considerable quantity still survives on external walls) as applied to the north-western quoins, has been fashioned to resemble regular stone quoins with false joints, whether it covers limestone or brick. A few putlog holes are visible in areas not covered by rendering. On the interior face of the north wall, near the ground, there is a small stone-lined niche.

The jambs of the tower arch, in their untidy execution resemble the eastern quoins (Pl. CXI). They are of limestone, with a chamfered leading edge. The arch itself has a double hollow chamfer, but no responds or imposts; its limestone is darker in tone than that of the jambs, suggesting the latter may have been remade at the same time as the eastern quoins. At its apex the tower has a relieving arch constructed of flint and radial bricks. It is noticeable that above this point, pebble flints are used to the exclusion of field flints and the coursing is more regular than below.

The same observation holds true for the west wall, the masonry above the west window appearing more regular, and using flint pebbles. Jambs and four-centred

Plate CXI. Godwick, All Saints: after the demolition of the chancel and nave, the 15th-century tower was restored in the 17th century to preserve it as a 'picturesque' ruin. This photograph was taken before the collapse of the eastern half of the tower in 1981. Photo: Hallam Ashley.

head of this window survive, but the sill, and a chunk of masonry below, have gone. The bricks of the jambs seem thinner than those of the arch and hood-mould. On the south side, the rendering is shaped to form hollow chamfers in the jamb; a fragment of tracery remains at the springing of the arch. On the inside, the rear arch has limestone hollow chamfered jambs and a brick head.

A stringcourse 6.5m from the ground divides lower from upper storey; it consists of two courses of brick, the upper one chamfered. The masonry above continues in the same technique as the upper part of the lower storey, with neater coursing and brick quoins. However, there is much greater use of brick, some laid herring-bone fashion, and of re-used limestone, with an apparent abundance of Norman engaged shafts speckling the walls.

Small windows in north, south and west walls make an apology for a middle storey; but this is really (and unusually) a two-storey tower. The sills of these windows are of limestone, but chamfered jambs (continuing into the pointed arch head) and hood-mould are of brick. On the east face of the tower, a limestone weathercourse marks a rather shallow roof-line (but apparently no scar for a roof underneath). Above are the belfry windows, again with stone sills and brick jambs; the bricks appear to define a double hollow chamfer. Only the south window retains its head: four-centred and part of the brick hood-mould. All tracery has gone. The parapet has also collapsed, leaving only three fragments, at the corners, of the concave brick stringcourse which ran below it. Bryant's photograph (1903, 95) shows the tower fully standing, with Y-tracery belfry windows and a crenellated parapet.

In June 1981, almost the whole of the east wall, and the eastern half of the south wall, collapsed, and the high pile of debris still remains at the foot of the tower where it has fallen. All the east wall above the tower arch has gone (although the two stones above the springing, on the north side, remain in place). Only the west jamb of the belfry south window and the western half of the south window below survive.

Interpretation and Dating

Apart from the tower, none of the church shows above ground; but eighty years ago, Bryant (*ibid.*) was able to trace the foundations in the grass. The measurements he gives are: nave 26ft by 19ft, chancel 15ft by 19ft. Judging from the number of Norman shafts built into the tower, part of this church dated back to the early 12th century. A church existed at Godwick at this time, since Ralph de Toni (d. 1101) gave the advowson to the priory at West Acre (Blomefield, 1805-10, IX, 159).

There are two phases of construction to the tower. Most of the masonry below the stringcourse, to which the nave west wall was attached, is late medieval in date; the jambs of the lower storey west window may belong to this phase, suggesting a late 15th or early 16th-century date. A thorough rebuilding then took place during the 17th century, involving a renewing of tower arch jambs, west window head, and total rebuilding of the upper storey of the tower. This reconstruction must have taken place after the church had fallen into ruins, since the limestone eastern quoins are clearly an attempt to patch the scars left by the removal of the nave walls. We know that the church was in ruins by the late 16th century, since in 1602 it is described as 'whollie ruynated and decaied long since, unknowne by whose negligence' (Tymms, 1866, 232).

It would appear that, during the 17th century, a decision was taken to demolish the nave and chancel, but rebuild the tower. The precise date when this took place is not known. There are some similarities with the brick west tower at nearby Litcham, built in 1669 (four-centred belfry windows, small windows to middle storey, use of mock quoins in rendering). Godwick tower may be a little earlier, perhaps rebuilt at the same time as the construction of the magnificent barn 200m to east (dateable to the first half of the 17th century). It looks as if the barn delineated the eastern boundary of a large yard on the north side of Godwick Hall (built in 1586; the last remains were unfortunately demolished in 1961). Blind windows with brick pediments decorate the western face of the barn (*i.e.* the side visible from the Hall; the doorway to the barn is on the other side), designed to fit in visually and architecturally with the Hall. Perhaps similar visual and aesthetic considerations were applied to the church, raising it from the stature of decaying ruin; like the barn, the church could be seen from the Hall. It may have been that the reconstruction of the tower fulfilled an obligation to maintain the structure — while actually reducing it to the status of a folly.

Causes of Abandonment
Godwick was always a small village, with 13 taxpayers in 1329 and in 1428 (Allison, 1955, 148). A map of 1596 shows the Hall and 8 or 9 houses (Holkham Hall MSS., Tittleshall Books, No.55), by which time some enclosure of land had been taking place. The barn is in fact sited across the path of the former main street, suggesting that little remained of the village. The parish was consolidated with Tittleshall in 1630 (Blomefield, 1805-10, IX, 509); the church had already fallen out of use in the 16th century (see above).

Condition
The remains are in a dangerous state; a large part of the tower collapsed in 1981. The fallen debris still lies in a heap. A barbed-wire fence surrounds the site.

Churchyard
The outline of the churchyard can be made out, although no monuments remain. A wide depression to north marks the line of the main street, running east-west; smaller streets flanked the churchyard to west and south, and a low mound forms the eastern boundary.

Archaeological Record
The church is set in the middle of the earthworks of an important and extensive DMV, with 17th-century barn and 16th-century Hall (site of) 200m east.

A large 13th-century clustered column base stands near the barn.

Archaeological and Architectural Assessment
The site is important in its context within the DMV. Below ground remains certainly would go back to the 12th century; a large quantity of Norman shafts were reused in the 17th-century reconstruction of the tower.

The restored tower must be one of the earliest examples of a 'folly' or ruin within a landscape. There are many that date from the 18th century, but I know of none as early as the first half of the 17th century.

Further References
Allison, 1955, 148.
Blomefield, 1805-10, IX, 159; 509.
Bryant, 1903, 95.
Cox, 1911, I, 59.
Cushion et al., 1982, 59.
Messent, 1931, 19.
Pevsner, 1962b, 173.
Tymms, 1866, 232.

III. Hindolveston, St George

Identification TG 0281 2915. *County No.*3093.
Diocese: Norwich. *Archdeaconry:* Norwich. *Deanery*: Sparham. *Parish*: Hindolveston. *Status*: parish church.
Date last in regular use: 1892.
Ownership and access: Diocese of Norwich.

Location and Setting
Hindolveston is a village of moderate size some 10km east of Fakenham. The parish church, dedicated to St George, stands towards the western end of the village. This brick and flint church was built in 1932, and incorporates a great deal of fabric reused from the old church. A small road south of the church leads to the ivy-clad half-tower which forms the principal remnant of the old church of St George, some 300m to south-east. Its enveloping churchyard is still in use.

Architectural Description
(Pls I, II)
Until the eastern half of the west tower collapsed and demolished the nave in 1892, this stately church consisted of chancel, vestry, nave, north aisle and west tower. In dramatic contrast, all that stands today is the western part of the tower, the vestry which abutted the south wall of the chancel, and a few low fragments of walling (Pls I and II).

Vestry. It is ironic that one of the comparatively late additions to the church fabric should survive. The vestry was built against the south wall of the chancel, and its east wall continued the line of the chancel east wall. Most of the gabled roof of the vestry survives, along with part of the flat plastered ceiling. Walls are built of flint interspersed with 18th-century brick. The two external corners have quoins made of reused blocks of limestone. A covered limestone cornice caps the gabled south wall.

On the north side, where it adjoined the chancel, the vestry is entirely open. The only other opening is the large square window in the south wall; the outer jambs and sill have been robbed; it has a wooden lintel. Above it is another square brick-lined opening, blocked with flint. The east wall also contains a square window with wooden lintel, now blocked with 19th-century brick.

Tower. First it is necessary to clarify how much of the tower survives. Its west wall stands to its full height, including parapet; the east wall has totally collapsed. North and south walls have half-collapsed, forming crudely stepped buttressings for the west wall. In fact, at its lowest storey the tower survives entire, including responds of tower arch; but at belfry level, the tower has collapsed east of the west jambs of the belfry windows.

A large mound of rubble stands at the foot of the east side of the tower. There are rather narrow half-columns from the tower arch responds, with round moulded bases and polygonal plinths. A flushwork base course (a cross of St George within a quatrefoil is the motif) goes round every external surface, including the diagonal buttresses (the eastern diagonal buttresses have largely gone), and the three sides of the polygonal stair-turret in the south-east corner. Immediately east of the stair-turret is an additional buttress of 18th-century or early 19th-century brick. This is in turn reinforced by a further flint buttress. On the inside a small pointed doorway, with limestone jambs and hood-mould, led into the stairway; it is now blocked and rendered.

The wide west doorway is likewise blocked. Its western side has limestone jambs with continuous mouldings, on the inside the pointed-segmental arch is lined with medieval brick; the door blocking contains flint, brick and fragments of reused limestone. Above the doorway is an exceptionally fine Perpendicular 3-light window within a pointed segmental rear arch. The main lights are stepped, each surmounted with a crenellated supertransom, and the side lights are subarcuated.

At first-floor level, a small sound-hole pierces the

west wall. At belfry level, only the west window survives, but it is totally intact. The two-centred rear arch is built of medieval brick. The tracery of the 3-light window is similar to that in the ground-storey below, but its crenellated supertransom surmounts the centre light only. A stone coping forms the parapet, surviving on the west wall.

Other fragmentary remains. Next to the tower and vestry, the largest visible remnant of the church is the diagonal north-east buttress of the chancel. It stands to a height of 1.3m, and is constructed, like the tower, of flint and square limestone edgings. Low fragments of the north and east walls of the chancel are discernible above the ground. The south-east buttress of the chancel survives to about 20cm high. All that remains of the south wall is the buttress which stood at right-angles to the wall, 2m west of the vestry; the buttress stands to 1.2m high.

The outline of the north aisle can be made out, especially its five straight buttresses. Nothing survives to enable an outline of the nave to be traced.

Interpretation and Dating
(Pl. I)

The church here is mentioned in *Domesday Book*, but nothing of this building survives. The style of window tracery in the tower points to a date after 1400. In fact, a certain John Swift of Hindolveston gave a legacy to the building of the new tower in 1445 (Blomefield, 1805-10, VIII, 239). It seems probable that chancel, nave and aisles belonged to the same sequence of building as the chancel. The responds of the chancel arch (now in the new church, see below) are identical to those of the tower arch. The style of the nave piers (also in the new church) would agree with this dating. Window tracery in other parts of the church (in Ladbrooke's drawing, Pl.I) also fits this pattern; note the supertransoms of the chancel's 4-light east window. It appears that we have a church consisting of chancel, nave, north and south aisles, and west tower, and built *c*.1430-1450.

At the time of the collapse of the tower in 1892, there was no south aisle. However, it was still standing in Blomefield's time and its outline can be traced on aerial photographs. This aisle burned down after being struck by lightning in 1804. A new wall was then built along the line of the south arcade. It is likely that the brick buttress at the south-east corner of the tower forms part of this scheme. It seems equally likely that the vestry was built against the south wall of the chancel at the same time.

Causes of Abandonment

The demise of the church of St George at Hindolveston was both dramatic and unexpected. On the afternoon of Sunday July 31st, 1892, part of the tower collapsed and demolished the nave. Messent records: 'No-one was hurt. A service which should have been held was for some reason cancelled.' (Messent, 1931, 22). At this stage, the chancel was unaffected, and the church was repaired. Subsequently a temporary wooden church was set up. Finally it was decided to build a new masonry church on a site 300m north-east of the old church, nearer the heart of the village. Materials were gathered from the old church and incorporated in the new. The new church of St George was completed in 1932.

There were many complaints at the time about the destructive way in which the stonework had been taken away. The chancel was still largely intact at this time. However, in 1933 permission was granted to destroy the chancel for the sale of its materials, and this wantonly unnecessary destruction took place. Strangely, the early 19th-century vestry was left standing.

Remains of the old church incorporated in the new church

The new church is a cruciform structure, built of flint interspersed with reused limestone fragments, with brick corners, buttresses and window surrounds. In the east wall, the inscribed foundation stone, dated 1932, states that 'This church was built largely from the fabric of the former which had become ruinous.' The four external doorways (one in each porch, one in each transept) make use of limestone from the old church, reworked in the case of those on the south side of the church. The old door of the north porch, with its ancient lock, is another survivor of the old church.

Inside, the church is a surprisingly successful blend of old materials worked in with the new. In the chancel, the two statue niches in the east wall are each capped with a triangular lintel carved with the figure of an angel holding a scroll, undoubtedly of 15th-century workmanship. Of probably the same date is the piscina in the south wall, at least the bowl and the western half of the piscina, with its nook-shaft and cusped arch (the plain eastern half is new). Further west are responds which must have belonged to the chancel arch of the old church; they are identical in type to the old church's tower arch responds, half-columns with round moulded bases on polygonal plinths, and polygonal capitals with rather attenuated bell.

The crossing makes use of four octagonal piers, with moulded base and capital, from the old church. Actually, only one (the south-east one) was originally a pier, the other three were responds from the ends of the nave arcades. The piscina in the south transept was possibly fashioned from a column piscina in the old church; the carved leaves give it the appearance of a 13th-century capital.

Halfway down the nave are two polygonal responds formed from octagonal piers from the old church. West of the respond in the south wall a fine 15th-century statue niche has been reassembled; its sill has two polygonal bases, and above is a cusped ogee arch and canopy, with a standing angle at either side. In the north porch, a canopied corbel has been made into a water-stoup; its niche has an ogee head and finial chancel with grotesque faces, crudely reassembled.

Funerary monuments and brasses were also removed to the new church. On the south wall, at the south-west corner, is the superb stone monument containing brasses of Edmon Hunt (d. 1558) and his wife Margaret (d. 1568). The rectangular stone is carved with a round-headed arch supported by responds, within which, in brass, is the kneeling figure of a man with ten sons and his wife with four daughters, and a shield above; the inscription below is in verse. This monument was formerly situated on the wall by the chancel arch according to Manning (1892, 78). On the north wall opposite are four brass inscriptions: Beatrice Bullye (d. 1621); John Bully (d. 1586), formerly at the east end of the south aisle (Martin, Rye MSS 17, 6, 86); Thome Warde (d. 1531); John Woodcrofte (d. 1491).

The font dates to the 15th century. It has an octagonal bowl, each face carved with figures now largely erased; one side shows a shield with the cross of St

George. The stem is carved with the crowned letters M and G.

Some bench ends, with carved poppyheads, also come from the old church.

Old Churchyard

The churchyard is rectangular, longer from north to south because an extension was added to the north side earlier this century. A flint wall capped with brick forms the western boundary, the other sides being hedged. There are several 18th-century headstones south of the church, most of the rest are of the 19th century. Southeast of the tower are two 18th-century table tombs; there are also two 19th-century table tombs south of the church.

Since the churchyard (or at least the southern part of it) is still in use, it is well tended. Sheep are used to assist in keeping down the grass, and they have succeeded in keeping it bare. The only place where saplings thrive is within the fence which surrounds the tower. There is but one tree, on the north boundary of the churchyard.

An engimatic small square building, constructed of flint and 18th-century brick is located at the south-east corner of the churchyard.

Condition

The tower is a potential danger, with crumbling upper surfaces. It is wisely fenced off. A profusion of ivy clings to the craggy walls.

The vestry is similarly bedecked with ivy. Most of the plastered ceiling and some of the roof timbers have collapsed.

Archaeological and Architectural Assessment

Before its destruction, the church was a remarkably fine example of Perpendicular architecture of the second third of the 15th century. It was lavish in scale and in carved detail. From the plan, drawings and the surviving remains (in the new church as well as on the old site) a fairly complete picture of the church can be built up.

Apart from the vestigial foliate capital used as a piscina in the new church, nothing remains of any earlier church. It is certain that there were earlier churches, since it is mentioned in *Domesday*.

Further References

Blomefield, 1805-10, VIII, 239.
Cox, 1911, I, 192.
Hudson, 1921, 179.
Manning, 1892, 78.
Messent, 1931, 22.
Pevsner, 1962b, 166.

IV. Panxworth All Saints

Identification TG 3473 1359 *County No.*8501
Diocese: Norwich. *Archdeaconry:* Norwich. *Deanery*: Blofield. *Status*: Parish church, now disused and partly demolished. *Date last in regular use*: 1959.
Ownership and access: Diocese of Norwich.

Location and Setting
(Pl. CXII)

The small village of Panxworth can be found 1km west of the Broadland village of South Walsham. All Saints stands on its own about 0.5km north of Panxworth village on the small road to Ranworth. A solitary flint tower rises gauntly within its isolated churchyard on the east side of the road, a sight enjoyed by day-trippers to Ranworth and the occasional discerning cyclist. The romantically wind-swept aspect which strikes today's visitors was the same for their 17th, 18th and early 19th-century counterparts; but in 1847 the lonely tower (as drawn by Ladbrooke, Pl. CXII) was incorporated into a new church with a new nave. However, since 1981 the nave has been demolished and the tower returned to its pre-1847 splendid isolation. A fence surrounds the tower, with attached notices warning of falling masonry.

Architectural Description
(Fig.38)

The remains consist of a square west tower with the attached west wall of the nave. Masonry is of coursed flint with limestone or brick dressings.

Nave west wall. The east face of this wall is covered with a thick buff rendering; stubs of the nave north and south walls (removed in 1981) are still visible. Moving to the west face, two types of masonry are apparent: the lower 3m consists of large cut flints, but the upper wall (mainly the gable) is built of smaller, uncut flints. The diagonal buttresses at either corner have two set-offs, and the masonry is of the same type as the lower walling described above; the corner dressings of these buttresses are of white 19th-century brick.

West tower. The unbuttressed west tower is constructed of flint with limestone quoins. The lower part of the exterior walls (*i.e.* the first storey) is faced in large cut flints similar in character to those of the nave west wall. There is a base course capped with chamfered limestone, just visible near the ground.

The east face is pierced by a tall tower arch; it has no projecting jambs, just a chamfered leading edge. The arch itself is four-centred, and springs from moulded polygonal corbels. Above the arch, the scar of the 19th-century roof is clearly visible, and 30cm above that the stone dripcourse of an earlier roof can be made out.

The remaining openings are fairly small. In the west wall, there is a first storey two-light window with cusped quatrefoil head. At second storey level, the masonry is more neatly coursed than lower down; it is pierced by a window in the west wall, a single cusped light with square

Plate CXII. Panxworth church by Ladbrooke (1822).

PANXWORTH

ELEVATION OF WEST FACE OF TOWER

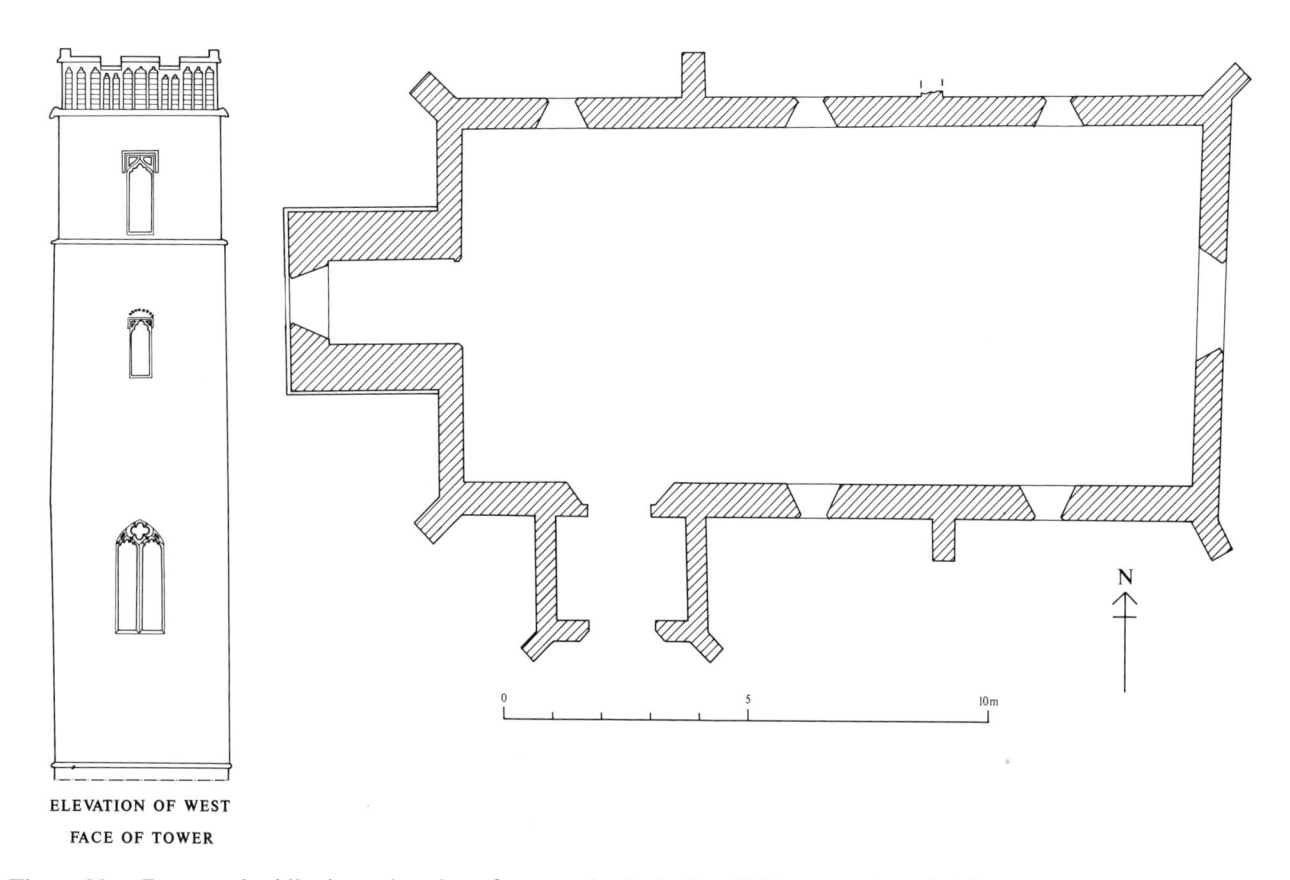

Figure 38. Panxworth, All saints: elevation of tower; plan including 1847 nave and porch (all except tower and west wall of nave demolished 1981). Scale 1:150.

hood-mould. Above this level, there is a limestone stringcourse and set-off. Each belfry window consists of a single-light opening with cusped ogee head and square hood-mould. This stage is capped by a hollow chamfered stringcourse, and carved animal head gargoyle at each corner.

The highest quality work is reserved for the parapet, with its fine flushwork crenellations (Fig. 38).

The 1847 church
Having survived as an isolated tower for centuries, it was decided to restore the church to parochial use. To this end, the sum of £530 was spent in 1847 on constructing a new nave, a single cell 16m by 8.5m plus porch, designed by James Watson (Pl. CXIII).

Watson's church was built of flint, neatly cut on exterior faces; the single-light windows and the door jambs were constructed of terracotta. The slate roof, of plainest construction, was already greatly decayed before its demolition, along with the walls of nave and porch, in 1981.

Interpretation and Dating
(Fig. 39)
The remains are not difficult to interpret: a late medieval (probably 15th-century) tower with 19th-century patching (notably in the gable wall of the nave). The 1847 nave and south porch were demolished in 1981. It is worth noting that a church existed here at the time of *Domesday*.

Apparently it was still made of wood in the mid 12th-century (Blomefield 1805-10, XI, 110).

Causes of Abandonment
All Saints church remains as isolated today as it did in the

Plate CXIII. Panxworth, All Saints: 15th-century tower with nave of 1847, prior to the latter's demolition in 1981.

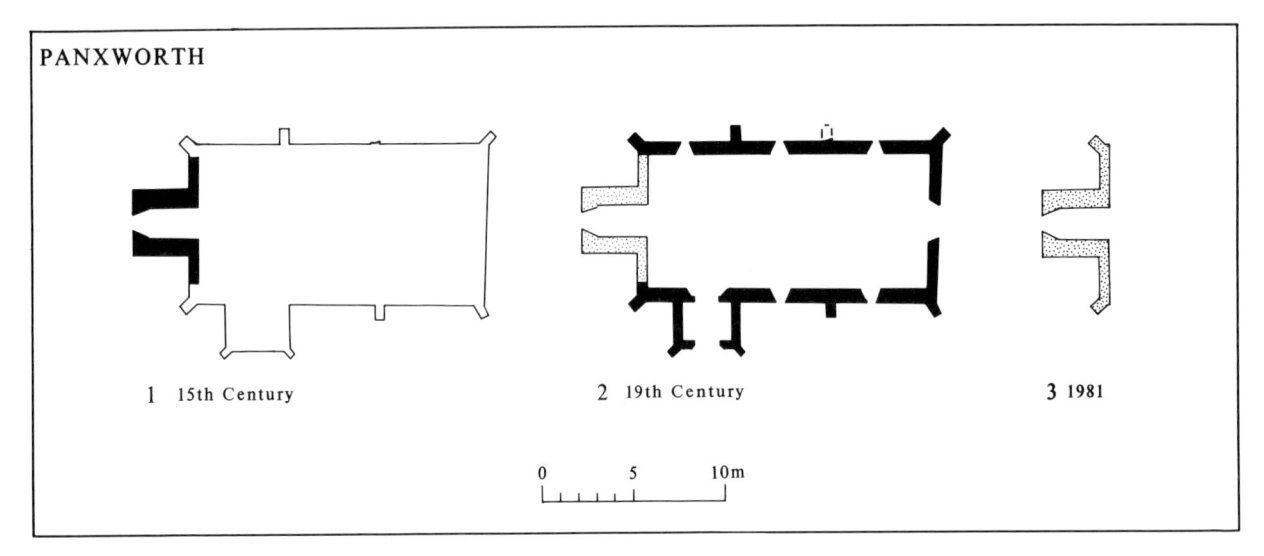

Figure 39. Panxworth, All Saints: phase plan. Scale 1:400.

17th century when it was first abandoned (the church had already been dissolved by 1603). The village of Panxworth is small and some 0.5km away from the church. Perhaps the building of the nave in 1847 was based on an assumption that the village would grow, which it did, but not enough to support a church situated at an inconvenient distance from the centre of population.

By 1959, the church had been closed for regular worship. Its condition soon deteriorated, partly due to vandalism; its isolation, combined with proximity to holiday-makers from the Broads, made it an easy target for the vandal. By 1969, the interior of the church had a ransacked appearance, with smashed windows and fittings. Before long, the structure was deteriorating, with loose slates and holes in the roof. Being in a dangerous condition, the nave and porch of 1847 were totally demolished in 1981.

Condition
Only the tower remains, and is in a fair state of preservation. The area around the tower arch is covered with thick rendering, and the west window is boarded up. The lower part of the tower has been reinforced with steel hawsers and wooden boarding to strengthen the quoins. To protect visitors from crumbling masonry, a fence now surrounds the tower, with a notice warning 'Danger. Falling stones'.

Churchyard
The rectangular churchyard is bounded on its north and west sides by a neat flint wall capped in brick (rather crumbling at the south-west corner). A hedge forms south and east boundaries. Most of the churchyard is grassed, and kept fairly neat, with some hawthorn and oak south of the church. Several headstones survive south and west of the tower, of late 19th and 20th-century date. Some of the graves are still tended (latest dates to 1956).

Archaeological and Architectural Assessment
The surviving tower is a significant landmark, but is architecturally unexceptional. It is perhaps the church site which is most important, since Panxworth in one of the Norfolk churches mentioned in *Domesday*. Furthermore, the *Domesday* church was undoubtedly a wooden one, since it is referred to in the mid 12th-century as a chapel to Ranworth built of wood (Blomefield *ibid.*). It remains open to question how much of this structure has survived later medieval and 19th-century rebuildings.

Further References
Blomefield, 1805-10, XI, 110.
Cox 1911, II, 12.
Messent 1936, 184.
Pevsner 1962a, 297.

V. Pudding Norton, St Margaret

Identification TF 9223 2775. *County No.*7111.
Diocese: Norwich. *Archdeaconry:* Lynn. *Deanery*: Burnham and Walsingham. *Parish*: Hempton with Pudding Norton. *Status*: parish church, now disused and ruined.
Date last in regular use: *c*.1570.
Ownership and access: private.

Location and Setting
Pudding Norton Hall, an 18th-century house with adjoining farm buildings, stands 2km south of Fakenham, just east of the B1146 road to Dereham. The extensive earthworks in the meadow south of the hall betray the presence of the former village. A shallow depression indicates a street running north-south, flanked by rectangular tofts. Only the ruined church provides any above-ground remains, standing at the western edge of the meadow some 300m south of the farm buildings; low earthworks mark the boundaries of the rectangular churchyard. The church is mentioned in the *Domesday Book*.

Architectural Description
(Pls XXII, CXIV)
The west tower and part of the nave north and south walls survive. Masonry consists of mortared flint (Pl. CXIV).

Nave. Apart from the south-west corner, all that remains of the nave south wall is a fragment of masonry about 2.5m high and 1m long. It is built of mortared flint, with occasional pieces of brown conglomerate; it is pierced by two large square putlog holes. From the inside, it can be seen that the eastern edge of this piece of wall has an internal splay, edged with limestone and conglomerate: clearly a large window, whose splay begins 0.5m from the ground and continues up to the full height of the surviving masonry.

Plate CXIV. Pudding Norton, St Margaret: the church, with 11th-century west tower, was abandoned in the second half of the 16th century. Photo: Hallam Ashley.

Between this wall and the piece forming the south-west corner, there is a gap some 2m wide, no doubt representing the site of the south doorway. The quoins are large squared stones, fourteen of them being conglomerate, the top two of limestone. In the south wall immediately east of the quoins, there is a long piece of conglomerate which may mark the springing-level of the former south doorway. The roof-line of a south porch can be seen cut into the wall at this point.

More survives of the nave north wall. There is a 2m gap like that in the south wall (but Bryant, 1900, 81, shows a round-headed opening, not a gap). West of the gap, there are twelve quoins at the corner, the top three of limestone, the rest conglomerate. East of the gap, the wall continues for 5m without any openings except four putlog holes. Level with the two lower putlog holes is a flat stringcourse. At the eastern extremity of this wall, there is a vertical line of conglomerate jambs on either face of the wall, suggesting a doorway at this point.

Tower. The nave is slightly wider than the west tower. Diagonally raked putlog holes pass through the thickness of the wall outside the line of the tower. There appears at first sight to be no tower arch connecting nave and tower. Access into the tower is only possible through an irregular opening 1.5m high in the nave west wall. However, the original tower arch has been blocked by neat flint and conglomerate masonry. The rough outline of a tower arch about 4.5m can be made out, but the break is difficult to see. It is impossible to tell whether the arch was round or pointed. Higher up, chamfered limestone forms the coping of the nave roof-line; below the roof-line, there is a great deal of masonry blocking in conglomerate and flint. Above the roof-line the east quoins of the tower are all of medium-sized limestone blocks.

The tower survives to a height of about 12m. It is of one build with the nave, and shares the same construction methods. Much of the masonry has been robbed near the bottom of the wall; the south-west quoins have been robbed to a height of 3m. Like the nave, the tower quoins (up to 5m from the ground) are of conglomerate, with limestone for the upper ones. Also like the nave, the tower is pierced by large square putlog holes, raking diagonally through the wall.

Up to the belfry stage, the only window is in the west wall of the lower storey. It is small, round-headed and single-splayed. It is constructed of 11 pieces of limestone: a sill, jambs of 2 upright stones and 6 flat ones, with 2 thicker blocks forming a split arched lintel (Pl. XXII). Internally, the splay is constructed in flint with no dressed stone.

The belfry windows have not survived. However, there are still remains of the chamfered jambs on the south and west sides. On the ground around the tower are pieces of limestone which probably came from the belfry windows. There are two chamfered pieces just north of the tower, one of which is part of a curving arch; no doubt these formed the Y-tracery visible in Bryant's day (*ibid*).

The south-west quoins extend as high as a concave stone cornice, which must mark the top of the belfry stage. Presumably only the parapet is missing. The other corners have crumbled away at a lower level.

Interpretation and Dating
Nave and west tower are unquestionably of one build. The character of the tower west window, with its upright stones and arched lintel, suggests an early Romanesque date: *c*.1050-1100.

The belfry windows are certainly later. If they had Y-tracery originally, as seems probable, then we should assign them to the late 13th or early 14th century. Perhaps the tower arch was blocked at the same time.

Causes of Abandonment
At the time of *Domesday*, *Nortuna* was a hamlet with its own church. It was never a large village, and was completely depopulated by the end of the 16th century.

The church was still in use up to the middle of the 16th century. In 1505 Andrew Williamson, the rector, willed to be buried in the chancel; in 1557 money was left for the repair of the church (Cushion *et al.*, 1982, 47). It must have been abandoned soon after, since in 1602 it is described as 'whollie ruinated and decaied long since, unknowne by whome it was pulled down' (Tymms, 1866, 232).

Condition
The masonry is in fairly poor condition. Debris from the belfry stage lies scattered around the tower; the bottom metre and a half of the tower has been heavily robbed; the tops of the nave walls are crumbly.

Churchyard
Slight banks mark the churchyard boundaries. It formed a rectangle around the church. No monuments remain.

Archaeological Record
The DMV around the church is a Scheduled Ancient Monument.

There are many pieces of squared and chamfered limestone around the church. On the ground, east of the tower is a piece which looks like a chamfered sill, with gouged slot for the window and pivot hole (presumably for shutters).

Archaeological and Architectural Assessment
The church is important for two reasons. Firstly, it is an unusually fine example of an 'overlap' church, *i.e.* *c*.1050-1100 with nave and square west tower. The west window is particularly interesting, using upright stone jambs and an arched lintel. It is quite possibly the very church mentioned in *Domesday*.

Secondly, it is of great importance as the only above-ground remnant of a very important DMV site. The archaeological potential of the whole site is very great indeed.

Further References
Allison, 1955, 154.
Blomefield, 1805-10, VII, 115.
Bryant, 1900, 81.
Cox, 1911, I, 201.
Cushion, Fenner, Goldsmith, 1982, 47.
Messent, 1931, 28.
Pevsner, 1962b, 285.
Tymms, 1866, 232.

VI. Wallington, St Margaret

Identification TF 6282 0768. *County No.*2421 c/1.
Diocese: Ely. *Archdeaconry:* Wisbech. *Deanery*: Fincham. *Parish*: Runcton Holme with South Runcton and Wallington and Thorpland. *Status*: parish church, now disused and ruined. *Date last in regular use*: *c*.1589.
Ownership and access: private.

Location and Setting
The surviving tower of Wallington church stands in an arable field a mere 100m north-east of Wallington Hall. The grounds of the Hall are sited on land which rises very gently from the Great Ouse River, less than 2km to west. No village can be traced; it was emparked in 1589. The Hall can be reached from the A10, 4km north of Downham Market. The church is mentioned in *Domesday Book*. Today, the tower is occasionally used as a vantage point for firing clays for shooting.

Architectural Description
(Pl. V)
The tower is built of rough blocks of ironbound conglomerate with late medieval brick and limestone edgings; some clunch is also used on the interior. Brick predominates over conglomerate higher up in the tower.

At the western corners, the stepped diagonal buttresses are made of medieval brick edged with squared limestone; where the stone has been robbed in the lower part of the buttresses, it has been replaced with 19th-century brick. At the south-east corner of the tower, three sides of the polygonal stair-turret protrude. The stair-turret has two small rectangular windows, and ends, like the buttresses, below belfry level. The eastern corners of the tower are abutted by the remains of the nave west wall, which projects north and south from the tower. At the south-eastern corner, 19th-century brick tidies up the scar left by the destruction of the nave south wall. The south-west quoins of the nave are still in place 1m further west, largish blocks of squared limestone; the intervening masonry is a mixture of medieval brick, flint and conglomerate, presumably the original masonry of the nave.

The tower arch remains open to the elements (Pl. V). There are no responds, and the double-chamfered brick arch merely dies into the wall. Chamfered late medieval brick forms the leading edge of the jambs, but the lower parts have been repaired with 19th-century brick. Above the arch, on the east face of the tower, a roofline with a brick drip-course can be made out. Inside the tower there is a low mitred arch of the stone doorway to the stair turret; newel and steps are also of limestone, whereas the outer casing is made of brick. In the west wall is a two-centred window with arch, jambs and sill intact; the mullion and tracery have gone, but fragments remain to show that this was a two-light window with a single quatrefoil reticulation. From the springing of the hoodmould, a limestone cornice proceeds round the entire church (including stair turret, but oddly omitting to go round the buttresses). The window has a pointed segmented rear arch, in medieval brick, and is blocked with 19th-century brick.

A small rectangular window pierces the north and west walls at second-storey level (the west one is blocked with brick). There is a large iron clock adorning the exterior of the south side, just below belfry level. The belfry windows survive on all four sides (although blocked on north and east sides). The pointed windows are each filled with cinque-foil cusped Y-tracery. At parapet level there is a large carved gargoyle at each corner. The crenellated parapet is built of brick capped with limestone. Until the second half of the 19th century, the remains of a small spire were visible, but had been removed by 1900 (Bryant, 1904, 299). There is still a small bronze bell in the belfry.

Interpretation and Dating
The masonry of the tower is chiefly characterised by the abundant use of brick; it is used to an extent unlikely before the 15th century. The windows are of cinque-foil cusped Y-tracery of common late Perpendicular type. A mid 15th-century date is likely.

From the fragmentary nave remains at the south-east corner of the tower, it seems that the nave was of the same build as the tower.

There is, however, evidence for remains earlier than these. Aerial photographs have revealed that the chancel had a rounded apse, a feature common in the 11th and 12th century but not used after. It is probable that, prior to demolition, the church had a Norman chancel.

Causes of Abandonment
The owner of Wallington Hall, the notorious Judge Gawdy, had the village emparked in 1589. Having profaned the church, the fate of the Judge (who died of apoplexy in 1606 in London), is described thus by Blomefield:

> 'and having made his appropriate parish church a hay-house, or a dog-kennel, his dead corps being brought from London to Wallington, could for many days find no place of burial, but growing very offensive, he was last conveyed to the church of Runcton, and buried there without any ceremony, and lyeth yet uncovered with so small a matter as a few paving stones' (Blomefield, 1805-10, VII, 412).

A warning to any would-be church profaners!

Condition
The tower is in surprisingly good condition. The most worrying feature is the parapet, which has loose masonry in places. Quite recently, a great deal of the north side of

the parapet fell down, and a scatter of brick and stone lies at the foot of the tower. The structure of the parapet was probably weakened by the growth of a rather large elder bush here, recently removed.

The roof of the tower is still intact, as is the first floor, although its timbers may be suspect.

Churchyard
There is no sign of the churchyard, but cropmarks reveal what may be a rectangular enclosure surrounding the church.

Archaeological Record
Aerial photographs taken in 1974 and 1976 reveal positive cropmarks of a modest nave and apsidal chancel east of the tower (Cambridge University Collection of Aerial Photographs, BQF 61-62, BYX 5-7). Since this reveals ditches and not walls, it would appear that any masonry has been entirely robbed out.

Wallington Hall, 100m south-west, is a stately house dating, in part, to 1525.

Late medieval bronze spout with dog's head found 50m west in 1979; many 13th and 14th-century sherds have been found in the area.

Archaeological and Architectural Assessment
The tower is an attractive ruin, well built, and of modest size. It is an example of thoroughly competent 15th-century design, although unspectacular. Of below-ground evidence for the rest of the church, it is likely that most was destroyed by Judge Gawdy's time and perhaps only robber trenches remain. Little is known of the size or disposition of the associated settlement. We know from *Domesday* that both a village and a church were here in the 11th century.

Further References
Blomefield, 1805-10, VII, 412.
Bryant, 1904, 299.
Messent, 1931, 37.
Pevsner, 1962b, 361.

Chapter 7. Category V

I. Burnham Sutton, St Ethelbert

Identification TF 8364 4176. *County No.* 1755.
Diocese: Norwich. *Archdeaconry*: Lynn. *Deanery*: Burnham and Walsingham. *Parish*: Burnham Sutton. *Status*: parish church, now disused and ruined. *Date last in regular use*: 1771.
Ownership and access: Diocese of Norwich (presumed).

Location and Setting
As the B1355 Fakenham road descends into Burnham Market, there is a small piece of apparently waste ground on the western side, in the triangle between the main road and the lane leading south towards Beacon Hill. Until 1966, fragments of the tower were still visible; but since its demolition, the remains of the church have been marked by nothing more than thick brambles. However, in 1984 the impenetrable brambles were cleared, and a few remnants of walling brought to light.

Architectural Description
(Fig. 40)
None of the walls stands to more than a metre high. The outline of the west tower and part of the nave can be made out, but nothing survives of the chancel (Fig. 40). Building materials are principally of mortared flint and clunch, and there is some medieval brick.

Nave. Most of the south wall is represented by a raised lump in the ground running in an east-to-west direction. Some coursed flint masonry protrudes above the surface at its south-east corner, where a diagonal buttress can be made out, with a piece of fallen masonry beside it. Further west are the remnants of two other buttresses, both appearing to be additions to the south wall; the more western one is faced with medieval brick. More of the north wall is visible, a trench having been dug (unofficially) along the north side of the wall. This has revealed a wall of small to medium-sized flints in neat courses; along its north side the wall has a 10cm wide set-off. As with the south wall, evidence for the western termination of the wall has gone; and in the case of the north wall, the masonry has been broken away before its eastern termination too.

Tower. Only the outline of the south wall of the tower is visible. The north wall is better preserved, and has had a trench dug along its south face. The masonry is very different from that of the nave, mainly consisting of clunch with some flint. At its eastern edge, the north respond of the tower arch can be made out, faced in chamfered brick.

The west wall of the tower does not appear to bond in with north and south walls, and continues north and south beyond the line of these walls. An angled fragment of masonry looks at first glance like part of a buttress at the north-west corner of the tower, but seems rather insubstantial.

Interpretation and Dating
(Fig.41; Pl. CXV)
There are clearly two phases of construction. The first is

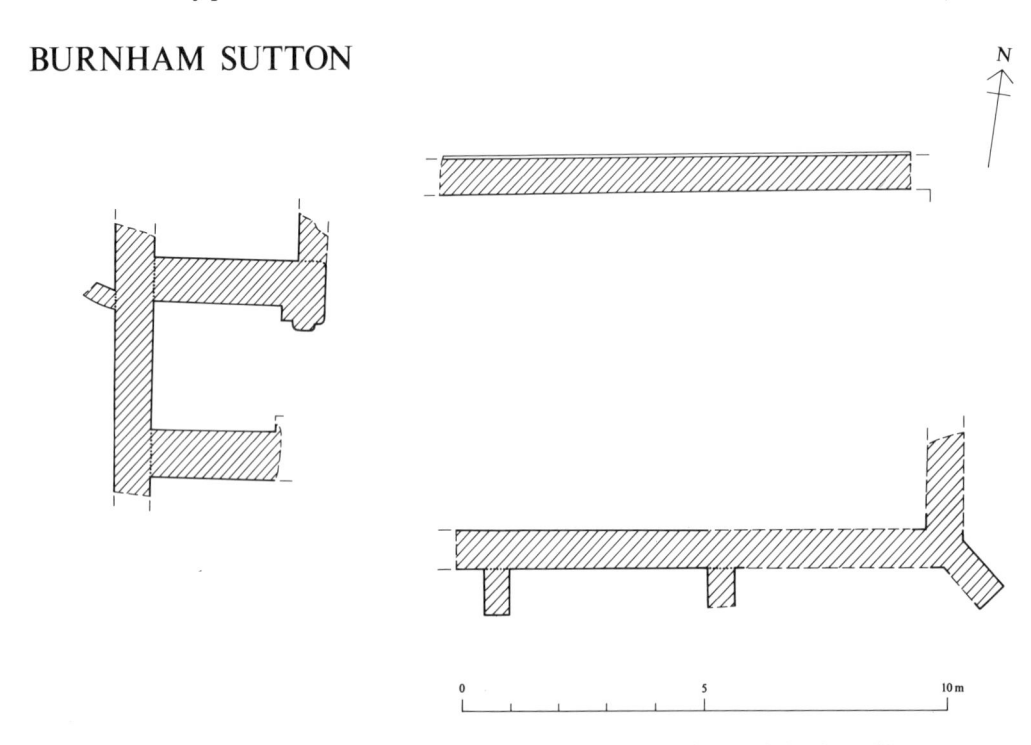

Figure 40. Burnham Sutton, St Ethelbert: plan, as revealed by excavation in 1985. Scale 1:150.

Plate CXV. Burnham Sutton church by Ladbrooke (*c.* 1825). The remains of the tower were demolished in 1958.

characterised by the use of neatly coursed flint, as found in the walls of the nave. The second is marked by the use of clunch and brick, as found in the north and south walls of the tower. Our reconstruction of the original form of the church is greatly helped by Ladbrooke's lithograph (*c.* 1825, Pl. CXV) which shows the ruined church with only tower and part of the nave north wall standing: the tower clearly stood within the west wall of the nave, rather than west of it.

The precise dating of the two phases is open to conjecture. In the broadest terms, diagonal buttresses are more likely after 1300, and the use of brick is more likely in the 15th than the 14th century. Thus, to provide a crude chronology, Phase 1 has been allocated to the 14th century and Phase 2 to the 15th century.

Causes of Abandonment
The Burnhams have always been (and perhaps still are) somewhat over-churched. Of nine medieval churches, St Peter's had been abandoned by the end of the 13th century, St Edmund's by the 14th century, and St Andrew's by the 15th century. Only one has been abandoned since the Reformation: St Ethelbert's at Burnham Sutton. The reasons for the closure of the latter are classic: serious decay of the fabric, combined with the proximity of another church which can easily accommodate the congregations of both churches. The case is clearly set out in the Faculty for the closure and partial demolition of Burnham Sutton church in 1771: the church is

'much decayed and cannot be repaired without great expense...the said church and chancel have been for some years last past so much decayed that it has not been safe for the Parishioners to assemble therein...the materials of the said church at Burnham Sutton are of so small a value as will little more pay the expense of taking down and clearing the same away and repairing the churchyard walls...the church of Burnham Ulph is sufficient to hold its own parishioners and those of Burnham Sutton...[permission was given to] pull down, demolish and lay waste to the said church and chancel of Burnham Sutton and to apply the materials therefrom arising for and towards repairing the said churchyard walls of Burnham Sutton...and to sell and dispose of the said bell belonging to the said church of Burnham Sutton and to apply the monies arising by such sale for and towards the repairing the said church of Burnham Ulph' (NRO, FCB/3, 158).

Burnham Ulph church is only 500m to north. Much of the fabric from Burnham Sutton church had been removed by the time Ladbrooke recorded it *c.* 1825 (Pl. CXV). Little but the tower survived, and this was finally demolished in 1966, despite local protests.

Churchyard
The shape of the churchyard is triangular, from the two roads which flank it to north-east and north-west. It is surrounded by a wire fence, with a gateway at the northern end. There are no surviving headstones or monuments. The whole area was cleared by a Manpower Services Commission team in 1984.

Archaeological Record
Unofficial excavation trenches were dug in 1985 (apparently by a local builder) next to the north walls of nave and tower. The walls revealed were recorded by the Norfolk Archaeological Unit in 1985. A large iron key was found on the site in 1962. The churchyard evidently extended further at some time, since human remains were found when the road to the new housing estate was widened in recent years.

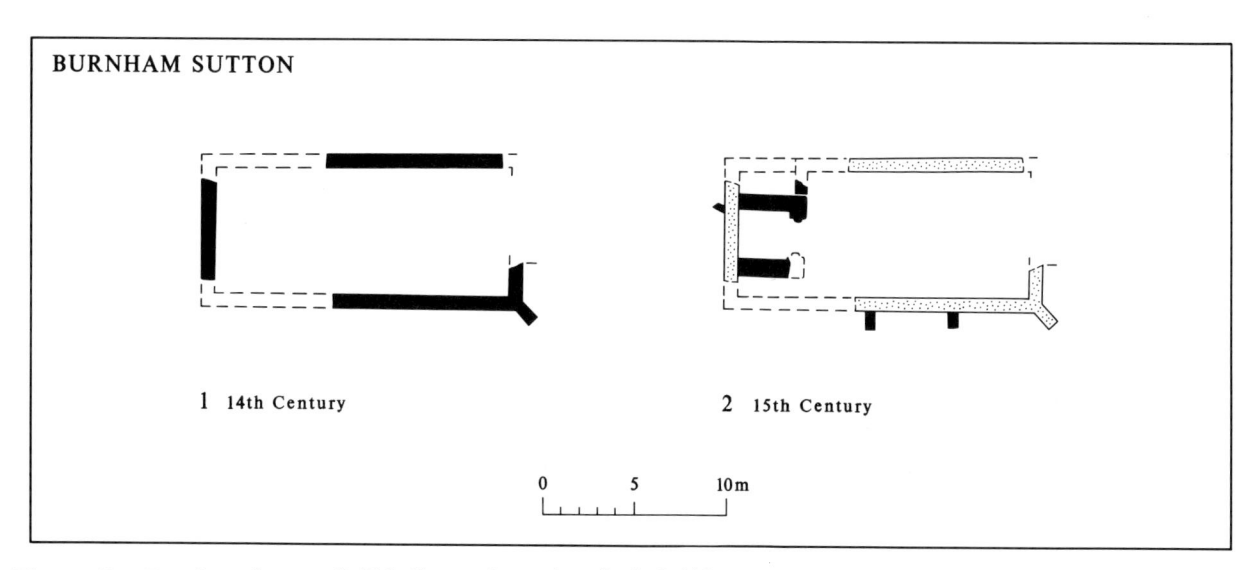

Figure 41. Burnham Sutton, St Ethelbert: phase plan. Scale 1:400.

Archaeological and Architectural Assessment
A church certainly existed here as early as 1254 (Norwich Taxation); the present nave may be as old as this, but is more likely to be a bit later; the tower probably goes back to the 15th century. Very little survives, although most of the churchyard has been retained. The site is mainly of local interest.

Further References
Blomefield, 1805-10, VII, 29
Cox, 1911, I, 76
Messent, 1931, 15.

II. Eccles-next-the-Sea, St Mary

Identification TG 4141 2883. *County No.* 8346
Diocese: Norwich. *Archdeaconry*: Norwich. *Deanery*: Waxham. *Parish*: Hempstead. *Status*: parish church, now disused and ruined. *Date last in regular use*: 1604. *Ownership and access*: on public beach.

Location and Setting
Much of the time, the remains are not at all visible, covered beneath the sands of Eccles beach; but the occasional tide will reveal the odd length of flint masonry. As recently as February 1987, the curved walling of the round tower could be made out. Assuming that the tides have been favourable, the remains can be found on the beach about halfway between Happisburgh and Sea Palling, 1km east of Hempstead church.

Architectural Description
(Pls XII, CXVI, CXVII)
It is difficult to describe the remains because no two visits are alike: sometimes there may be nothing to see, at other times a few lumps of flint masonry protrude above the surface (Pl. CXVI), and occasionally it is possible to make out the curving wall of the round tower (Pl. XII). Since the 17th century, only the round west tower has survived. Old drawings and photographs show that the latter was round for two thirds of its height, with an octagonal belfry stage and crenellated parapet (Pl. CXVII). It eventually collapsed during a raging storm in 1895.

A storm in 1862 brought to light the foundations of the rest of the church, which consisted of chancel, nave, 5-bay arcade and south aisle, and south porch. By 1869, the eastern foundation of the chancel had been undermined, and the remaining foundations continued to deteriorate (Danby-Palmer 1895, 305). At the beginning of this century, Cox (1911, I, 222) was able to describe the surviving fragment of tower:

'The fragment now remaining stands 6 feet 9 inches above the sand drifts; it consists of about half of the west side of a circular Norman tower of pebble formation. The wall is 4 feet 7 inches thick, and is 18 feet in outside diameter. Two or three large disjointed fragments of this tower rise from the sand near the tower base.'

Pevsner had much less to go on, since all he was able to record were 'two heaps of flint on the beach the size of two beginners' sandcastles' (Pevsner, 1962a, 125).

Interpretation and Dating
Old photographs of the tower show that the masonry of the lower part of the round tower was of flint in neat clearly-defined courses, of a character very like surviving

Plate CXVI. Eccles-next-the-Sea, St Mary: 'two heaps of flint on the beach the size of two beginner's sandcastles.'

Plate CXVII. Eccles-next-the-Sea by Ladbrooke (1823).

11th/12th-century work in the county. The octagonal belfry was probably added in the 14th or 15th century.

Causes of Abandonment
A tremendous storm in 1604 destroyed the church along with the whole village; before then, the village comprised 1300 acres of land, but after the storm a mere 300 acres remained (Blomefield 1805-10, IX, 293).

Archaeological Record
Church and churchyard were exposed after storms in 1862, 1874 and 1912. In 1912, thirty-eight skeletons from the churchyard were uncovered, as well as a Roman coin. Medieval coins, spurs, escutcheons *etc.* were found on the site in 1918.

Archaeological and Architectural Assessment
The church remains date from the 11th/12th to the 15th century. It is difficult to know how much of the church, churchyard and village still lie beneath the sand.

Further References
Allison, 1955, 116.
Blomefield, 1805-10, IX, 293.
Cox, 1911, I, 222.
Danby-Palmer, 1895, 305.
Messent, 1931, 18.
Pevsner, 1962a, 125.

III. Hackford, All Saints

Identification TG 1011 2283. *County No.*7471.
Diocese: Norwich. *Archdeaconry:* Norwich. *Deanery*: Sparham. *Parish*: Reepham and Kerdiston with Hackford and Whitwell. *Status*: parish church, now disused and ruined. *Date last in regular use*: 1543.
Ownership and access: Diocese of Norwich.

Location and Setting
(Pl. XVI)
Reepham is unique in having three parish churches within one churchyard. All three used to have separate and distinct parishes: the parish of Hackford went west from the churchyard, Whitwell went south, and Reepham north-east (Pl. XVI). Reepham and Whitwell churches are still in use, but Hackford church burned down in 1543. Its remains can be found under a yew tree, just south of Whitwell church.

Architectural Description
(Pl. CXVIII)
The remains consist of one piece of wall, running north-south, about 6m high and covered in ivy. It is 3.7m long and 42cm thick, and built of coursed flint. On its west face, a blocked window opening 1.5m wide can be made out, framed in chamfered medieval brick. The stone base of a wall monument is set into the blocking. On the east face, the wall is inset with three memorial stones, the only legible one dating to 1729.

Messent describes this surviving wall as the east wall of one of the aisles (Messent, 1931, 19), but it cannot be so. A drawing made by Miss E.F.Boon in 1784, (Pl. CXVIII), shows only tower, south porch and western parts of nave walls surviving. The east wall of the porch was already inset with memorials at this date, although this does not appear to be the wall remaining today since the latter survives to a greater height. We must be left, therefore, with the west wall of the porch as the sole witness to the parish church of Hackford.

More evidence for the form of the church is provided by the 1784 drawing. Evidently, the tower had a chequerboard parapet and diagonal buttresses. The tracery had already gone from the belfry windows. The south wall of the tower had a square sound-hole. The roof-line of the nave was clearly visible and the porch had an elaborate doorway. The tower was demolished in 1796. Martin (1771) provides us with a sketch plan of the church c.1750 (Pl. XIX). The complete outline was still traceable then: chancel, nave, porch and tower; doors and buttresses are also indicated.

Interpretation and Dating
The brickwork in the porch suggests a 14th or 15th-century date for the surviving remains.

Causes of Abandonment
The cause is quite clear: natural disaster. The church was destroyed by the devastating fire of 1543, which also burned down most of the surrounding houses. The parish was then consolidated with Whitwell.

The 1552 Inventory of Church Goods (Walter, 1945, 14) records the selling of the church plate in 1547 for £20, 'Whereof thei have bestowed in Bricke and lede towards the making of an Ele by reason that the church of Hackford was brent and is nowe uned to Whitwell.' Some of the materials were also used for repairing the highways.

Plate CXVIII. Hackford, All Saints: drawing by E.F.Boon, 1784. Nave and chancel were burned down in 1543; the tower was demolished in 1796; only the west wall of the porch survives today.

The tower and most of the remaining masonry was pulled down in 1790.

Churchyard
The site of Hackford church is part of the cemetery of Reepham and Whitwell, and is scattered with 18th and 19th-century gravestones. A large 19th-century brick table tomb (to the Sewells) stands north-west of the surviving wall, probably covering part of the site of the tower.

Archaeological Record
Materials from the church were used to build the transept of Whitwell church in the 16th century. Much material from All Saints must have been used to build the churchyard south wall, which is speckled with reused limestone.

Archaeological and Architectural Assessment
Given the uniqueness of Reepham's three parish churches in one combined churchyard, the surviving remains of Hackford church assume considerable importance.

Further References
Blomefield, 1805-10, VIII, 223.
Cox, 1911, I, 192.
Messent, 1931, 19.

IV. King's Lynn, St James

Identification TF 6215 1978. *County No.*5484.
Diocese: Norwich. *Archdeaconry:* Lynn. *Deanery*: Lynn. *Parish*: King's Lynn, St Margaret. *Status*: parochial chapel, now disused and ruined. *Date last in regular use*: c.1540. *Ownership and access*: private.

Location and Setting
The parochial chapel of St James was built by Bishop Eborard (1121-45) 400m east of St Margaret's, the priory

and parish church founded by Bishop de Losinga soon after 1100. No doubt St James's was intended to serve the rapidly expanding town and port of Lynn; under Bishop Turbe (1146-74) the marshy area north of the town was enclosed and drained; this addition, known as 'the Newland' and served by a new chapel dedicated to St Nicholas, nearly doubled the size of Lynn. The eastern part of the town, which was served by St James's, was always sparsely populated; even today there is a surprising amount of parkland in the vicinity of St James's, with The Walks to east, the Greyfriars gardens to west, and the small park to north which was formerly the cemetery of St James.

There still exists a chapel of St James, on London Road, but this is a Methodist church built on the site of the parochial chapel in 1858. Only one piece of walling belonging to the original chapel survives, situated immediately north of the Methodist church hall (built in 1978 at the east side of the Methodist church, replacing the Sunday School of 1875). It can best be viewed from the north side, in a small field belonging to a nursery school.

Architectural Description
(Pl. CXIX)
Part of the north wall of the north transept survives, fenced off from the small playing field of the nursery school and standing within 1.5m of the Methodist church hall (Pl. CXIX).

The masonry is of mortared rubble, largely flint but with a great quantity of reused limestone; many of the limestone pieces have diagonal tooling, and some are shaped voussoirs, angle shafts, roll-mouldings; one of the pieces may be part of a cushion capital. A large angle buttress in squared limestone forms the north-west corner of the transept, with a chamfered base-course just visible above the ground, and a single set-off higher up. The north-east corner of the transept does not survive.

A very wide rectangular window occupies most of the wall. It is lined all round with chamfered limestone. Above it there is an equally wide four-centred relieving arch, constructed (along with the intervening tympanum) of 16th-century brick. The window has subsequently been modified by the infilling of either end and the insertion of a wooden window frame, with three wooden mullions and a heavy wooden transom; this window is the same height as the earlier one, but not quite so wide. On the inner face, the offset window sill is capped with reused tiles, one of which is of glazed late medieval type.

Plate CXIX. King's Lynn, St James: north wall of north transept; the wooden window belongs to its post-medieval transformation into a workhouse.

Nothing else remains of this transept, but a fragment of odd wall 20m further south may have belonged to the original church. Its masonry is of flint with many reused limestone pieces, running in an east-west direction. Niches and fireplaces built into the south face of this wall suggests modification for domestic use.

Interpretation and Dating
(Pls CXX, CXXI)
The surviving wall contains reused 12th-century material. The plain angle buttress seems to be of 13th or early 14th-century type. Into this wall a wide window was inserted in the 16th century, to judge from the brickwork of the four-centred arch and tympanum. The window was in turn remodelled, with wooden frame and mullions: surely no later than the 17th century.

The chapel of St James was founded by an unnamed Bishop of Norwich (Blomefield, 1805-10, VIII, 512). Beloe (1899, 163) has argued that, since its foundation was confirmed by Bishop Turbe, its construction must belong to the latter years of his predecessor Eborard (1121-45). The only part of Eborard's church still on site must be the reused limestone pieces described above. Until the collapse of the crossing tower in 1854, the 12th-century compound piers of the crossing were still intact. Illustrations published by Beloe show that the piers had two or three orders of round engaged shafts with cushion capitals (Beloe, 1899, Pl. 37, 40); a Norman corbel table and engaged shaft were visible on the east wall of the south transept. The moulded pointed arches of the crossing must belong to a later reconstruction, in the late 13th or early 14th century. The transepts must have been remodelled at the same time, including the large buttresses of which one survives. According to Beloe (1899, 164-5), the choir had aisles; he also reports that the outer walls of the nave-aisles were as high as the nave arcade, leaving no room for a clerestorey, but that the aisles were probably an addition to the old Norman nave.

There can be no doubt that St James's was a large cruciform church, modified and partly rebuilt c.1300. The nave was pulled down in 1549, and was apparently 100 feet long and 24 feet wide; the east end contained a revered image of Christ (Richards, 1812, 564-5). At the Dissolution, the control of the church was transferred from the Priory of Norwich to the Dean and Chapter of Norwich Cathedral; in 1566 it was made over to the mayor and corporation of Lynn (*ibid*, 566). They decided to keep the choir and transepts, which were re-roofed in 1561 (Beloe, 1899, 162). These premises were modified in 1581 at a cost of £600 for use as a workhouse for the manufacture of baize (Hillen, 1907, 871); the wide window at the end of the north transept probably belongs to this phase.

Further alterations took place in 1682, when the structure was restored and an octagonal belfry with lantern built above the crossing (by Henry Bell, Pl. CXX). Mackerell (1737, 177) records the marble inscription above the door: 'E RUINIS CAPELLAE S^{TI} JACOBI ORPHANOTROPHIUM HOC EREXIT S.P.Q.L. SIMONE TAYLOR MAIORE MDCLXXXII.' Old drawings show that the octagonal belfry was supported on squinches. It seems probable that the surviving wooden window in the north transept dates to this remodelling. The workhouse was enlarged in 1782 (Hillen, 1907, 551), and more alterations were made soon after 1835: £750 was spent, raising its accommodation to 200 inmates; the stone Royal coat of arms of Elizabeth I which

Plate CXX. King's Lynn, St James: transepts and crossing of the church used as a workhouse after the demolition of the nave in 1549; the belfry with lantern was added in 1682; tragically, the tower collapsed in 1854, killing two people.

Plate CXXI. King's Lynn, St James: crossing and transept used as a dormitory.

had surmounted the main entrance, was at this time removed to the Guild Hall (Hillen, 1907, 594). The chancel and transepts of St James's had been divided into three storeys to provide the required accommodation (Pl. CXXI). From 1835, St James's served as workhouse for the whole of King's Lynn, and not just the parish of St Margaret.

After nearly three hundred years as a workhouse came the sudden and tragic end. On August 20th 1854, it was noticed that the tower clock had stopped; on closer inspection it could be seen that the tower wall was listing. An attempt was made to correct this, using a rope; but all in vain. 'Without further warning the wall, tower and central arches of the old building collapsed ... Mr Andrews and an inmate of the workhouse were killed' (Tuck, 1981, 13). The site was sold in 1856, and a new workhouse was built on a new site. The site of St James's was occupied by a Methodist chapel (built in 1858, with Sunday School added in 1875), the County Court (in 1864) and two assembly rooms (built in 1887, destroyed by fire in 1904).

Causes of Abandonment
St James's, since its foundation, was a chapel-of-ease to St Margaret's in King's Lynn. We are told that it was closed at the Dissolution, that the nave was pulled down in 1549, and that its contents (4 bells worth £200, stone, iron and glass worth 100 marks, timber and lead worth £300, plate, jewellery and stock worth £200) came into the hands of the mayor and corporation of Lynn and were later sold (Richards, 1812, 565). The precise reasons for the closure of St James's are difficult to discern. Perhaps it was mistakenly thought to be a monastic foundation, since it was owned by the Priory of Norwich, had the status of chapel, and contained a revered image. More likely it fell victim to the parochial reorganisation of the time, and was regarded as superfluous to parochial needs; Lynn could be adequately served by St Margaret's and St Nicholas.

By 1566, St James's was in the hands of the corporation of Lynn, and had certainly ceased to function as a place of worship. The materials of the demolished nave were dispersed, some to repair St Margaret's. Of additional interest (and showing the scarcity of building stone in Norfolk) is the record, dated 1569, of the Duke of Norfolk removing '20 loads of free-stone of the Chapel of St James' (Hillen, 1907, 291) for the construction of his palace at Norwich.

Converted to use as a workhouse from 1581, the chancel and transepts of St James's remained intact until its final collapse in 1854.

Condition
All that remains *in situ* is the lower part of the north wall of the north transept. The masonry is in reasonable condition, but the exposed top of the wall is crumbly.

Churchyard
None of the original churchyard remains, although it continued in use through the 16th and possibly also the 17th century; 200 plague victims were buried in it in 1597 (Hillen, 1907, 298). The field next to the workhouse was bought for use as a burial ground, with its own chapel, in 1805 (ibid. 543-4). This is no longer in use, but part of the burial ground, with stacked gravestones, can be seen north-east of the site.

Archaeological Record
Some details of measurement were revealed by (unrecorded) excavations which took place in 1905. They confirm that the chancel did indeed have aisles (7 feet wide); the chancel itself was 15 feet wide. Hillen (1907, 595) records it thus:

'The St James's Hall and Assembly Room built in 1887 were destroyed by fire (12th November 1904). During the excavations before the rebuilding of the hall, the bases of the columns forming the entrance to the chancel of St James's church were discovered, besides a wall two feet thick, and other remains. The width of the chancel arch was 15 feet, and the chancel side aisles 7 feet; the pillars supporting the chancel roof were 15 feet apart. Four bases *in situ* may be seen beneath the present platform, abutting upon the original transept (100 by 24 feet in 1561) which was incorporated in the old workhouse.'

New law courts now cover the site, and the bases uncovered in 1905 do not seem to have survived.

Several limestone pieces of Norman workmanship have been reused in the masonry of the surviving north transept wall. Even more pieces can be found 10km away (to south-west) at St Peter's Lodge in the parish of Walpole St Peter. After the collapse of the workhouse in 1854, the site of St James' came into the possession of Richard Munson of St Peter's Lodge. When the Methodists wanted a site for a new chapel, they bought the western half (a piece of land 108ft by 60ft) from Munson in 1858 for £350 (Hillen, 1907, 646). Many medieval fragments were built into the 19th-century porch of St Peter's Lodge, including much Norman limestone shafting.

Further References
Beloe, 1899.
Blomefield, 1805-10, VIII, 512.
Hillen, 1907.
Mackerell, 1737, 177.
Richards, 1812, 564-6.
Tuck, 1981, 13.

V. Great Walsingham, All Saints

Identification TF 9395 3785 *County No.*2057
Diocese: Norwich. *Archdeaconry:* Lynn. *Deanery*: Burnham and Walsingham. *Parish*: Great Walsingham. *Status*: parish church, now disused and ruined. *Date last in regular use*: second half of 16th century.
Ownership and access: private, meadow.

Location and Setting
Walsingham, perhaps the most important pilgrimage centre in the country, lies in the gentle valley of the River Stiffkey, half-way between Fakenham and Wells. Shrines, priory, friary, museum and inn are all located at Little Walsingham. Few pilgrims venture as far as Great Walsingham, 0.7km to north-east, which is fortunate in remaining undeveloped and unspoilt. In the church of St Peter, Great Walsingham possesses one of the finest Decorated churches in the county (designed in the 1340s by the anonymous 'Architect of Great Walsingham', whose work has been analysed by Fawcett, 1980). Remains of a second church can be found in a meadow 250m north-east of St Peter's. This was a separate parish church, dedicated to All Saints. Much of the churchyard wall can

Plate CXXII.   Great Walsingham, All Saints: low walls remaining of the church of *c.* 1340, abandoned in the 16th century. Cambridge University Collection BUE 59, copyright reserved.

be traced; its east boundary is the minor road which bends back to the Wells road, 300m to west.

Architectural Description
(Pl. CXXII)

Most of the walls can be traced, standing just above the level of the surrounding meadow (up to 30cm high in places). It presents a rather unusual outline, with very wide nave, narrow west tower and very short chancel (Pl. CXXII).

No masonry protrudes above ground in the chancel, but its plan is clearly suggested by humps. The nave outline is very clear with much of its 90cm wide walling of mortared flint showing through. Between north and south walls is a slight depression. The two walls are nearly 11m apart, with no sign of an intervening arcade. It can be seen that the nave south wall had diagonal buttresses at its corners. Traces of north and south porches are also visible. The tower is outlined by humps.

Interpretation and Dating
(Pl. CXXII)

An aerial photograph (Pl.CXXII; Cambridge University Collection of Air Photographs BUE 59) reveals the outline of all but the chancel. Extra details, such as the location of buttresses along the nave, can be made out. However, there are no indications of any arcade walls within the outer walls of the nave. Thus the nave would appear to have been wide and aisleless.

In the absence of significant standing remains or documentation, the date of this structure can only be guessed. The outline, with its diagonal corner buttresses, suggests a 14th or 15th-century date. Furthermore, it seems that a date for its construction before 1360 would be likely: until then it was served by a vicar, but in 1360 the parish was merged with St Peter's and served by only a curate (Blomefield, 1805-10, IX, 271). It is probable that, considering the scale of All Saints, it was built prior to this diminution in status.

Fawcett has given sound reasons for dating St Peter's church to the 1340s or 1350s (Fawcett, 1980, 292-3). Although All Saints is clearly not of the same design, it is possible that both were being built at the same time (perhaps by rival patrons). The design of All Saints, while not resembling St Peter's, is strikingly similar in its planning to another church being built in the 1330s and 1340s: St Mary's at Elsing. The latter church has an aisleless nave of extraordinary width (nearly 40ft; Pevsner, 1962b, 157); there is no other church of comparable dimensions in the county apart from All Saints at Great Walsingham with its nave about 36 ft wide. Furthermore, Elsing church has a similar disposition of tower and chancel, possesses a north and south porch, and has diagonal buttresses at the nave corners. The similarities are so strong that it prompts questions about a connection between Elsing and Walsingham All Saints, and suggests that the latter was built *c.*1340.

Causes of Abandonment

The most obvious cause of abandonment is the presence of another very large church only 250m away within the same parish. All Saints was served by vicars until 1360, when it was demoted to a curacy dependent on St Peter's. It was abandoned shortly before 1552, as the Inventory of Church Goods presents a certificate of sale of its goods; the money was used to repair the bridge and roads in the town (Walters, 1945, 224).

Condition

Masonry, where it survives, protrudes above the ground to a maximum height of 30cm.

Churchyard

Fragments of the mortared flint west and south walls of the churchyard survive. The line of these walls is clearly visible from the air. The churchyard would have formed a wide rectangle around the church, its east boundary formed by the road running very near to the chancel east wall. No monuments survive.

Archaeological Record

There are many odd pieces of freestone built into the flint wall flanking the road east of the church; it is highly probable that these pieces came from the church.

Messent believed there to have been another church, of Saxon date, 100 yards north of All Saints (1931, 37), but there is no evidence for this. He follows Bryant (1898, II, 85), who seems to have been misled on this point.

Archaeological and Architectural Assessment

All Saints was a large and undoubtedly fine medieval church. Surviving remains belong to the 14th-century church, which may have been aisleless resembling Elsing. The 14th-century church replaced an older one, of which there may be below-ground remains.

The fragmentary remains which exist today only do so because the surrounding land is pasture, and has not been ploughed up. Any change in the use of this field would clearly have serious implications for the site, both church and churchyard.

Further References
Blomefield, 1805-10, IX, 271.
Bryant, 1898, II, 85.
Cox 1911, I, 209.
Fawcett, 1980.
Messent, 1931, 37.

Pevsner, 1962a, 141.
Walters, 1945, 224.

VI. Weeting, All Saints

Identification TL 7756 8869. *County No.* 5625.
Diocese: Ely. *Archdeaconry:* Wisbech. *Deanery*: Feltwell.
Parish: Weeting. *Status*: parish church, now disused and ruined. *Date last in regular use*: c. 1700.
Ownership and access: public land under the control of Breckland District Council.

Location and Setting
(Fig.42)
The village of Weeting stands in a gap in the Breckland forest 2km north-west of Brandon. At the eastern edge of the village, near the remains of the Norman castle, is the parish church of St Mary. The unlikely location for the church of All Saints is 500m south of St Mary's, in the middle of a public recreation ground, not far from the club-house. Most of the site has been levelled and grassed over, but there are two raised lumps of masonry which form the only clues to the existence of the church (Fig.42).

Architectural Description
The eastern lump of the two consists of mortared flint masonry 1.5m high. There is the beginning of a narrow spiral stair, with four steps on the south-west side. To the north, the exterior of the stairway is indicated by a neatly finished piece of walling forming two sides of a polygon, and containing a stretch of limestone stringcourse. The eastern face is also neatly finished, forming the west jamb of a (now demolished) doorway; the moulded limestone base jambs still survive.

Moving to the western lump of masonry, this stands to the same height (about 1.5m) but the scattering of rubble covers a wider area. Two diagonal buttresses can be discerned, evidently forming the north-west and south-west corners of the church. Just east of the south-west buttress, the remains of another spiral stairway can be made out; this one has polygonal external walling on the south side, faced with small flints and limestone quoining at the angles.

Interpretation and Dating
What can these two lumps of masonry tell us about the form of the church, apart from the fact that the stairways were evidently the strongest part of the structure? The answer: a great deal. With its diagonal buttresses and stair-turret, the western lump forms the remains of the west tower. Equally clearly, the eastern lump must represent the north-east corner of the nave, with its rood-stair, and chancel (with priest's door) to east. We therefore have an outline of tower and nave, broadly datable to the 14th or 15th century (buttresses, jambs, masonry).

Our knowledge of the site is supplemented by Blomefield's description of it *c.* 1740, shortly after the tower had collapsed. He gives us the size of the chancel and informs us that there was a south aisle:

'This church stood in the south part of the town, and is now in ruins, by the fall of the tower on it, about 40 years past; it was the neatest, the most regular, and modern church of the two, built of flint, chalk, etc. and consisted of a nave, about 35 feet in length, and (including the south isle) about 31 in breadth, having on that side three neat arches, supported by pillars, formed of four pilasters united together. At the west end of the nave stood an handsome square tower of flint, with quoins etc. of freestone, as appears from what is still remaining: the nave is divided from the chancel by a neat and lofty arch of stone work, still standing; the length of the chancel was about 33 feet, and the breadth about 18: the greatest part of the walls, both of the church and chancel, is still standing, but the roof is totally decayed and gone' (Blomefield 1805-10, II, 170).

The accuracy of Blomefield's description was confirmed during the hot summer of 1983, when parchmarks revealed the outline of the church with such clarity that it was possible to plot the plan on the ground. The only feature which Blomefield had not mentioned was the south porch, attached to the south aisle.

Causes of Abandonment
The collapse of the tower *c.* 1700 resulted in the abrupt abandonment of the church. No doubt attempts might have been made to repair it if it had only been the only church in the village; but the presence of St Mary's only 500m away rendered this an unnecessary expense, and it was allowed to decay. The churchyard, however, continued in use until at least *c.* 1900.

Condition
The site of chancel nave and aisle is under mown grass, and used as part of the playing field; whereas the rubble-strewn tower site cannot be mown, and is covered with moderate weeds. Local inhabitants say that, as late as the 1960s, the tower was still standing up to several metres in height.

Churchyard
Today the churchyard forms part of the playing field. The fenced boundaries to east and south of the church undoubtedly mark the limits of the churchyard; that to south is lined with 18th and 19th-century headstones (there is also a ledger slab, dated 1678, which came from the church). The latest surviving headstone dates to 1890, proving that the churchyard remained in use to at least this date. Again, local inhabitants recall that the churchyard remained separate from the playing field until at least the 1950s.

Archaeological and Architectural Assessment
As indicated by the 1983 parchmarks, the foundations (and probably also the lower rising walls) of the entire church lie just below the surface. It was obviously a reasonably grand church of 14th or 15th-century date.

Further References
Blomefield, 1805-1810, II, 170.
Cox 1911, II, 74.
Messent 1931, 39.
Pevsner, 1962b, 369.

WEETING

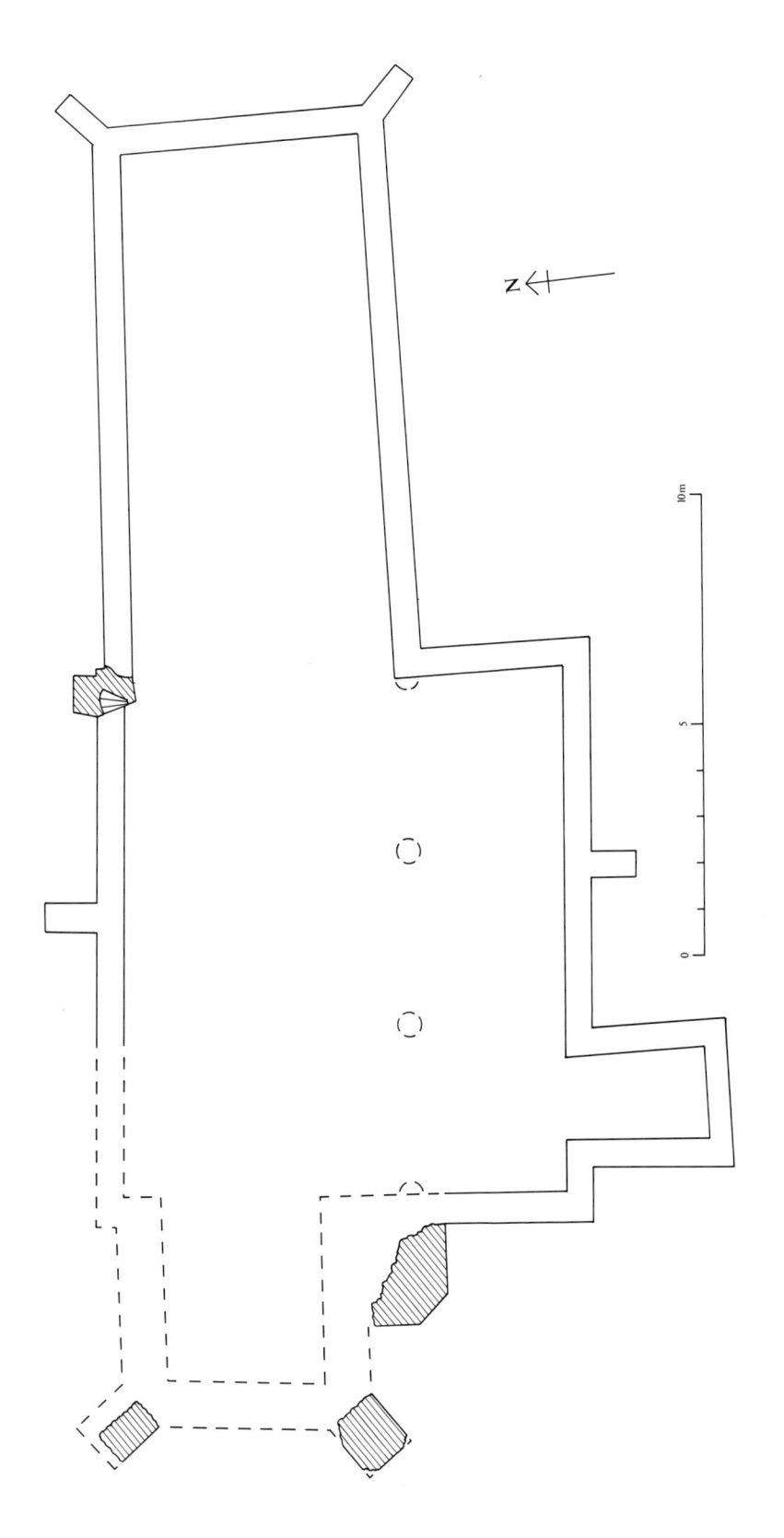

Figure 42. Weeting, All Saints: late medieval church whose tower collapsed c. 1700; mound of rubble around tower and fragment of rood-stair are all that remain; rest of church revealed in outline by parchmarks in 1983.

Chapter 8. Category VI

I. Ashby St Mary

Identification TH 4229 1522 *County No.*8542
Diocese: Norwich. *Archdeaconry:* Norwich. *Deanery*: Flegg. *Parish*: Ashby, Oby and Thurne. *Status*: parish church, now disappeared. *Date last in regular use*: mid 18th century.
Ownership and access: private, arable field.

Location and Setting
The site of the church is in arable field 0.75km west of the B1152 road from Acle to Martham, immediately north of the small road to Thurne. Part of this field is marked as 'Church Yard' in the 1845 tithe map, and today the site can be identified by a thin scattering of pieces of limestone and brick. Ashby Hall still stands 0.5km northwest of here, and the village (completely deserted by the 18th century) was situated between the Hall and the church. It is an exceedingly isolated location today.

Architectural Description
(Pl. CXXIII)
Apart from the scattered debris on the surface of the field, there are no above-ground remains. The site was excavated in the late 19th century, but the only record of it is by Bryant (1899, IV, 114):

> 'In the autumn of 1822, when some trenches were made in the ground, there were found remains of the church and some pieces of encaustic tile pavement, yellow and black, in perfect condition, and laid in zig-zag fashion, similar to those used in Martham church, only smaller. A wall was traced, east and west for 90 feet, and another wall north and south for 30 feet. To the west of the latter there was found what appeared to be the foundations of a square tower with buttresses at the angle'.

However, much more information about the church was available after aerial photographs were taken of the site during the drought of 1976. These revealed in the negative cropmarks, not only the outline of the church as it existed before its demolition in the 18th century, but also, most excitingly, the earlier construction phases, exposing the plan of the church as early as c. 1100 (Pl. CXXIII).

This early church resembled that at Hales, with rectangular nave, apsidal chancel and round west tower. Later on, the chancel was evidently enlarged by a new rectangular chancel almost twice as long as the old one, and as wide as the old nave; this chancel had three bays, as suggested by the buttresses. The west end of the church had been as thoroughly altered as the east: the round west tower must have been demolished to allow for a western extension of the nave; west of this new longer nave, a square west tower had been added; a south porch adjoined the west bay of the nave. Thus the church, as it stood prior to its demolition in the 18th century, comprised a long chancel and nave, with south porch and square west tower.

Plate CXXIII. Ashby, St Mary: cropmarks show not only the late medieval form of the church, but also its earlier plan with apsidal chancel and round west tower. Cambridge University Collection BYY 80, copyright reserved.

Interpretation and Dating
It is interesting to reflect that, had the church survived today, there would have been little or no evidence to suggest a church with apsidal chancel and round tower of the Hales type. Since Hales church belongs to the first half of the 12th century, there is no reason to doubt that the earlier church at Ashby is of similar date. The extensions of chancel and nave, and additions of tower and porch, are more difficult to date accurately from the evidence available. It is likely that they cover several phases from the 13th to the 15th century.

Causes of Abandonment
When Blomefield recorded the church c. 1740, it was still standing; he gave few details of the appearance of the church, but described many of the gravestones inside, and also the font (Blomefield 1805-10, XI, 148). However, the village of Ashby had virtually disappeared by this time, since he noted: 'Many years past there were no houses standing but that of the manor; the inhabitants of Oby came to this church' (*ibid*).

This latter fact led to a confusion in identification of the church, since the village of Ashby was almost wholly depopulated, and therefore the church was used by the inhabitants of the hamlet of Oby (1km south-west) who had lost their church two centuries earlier: thus Faden's map of 1797 marks St Mary's at Ashby as the 'site of Oby Ch.'. Although Faden's identification is incorrect, it suggests that the church was no longer in use by 1797. Rather tenuous evidence that the church was at least partly standing, but not in use, in the second half of the 18th century is provided by Bryant (1899, IV, 114): 'The Rev.W.C.Davie, Rector here, was told by a man living in Thurne, over 80 years of age, that he had heard his grandfather speak of boiling a kettle in the tower of the church in Oby (*sic.*) churchyard'.

The principal cause of the abandonment of the church at Ashby is clearly the lack of parishioners, first of all in Ashby itself, and later from neighbouring Oby. It is, however, curious for a church still standing in the 18th century to leave no trace about ground today. Such thorough demolition is unusual in rural locations; it is therefore possible that the fact that the land the church stood on was coveted, no doubt by a local landowner, may have had an influence on its abandonment in the 18th century.

Archaeological and Architectural Assessment
The site is a very important one, with remains of a medieval church of several phases lying below ground, the phases going back at least to the early 12th century. It acquires additional importance from its relationship with Ashby DMV, north-west of the church.

Further References
Allison 1955, 142.
Blomefield, 1805-10, XI, 148.
Bryant, 1899, IV, 114.
Cox 1911, I, 88.
Messent 1931, 12.

II. Fincham St Michael

Identification TF 6857 0635. *County No.*4358.
Diocese: Ely. *Archdeaconry:* Wisbech. *Deanery*: Fincham.
Parish: Fincham. *Status*: parish church, now disappeared. *Date last in regular use*: 1744-5.
Ownership and access: Diocese of Norwich.

Location and Setting
The village of Fincham is spread along the A1122 road from Swaffham, 7km north-east of Downham Market. The magnificent parish church of St Martin's stands on the north side of the road (originally a Roman road cutting across Norfolk and linking with the Fen Causeway of Denver) at the eastern end of the village. Towards the western end of the village, and south of the road, is the old Rectory, a building of the 17th and 19th centuries. The western part of the Rectory garden was fenced off in 1980 for the construction of a new Rectory, allowing the old one to be sold off. A wall at the northern edge of the new Rectory garden (and formerly belonging to the old Rectory) incorporates a stone with this inscription (rather faded): 'Here stood formerly the ancient Church of Saint Michael in this village, dilapidated and destroyed, A.D.1744'.

Architectural Description
There are no coherent church remains. Some odd pieces of limestone and brick have been incorporated into the garden walls, including some window tracery in the garden of the old Rectory. The new Rectory garden contains a massive piece of carved limestone; the stone appears to be the springing of four arches and four diagonal ribs, no doubt originally supported by a free-standing pier at the centre of four vaulted compartments (such as one finds in a medieval undercroft or cellar).

It must be presumed that the church stood north of the new Rectory, in the garden. When the foundations for the new house were dug in 1980, no remaining walls were uncovered; some possible robber trenches were noticed but could not be interpreted as church remains. Plenty of inhumations were uncovered, however (info. Norfolk Archaeological Unit).

Fortunately, Parkin was able to describe the church before its demise in 1744, and it is worth quoting from him at length.

'This church is built of flint and boulder, and consists only of a nave, or body, with a chancel covered with lead. At the west end of the nave stands a large square tower embattled with quoins and copings of freestone, and a pinnacle at each corner; and herein hang three bells. The length of the nave, from the west door to the chancel, is about 60 feet, and in breadth about 27. The roof is supported by oaken principals; on the head of which have been the effigies of religious persons in their habits; but their heads are broken off ... The chancel is in length about 33 feet, and in breadth about 18; the upper part of the wall on the north side is of brick embattled, and coped with free-stone; also a little freestone porch or passage into the chancel; in the centre of the arch there seem to be cinquefoils cut, the arms of the Lords Bardolphs.'

[There follows a transcription of a gravestone, Robert and Sarah King, d. 1683 (now in St Martin's); communion table given in 1623 (also in St Martin's); arms of Dereham Abbey in the east window; monument against north chancel wall, in black marble, Rev.Daniel Baker, d.1722].

'Against the said wall, east from this, is an arched monument of stone: in this arch is a raised tomb 2 feet from the ground; on each side of this arch, on the summit, is a niche carved for some statue; there is no inscription or arms about it, and probably it was the Sepulchram Domini, or the sepulchre of our Lord. Opposite to this, on the south wall of the chancel, are three stone seats or stalls, raised within the wall, having 3 arches, one over each seat; which seats are about 2 feet in depth, and above 3 in height; on the summit of each rises a pyramid of stone, carved, and pointing to the cornish, which juts out from the wall about 3 inches. Such seats and stalls are still to be seen in many old churches, and were for the bishop, priest and deacon, or the rector, curate, or chantry priests. The stalls here differ in this; that of the bishop or rector is about two inches higher than that of the priest; and the stall of the priest is the same, in respect of the deacon. Over the stall of the bishop are these two shields... in a bordure of the last, eight mitres of the 2d Spencer's arms, Bishop of Norwich in the reign of Edward III. and Richard II. when I conceive this church was built.' (Blomefield,1805-10, VII, 359-361).

He adds (*ibid*, 363) that 'This church was a few years past, pulled down, and the two parishes consolidated.'

Interpretation and Dating
Parkin is evidently describing a largish church with chancel, nave, west tower and porch attached to the chancel north wall. From his observations, a 14th or 15th-

century date for the church seems likely, and the presence of Bishop Despenser's arms above the sedilia makes it probable that the chancel at least dates to his episcopacy (1370-1406). We know that in 1511 40d was given for the reparation of the steeple and 5 marks in 1525 to make the chancel roof (Cattermole and Cotton, 1983, 247), but this need not suggest major rebuilding.

Bryant (1904, 123) calls the church 'Norman and Early English in style', but it is difficult to know why. There were a few more remains in his day, but the only evidence he has for a Norman date is provided by the large stone (described above) which he regarded (quite erroneously) as an 'old Norman boss' (*ibid.* 124), 'probably the central stone of the porch roof': an absurd assertion. He also claims that the church was mentioned in a deed of *c.*1160, which may be true. Cox (1911, II, 92) follows Bryant's errors, and perhaps adds one of his own in calling the tower 15th-century.

Causes of Abandonment
St Martin's was the larger of the two churches, and stands only 200m east of the site of St Michael's. The cost of supporting two churches must have been a burden on a parish of average size. Martin (1771 2, 102) indicates that St Michael's was falling into decay early in the 18th century: 'The Ch. is in a decaying condition, especially on ye south side, occasioned by suffering ye ivy to root into ye walls etc.,'; he also observed that there was 'a tree upon ye steple or elder bush'.

If Bryant's account is to be believed (*ibid*, 124) the decision to abandon St Michael's followed after the unfortunate incident in 1745, when the Rector, the Rev.William Harvey, was married in St Michael's: the tower fell, narrowly missing Mrs.Harvey. The two Fincham parishes were formally consolidated in 1787, and permission was granted to pull down the ruins of St Michael's and apply the materials for repairing St Martin's or for sale (NRO, FCB/4, 6, 49).

Archaeological Record
During the digging of trenches for a new Rectory in 1980 many inhumations were uncovered but no positive remains of the church. One post-medieval wall was uncovered, built of brick with a large reused slab of ashlar. Three Roman sherds, one Thetford Ware sherd, and two fragments of floor-tile were found (info. Norfolk Archaeological Unit).

Part of the Rectory, immediately west of the site dates to 1624, but most belongs to a rebuilding of 1827. Blocks of reused stone are built into a wall east of the house; a garden seat is also made from reused fragments, and pieces of Perpendicular tracery are built into the round tower (perhaps a dovecote) of flint and reused stone.

Line of Roman road immediately north of site.
Ridge-and-furrow field to south.

It is claimed (by Bryant, Cox and Pevsner) that the superb Norman font in St Martin's church originally came from St Michael's. Bryant (1904, 125) states that from 1807 to 1842, the font stood in the Rectory garden. Yet in Parkin's time, it was evidently standing in St Martin's (Blomefield, 1805-10, VII, 355). If Bryant's information is correct, then it must have been removed from St Martin's church in 1807, and returned there in 1842.

Archaeological and Architectural Assessment
It may be that robber trenches are all that survive of St Michael's, as nothing was recovered in 1980; perhaps the precise site of the church is north of the new Rectory, in the garden. Much is already known about the church prior to its demolition, thanks to Parkin and Martin.

Further References
Blomefield, 1805-10, VII, 359-363.
Bryant, 1904, 123-5.
Cattermole and Cotton, 1983, 247.
Cox, 1911, II, 92.
Messent, 1931, 18.

III. Holverston, St Mary

Identification TG 3041 0309 *County No.*10331
Diocese: Norwich. *Archdeaconry:* Norfolk. *Deanery*: Loddon. *Parish*: Holverston. *Status*: Parish church, now disappeared. *Date last in regular use*: mid-16th century. *Ownership and access*: Private, arable field.

Location and Setting
All that remains of the village is Holverston Hall, 8km south-east of Norwich on the A146 Beccles road. As the road from Norwich breasts a slight hill, a track forks north-east towards Holverston Hall; after 400m, the track bends to the right, and the site of the church is at the edge of the arable field on the left, not far from a concrete platform used for storing muck. The Hall, which largely dates from the 16th century, stands a further 400m north-east.

Architectural Description
(Pl. CXXIV)
There are no above-ground remains. As early as *c.* 1740 the ruins of St Mary's had been razed to the ground, although Blomefield (1805-10, V, 487) was able to provide a few details:

'the church hath been so totally demolished, that it is now ploughed over: it was about 24 yards long, and stood on the west side of the road leading from Holverston-hall to Yelverton-heath, right between them, on the very pitch of the hill, from which place, the road to the heath is mended with its ruins, which were pulled down in memory of many now living, for that purpose; the road formerly joined to the south-east part of the churchyard, which it now doth not touch by about 50 yards'.

Bryant (1910, VII, 38) was able to furnish even more information, although he does not specify his source:

'An old MS says it was 24 yards long and 8 yards wide, and consisted of chancel and nave-continuous, south porch, and a round western tower, with one bell. The east window was lancet-shaped, and of one light, and contained the Arms of the Brothertons and the Mannys; the windows in the nave were small (circular and lancet) and widely splayed. In the chancel was an aumbry, a Norman piscina, and a sedilia, and there was a fair rood-screen. The whole building was thatched'.

Whatever his source (and it must be much older than Blomefield's), Bryant's description has been shown to be accurate (at least in outline) by aerial photographs taken in 1977 (Pl. CXXIV). The cropmarks revealed the plan of the church which, like Ashby, originally resembled Hales: round west tower, rectangular nave and apsidal chancel, all of rather short proportions; the round

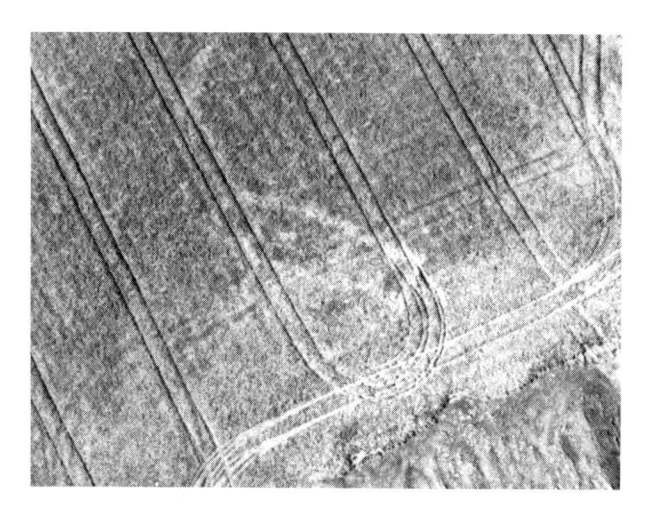

Plate CXXIV. Holverston, St Mary: a church with round tower and apsidal east end revealed by cropmarks. Norfolk Archaeological Unit 1983 TG3003/N/ATB26.

windows and wide splays described by Bryant enhance the link with Hales. It can be seen from the photograph that the church was extended to the east with a straight east wall; the thicker foundation of the extension suggests that the western part of the old chancel was retained. Towards the west end of the nave, a circular mark probably indicates the foundation of a font. A porch joined the south wall at this point. It is possible that not all the church materials have been destroyed: a quantity of squared limestone, and Norman or Early English shafts and mouldings, are incorporated into the fabric of Holverston Hall.

Interpretation and Dating
It is probable that, like Hales, this church goes back to the early 12th century (a late 11th-century date is also possible). The extended chancel, with its straight east wall and lancet window, would seem to be an addition of late 12th or early 13th-century date. With the possible exception of the porch, which is undated, there is no evidence of later medieval alteration to the fabric, unlike Ashby.

Whilst similarities with Hales are obvious, the rather squat proportions at Holverston have an even closer resemblance to a much nearer church: St Andrew's at Framingham Earl, only 2.5km to the west. Furthermore, the dimensions at Holverston given by Bryant (24 yards by 8 yards) are identical to Framingham Earl; the latter church still retains its round windows in the chancel, which, like Holverston, was originally apsidal. Harris is surely correct in dating the Phase I church at Framingham Earl to the late 11th/early 12th century (Rogerson 1987, 82). It is also worth noting that Harris's Phase 2 consists of replacing the apse with a square east end, and adding a south porch (ibid.), but no evidence is advanced for supplying a 15th-century date for this phase; it is possible that the squaring of the east end occurred at around the same time as the neighbouring church at Holverston. The similarities between the two churches are very striking.

Causes of Abandonment
The whole village had disappeared by Blomefield's time, and the church with it, the ruins of which had finally been demolished c. 1700. It seems probable that the village had already greatly declined by the 14th century, since there was little or no enlargement of the rather small parish church after the 13th century. Indeed, the parish was united with Rockland St Mary in 1358 (Blomefield, 1805-10, V, 488), but probably continued in use until the 16th century. By the second half of that century, it is likely that partial demolition of its fabric had begun, since ashlar and carved stone found its way into the fabric of Holverston Hall (400m away) which was being built at this time. Any parishioner had a phlethora of alternative churches to attend: Hellington, 0.9km to east; Rockland St Mary (formerly with two churches) 1.1km to north-east; Bramerton 1.8km to north-west; Yelverton 1.4km to south-west. A radius of 3.5km from Holverston church takes in another sixteen churches, including two that are ruined and two that have disappeared, making a total of twenty-one medieval churches less than a 2¼ mile walk away.

Archaeological and Architectural Assessment
The aerial photographs have made clear that there are still remains of Holverston church below ground. These remains appear to belong to the early 12th century, with 13th-century alterations, but little additional work before its demolition during the 16th and 17th centuries; some of the robbed material survives at Holverston Hall. The plan of the early 12th-century church suggests an interesting sub-group of the 'Hales' type, with rather stocky proportions, as in the neighbouring church of Framingham Earl.

Further References
Blomefield, 1805-10, V, 487-8.
Bryant, 1910, VII, 38.
Harris, in Rogerson, 1987, 82.
Messent, 1931, 22.

IV. Itteringham, St Nicholas

Identification TG 154 303. *County No.*12525
Diocese: Norwich. *Archdeaconry:* Norwich. *Deanery*: Ingworth. *Parish*: Itteringham. *Status*: presumed parish church, later chapel, now disappeared. *Date last in regular use*: 14th century.
Ownership and access: private, arable field.

Location and Setting
Itteringham is a small village in the valley of the River Bure 5km north-west of Aylsham. Most of the parish lies on the north side of the Bure, but Itteringham Common is on the south side, adjoining Blickling park. The parish church of St Mary is near the northern end of the village; the site of the church of St Nicholas is an arable field 1km to south-east, still north of the Bure. A footpath from Itteringham Common crosses the river by means of a plank and skirts the riverbank before forking north; about 250m north of the plank bridge, and at the top of a slight rise, the unmarked site of the church is located about 20m into the arable field.

Architectural Description
(Pl. III)
Until the summer of 1986, there was no information about the form of the church of St Nicholas; the only indication of its location was that it had stood in land belonging to the Bishop of Norwich's Blickling estate (interestingly, the Bishop's palace at Blickling was revealed by aerial photographs to be only 1.5km east of this

site). It was therefore startling to discover a complex of buildings, including a church, coming to light in Derek Edwards's photograph of 1986 (Pl. III). The presence of these below-ground structures was revealed by parchmarks on a crop of ripening wheat, outlining three buildings in such clarity that they could be seen (and measured) from the ground as well as from the air.

From its form, the northernmost structure must have been a church: its rectangular nave measured 36ft by 20ft; to east, its apsidal chancel measured 20ft long by 18ft wide (the building is oriented); if the marks provided an accurate indication (which they appeared to) the walls were 2 ft thick. At the southern end of the complex, and parallel to the church, was a more substantial rectangular outline suggesting a hall, and measuring 60ft by 22ft, with walls 3ft wide. Between these two 'outlined' structures there was a third; this did not resemble a complete building, merely its rectangular east end.

It needs to be repeated that none of these 'buildings' showed up at all on the ground itself (no protruding stretches of masonry) since the site had been ploughed for many years. However, sherds of medieval pottery and green-glazed Flemish tile were recovered from the site of the southern structure.

Interpretation and Dating
The church is most likely to be the chapel of St Nicholas at Itteringham, formerly the second parish church of the village. The parish of Itteringham had three separate rectors, one of which was in the patronage of 'Nower's Manor'. In 1310, William de Briston was presented as rector of this portion, 'and the chapel of St Nicholas annexed' (Blomefield, 1805-10, VI, 475). In the 1368 Inventory of Church Goods (Watkins, 1947, 56) we learn that a certain Richard de Gateley served at the parish church of St Mary, Itteringham, and was also chaplain of the 'other church' at Itteringham. Presumably this 'other church' is the same as the chapel of St Nicholas, which no doubt had been parochial at one time, but whose status was now that of a chapel served by a chaplain. The chapel was still standing in the 15th century, since the feoffees were presented to the manor, 'with St Nicholas's chapel', in 1430 (Blomefield 1805-10, VI, 472). Perhaps the chapel had been reduced to private status by this time. The impression from the documents is that the chapel of St Nicholas at Itteringham was very closely linked to Nower's Manor. It seems probable that the site revealed by aerial photographs is a manorial complex, the main structures comprising of hall and chapel. The hall would have been quite grand in scale, with at least part of it floored with glazed tiles. The tile fragments are of 15th-century date, which is the only dating evidence we have for this structure. The odd intermediate building may have belonged to an outbuilding, or may even have been a fireplace in an otherwise timber structure unrecorded by cropmarks. The complex may indeed be Nower's Manor, as it appeared in the 15th century, incorporating an old church alongside a newer hall.

This identification makes topographical sense, since Nower's Manor belonged to the Bishop of Norwich's Blickling estate, most of which lay just across the River Bure from this site. At the time of the *Domesday* survey, this estate belonged to Bishop Beaufoe, and before 1066 to King Harold (Blomefield 1805-10, VI, 473). There is no evidence for the dating of the chapel apart from its plan. Assuming that we are not dealing with a pre-Danish church (a little incongruous in the context of a late medieval manorial complex) we are left with a *c.* 1040-1150 dating parameter. Apsidal chancels were out of fashion by the latter date, and churches (even abbeys and cathedrals) in Norfolk seem to have been constructed exclusively of wood before the former date. The church at Itteringham would probably fall into the first half of this date bracket, having none of the scale or complexity of later Norman churches. To speculate further, if built before 1066 it would have belonged to King Harold, if after 1066 to the Bishops of Thetford/Norwich.

Causes of Abandonment
It is interesting that the church was never altered or enlarged. There was clearly no need to increase its capacity. Indeed, by the 14th century it had probably lost its parochial status (see above), being served only by a chaplain dispatched from St Mary's. By the 15th century, full privatisation had taken place, and the church of St Nicholas served as manorial chapel to a smartly rebuilt new Hall. It is not known when the manorial complex was demolished.

Archaeological and Architectural Assessment
The below-ground remains of this site are of very great importance. It consists of not only a late medieval manorial complex with tiled hall and chapel, but also an even earlier church site going back to the 11th century.

Further References
Blomefield, 1805-10, VI, 472, 475.
Bryant, 1905, 14, 275.
Watkins, 1947, 56.

V. Ormesby, St Peter

Identification TG 4913 1468 *County No.*8648
Diocese: Norwich. *Archdeaconry:* Norwich. *Deanery*: Flegg. *Parish*: Ormesby St Margaret. *Status*: parish church, now disappeared. *Date Last In Regular Use*: c. 1591. *Ownership and access*: private, arable field.

Location and Setting
Ormesby St Margaret is the seaward of the two Ormesbys. Sandwiched between Hemsby to the north and Caister-on-Sea to the south, it is one of the less well-known resorts of the Norfolk east coast Riviera. The eastern edge of the parish is a sandy coastal strip (appropriately named 'California'), and has seen much housing development this century. To the west is the parish of Ormesby St Michael (or Little Ormesby), more broadland than seaside, and abutting Ormesby and Rollesby Broads.

The site of St Peter's church is about halfway between the two Ormesby parish churches of St Michael and St Margaret, in an arable field 100m south of the A149 Caister road, very close to some allotments.

Architectural Description
(Pl. CXXV)
Without identifying it, Blomefield personally visited and described the remains of St Peter's church during a journey he made in 1726 (Linnell 1951, 65). Travelling from Caister, he came west to Ormesby:

'Coming from Great Ormesby [*i.e.* St Margaret] to Little Ormesby [*i.e.* St Michael] between them both on the right hand of the road I saw a church thatched and in tolerable repair turned into a barn, the foundations of a round steeple are visible at the west end, and in short I think it might with little charge be made fitt for service...quaere if this be not Scroutby church...the inhabitants near it could give me no account of it which makes me rather think it was some small religious house dissolved either by H8 or E6.'

It is more likely that Blomefield had encountered one of the two parish churches, either St Peter's or St Andrew's, abandoned since the late 16th century; Scratby church was right by the coast. It is not known when the church/barn noticed by Blomefield became dilapidated, but the site was marked as 'church in ruins' on the Ordnance Survey map of 1838; later OS maps identified this as St Peter's rather than St Andrew's, but the basis of this attribution remains unknown.

Little else could be said about the church until the dry summer of 1976, when cropmarks revealed the outline of the same church described by Blomefield. The aerial photograph (Pl. CXXV) indicates a church with round west tower, nave and rectangular chancel. Within the nave the outline of an earlier, narrower chancel can be made out, terminating in an apse. Even the buttresses of nave and chancel stand out clearly. On inspection on the ground, the site yielded a fragment of medieval glazed tile (Flemish), and a scattering of limestone and medieval brick.

Interpretation and Dating
The church with nave, apsidal chancel and round west tower is of the same plan as Hales, and likewise undoubtedly goes back to the early 12th century. It is difficult to be more precise about the date of the new rectangular chancel which replaced the apsidal one: somewhere between the 13th and the 15th century. The glazed tile is probably of the 15th century, which may indicate that reconstruction was taking place at this time.

Causes of Abandonment
Throughout the medieval period, Ormesby possessed four parish churches (five if Scratby is included). All of the Ormesby churches were still in use in 1591 (Blomefield 1805-10, XI, 239), but both St Andrew's and St Peter's were withdrawn from use by the end of the century. The reason was no doubt that there was an insufficient population to support five churches: in 1603 the combined parish of Ormesby-cum-Scratby served 220 communicants. Clearly, any parochial reorganisation would be very easy given the short distances between the churches, with St Peter's only 0.8km from either St Margaret's or St Michael's.

This was a planned redundancy, since the most westerly church and the most easterly church were the ones retained, whilst the two in the middle were given up. St Peter's became a barn, which was its state when Blomefield visited it in 1726. There were still visible ruins in 1838, which were subsequently razed to the ground.

Archaeological and Architectural Assessment
The aerial photographs have revealed that there are below-ground remains of the church, and that these go back to at least the early 12th century. It is open to question how much of the tiled floor survives since it is in an arable field. The early church followed the same plan as that at Hales.

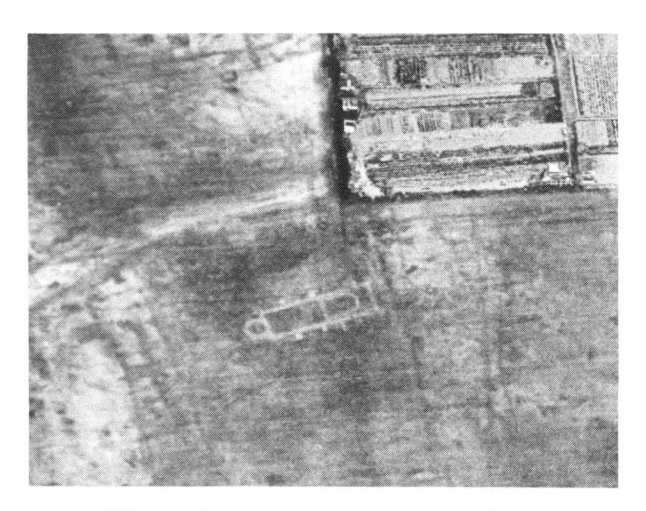

Plate CXXV. Ormesby, St Peter: cropmarks again revealing a 'Hales' plan with apse and round west tower. Cambridge University Collection BYJ 29, copyright reserved.

Further References
Blomefield, 1805-10, XI, 239.
Cox 1911, I, 101.
Linnell, 1951, 65.
Messent, 1931, 28.

VI. Thetford, St Giles

Identification TL 8705 8310. *County No.*5894.
Diocese: Norwich. *Archdeaconry:* Norfolk. *Deanery*: Thetford and Rockland. *Parish*: Thetford. *Status*: parish church, later hermitage, now disappeared. *Date last in regular use*: c.1470.
Ownership and access: private, Halifax Building Society (in 1984).

Location and Setting
King Street, north of the Little Ouse, is one of the main shopping streets of Thetford. About 100m east of St Peter's, St Giles Street forks north-eastward from King Street; the building occupying the angle of the two streets belongs at present to the Halifax Building Society: according to Martin's map (in the Ancient House museum), the yard behind this was the site of the church of St Giles, still standing in the 18th century.

Architectural Description
(Pl. CXXVI)
There do not appear to be any *in situ* remains but the external walls of the building society premises are studded with reused limestone blocks. On the King Street side, the lowest 1m of the building is constructed of flint with occasional carved limestone pieces, including what appears to be a piece of 12th-century chip-carved voussoir.

There are two good illustrations of the church as it appeared in the 18th and early 19th century. One is by Martin, dated 1780, showing it from the south-east. It depicts a rectangular structure, perhaps just the chancel of the original church, with a diagonal buttress at each corner; it is roofed rather strangely, with thatch for its upper part, tiles lower down; there is a buttress near the middle of the south wall, with two-light windows east of it

Plate CXXVI. Thetford, St Giles: east end by Wilkinson (1822).

and a statue-niche and another window to west. Underneath the drawing is the note: 'This is now and has been for some years a wheelwright's shop' (Martin, 1771, 6, 131). The second depiction is by Wilkinson in 1822 (Pl. CXXVI), and shows the church from the east: the tracery of the east window is clearly revealed, three-light and Perpendicular in style, of the late 14th century.

Our knowledge of the structure is augmented by Blomefield and Martin. The latter (1779, 82) records that 'The east window is rich, consisting of three bays, and there is a south window of two. At the east end within is a holy water stone, and something like a square recess for a monument with a neat architrave above it, but defaced.' Blomefield (1805-10, II, 75) comments that 'it is turned into a barn, the steeple (if there was one) being quite down, and a new gable in its place'. This last piece of information is particularly useful, since it tells us that the building depicted in the 18th century is a truncated form of the original church, with a 'new gable' at its west end. No doubt nave (and tower if it had one) were demolished and the chancel converted for use by a hermit in the latter half of the 15th century. The late 14th-century east window must therefore belong to when it was used as a parish church.

Causes of Abandonment
St Giles is listed in 1291 and in 1368, by which time it had been appropriated to the Canons (priory of Augustinian canons) and was served by a curate. It presumably continued to function as a parish church until *c*.1470, since Blomefield (*ibid.*) tells us that in the reign of Edward VI 'the parish was annexed to St Cuthbert's, and the church let to a hermit, who lived in it, and performed service there for his own profit.' Sir Richard Fulmerston acquired the site at the Dissolution; Martin (1779, 81) adds that it was sold in 1563, was made a barn in 1598, and had become a wheelwright's shop by the 18th century. It was still standing in 1822 (Wilkinson, 1822).

Archaeological and Architectural Assessment
St Giles was perhaps a post-Conquest foundation. The fragments of 12th-century arch reused in adjacent buildings may belong to the original doorway. Some rebuilding took place in the late 14th century. Part of the church was destroyed in the 15th century, and it had become a barn by the late 16th century.

Any further remains of the church presumably lie below the yards at the back of the shops in King Street.

Further References
Blomefield, 1805-10, II, 75.
Cox, 1911, II, 224.
Davison, 1986.
Martin, 1771, 6, 131.
Martin, 1779, 82.
Messent, 1931, 36.
Pevsner, 1962b, 342.
Wilkinson, 1822.

Glossary

Apse	semi-circular termination to chancel
Arcade	a series of arches
Arch	an opening with round or pointed head. *Three-centred arch:* set out from three centres. *Two-centred arch:* pointed. *Four-centred arch:* set out from two pairs of centres. *Ogee arch:* counter-curving arch, rising to a sharp point. *Segmental arch:* a low, two-centred arch, forming the segment of a pointed arch. *Stilted arch:* arch whose impost or capital is below the level of springing
Archlet	small arch, e.g. head of a single window light
Arris	the sharp edge forming the angle of two surfaces
Articulation	division of an elevation into architectural features
Ashlar	masonry of squared stone blocks
Aumbry	cupboard within wall for sacred vessels
Axial tower	tower on main axis of church, between chancel and nave
Baldacchino	canopy supported on columns
Baluster	small turned pillar
Balustrade	series of balusters supporting a handrail or coping
Base	moulded foot of column, shaft or pilaster
Batement light	upper light of Perpendicular window
Bay	division of a church longitudinally by a regular vertical feature, usually an arch or window
Beakhead	Romanesque motif consisting of a row of beast heads with beaks biting into a roll-moulding
Belfry	stage of tower (usually 3rd storey) where bells are hung
Bellcote	small housing for bells on gable or roof
Bench	open seat
Billet	Romanesque decorative motif consisting of short rectangular (or cylindrical) blocks placed at regular intervals
Blind arcading	arcade in relief on wall, not pierced by openings
Bobbin	motif like a string of bobbins
Buttress	a structure of stone or brick built against a wall to strengthen it. *Angle buttress:* two buttresses set at right angles to one another to support a corner. *Clasping buttresses:* buttresses encasing the angles of the tower. *Diagonal buttress:* single buttress set diagonally and radiating away from the corner it is supporting. *Set-back buttresses:* like angle buttresses, but set back a little to allow the arris of the corner to show through
Cable	decorative moulding carved in the form of a rope
Canopy	projection above an altar tomb or niche
Capital	head of column, pier or respond. *Corinthian capital:* classical, with acanthus leaf decoration. Cushion capital: Romanesque block capital with rounded lower angles. Moulded capital: round or polygonal capital formed of superimposed mouldings
Casement	*see* moulding
Chamfer	surface produced by bevelling a square edge (or arris), usually at an angle of 45°; called a hollow chamfer when concave; sunk chamfer when recessed
Chancel	east arm of the church, used by the officiating clergy
Chantry	chapel for celebration of masses for the soul of the founder
Chevron	three-dimensional zig-zag motif
Cinquefoil	cusping forming a shape with five lobes
Clerestorey	wall above an arcade, usually pierced by windows
Conglomerate	an iron-bound conglomerate stone, brown in colour
Console	bracket with curved outline
Corbel	a cantilevered block of stone or wood projecting from the surface of the wall
Corinthian	*see* Orders
Cornice	horizontal moulding at the top of a building or feature
Coping	stone or brick masonry covering the top of a wall
Course	layer of masonry in a wall
Crenellated	in the form of battlements
Crocket	leaf-shaped lobes projecting from a surface
Crossing	central space at junction of chancel, nave and transepts
Cupola	a small dome
Cusp	projecting point (usually) in tracery. *Sub-cusp:* cusps within larger cusping
Dagger	a tear-shaped tracery motif constricted by two cusps
Dentil	decoration in the form of a series of small squared blocks
Dogtooth	ornamental motif of late 12th and 13th century, consisting of four petal shapes forming a pyramid
Doric	*see* Orders
Double-splayed	window with splay from exterior as well as interior wall surface
Dressings	stone or brickwork used at the angles of a feature
Dripstone	stone or brick projection above an arch, window or roof
Eaves	the projecting edge of a roof which overhangs the wall
Effigy	in funerary monuments, a representation of the deceased
Entablature	horizontal member supported by columns; in classical architecture, divided into architrave, frieze and cornice
Eyelet	a small tracery opening, usually lozenge-shaped
Faculty	a license granted by the diocese to allow alterations to the fabric or contents of a church
Fillet	narrow flat band projecting from a shaft or moulding
Finial	ornament surmounting a pinnacle, gable or canopy
Fleur-de-lys	decorative motif in the form of a stylised lily
Flowing	*see* Tracery
Flushwork	decorative use of stone traceried panels inlaid with flint
Fluting	concave channels in column or pilaster
Foliate	decorated with leaves
Font	receptacle for water used in baptism; usually consists of stone bowl and stem
Frieze	middle division of a classical entablature, often adorned with reliefs
Gable	end wall, usually triangular to support a double-pitched roof
Gable cross	stone cross surmounting apex of gable
Galleting	small stones (especially flint flakes) set into mortar
Gargoyle	projecting spout for rainwater
Geometrical	*see* Tracery
Hammerbeam	*see* Roof elements
Herringbone	masonry laid diagonally in horizontal courses
Hood-mould	projecting moulding above a window or doorway
Impost	horizontal moulding at the springing of an arch
Indent	the sinking for a brass in a tomb slab
Interlace	decorative motif of entwined bands
Intersecting	*see* Window tracery

Jamb	side-post (in stone or wood) of a doorway or window	Quatrefoil	shape formed of four lobes
Keel moulding	see Moulding	Quirk	incised groove
Knapped flint	cut flint forming a smooth surface to a wall	Quoins	(usually dressed) stones forming the angles of the building
Kneeler	cantilevered stone at the wall-plate level of a gable wall	Rear-arch	arch on inner wall of doorway or window
Label-stop	small stone block (often carved) at the termination of a hood-mould (or label)	Rebate (or Rabbet)	a rectangular recess made along a stone or timber edge to receive a window or door
Lancet	pointed-arched window of one light	Rendering	exterior wall plastering
Lectern	desk for reading the Scriptures	Reredos	screen above and behind the altar
Light	a single compartment of a traceried window	Respond	half-pier at end of an arcade, or at either side of a single arch
Lintel	horizontal beam of stone, timber, steel or concrete	Reticulated	see Tracery
Lowside window	window in chancel with lower sill than others	Reveal	the vertical side of a window-opening or doorway
Lunette	semi-circular window	Rood	large carved cross over entry into chancel, usually set on a beam. *Rood loft:* platform before rood beam. *Rood screen:* carved (and often painted) screen beneath rood beam. *Rood stair:* stairway giving access to rood loft
Mansard	roof with double slope, the lower slope being steeper		
Mouchette	in tracery, a curved dagger		
Moulding	ornament of continuous section decorating an arch, respond, jamb, cornice or stringcourse. *Casement moulding:* wide and shallow hollow moulding. *Keel moulding:* pointed, like the keel of a ship. *Ogee moulding:* concave curve merging into a convex curve. *Quadrant moulding:* quarter of a circle section. *Roll moulding:* moulding of circular section. *Scroll moulding:* roll moulding with overlap, like a wrapped scroll. *Wave moulding:* convex moulding flanked by hollows	Roof elements	*Arched braces:* curved braces supporting the principal rafters. *Collar-beam:* horizontal timber connecting rafters between the wall-plate and the apex. *Collar-purlin:* longitudinal timber carrying collar beams. *Crown-post:* vertical timber standing centrally on tie-beam and supporting a collar purlin. *Hammerbeam:* cantilevered bracket projecting at wall-plate level, giving the appearance of a tie-beam with the centre cut away. *King-post:* vertical timber standing on tie-beam and rising to apex. *Through purlin:* longitudinal timber resting in slots in the rafters. *Tie-beam:* horizontal beam connecting two walls at wall-plate level. *Wall-plate:* timber laid longitudinally on top of a wall to receive the rafters. *Wall-post:* vertical timber supporting tie-beam or hammerbeam
Mullion	Vertical member dividing lights of a window or screen		
Narthex	enclosed vestibule at entrance		
Nave	the main body of the church, for the accommodation of the congregation		
Niche	arched recess, often used to house a statue		
Nook-shaft	shaft set into angle of wall, pier, respond, doorway or window		
Oculus	round opening or reticulation at apex of window		
Ogee	a double curved arch or moulding (i.e. curve or reverse-curve or concave or convex)	Roundel	round ornament in shallow relief
Openwork	pierced panelling	Salient tower	axial tower wider than nave, and therefore projecting salient corners
Order	series of recessed arches or shafts	Saltire cross	the cross of St Andrew, in the form of an X
Orders	the formalized versions of trabeated structures in classical architecture consisting of base, column, capital and entablature; in the Doric order, the capitals are moulded; in the Ionic order, the capitals have volutes; in the Corinthian order, the capitals have foliate (acanthus) decoration	Sarcophagus	stone coffin
		Sedilia	seats for clergy, usually set into the south wall of the chancel
		Set-off	sloped horizontal surface (on sills, buttresses) to throw off rainwater
		Shaft	round (or polygonal) vertical member, usually monolithic
Pamments	large, square quarry tiles		
Parapet	low wall rising above gutter-level of roof	Sill	horizontal base of a window or doorway
Parclose screen	separating a chapel from the rest of the church	Sill-sedile	seat set at or below a window sill
Patera	round or oval ornament, especially in a frieze	Situ	*in situ* means still in original location. *Ex situ* means removed from original location
Pedestal	base block supporting column or statue		
Pediment	low-pitched gable above a portico, door or window. *Broken pediment:* with the centre portion of the base left open	Soffit	underside of an arch
		Spandrel	triangular surface between two arches
		Splay	angled reveal
Pier	masonry support for an arch or architrave	Springing	level at which an arch rises from its supports
Pilaster	flat column in shallow relief against a wall	Squint	angled piercing of wall, usually to allow view of altar
Pinnacle	vertical extension to buttress, corners of tower etc. usually decorated, and terminating in a pyramid or cone		
		Stoup	basin for containing holy water
		Stringcourse	horizontal course projecting from a wall
Piscina	stone basin with drainage hole, used for washing sacred vessels; usually set into the wall south of the altar. *Angle piscina:* piscina hollowed into an arris, and accessible from either plane	Supermullion	a mullion rising from the apex of an archlet, or a mullion extending above the main lights
		Supertransom	a transom above the springing of a window
		Tester	horizontal sounding board over pulpit
		Three-light	window having tracery of three main lights
Plinth	projecting course at the foot of a wall or column	Tie-beam	see Roof elements
Poppy-head	finial surmounting bench-end	Tomb chest	stone funerary monument in the form of a chest
Portico	classical 'temple' facade of columns supporting a pediment	Tower	usually of three storeys, the uppermost (the belfry) used for housing the bells
Priest-door	small doorway in chancel for access of clergy	Tracery	the pattern of the stone or wooden subdivision of the upper part of a window. *Drop-tracery:* tracery filling a stilted arch. *Flowing tracery:* continuous curvilinear form. *Geometric tracery:* foiled circles and other regular shapes. *Intersecting tracery:* the mullions divide into branches parallel to the window arch and form simple intersections.
Pulpit	raised and enclosed platform for delivering sermons. *Two-decker pulpit:* pulpit with reading desk below		
Putlog hole	small recess in masonry wall for receiving scaffolding timber		
Putto	cherub (small naked boy)		
Quadrant	see Moulding		

	Plate tracery: decoratively shaped openings cut through the solid stone filling in a window head.	Upright-and-flat	quoins or jambs formed of rectangular stones placed (not necessarily regularly) with the longer axis alternately vertical and horizontal
	Reticulated tracery: forming a net-like pattern of ogee quatrefoils.	Vault	stone ceiling.
	Y-tracery: a single mullion which branches into a Y shape		*Barrel vault:* a continuous round-headed arch. *Rib vault:* having a skeletal framework of transverse and diagonal members.
Transept	transverse arm of church, at right angles to the nave		*Tierceron vault:* having secondary ribs
Transom	horizontal member of window tracery	Vestry	room for the robing of clergy or choir
Trefoil	three-lobed	Voussoir	wedge-shaped stone forming part of an arch
Triglyph	in the Doric frieze, blocks with vertical grooves	Wall-plate	*see* Roof elements
Two-light	window having tracery of two main lights	Waterholding base	base of two rolls separated by a hollow deep enough to hold water
Tympanum	a thin fill of masonry blocking the head of an arch		

Appendix I

Parish Churches and Chapels-of-Ease Founded after 1800 A.D.

In Use:

Blofield
Plumstead, Great, St David
Rackheath, Holy Trinity

Flegg
Caister, West, St Edmund II
Gorleston, St Mary Magdalen
Southtown, St Mary
Southtown, St Luke
Yarmouth, Great, St James
Yarmouth, Great, St John
Yarmouth, Great, St Paul
Yarmouth, Great, St Peter (leased to Greek Orthodox)

Ingworth
Hainford, All Saints II
Hautbois, Great, Holy Trinity

Norwich, North
Beeston, St Andrew II
Catton, New, Christ Church
Catton, New, St Luke
Costessey, St Helen
Hellesdon, St Michael
Hellesdon, St Paul
Mile Cross, St Catherine
Sprowston, St Catherine

Norwich, South
Bowthorpe II
Earlham, St Anne
Earlham, St Elizabeth
Eaton, Christ Church
Heigham, Holy Trinity
Heigham, St Barnabas
Heigham, St Thomas
Lakenham, St Alban
Tuckswood

Norwich, East
Heartsease
Lakenham, St Mark
Norwich, St Mary Magdalen
Thorpe-by-Norwich, St Andrew II
Thorpe-by-Norwich, The Good Shepherd
Thorpe Hamlet, St Matthew II

Repps
Cromer, St Martin
Sheringham, Lower, St Peter II
Sidestrand, St Michael II

Sparham
Hindolveston, St George II
Lenwade All Saints

Depwade
Forncett St Edmund
Pirnough, All Hallows

Humbleyard
Silfield
Spooner Row

Lothingland (in Norfolk)
Hopton, St Margaret II

Redenhall
Diss Heywood, St James
Harleston, St John II

Burnham and Walsingham
Fulmodestone, Holy Trinity
Hempton, Christ Church

Heacham and Rising
Hunstanton, St Edmund

Holt
Beckham, St Helen and All Saints
Burgh Parva, St Mary II
Edgefield, SS Peter and Paul II
Kelling, High, All Saints

Lynn
Lynn, King's, St Edmund
Lynn, King's, St John the Evangelist

Feltwell
Whitington, Christ Church

Fincham
Hilgay, Ten Mile Bank, St Mark
Nordelph, Holy Trinity
Southery, St Mary II
Stow Bridge, St Peter

Lynn Marshland
Marshland, St James
Walpole Cross Keys, St Helen
Walpole Highway, St Edmund

Ely
Little Ouse, St John

Disused/Ruined/Demolished

Flegg
Yarmouth, Great, St Andrew (built 1860; now demolished)

Norwich, South
Heigham, St Philip (built 1871, Pls CXXVI, CXXVII; demolished 1978: extra to parochial needs, and on prime value development land).

Norwich, East
Thorpe Hamlet, St Leonard (demolished)
Thorpe Hamlet, St Matthew I (built in 1951, Pls CXXVIII, CXXIX; declared redundant and converted to use as offices in 1982).

Repps
Overstrand, Christ Church (built 1867 in same churchyard as St Martin; St Martin restored to use in 1914, Christ Church abandoned and finally demolished in 1960).
Sheringham, Lower, St Peter I (mission chapel built in 1842, abandoned in 1897 when new St Peter's consecrated).

Humbleyard
Wymondham, Downham, St Edmund (converted to house)
Wymondham, Silfield, St Helen (converted to house)

Heacham and Rising
Babingley, St Felix II (corrugated iron church built in 1894-5; serves only a small hamlet, abandoned c. 1977, and remains disused).

Lynn
Lynn, South, St Michael (built in 1901, closed in 1965, declared redundant in 1972 and demolished apart from low walls).
Setchey, St Mary (built in 1844 as chapel-of-ease to North Runcton; abandoned in 1978, remains disused and boarded up).

Plate CXXVII.   Heigham, St Philip: from the west in 1976. Sadly, it was demolished to make way for a housing estate in 1977. BB77/5872 copyright Royal Commission on Historical Monuments (England).

Plate CXXVIII.   Heigham, St Philip: interior in 1976: in good condition and a good example of Edward Power's work (1871), demolished in 1977. BB77/5878 copyright Royal Commission on Historical Monuments (England).

Plate CXXIX. Thorpe Hamlet, St Matthew: from the south-east in 1976. After receiving a generous legacy, the parish decided to build a new church nearer the parish centre; the old church was converted into offices in 1982. BB78/9643 copyright Royal Commission on Historical Monuments (England), 1976.

Plate CXXX. Thorpe Hamlet, St Matthew: interior in 1976. Although not destroyed, John Brown's design of 1851 has been divided into several storeys of offices. BB78/9643 copyright Royal Commission on Historical Monuments (England), 1976.

Appendix II

Parish Churches of Norfolk Founded before 1800 A.D.

(all medieval foundations except Yarmouth St George; post-medieval total rebuildings indicated)

1. Deanery of Blofield
In Use
Acle
Beighton
Blofield
Braydeston
Brundall
Burlingham, North
Burlingham, South
Cantley
Fishley
Freethorpe
Halvergate
Hassingham
Hemblington
Limpenhoe
Lingwood
Plumstead, Great
Plumstead, Little
Postwick
Ranworth
Reedham
Salhouse
Strumpshaw
Upton
Walsham, South, St Mary
Wickhampton
Witton
Woodbastwick

Disused/Ruined
Category I
Buckenham Ferry
Moulton St Mary
Rackheath All SS
Category II
Burlingham, North, St Peter
Southwood
Tunstall
Walsham, South, St Lawrence
Category IV
Panxworth
Category VI
Brundall, St Clement
Rackheath, Little

2. Deanery of Flegg
In Use
Belton
Billockby
Bradwell
Burgh St Margaret
Burgh Castle
Caister
Clippesby
Filby
Gorleston
Hemsby
Martham
Mautby
Ormesby, St Margaret
Ormesby, St Michael
Repps
Rollesby
Runham
Somerton, West
Stokesby
Thrigby
Thurne
Winterton
Yarmouth, Great, St Nicholas

Disused/Ruined
Category I
Yarmouth, Great, St George (post-medieval)
Category II
Somerton, East
Category IV
Bastwick
Burgh St Mary
Caister, West, St Edmund
Category VI
Ashby
Herringby
Oby
Ormesby, St Andrew
Ormesby, St Peter
Scratby
Southtown
Yarmouth, Great, St Benedict

3. Deanery of Ingworth
In Use
Alby
Aylsham
Barningham, Little
Belaugh
Blickling
Brampton
Burgh-next-Aylsham
Buxton
Calthorpe
Cawston
Coltishall
Erpingham
Felthorpe
Haveringland
Hevingham
Heydon
Horstead
Ingworth
Itteringham
Lammas
Marsham
Oulton
Oxnead
Saxthorpe St Andrew
Stratton Strawless
Thwaite
Wickmere

Disused/Ruined
Category I
Corpusty
Category II
Hautbois, Great, St Mary
Mannington
Category IV
Hainford I
Wolterton
Category VI
Hautbois, Little
Irmingland
Itteringham, St Nicholas
Saxthorpe, St Dunstan

4. Norwich North
In Use
Catton, Old
Costessey
Crostwick
Drayton
Frettenham
Hellesdon
Horsford
Horsham St Faith
Ringland
Spixworth
Sprowston
Taverham

Disused/Ruined
Category III
Stanninghall
Category VI
Beeston, St Andrew

5. Norwich South
In Use
Colney
Earlham, St Mary
Eaton
Lakenham, St John the Baptist

Disused/Ruined
Category II
Bowthorpe I
Category IV
Heigham, St Bartholomew
Category VI
Bracondale
Carrow

6. Norwich East
In Use
Norwich, St Andrew
Norwich, St Augustine
Norwich, St George Colegate
Norwich, St George Tombland
Norwich, St Giles
Norwich, St Helen II
Norwich, St John the Baptist, Maddermarket
Norwich, St John the Baptist, Timberhill
Norwich, St John de Sepulchre
Norwich, St Julian
Norwich, St Peter Mancroft
Norwich, St Stephen

Ruined/Disused
Category I
Norwich:
All SS Timberhill
St Clement, Fye Bridge
St Edmund
St Etheldreda
St Gregory
St James
St Lawrence
St Margaret Westwick
St Martin at Oak
St Martin at Palace
St Mary Coslany
St Mary the Less
St Michael Coslany
St Michael at Pleas
St Peter Hungate
St Peter Parmentergate

St Saviour
SS Simon and Jude
St Swithin
Category II
Thorpe-by-Norwich, St Andrew I
Category III
St Peter Southgate
Category IV
Norwich, St Benedict
Category V
Norwich, St Bartholomew
Norwich, St Mary in the Marsh
Category VI
All SS Fybridgegate
St Anne
St Botolph
St Christopher
St Clement, Conesford
St Crowche
St Cuthbert
St Edward
St Ethelbert
Holy Trinity
St Helen I
St John the Baptist, Colegate
St John the Evangelist, Conesford
St Margaret, Newbridge
St Margaret, Fye Bridge
St Martin in Balliva
St Mary Unbrent
St Mathew the Apostle
St Michael Conesford
St Michael Tombland
St Michael at Thorn
St Olave Colegate
St Olave Conesford
St Paul
St Vedast
St Winwaloy/St Catherine
Church in Castle Bailey
Thorpe-by-Norwich, Old Thorpe Church

Eising
Foulsham
Foxley
Guestwick
Guist
Lyng
Reepham
Salle
Sparham
Swannington
Themelthorpe
Thurning
Twyford
Weston Longville
Whitwell
Witchingham, Great
Witchingham, Little
Wood Dalling
Wood Norton, All Saints

Category III
Wood Norton, St Peter
Category IV
Hindolveston I
Category V
Hackford, All SS
Category VI
Guist Thorpe
Helmingham
Kerdiston

9. Tunstead
In Use
Ashmanaugh
Bacton
Banningham
Barton Turf
Beeston St Lawrence
Colby
Crostwight
Dilham
Edingthorpe
Felmingham
Honing
Horning
Hoveton St John
Hoveton St Peter (post-medieval)
Irstead
Knapton
Neatishead
Paston
Ridlington
Scottow
Skeyton
Slolely
Smallburgh
Suffield
Swanton Abbot
Tunstead
Tuttington
Walsham, North
Westwick
Witton
Worstead
Wroxham

Disused/Ruined
Category II
Sco Ruston
Category VI
Barton Turf B
Keswick, St Clement
Worstead, St Andrew

7. Repps
In Use
Aldborough
Antingham, St Mary
Aylmerton
Barningham
Beeston Regis
Bessingham
Bradfield
Cromer SS Peter and Paul
Felbrigg
Gimingham
Gresham
Hanworth
Matlaske
Melton
Mundesley
Northrepps
Overstrand, St Martin II
Roughton
Runton
Southrepps
Sustead
Swafield
Thorpe Market (post-medieval)
Trimingham
Trunch

Disused/Ruined
Category I
Barningham, North
Gunton (post-medieval)
Thurgarton
Category III
Antingham, St Margaret
Category VI
Overstrand, St Martin I
Shipden
Sidestrand I

10. Waxham
In Use
Brumstead
Catfield
Happisburgh
Hempstead
Hickling
Horsey
Ingham
Lessingham
Ludham
Palling
Potter Heigham
Stalham
Sutton
Walcot
Waxham

Disused/Ruined
Category I
Ruston, East
Category V
Eccles, St Mary
Category VI
Waxham, Little

Archdeaconry of Norfolk

8. Sparham
In Use
Alderford
Attlebridge
Bawdeswell (post-medieval)
Bintree
Bylaugh

Disused/Ruined
Category I
Booton (post-medieval)
Brandiston
Category II
Morton-on-the-Hill

11. Depwade
In Use
Aslacton
Bedingham, St Andrew

Disused/Ruined
Category I
Forncett, St Mary

Brooke
Broome
Bunwell
Carleton Rode
Ditchingham
Forncett St Peter
Fritton
Fundenhall
Hardwick
Hedenham
Hempnall
Kirstead
Morningthorpe
Moulton, Great
Saxlingham Nethergate
Shelton
Shotesham, All Saints
Shotesham, St Mary
Stratton, St Michael
Stratton, Long, St Mary
Tacolneston
Tasburgh
Tharston
Topcroft
Wacton, Great
Woodton

Category II
Shotesham, St Martin
Category III
Saxlingham Thorpe
Category V
Shotesham, St Botolph
Category VI
Bedingham, St Mary
Carleton Rode B
Hempnall, St Andrew
Langhale
Moulton, Little
Stratton, St Peter
Topcroft, St Giles
Wacton, Little

12. Hingham and Mitford
In Use
Barford
Barnham Broom, SS Peter and Paul
Bradenham, East
Bradenham, West
Brandon Parva
Carlton Forehoe
Colton
Cranworth
East Dereham
Easton
Garveston
Hardingham
Hingham
Hockering
Hoe
Honingham
Kimberley
Mattishall
Mattishall Burgh
Reymerston
Runhall
Shipdham
Southburgh
Thuxton
Tuddenham, East
Tuddenham, North
Welbourne
Westfield
Whinburgh
Wramplingham
Yaxham

Disused/Ruined
Category I
Coston
Category III
Bickerston
Category V
Barnham Broom, St Michael
Letton

13. Humbleyard
In Use
Ashwellthorpe
Bawburgh
Braconash
Carleton, East, St Mary
Cringleford
Deopham
Flordon
Hackford
Hapton
Hethel
Hethersett
Intwood
Keswick
Ketteringham
Marlingford
Melton, Great, All Saints

Disused/Ruined
Category I
Crownthorpe
Category IV
Melton, Great, St Mary
Category V
Carleton, East, St Peter
Category VI
Algarsthorpe
Cantelose
Dykebeck
Gowthorpe
Keningham
Nelonde
Swainsthorpe, St Mary
Wicklewood, St Andrew
Wreningham, Little

Melton, Little
Morley St Botolph
Morley St Peter
Mulbarton
Newton Flotman
Swardeston
Swainsthorpe, St Peter
Wicklewood
Wreningham
Wymondham

14. Loddon
In Use
Aldeby
Arminghall
Ashby, St Mary
Bergh Apton
Bixley
Bramerton
Burgh St Peter
Caister St Edmund
Carleton St Peter
Claxton
Chedgrave
Dunston
Ellingham
Framingham Earl
Framingham Pigot
Gelderston
Gillingham, St Mary
Haddiscoe
Hardby
Heckingham
Hellington
Howe
Kirby Bedon, St Andrew
Kirby Cane
Langley
Loddon
Mundham, St Peter
Norton Subcourse
Poringland, Great
Raveningham
Rockland, St Mary
Seething
Sisland
Stockton
Stoke Holy Cross
Surlingham, St Mary
Thorpe-next-Haddiscoe
Thurlton
Thurton
Thwaite
Toft Monks
Trowse
Wheatacre
Yelverton

Disused/Ruined
Category I
Hales
Category III
Kirby Bedon, St Mary
Mundham, St Ethelbert
Surlingham, St Saviour
Whitlingham
Category IV
Gillingham, All SS
Category V
Rockland St Mary, St Margaret
Category VI
Alpington/Apton
Holverston
Markshall
Poringland, East, I
Porlingland, West
Seething B
Stoke Holy Cross B
Thurketeliart
Windle
Winston

15. Lothingland (Norfolk)
In Use
Fritton

Disused/Ruined
Category II
Hopton St Margaret I

16. Redenhall
In Use
Alburgh
Billingford
Bressingham
Brockdish
Burston
Denton
Dickleburgh
Diss
Earsham
Fersfield
Gissing
Lopham, North
Lopham, South
Needham
Pulham Market

Disused/Ruined
Category I
Frenze
Shimpling
Category II
Tivetshall, St Mary
Category IV
Thorpe Parva
Category VI
Harleston I

172

Pulham St Mary
Redenhall
Roydon
Rushall
Scole
Shelfanger
Starston
Thelveton
Thorpe Abbots
Tibenham
Tivetshall, St Margaret
Winfarthing

17. Thetford and Rockland

In Use
Attleborough
Banham
Besthorpe
Blo Norton, St Andrew
Brettenham
Bridgham
Buckenham, New
Buckenham, Old
Croxton
Eccles
Ellingham, Great
Ellingham, Little
Garboldisham, St John
Harling, East
Hockham
Kenninghall
Kilverstone
Larling
Quidenham
Riddlesworth
Rockland, All Saints
Rockland, St Peter
Rushford
Shropham
Thetford, St Cuthbert
Thetford, St Mary
Thetford, St Peter
Wilby
Wretham, East

Disused/Ruined
Category I
Harling, West
Illington
Snetterton, All SS
Stanford
West Tofts
Category II
Hargham
Roudham
Wretham, West
Category III
Buckenham, New, St Mary
Gasthorpe
Snarehill
Category IV
Garboldisham, All SS
Rockland, St Andrew
Category VI
Blo Norton, St Margaret
Bradcar
Buckenham, Old, St Nicholas
Buckenham Tofts
Harling, Middle
Hockham, Little
Snetterton, St Andrew
Thetford:
All Saints
St Andrew
St Benet
St Edmund
St Etheldreda
St George
St Giles
St Helen
Holy Trinity
St John
St Lawrence
St Margaret
St Martin
Great St Mary
St Michael
St Nicholas
Church at Red Castle Site
Church at Gas Works site, Bury Road
Church on site of St Michael's Close

18. Breckland

In Use
Ashill
Bodney
Breckles
Carbrooke
Caston
Cockley Cley, All SS
Cranwich
Cressingham, Great
Cressingham, Little
Didlington
Foulden
Gooderstone
Griston
Hilborough
Holm Hale
Ickburgh
Merton
Mundford
Necton
Ovington
Oxborough, St John
Pickenham, North
Pickenham, South
Wood Rising
Saham Toney
Scoulton
Sporle
Stow Bedon
Swaffham
Thompson
Threxton
Watton

Disused/Ruined
Category I
Langford
Tottington
Category II
Houghton-on-the-Hill
Category III
Oxborough, St Mary Magdalen
Category V
Colveston
Foulden, St Edmund
Category VI
Breccles, Little
Caldecote
Carbrooke, Little
Cockley Cley, St Peter

Cressingham, Great, St George
Holm
Lynford
Palgrave, Little
Pickenham, South, St Andrew
Sturston

19. Brisley and Elmham

In Use
Beeston-next-Mileham
Beetley
Billingford
Bilney, East
Bittering, Little
Brisley
Castle Acre
Colkirk
Dunham, Great
Dunham, Little
Elmham, North, II
Fransham, Great
Fransham, Little
Gressenhall
Harpley
Helhoughton
Horningtoft
Lexham, East
Lexham, West
Litcham
Longham
Massingham, Great
Massingham, Little
Mileham
Newton-by-Castleacre
Raynham, East
Raynham, South
Raynham, West
Rougham
Scarning
Southacre
Stanfield
Swanton Morley
Weasenham All SS
Weasenham St Peter
Wellingham
Wendling
Whissonsett
Worthing

Disused/Ruined
Category II
Kempstone
Oxwick
Category III
North Elmham I
Raynham, West
Category IV
Godwick
Category VI
Bitteringham, Great
Dunham, Great, St Mary
Massingham, Great, All SS
Pattesley
Weasenham, St Paul

20. Burnham and Walsingham

In Use
Barsham, East
Barsham, North
Barsham, South
Burnham Westgate
Burnham Norton
Burnham Overy
Burnham Thorpe
Burnham Ulph
Creake, North
Creake, South
Fakenham
Gateley
Holkham
Houghton
Houghton, St Giles
Kettlestone
Rudham, East
Ryburgh, Great
Sculthorpe

Disused/Ruined
Category I
Barmer
Dunton
Rudham, West
Category II
Croxton, St John the Baptist
Fulmodestone, St Mary
Category III
Ryburgh, Little
Category IV
Egmere
Pudding Norton
Snoring, Little
Testerton
Category V
Burnham Sutton
Creake, North, St Michael
Hempton, St Andrew
Penstorpe

Shereford
Snoring, Great
Snoring, Little
Stibbard
Syderstone
Tatterford (post-medieval)
Tattersett
Toftrees
Walsingham, Great, St Peter
Walsingham, Little
Waterden
Warham, All SS
Warham, St Mary Magdalen
Wighton
Wells

Quarles
Tattersett, St Andrew
Thorpland
Walsingham, Great, All SS
Category VI
Alethorpe
Broomsthorpe
Burnham, St Andrew
Burnham, St Edmund
Burnham Thorpe, St Peter
Doughton
Warham, St Mary the Virgin

21. Heacham and Rising
In Use
Anmer
Bircham, Great
Bircham Newton
Brancaster
Burnham Deepdale
Castle Rising II
Dersingham
Docking
Flitcham
Fring
Heacham
Hillington
Holme
Hunstanton, St Mary
Ingoldisthorpe
Newton, West
Ringstead, Great
Sandringham
Sedgeford
Shernborne
Snettisham
Stanhoe
Thornham
Titchwell
Wolferton

Disused/Ruined
Category I
Bagthorpe
Category II
Appleton
Babingley
Bircham Tofts
Ringstead, Little
Category III
Castle Rising I
Category IV
Ringstead, Great, St Peter
Category V
Barwick, Great
Category VI
Choseley
Summerfield

22. Holt
In Use
Baconsthorpe
Bale
Barney
Binham
Blakeney
Bodham
Briningham
Brinton
Briston
Cley
Field Dalling
Glandford
Gunthorpe
Hempstead
Hindringham
Holt
Hunworth
Kelling
Langham
Letheringsett
Melton Constable
Morston
Plumstead
Saxlingham
Salthouse
Sharrington
Sheringham, Upper
Stiffkey
Stody
Swanton Novers
Thornage
Thursford
Weybourne
Wiveton

Disused/Ruined
Category I
Cockthorpe
Category II
Bayfield
Category III
Burgh Parva
Category IV
Edgefield I
Category V
Beckham, East
Beckham, West
Category VI
Langham Parva
Stiffkey, St John

23. Lynn
In Use
Ashwicken
Bilney, West
Congham, St Andrew
Gayton
Gayton Thorpe
Gaywood
Grimston
Lynn, King's, St Margaret
Lynn, King's, St Nicholas
Lynn, South
Lynn, West, II
Middleton
Narborough
Pentney
Roydon
Runcton, North (post-medieval)
Walton, East
Westacre
Winch, East
Winch, West
Wootton, North
Wootton, South

Disused/Ruined
Category I
Narford
Category III
Bawsey
Mintlyn
Walton, East, St Andrew
Category V
Leziate
Lynn, King's, St James
Category VI
Congham, All SS
Congham, St Mary
Hardwick
Lynn, North
Lynn, West, I
Setchey, I

Diocese of Ely

Feltwell
In Use
Feltwell, St Mary
Methwold
Northwold
Stoke Ferry
Weeting
Wilton
Wretton

Disused/Ruined
Category I
Feltwell, St Nicholas
Hockwold
Category V
Weeting All SS
Category VI
Methwold Hythe

Fincham
In Use
Barton Bendish, St Andrew
Beachamwell, St Mary
Bexwell
Boughton
Crimplesham
Denver
Dereham, West
Downham Market
Fincham, St Martin
Fordham
Hilgay
Marham
Runcton Holme
Runcton, South
Ryston
Shouldham
Shouldham Thorpe
Stow Bardolph
Stradsett
Tottenhill/West Briggs
Watlington
Wereham
Wimbotsham
Wormegay

Disused/Ruined
Category I
Barton Bendish, St Mary
Shingham
Category II
Southery, St Mary
Category III
Beachamwell, All SS
Category IV
Beachamwell, St John
Wallington
Category VI
Barton Bendish, All SS
Dereham, West, St Peter
Fincham, St Michael
Foston
Marham, St Andrew
Roxham
Shouldham, St Margaret
Thorpland
Tottenhill

Wisbech (in Norfolk)
In Use
Emneth
Outwell
Upwell
Walsoken

March
In Use
Welney (post-medieval)

Mildenhall (in Norfolk)
In Use
Santon (post-medieval)

Lynn Marshland

In Use
Clenchwarton
Terrington St Clement
Terrington St John
Tilney All Saints

Disused/Ruined
Category I
Walpole St Andrew
Wiggenhall, St Mary the Virgin
Category II
Walpole St Peter
Walton, West
Wiggenhall, St Germans
Wiggenhall, St Mary Magdalen

Islington
Wiggenhall St Peter
Category VI
Clenchwarton, South
Kenwick

Appendix III

Disused/Ruined/Disappeared Medieval Churches within the City Walls of Norwich

1. **All Saints, Fyebridgegate.** Added to St Paul's, demolished 1550. Co-op site.
2. **All Saints, Timberhill.** Redundant in 1976; ecumenical centre.
3. **St Anne.** Added to St Clement's (Conesford) c. 1370. Chapel demolished some time after 1389.
4. **St Bartholomew.** Fell into ruin after 1549. Added to St John de Sepulchre c. 1550. Partly intact until 1930s.
5. **St Benedict.** Bombed April 1942; excavated 1972.
6. **St Botolph.** Added to St Saviour's, 1548; demolished 1549. Odeon site.
7. **St Christopher.** Added to St Andrew's later 13th century; burned and destroyed.
8. **St Clement Conesford.** Advowson given to St Julian 1472; added to St Julian's 1482. 1560 church and churchyard sold. Still standing 1744.
9. **St Clement, Fye Bridge.** Declared redundant 1976, rented as centre for prayer and meditation since 1978.
10. **St Crowche.** Added to St John Maddermarket c. 1551, and demolished.
11. **St Cuthbert.** Added to St Mary the Less 1492, St George Tombland 1542. Demolished c. 1530.
12. **St Edmund.** Redundant since 1980; store, to be converted to offices.
13. **St Edward.** Added to St Julian's before 1305.
14. **St Ethelbert.** Added to St Mary in the Marsh late 13th century. Destroyed by riot 1272.
15. **St Etheldreda.** Redundant since 1975; artist's studio.
16. **St Gregory.** Redundant since 1974; arts centre.
17. **St Helen I.** First site demolished 13th century; new church in transept of St Giles hospital.
18. **Holy Trinity.** Demolished c. 1100; cathedral site.
19. **St James Pockthorpe.** Redundant since 1972. Excavated 1974. Puppet Theatre.
20. **St John the Baptist Colegate.** Added to St George Colegate 13th century. Absorbed into Dominican Friary (first site).
21. **St John the Evangelist, Conesford.** Added to St Peter's Parmentergate c. 1300. Destroyed.
22. **St Lawrence.** Redundant since 1974; no use yet.
23. **St Margaret at Newbridge.** Parish depopulated by plague 1349. Added to St George Colegate after 1349. Valued in 1368, but probably not in parochial use at this date.
24. **St Margaret, Fye Bridge.** Added to All Saints c. 1468, and St Paul's 1550; demolished 1547. Excavated 1987.
25. **St Margaret, Westwick.** Redundant since 1974; fitness centre (gymnasium).
26. **St Martin in Balliva.** Desecrated 1562; added to St Michael at Thorn 16th century.
27. **St Martin at Oak.** Redundant since 1976; night shelter.
28. **St Martin at Palace.** Redundant since 1974; excavation begun 1987-8. Conversion to probation day centre.
29. **St Mary Coslany.** Redundant since 1975; art and craft centre.
30. **St Mary in the Marsh.** Founded by de Losinga; pulled down 1564; bits still there.
31. **St Mary the Less.** Redundant; store.
32. **St Mary Unbrent.** Added to St Saviour's c. 1540, and demolished.
33. **St Matthew the Apostle.** Church ruinous in 1368; since plague parishioners attended St Martin's. Added to St Martin at Palace c. 1377. Last rector died 1377-8; church later demolished.
34. **St Michael Coslany.** Redundant since 1976. Martial Arts Centre (Sports Hall).
35. **St Michael Conesford.** Added to St Peter's Parmentergate and demolished 1360. Absorbed into Augustinian Friary.
36. **St Michael at Pleas.** Redundant since 1974; exhibition centre.
37. **St Michael Tombland.** Demolished c. 1100. Richest church at Domesday; site partly destroyed by public lavatories, 1871.
38. **St Michael at Thorn.** Bombed 1942; Norman doorway into St Julian's. Car park.
39. **St Olave Colegate.** Chapel probably by 1482. Added to St George Colegate, 1546, and demolished.
40. **St Olave, Conesford.** Added to St Peter's Southgate before 1345. Destroyed.
41. **St Paul.** Bombed 1942.
42. **St Peter Hungate.** Redundant since 1932; ecclesiastical museum.
43. **St Peter Parmentergate.** Redundant since 1979; organ builder's workshop.
44. **St Peter Southgate.** Demolished 1887.
45. **St Saviour.** Redundant since 1976; badminton hall.
46. **SS Simon and Jude.** Redundant; used by Boy Scouts Association since 1952.
47. **St Swithin.** Redundant since 1974; Norwich Arts Centre.
48. **St Vedast.** Added to St Mary in the Marsh c. 1272; St Peter Parmentergate c. 1562.
49. **St Winwaloy.** Parish depopulated by plague in 1349; became a chapelry attached to Carrow Priory. Demolished in 16th century.
50. **Church in castle bailey.** Abandoned early in 12th-century (Ayers).

Appendix IV

Erroneous Attributions of Parochial Status

Very few of the chapels in existence in the Middle Ages had parochial status, with full rights of baptism and burial. Most were either chantries (private chapels for masses for the dead) or private chapels owned by manorial lords. There were also a number of chapels serving a small monastic cell, and occasionally a secular guild chapel.

Messent included many such chapels in his book 'The Ruined Churches of Norfolk' (1931). The fifty-four erroneous attributions are:

Ashwell	guild chapel
Bale, St Botolph	no evidence of parochial use
Barsham, North, St Catherine	no evidence of parochial use
Barwick Parva	no evidence of a church existing
Bawburgh, St Walstan	pilgrimage chapel attached to the parish church
Belhaugh, St Andrew	no evidence of parochial use
Berking	no evidence of parochial use
Billockby, All Saints	church still in use, although nave ruined
Catsholm, St Catherine	Messent's reference is from White's Directory; the latter appears to have muddled it with Slevesholm
Cockley Cley, St Mary	no evidence of parochial use
Custhorpe, St Thomas Becket	was part of a monastic cell
Dereham East, St Withburga	shrine over a spring
Dersingham	no evidence of parochial use
Diss, St Nicholas	guild chapel
Eastmore	no evidence of parochial use
Gissing, All Saints	chantry chapel
Glosthorpe, St Peter	no evidence of parochial use
Guton, St Swithin	a misreading of Blomefield; the description of St Swithin's at Bintree follows Blomefield's account of Guton
Hilborough, St Margaret	a chantry chapel
Hunstanton, St Edmund	no evidence of parochial use
Ickburgh, St Lawrence	leper-house and hermitage
Keburn	no evidence of parochial use
Kimberley, St Mary	chantry chapel
Kirstead, St Andrew	no evidence of a second church here
Loddon, St Mary	chantry chapel
Lynn, King's, Our Lady on the Bridge	bridge chapel
Lynn, King's, St Ann	no evidence of parochial use
Lynn, King's, St Catherine	no evidence of parochial use
Narborough	no evidence of parochial use
Narford, St Mary	no evidence of parochial use
Palgrave, Great	the parish church was at Little Palgrave
Pickenham, North, St Paul	hermit's chapel
Pulham St Mary, St James	guild chapel
Rougham	no evidence of parochial use
Rougholm (Gressenhall), St Nicholas	chantry chapel
Roydon, St Mary	chantry chapel
Rudham, West, All Saints	no evidence of parochial use
Sallow	it remains a parish church, the village is now spelled 'Salhouse'
Scornston	an ancient spelling for Sco Ruston
Shelfanger, St Andrew	no evidence of parochial use
Shimpling Hythe, St Mary	no evidence of parochial use
Slevesholm	site of priory
South Acre, St Bartholomew	leper chapel
Stow, St Guthlac	hospice of Castle Acre
Swaffham	chantry chapel
Swathing	no evidence of ever possessing a church
Tasburgh, St Michael	private chapel
Terrington, St James	chantry chapel
Tibenham, St Mary	no evidence of parochial use
Trowse Millgate	no evidence of a church, perhaps confused with Carrow?
Tuttington St Botolph	no evidence of parochial use
Wighton	probably a private chapel
Wimpwell	no evidence of ever possessing a church
Wiveton, St Mary	no evidence of parochial use

Appendix V

Statistics for the Diocese of Norwich
a) Churches in use, disused, ruined or disappeared (including chapels-of-ease)

Lynn   Norfolk   Norwich

Archdeaconry Deanery	In use	I	II	III	IV	V	VI	Total
Blofield	29	3	4	—	1	—	2	39
Flegg	31	1	1	—	3	—	9	45
Ingworth	29	1	2	—	2	—	4	38
Norwich North	20	—	—	1	—	—	1	22
Norwich South	13	—	1	—	1	—	3	18
Norwich East	18	20	1	1	1	2	29	72
Repps	28	3	—	1	—	—	5	37
Sparham	26	2	1	1	1	1	3	35
Tunstead	32	—	1	—	—	—	3	36
Waxham	15	1	—	—	—	1	1	18
Depwade	30	1	1	1	—	1	8	42
Hingham and Mitford	31	1	—	1	—	2	—	35
Humbleyard	28	3	—	—	1	1	9	42
Loddon	44	1	—	4	1	1	10	61
Lothingland	24	—	1	1	—	—	2	28
Redenhall	29	2	1	—	1	—	1	34
Thetford and Rockland	29	5	4	3	2	—	26	69
Breckland	32	2	1	1	—	2	10	48
Brisley and Elmham	39	—	2	2	1	—	5	49
Burnham and Walsingham	38	3	2	1	4	8	7	63
Heacham and Rising	26	2	4	1	1	1	2	37
Holt	38	1	1	1	1	2	2	46
Lynn	24	2	—	3	—	3	6	38
Total	653	54	28	23	21	25	148	952

b) Parishes outside the county of Norfolk, but within the diocese of Norwich (excluding parishes in Norfolk; see Appendices I and II.)

1. The Deanery of Lothingland

In Use
Ashby
Blundeston
Carlton Colville
Corton
Gisleham
Gunton, St Benedict (post-medieval)
Gunton, St Peter
Herringfleet
Kessingland
Kirkley (post-medieval)
Lound
Lowestoft, Christ Church (post-medieval)
Lowestoft, St Andrew (post-medieval)
Lowestoft, St Margaret
Lowestoft, The Good Shepherd (post-medieval)
Mutford
Oulton
Oulton Broad, St Luke (post-medieval)
Oulton Broad, St Mark (post-medieval)
Pakefield
Rushmere
Somerleyton

Disused/Ruined
Category III
Flixton
Category VI
Lowestoft, St John (post-medieval)
Lowestoft, St Peter (post-medieval)

2. The Deanery of Thetford and Rockland

Disused/Ruined
Category II
Knettishall

Appendix VI

Major Building Operations

Romanesque c. 1040-1180 (52)

Antingham
Appleton
Barningham, North
Barton Bendish, St Mary
Bawsey
Bayfield
Beachamwell, All Saints
Bickerston
Brandiston
Buckenham Ferry
Buckenham, North, St Mary
Burgh Parva
Burgh St Mary
Castle Rising
Cockthorpe
Islington
Kempstone
Kirby Bedon
Langford
Lynn, King's, St James
Mannington
Mintlyn
Morton-on-the-Hill
Narford
Oxborough
Pudding Norton
Rackheath
Ringstead, Great
Ryburgh, Little
Saxlingham Thorpe
Crownthorpe
Croxton
Edgefield
Egmere
Elmham, North
Feltwell
Forncett St Mary
Fulmodestone
Hautbois, Great
Hales
Houghton-on-the-Hill
Illington
Shimpling
Shingham
Shotesham, St Martin
Snarehill
Snoring, Little
Southwood
Stanford
Surlingham
Walton, East
Whitlingham

Transitional and Early English c. 1170-c.1300 (29)

Appleton
Barmer
Barningham, North
Buckenham Ferry
Mundham
Rackheath
Ringstead, Little
Rockland, St Andrew

Croxton	Rudham, West	Burnham Sutton	Ryburgh, Little
Cockthorpe	Saxlingham Thorpe	Caister, West	Saxlingham Thorpe
Coston	Shimpling	Cockthorpe	Sco Ruston
Crownthorpe	Snarehill	Corpusty	Shimpling
Feltwell	Snetterton	Coston	Shotesham, St Botolph
Fulmodestone	Southwood	Crownthorpe	Shotesham, St Martin
Gasthorpe	Tivetshall	Croxton	Snetterton
Harling, West	Walton, East	Dunton	Somerton, East
Hautbois, Great	Walton, West	Edgefield	Southery
Islington	Wiggenhall, St Mary the Virgin	Feltwell	Southwood
Kirby Bedon		St Mary	Stanford
		Frenze	Stanninghall

Decorated c. 1280-c. 1370 (39)

Antingham	Moulton St Mary
Appleton	Narford
Babingley	Oxwick
Barmer	Pudding Norton
Barningham, North	Rackheath
Barton Bendish, St Mary	Raynham, West
Bowthorpe	Roudham
Brandiston	Rudham, West
Buckenham Ferry	Ruston, East
Burlingham, North	Sco Ruston
Dunton	Shingham
Edgefield	Stanford
Egmere	Surlingham
Frenze	Tivetshall
Harling, West	Thurgarton
Hautbois, Great	Tottington
Hockwold	Walsingham, Great
Hopton	West Tofts
Kempstone	Wretham, West
Morton-on-the-Hill	

Fulmodestone	Surlingham
Garboldisham	Testerton
Gasthorpe	Thorpe
Gillingham	Thorpland
Godwick	Thorpe Parva
Hainford	Thurgarton
Hargham	Tivetshall
Harling, West	Tottington
Hautbois, Great	Tunstall
Heigham, St Bartholomew	Wallington
Hindolveston	Walpole St Andrew
Hockwold	Walsham, South
Hopton	West Tofts
Houghton-on-the-Hill	Wretham, West
Illington	Whitlingham
Islington	Wiggenhall, St Mary the Virgin
Kirby Bedon	Wiggenhall, St Peter
Melton, Great	Wolterton
Mintlyn	Wood Norton

Post-Medieval c. 1540-today (22) (excluding churches newly founded 1800-today)

Babingley	Mintlyn
Bagthorpe	Panxworth
Barmer	Ruston, East
Booton	Sco Ruston
Bowthorpe	Setchey
Burlingham, North	Shimpling
Croxton	Southery
Egmere	Stanford
Godwick	Tunstall
Gunton	West Tofts
Houghton-on-the-Hill	Yarmouth, St George

Perpendicular c. 1350-c. 1540 (82)

Antingham	Morton-on-the-Hill
Appleton	Moulton St Mary
Barningham, North	Narford
Bastwick	Oxborough
Bayfield	Panxworth
Beachamwell, St John	Rackheath
Bircham Tofts	Raynham, West
Brandiston	Roudham
Burgh Parva	Rudham, West
Burlingham, North	Ruston, East

Appendix VII

Quality of Church Architecture (excluding City of Norwich)

I. Of National Importance

Gunton
Hales
West Tofts
Walton, West (tower)

II. Of County Importance

Appleton	Langford
Barmer	Lynn, King's, St James
Babingley	Morton-on-the-Hill

North Barningham	Moulton St Mary
Barton Bendish, St Mary	Narford
Bawsey	Pudding Norton
Booton	Rackheath
Brandiston	Roudham
Buckenham Ferry	West Rudham
Castle Rising	East Ruston
Cockthorpe	Saxlingham Thorpe
Corpusty	Shimpling
Coston	Shingham
Crownthorpe	Snarehill
Dunton	Snetterton
Edgefield	Snoring, Little
Egmere	Stanford
Elmham, North	Surlingham, St Saviour
Feltwell	Thurgarton
Forncett, St Mary	Tivetshall St Mary
Frenze	Tottington

178

Fulmodestone
Hargham
West Harling
Hautbois, Great
Hockwold
Hopton
Houghton-on-the-Hill
Illington
Islington
Kempstone
Tunstall
Walton, East, St Andrew
Wallington
Walpole St Andrew
Wiggenhall, St Mary the Virgin
Wiggenhall, St Peter
Wretham, West
Wolterton
Yarmouth, St George
Croxton
Garboldisham
Gasthorpe
Gillingham, All Saints
Godwick
Hainford
Heigham, St Bartholomew
Hindolveston
Kirby Bedon, St Mary
Mannington
Somerton, East
Southery
Southwood
Stanninghall
Testerton
Thorpe-by-Norwich
Thorpe Parva
Walsham, South, St Lawrence
Whitlingham
Wood Norton

III. Of Local Importance

Antingham St Margaret
Bagthorpe
Bastwick
Bayfield
Beachamwell, All Saints
Beachamwell, St John
Bickerston
Bircham Tofts
Bowthorpe
New Buckenham, St Mary
Burgh Parva
Burgh St Mary
Burlingham St Peter
West Caister
Melton, Great, St Mary
Mintlyn
Mundham, St Ethelbert
Oxborough, St Mary Magdale
Oxwick
Panxworth
Raynham, West
Ringstead, Little
Ringstead, Great
Rockland St Andrew
Ryburgh, Little
Sco Ruston
Setchey
Shotesham St Martin

IV. Of Importance Only to the Very Dedicated

Barnham Broom, St Michael
Barwick, Great
Beckham, East
Beckham, West
Burnham Sutton
Carlton, East
Colveston
Creake, North, St Michael
Eccles
Foulden
Hackford, All Saints
Hempton
Letton
Leziate
Pensthorpe
Quarles
Rockland St Mary, St Margaret
Shotesham, St Botolph
Tattersett, St Andrew
Thorpland
Walsingham, Great, All Saints
Weeting, All Saints

Appendix VIII

Church Contents

I. Of National Importance
North Barningham
Frenze (Brasses, font, pews, pulpit)
Rudham, West (glass)
West Tofts (monument, screens, stalls)
Wiggenhall St Mary the Virgin (benches, font cover, lectern, monument, screen)

II. Of County Importance
Bagthorpe (font)
Barton Bendish, St Mary (paintings)
Booton
Cockthorpe (monument)
Corpusty (screen)
Gunton (decor)
West Harling (brasses, font, monuments, reredos)
Hales (font, paintings)
Hockwold (monuments)
Langford (monument)
Moulton St Mary (benches, font, monument, paintings)
Rackheath (monuments)
East Ruston (font, screen)
Shimpling (font, glass)
Shingham (benches, pulpit)
Thurgarton (benches)
Walpole St Andrew (pulpit)

III. Of Local Importance
Barmer
Booton
Brandiston
Buckenham Ferry
Burlingham St Peter
Coston
Crownthorpe
Dunton
Feltwell
Hargham
Islington
Morton-on-the-Hill
Snetterton
Stanford
Tottington
Tunstall

179

Appendix IX

Condition of Churches (excluding Norwich)

Good Condition

Bagthorpe
Barmer
North Barningham
Barton Bendish
Booton
Bowthorpe
Brandiston
Buckenham Ferry
Castle Rising
Cockthorpe
Coston
Dunton
North Elmham
Feltwell
Forncett
Frenze
Gunton
Hales
West Harling
Hockwold
Islington
Moulton St Mary
Rackheath
West Rudham
East Ruston
Shimpling
Snetterton
Thorpe Hamlet
Thurgarton
Wiggenhall St Mary
Yarmouth St George
Tottington
Tunstall
South Walsham
Walpole St Andrew

Average Condition

Bastwick
Bayfield
New Buckenham
Crownthorpe
Hainford
Heigham
Great Hautbois
Langford
Mannington
Morton-on-the-Hill
Sco Ruston
Setchey
Shingham
Snarehill
Stanford
West Tofts

Poor Condition

Beachamwell All Saints
Bickerston
Corpusty
Edgefield
Hackford
King's Lynn St James
Mintlyn
Mundham
Oxborough
Oxwick
Little Ryburgh
Southery
Surlingham
Thorpe-by-Norwich
Tivetshall
East Walton
Wood Norton

Dangerous Condition

Antingham
Appleton
Babingley
Bawsey
Beachamwell St John
Bircham Tofts
Burgh Parva
Burgh St Mary
Burlingham St Peter
West Caister
Croxton
Egmere
Fulmodestone
Garboldisham
Gasthorpe
Godwick
Hindolveston
Hopton
Houghton-on-the-Hill
Kempstone
Kirby Bedon
Great Melton
Panxworth
Pudding Norton
West Raynham
Great Ringstead
Little Ringstead
Rockland
Roudham
Saxlingham Thorpe
Shotesham St Martin
East Somerton
Southwood
Stanninghall
Testerton
Thorpe Parva
Wallington
Whitlingham
Wiggenhall St Peter
Wolterton
West Wretham

Appendix X

Dates of Abandonment of Parish Churches

This section provides more detail about the factual base for Fig. 4. Most of the dates are reasonably precise, but there is a measure of uncertainty for a number of entries before 1500. In particular, it is difficult to be certain about those churches for which *Domesday Book* provides the sole mention: it has been presumed that they would have been listed in 1254 if they had still existed, but they may have been abandoned at any time between *c.* 1100 and *c.* 1250. Problematic datings are indicated by the letter (P). Site numbers follow the catalogue. Churches within the City of Norwich follow the numbering in Appendix III, and are preceded by the letter N. Additional sites are numbered according to Appendix XI, and are preceded with the letter A.

Churches abandoned 1051-1100
Category VI

N18. Norwich, Holy Trinity. Demolished *c.* 1100 to build new cathedral.
N37. Norwich, St Michael Tombland. Demolished *c.* 1100 to make way for cathedral precinct.
A4. Poringland, East, I. Church moved to a more convenient site in reign of William II (Blomefield).
234. Thetford, St Martin. Recorded in *Domesday*. Probably abandoned soon after the transference of the See in 1094 (Davison).
235. Thetford, Great St Mary. Parish church until 1072, cathedral until 1094, then part of Cluniac priory.
254. Yarmouth, Great, St Benedict. Replaced by de Losinga's church *c.* 1100.

Churches abandoned 1101-1150
Category VI

138. Barton Turf B (P). Sole mention in *Domesday*.
155. Carleton Rode B (P). Sole mention in *Domesday*.
167. Dykebeck (P). Sole mention in *Domesday*.
N50. Church in castle bailey. Abandoned early in 12th century (Ayers).

Category IV
104. Snoring, Little, tower. Church rebuilt to north in 12th century.

Category III
71. Castle Rising, church in castle bailey. Abandoned during construction of castle *c.* 1150.
72. Elmham, North, I. Became parish church after 1071, replaced by a new church early in 12th century.

Churches abandoned 1151-1200
Category VI
210. Seething B (P). Sole mention in *Domesday*.
217. Stoke Holy Cross B (P). Sole mention in *Domesday*.
227. Thetford, St George. Became the church of the Nunnery *c.* 1160.
238. Thetford, church at Red Castle site. Probably abandoned by late 12th century (Knocker).
239. Thetford, church on site of Gas Works. Destruction layer postdates a piece of early medieval ware.
240. Thetford, church on site of St Michael's Close. Pottery finds suggest it went out of use towards the end of the 12th century.
243. Thurketeliart. *Domesday* sole mention.

Churches abandoned 1201-1250
Category VI
163. Cressingham, Great, St George (P). Form suggests no extensions after 1150. Became a hermit's chapel (Blomefield).
176. Helmingham (P). Mentioned only in *Domesday*.
186. Kerdiston, St Mary (P). Mentioned in *Domesday*, abandoned before 14th century.
195. Methwold Hythe (P). Controversy over its patronage in late 12th century; silence after.
224. Thetford, St Benet (P). Donated to Nunnery *c.* 1160, went out of use in 13th or 14th century (Davison).

Category III
69. Buckenham, New, St Mary. Served town until new parish church of St Martin built in 1240s.

Churches abandoned 1251-1300
Category VI
N7. Norwich, St Christopher. Destroyed after being added to St Andrew's in late 13th century.
N13. Norwich, St Edward. Added to St Julian's before 1305.
N14. Norwich, St Ethelbert. Destroyed by riot in 1272.
N17. Norwich, St Helen I. Demolished in 13th century.
N20. Norwich, St John the Baptist Colegate. Added to St George Colegate in 13th century, and absorbed into friary.
N21. Norwich, St John the Evangelist Conesford. Added to St Peter's Parmentergate *c.* 1300 and destroyed.
A3. Lynn, West, St Peter I. Inundated by sea, moved to new site in 1271.

Churches abandoned 1301-1350
Category VI
151. Burnham, St Edmund (P). List of rectors terminates *c.* 1345.
165. Doughton (P). Reduced to chapel status in 1325 (Blomefield).
N40. Norwich, St Olave Conesford. Added to St Peter's Southgate before 1345, and destroyed.
204. Pickenham, South, St Andrew (P). Standing in 1291, but silence after.
231. Thetford, St John. Became a leper chapel before 1307 (Knowles and Hadcock).
233. Thetford, St Margaret. Became a leper chapel before 1304 (Davison).

Category V
110. Barnham Broom, St Michael (P). Consolidated with SS Peter and Paul in 1347.

Churches abandoned 1351-1400
Category VI
142. Blo Norton, St Margaret. Abandoned in 1394.
152. Burnham Thorpe, St Peter (P). Consolidated with All Saints in 1364.
159. Clenchwarton, South. Destroyed by sea shortly before 1368 (Watkin).
187. Keswick, St Clement. Washed away by sea shortly after 1382 (Blomefield).
N3. Norwich, St Anne. Added to St Clement's *c.* 1370, chapel demolished after 1389.
N23. Norwich, St Margaret at Newbridge. Depopulated by plague in 1349, added to St George Colegate, not in parochial use by 1368 (Watkin).
N33. Norwich, St Matthew the Apostle. Depopulated by plague in 1349, added to St Martin at Palace *c.* 1377, church later demolished.
N35. Norwich, St Michael in Conesford. Added to St Peter's Parmentergate and demolished 1360.
201. Overstrand, St Martin I. Washed away by sea *c.* 1398.
212. Shipden. Washed away by sea *c.* 1400.
222. Thetford, All Saints. Out of use in 1368 (Watkin).
229. Thetford, St Helen (P). Probably disused by end 14th century.
232. Thetford, St Lawrence. Impropriated to the Canons *c.* 1400 (Davison).
247. Waxham, Little, St Margaret (P). List of rectors until 1383; possibly engulfed by the sea (Messent).
249. Wicklewood, St Andrew. Consolidated to All Saints in 1367, demolished soon after (Blomefield).

Churches abandoned 1401-1450
Category VI
145. Breccles, Little (P). Demolished before Edward III's time (Blomefield).
150. Burnham, St Andrew. Consolidated with Burnham Overy in 1421; rectors continued until 1447.
156. Carbrooke, Little. Consolidated with Great Carbrooke and demolished in 1424 (Blomefield).
179. Hockham, Little, St Mary. In use *c.* 1390, allowed to decay soon after (Bryant).
250. Windle, St Andrew. United to Gillingham All Saints in 1440.
253. Wreningham, Little, St Mary. Annexed to Nelonde in 1406, became a chapel, pulled down soon after (Blomefield; Nelonde was in turn demolished in the 16th century).

Churches abandoned 1451-1500
Category VI
180. Holm, St Andrew. Consolidated with Hale in 1352, rectors continued until 1470, fell into decay soon after (Bryant).
183. Itteringham, St Nicholas. Reduced to chapel status by 1430, the church and manor were probably both abandoned by the end of the 15th century.
184. Kenningham. United with Mulbarton in 1452; demolished long before the Dissolution (Blomefield).
225. Thetford, St Edmund. Reduced to chapel status temp. Henry IV; demolished before Reformation (Blomefield).
228. Thetford, St Giles. Let to a hermit *c.* 1470; made a barn by 1598 (Martin).
236. Thetford, St Michael (P). Abandoned 15th century or early 16th century (Davison).
242. Thorpeland, St Thomas. In use in 1488, but in ruins by 1500 (Bryant).

Churches abandoned 1501-1550
Category VI
134. Algarsthorpe, St Mary Magdalen. United to Great Melton in 1476; abandoned at the Dissolution (Blomefield).
139. Bedingham, St Mary (P). Probably abandoned at Reformation.
140. Beeston, St Andrew. Consolidated with Sprowston in 1543; long abandoned by 1603 (Jessopp).
141. Bittering, Great, St Nicholas (P). Probably abandoned in 16th century.
143. Bracondale, St Nicholas. In use in 1428; pulled down at Dissolution (Blomefield).
144. Bradcar, St Andrew. Annexed to Shropham in 1332; reduced to chapel status 1519.
146. Broomsthorpe. Parishioners had licence to go to East Rudham church in 1536.
147. Brundall, St Clement. A chapel-of-ease, but suppressed with other chapels in 1547.
148. Buckenham, Old, St Andrew. Abandoned in 1536; decayed 3 score years in 1602 (Tymms).
154. Cantelose, All Saints. Consolidated with Hethersett in 1397;

continued as a chapel until Reformation (Blomefield).
157. Carrow, St James. In use in 1520, but abandoned at Reformation (Blomefield).
158. Choseley (P). Mentioned in 1267, but gone by end of 16th century.
161. Congham, All Saints. Abandoned soon before 1552 (Walters).
164. Dereham, West, St Peter. Only St Andrew's standing by 1552.
166. Dunham, Great, St Mary. Still in use in 1514; abandoned at Dissolution (Blomefield).
169. Foston, St Peter. Rectors until 1449, then a curate until the Dissolution (Bryant).
171. Guist Thorpe, All Saints. Demolished in 1547 (Walters).
172. Hardwick. Chapel still standing in 1528; abandoned at Dissolution (Blomefield).
174. Harling, Middle, St Andrew. Consolidated to West Harling in 1457. Entirely taken down in 1543 (Blomefield).
177. Hempnall, St Andrew (P). In use in 1379; not listed in 1552.
185. Kenwick, St Thomas (P). Chapel-of-ease to Tilney All Saints in 1368.
189. Langham Parva, St Mary. No mention in 1552. Ruined 'long since' in 1602 (Tymms).
190. Lynford. Served by rectors until 1455, then by curates until the Dissolution (Blomefield).
192. Marham, St Andrew. Still in use in 1428. Not mentioned in 1552.
193. Markshall, St Edmund. Became a free chapel in 1525; demolished at the Dissolution (Blomefield).
194. Massingham, Great, All Saints. List of rectors until 1427; still in use in 1514.
197. Nelonde, St Peter. United to Little Wreningham in 1406, to Great Wreningham in 1414, demolished at the Dissolution (Blomefield).
N1. Norwich, All Saints, Fybridgegate. Demolished 1550.
N6. Norwich, St Botolph. Demolished 1549.
N11. Norwich, St Cuthbert. Demolished c. 1530.
N24. Norwich, St Margaret Fye Bridge. Demolished 1547.
N32. Norwich, St Mary Unbrest. Added to St Saviour's c. 1540 and demolished.
N39. Norwich, St Olave, Colegate. Added to St George Colegate in 1546 and demolished.
N49. Norwich, St Winwaloy. Became a chapel after 1349; demolished 16th century.
203. Pattesley, St John the Baptist. A sinecure in 1521, demolished in 1571.
205. Poringland, West, St Michael. Still in use in 1505. Demolished before 1540 (Blomefield).
206. Rackheath, Little, Holy Trinity. Consolidated with Great Rackheath in 1407; mentioned in 1517.
208. Saxthorpe, St Dunstan. Parochial, but also used as a chantry chapel; therefore dissolved 1547-8.
209. Scratby, All Saints. Consolidated with Ormesby in 1548 and licence obtained to demolish.
211. Setchey. Lead, bells and chalice sold in 1548 (Walters).
215. Snetterton, St Andrew. Consolidated with All Saints in 1435; pulled down temp. Henry VIII (Blomefield).
218. Stratton, St Peter. Consolidated with Stratton St Michael in 1449; 'utterly decayed about three or four score years since' in 1602 (Tymms).
221. Swainsthorpe, St Mary. Consolidated with St Peter in 1406; demolished at Reformation (Blomefield).
223. Thetford, St Andrew. Consolidated with St Peter's in 1546 and soon demolished (Blomefield).
226. Thetford, St Etheldreda. Rectors instituted until 1528. Attracted pilgrims to its relic of St Etheldreda, therefore demolished c. 1540.
230. Thetford, Holy Trinity. Consolidated with St Cuthbert's in 1547, fell out of use soon after (Blomefield).
237. Thetford, St Nicholas. Consolidated with St Peter's in 1547, then demolished (Blomefield).
241. Thorpe-by-Norwich, Old Thorpe church. 'Systematically dismantled in 16th century' (Clarke).
244. Topcroft, St Giles. A chapel with list of vicars until c. 1540 (Blomefield).
A5. Tottenhill (P). Mentioned in 1397.
245. Wacton, Little, St Mary. In use until c. 1500; in decay 1510; fell down after 1520.
248. Weasenham, St Paul (P). Abandoned after 1368.
251. Winston, St Andrew (P). Consolidated with Gillingham All Saints 1440. Still in use probably until 16th century.
252. Worstead, St Andrew. Still in use in 1529; abandoned after 1536 (Blomefield).

255. Yarmouth, Southtown, St Nicholas. United with Gorleston in 1511.

Category V
111. Barwick, St Mary. Consolidation with Stanhoe in 1511 refused, despite only having one parishioner; abandoned soon after.
115. Carlton, East, St Peter. United with St Mary's in 1441. Dilapidated c. 1550 (Blomefield).
117. Creake, North, St Michael. The vicar Richard Vowel (d. 1550) allowed his brother to dilapidate the church.
119. Foulden, St Edmund (P). Abandoned by 16th century.
120. Hackford, All Saints. Burned down in 1543.
124. Lynn, King's, St James. Closed c. 1540, nave demolished 1549.
N4. Norwich, St Bartholomew. Fell into ruin after 1549.
125. Pensthorpe (P). No church by 1633 (Blomefield).
127. Rockland St Mary, St Margaret. Last mentioned in 1514.
128. Shotesham, St Botolph. Pulled down at the Reformation (Blomefield).
129. Tattersett, St Andrew. List of rectors to c. 1450; only neighbouring church of All Saints mentioned in 1552.

Category IV
88. Beachamwell, St John. In use in 1535, not mentioned in 1552.
106. Thorpe Parva, St Mary. Described as ruined for 60 years in 1602.

Category III
77. Oxborough, St Mary Magdalen (P). Reduced to chapel status in late 14th century; probably continued until 16th century.
81. Snarehill, Great. In use 1525-6. No further mention.
84. Walton, East, St Andrew (P). Still in use in 1368; abandoned by 16th century.
86. Wood Norton, St Peter. In use in 1417; not mentioned in 1552.

Category II
52. Ringstead, Little, St Andrew. Reduced to status of chapel in 1349; continued until 16th century.

Category I
31. Norwich, St Mary the Less. Made over to Corporation of Norwich c. 1540.

Churches abandoned 1551-1600
Category VI
133. Alethorpe, All Saints. In use in 1552. Used as a barn by 1602 (Tymms).
135. Apton, St Martin. In use in 1552, abandoned soon after.
149. Buckenham Tofts, St Andrew. Long since decayed in 1602 (Tymms).
153. Caldecote, St Mary. Still in use in 1496. Profaned before 1603 (Jessopp).
160. Cockley Cley, St Peter. Accidentally burned down in reign of Elizabeth (Blomefield).
162. Congham, St Mary. In use in 1552. Profaned by 1603 (Jessopp).
170. Gowthorpe, St James. Consolidated with Intwood 1401, with Keswick 1597; in use until c. 1590 (Blomefield).
175. Hautbois, Little, St Mary. In use in 1552; gone by 1603 (Jessopp).
178. Herringby, St Ethelbert. Last vicar installed in 1541. Dilapidated before 1603 (Jessopp).
181. Holverston, St Mary. United to Rockland St Mary 1358. Demolition under way in second half of 16th century: stone from church used in Holverston Hall (Elizabethan).
182. Irmingland, St Andrew. In use in 1557. Long decayed by 1602 (Tymms).
196. Moulton, Little, All Saints. In use in 1552; destroyed, stones used to make a road before 1602 (Tymms).
N8. Norwich, St Clement Conesford. Added to St Julian's 1482. Church and churchyard sold 1560.
N10. Norwich, St Crowche. Added to St John Maddermarket c. 1551 and demolished.
N26. Norwich, St Martin in Balliva. Desecrated 1562.
N48. Norwich, St Vedast. Added to St Mary in the Marsh c. 1272, to St Peter Parmentergate c. 1562.
198. Oby. In use in 1552; referred to as 'Ashby-cum-Oby' from 1597.

199. Ormesby, St Andrew. In use in 1591. Abandoned by 1603 (Jessopp).
200. Ormesby, St Peter. In use in 1591. Abandoned by 1603 (Jessopp).
202. Palgrave, Little. Consolidated with Sporle 1581.
207. Roxham, St Michael. United with Ryston 1555.
213. Shouldham, St Margaret. In use in 1519, 1552. Abandoned by end of century.
216. Stiffkey, St John the Baptist. List of rectors until 1559. In ruins by 1602 (Tymms).
220. Summerfield, All Saints. No churchwardens or inhabitants in 1554. In ruins *temp.* Elizabeth (Blomefield).
246. Warham, St Mary the Virgin. In use in 1552. In ruins by 1562 (Blomefield).

Category V
121. Hempton, St Andrew. In use in 1552; destroyed before 1623.
122. Letton, All Saints. Consolidated with Cranworth in 1546. In ruins by 1560-1.
N30. Norwich, St Mary in the Marsh. Pulled down in 1564.
126. Quarles. In ruins by 1571 (Blomefield).
130. Thorpland, St Thomas. In use in 1492; a barn by 1611.
131. Walsingham, Great, All Saints. All church goods sold in 1552.

Category IV
89. Burgh, St Mary. Had a rector until 1554; used as a barn by 1602 (Tymms).
90. Caistor, West, St Edmund. Made into a barn by 1602 (Tymms).
92. Egmere, St Edmund. Abandoned *c.* 1580.
95. Godwick, All Saints. Ruined 'long since' by 1602 (Tymms).
101. Pudding Norton, St Margaret. In use in 1557; long ruined by 1602 (Tymms).
107. Wallington, St Margaret. Largely demolished *c.* 1589.

Category III
82. Stanninghall. Ruined by 1602 (Tymms).

Churches abandoned 1601-1650
Category VI
188. Langhale, St Christopher. Consolidated to Kirstead 1421. Demolished temp. James I (Blomefield).

Category V
118. Eccles, St Mary. Destroyed by sea in 1604.

Category IV
87. Bastwick, St Peter. Stones removed from site in 1618.

Category III
68. Bickerston, St Andrew. Abandoned by 1633.
80. Saxlingham Thorpe, St Mary. Registers end in 1640.
85. Whitlingham, St Andrew. Decayed by 1630; consolidated to Kirby Bedon in 1653.

Churches abandoned 1651-1700
Category VI
191. Lynn, North, St Edmund. Recorded in 1685 as demolished after flooding.

Category V
112. Beckham, East, St Helen. Abandoned *c.* 1700.
116. Colveston, St Mary. Consolidated with Didlington in 1676; 'long ruined' by *c.* 1740 (Blomefield).
132. Weeting, All Saints. Recorded *c.* 1740 as being demolished 40 years ago (Blomefield).

Category IV
103. Rockland, St Andrew. Consolidated with All Saints in 1691, and allowed to fall down.
105. Testerton, St Remigius. Continuous dilapidation through 17th century.

Category III
65. Antingham, St Margaret. Abandoned late 17th century.

Churches abandoned 1701-1750
Category VI
168. Fincham, St Michael. Demolished in 1744.
219. Sturston, Holy Cross. Chancel and tower in ruins in 1738; nave abandoned soon after.

Category IV
93. Garboldisham, All Saints. Demolished in 1736.
94. Gillingham, All Saints. Demolished in 1748.
109. Wolterton, St Margaret. Demolished *c.* 1740.

Category III
74. Kirby Bedon, St Mary. Vicarage abolished in 1721.
76. Mundham, St Ethelbert. Abandoned in 1749.
78. Raynham, West, St Margaret. Abandoned *c.* 1735.
79. Ryburgh, Little, All Saints. Consolidated with Great Ryburgh 1750 and abandoned.
83. Surlingham, St Saviour. Abandoned soon after 1705.

Category II
53. Roudham, St Andrew. Burned down in 1734.
67. Beachamwell, All Saints. Abandoned in 1688.
70. Burgh Parva, St Mary. Abandoned *c.* 1655.
73. Gasthorpe, St Nicholas. Very decayed by 1691.
75. Mintlyn, St Michael. Ruined by *c.* 1680.

Category II
35. Appleton, St Mary. Abandoned in late 17th century.
37. Bayfield, St Margaret. In use in 1603; abandoned by late 17th century.
55. Shotesham, St Martin. In use in 1603; in ruins by early 18th century.
56. Somerton, East, St Mary (P). Out of use by late 17th century.

Churches abandoned 1751-1800
Category VI
136. Ashby, St Mary. Demolished before *c.* 1800.
137. Barton Bendish, All Saints. Demolished in 1789.

Category V
114. Burnham Sutton, St Ethelbert. Demolished in 1771.
123. Leziate, All Saints. In use *c.* 1740, long in ruins by 1808.

Category IV
102. Ringstead, Great, St Peter. Demolished in 1772.

Category III
66. Bawsey, St James. Abandoned in the 1770s.

Category II
39. Bowthorpe, St Michael. Abandoned in 1792.
49. Mannington. In decay by the 1750s.
64. Wretham, West, St Lawrence. Abandoned in 1792.

Churches abandoned 1801-1850
Category IV
96. Hainford, All Saints. Demolished in 1839.

Churches abandoned 1851-1900
Category VI
173. Harleston. Demolished in 1873.
214. Sidestrand, St Michael. Dismantled in 1890 and rebuilt further inland.

Category V
113. Beckham, West, All Saints. Demolished in 1890 and rebuilt on new site.

Category IV
91. Edgefield, SS Peter and Paul. Dismantled and moved to new site in 1883.

98.	Hindolveston, St George. Collapsed in 1892.
99.	Melton, Great, St Mary. Demolished in 1883.
N44.	Norwich, St Peter Southgate. Demolished in 1887.

Category II

36.	Babingley, St Felix. Abandoned in 1895.
41.	Croxton, St John the Baptist. Replaced by new church in 1882.
42.	Fulmodestone, St Mary. Replaced by new church in 1882.
44.	Hautbois, Great, St Mary. Replaced by new church in 1863.
45.	Hopton, St Margaret. Burned down in 1865.
57.	Southery, St Mary. Replaced by new church in 1858.
58.	Southwood, St Edmund. Abandoned in 1881.
59.	Thorpe-by-Norwich, St Andrew. Replaced by new church in 1866; reduced to 'picturesque' ruin in 1881.
62.	Walsham, South, St Laurence. Used as schoolroom from 1890.

Churches abandoned 1901-1950

Category VI

N38.	Norwich, St Michael at Thorn. Bombed in 1942.
N41.	Norwich, St Paul. Bombed in 1942.

Category IV

97.	Heigham, St Bartholomew. Bombed in 1942.
N5.	Norwich, St Benedict. Bombed in 1942.

Category II

38.	Bircham Tofts, St Andrew. Abandoned in late 1940s.
40.	Burlingham, St Peter. Abandoned in 1935.
46.	Houghton-on-the-Hill, St Mary. Abandoned *c.* 1945.
48.	Kempstone, St Paul. Abandoned for normal worship *c.* 1901, continued as mortuary chapel to 1950s.
51.	Oxwick, All Saints. Abandoned in 1940.
60.	Tivetshall, St Mary. Abandoned in 1947.
63.	Wiggenhall, St Peter. Abandoned in 1929.

Category I

20.	Langford, St Andrew. Forcibly abandoned in 1942.
N42.	Norwich, St Peter Hungate. Converted to ecclesiastical museum in 1932.
23.	Rackheath, All Saints. Abandoned in 1948, leased to Norfolk Churches Trust in 1981.
27.	Shingham, St Botolph. Abandoned in 1941.
29.	Stanford, All Saints. Forcibly abandoned in 1942.
31.	Tottington, St Andrew. Forcibly abandoned in 1942.
32.	West Tofts, St Mary. Forcibly abandoned in 1942.

Churches abandoned 1951-1987

Category IV

100.	Panxworth, All Saints. Demolished in 1981.

Category II

43.	Hargham, All Saints. Leased to Norfolk Churches Trust in 1979.
47.	Islington, St Mary. Vested in Redundant Churches Fund in 1973.
50.	Morton-on-the-Hill, St Margaret. Partial collapse in 1959; leased to Norfolk Churches Trust in 1980.
54.	Sco Ruston, St Michael. Abandoned *c.* 1970.
61.	Tunstall, St Peter and St Paul. Declared Redundant in 1980.

Category I

1.	Bagthorpe, St Mary. Abandoned in 1970. Leased to Norfolk Churches Trust in 1979.
2.	Barmer, All Saints. Abandoned in 1977. Leased to Norfolk Churches Trust in 1978.
3.	Barningham, North, St Peter. Vested in Redundant Churches Fund in 1976.
4.	Barton Bendish, St Mary. Vested in Redundant Churches Fund in 1976.
A1.	Booton, St Michael. Vested in Redundant Churches Fund in 1987.
5.	Brandiston, St Nicholas. Closed in 1971. Vested in Redundant Churches Fund in 1981.
6.	Buckenham Ferry, St Nicholas. Abandoned in 1968. Vested in Redundant Churches Fund in 1979.
7.	Cockthorpe, All Saints. Leased to Norfolk Churches Trust in 1978.
8.	Corpusty, St Peter. Abandoned since 1965. Leased to Friends of Friendless Churches.
9.	Coston, St Michael. Abandoned in 1970. Vested in Redundant Churches Fund in 1979.
10.	Crownthorpe, St James. Abandoned *c.* 1970.
11.	Dunton, St Peter. Leased to Norfolk Churches Trust in 1978.
12.	Feltwell, St Nicholas. Vested in Redundant Churches Fund in 1975.
13.	Forncett, St Mary. Abandoned in 1979.
14.	Frenze, St Andrew. Abandoned in 1976. Leased to Norfolk Churches Trust in 1980.
15.	Gunton, St Andrew. Abandoned in 1976. Vested in Redundant Churches Fund in 1977.
16.	Hales, St Margaret. Abandoned in 1967. Vested in Redundant Churches Fund in 1974.
17.	Harling, West, All Saints. Vested in Redundant Churches Fund in 1977.
18.	Hockwold, St Peter. Vested in Redundant Churches Fund in 1974.
19.	Illington, St Andrew. Declared Redundant in 1987.
21.	Moulton, St Mary. Abandoned in 1965. Vested in Redundant Churches Fund in 1980.
22.	Narford, St Mary. Closed *c.* 1960.
N2.	Norwich, All Saints. Redundant in 1976.
N9.	Norwich, St Clement. Redundant in 1976.
N12.	Norwich, St Edmund. Redundant in 1980.
N15.	Norwich, St Etheldreda. Redundant in 1975.
N16.	Norwich, St Gregory. Redundant in 1974.
N19.	Norwich, St James Pockthorpe. Redundant in 1974.
N22.	Norwich, St Lawrence. Redundant in 1974.
N25.	Norwich, St Margaret, Westwick. Redundant in 1974.
N27.	Norwich, St Martin at Oak. Redundant in 1976.
N28.	Norwich, St Martin at Palace. Redundant in 1974.
N29.	Norwich, St Mary Coslany. Redundant in 1975.
N34.	Norwich, St Michael Coslany. Redundant in 1976.
N36.	Norwich, St Michael at Pleas. Redundant in 1974.
N43.	Norwich, St Peter Parmentergate. Redundant in 1979.
N45.	Norwich, St Saviour. Redundant in 1976.
N46.	Norwich, SS Simon and Jude. Redundant in 1952.
N47.	Norwich, St Swithin. Redundant in 1974.
24.	Rudham, West, St Peter. Leased to Norfolk Churches Trust in 1979.
25.	Ruston, East, St Mary. Abandoned in 1975. Vested in Redundant Churches Fund in 1981.
26.	Shimpling, St George. Vested in Redundant Churches Fund in 1985.
28.	Snetterton, All Saints. Leased to Norfolk Churches Trust in 1978.
30.	Thurgarton, All Saints. Vested in Redundant Churches Fund in 1982.
A2.	Walpole, St Andrew. Vested in Redundant Churches Fund in 1987.
33.	Wiggenhall, St Mary the Virgin. Vested in Redundant Churches Fund in 1981.
34.	Yarmouth, Great, St George. Last used in 1959.

Appendix XI

Causes of Abandonment of Churches
The churches have been classified according to the probable principal cause of abandonment.

Stanford Training Area
20.	Langford, St Andrew.
29.	Stanford, All Saints.
31.	Tottington, St Andrew.
32.	West Tofts, St Mary.

Isolated Site
2.	Barmer, All Saints.
3.	Barningham, North, St Peter.
112.	Beckham, East, St Helen.
8.	Corpusty, St Peter.
16.	Hales, St Margaret.
21.	Moulton, St Mary.
100.	Panxworth, All Saints.
23.	Rackheath, All Saints.
24.	Rudham, West, St Peter.
25.	Ruston, East, St Mary.
28.	Snetterton, All Saints.
58.	Southwood, St Edmund.
30.	Thurgarton, All Saints.
33.	Wiggenhall, St Mary the Virgin.

Inconvenient Site
113.	Beckham, West, All Saints.
71.	Castle Rising.
41.	Croxton, St John the Baptist.
91.	Edgefield, St Peter and St Paul.
72.	Elmham, North, I.
42.	Fulmodestone, St Mary.
96.	Hainford, All Saints.
173.	Harleston.
44.	Hautbois, Great, St Mary.
77.	Oxborough, St Mary Magdalen.
A4.	Poringland, East, I.
214.	Sidestrand, St Michael.
57.	Southery, St Mary.
59.	Thorpe-by-Norwich, St Andrew I.
241.	Thorpe-by-Norwich, Old Thorpe Church.
254.	Yarmouth, Great, St Benedict.

Disaster
159.	Clenchwarton, South.
160.	Cockley Cley, St Peter.
118.	Eccles, St Mary.
120.	Hackford, All Saints.
97.	Heigham, St Bartholomew.
98.	Hindolveston, St George.
45.	Hopton, St Margaret.
187.	Keswick, St Clement.
191.	Lynn, North, St Edmund.
A3.	Lynn, West, St Peter I.
50.	Morton-on-the-Hill, St Margaret.
N5.	Norwich, St Benedict.
N7.	Norwich, St Christopher.
N14.	Norwich, St Ethelbert.
N38.	Norwich, St Michael at Thorn.
N41.	Norwich, St Paul.
201.	Overstrand, St Martin, I.
53.	Roudham, St Andrew.
212.	Shipden.
132.	Weeting, All Saints.

Shrunken Village
1.	Bagthorpe, St Mary.
87.	Bastwick, St Peter.
38.	Bircham Tofts, St Andrew.
A1.	Booton, St Michael.
5.	Brandiston, St Nicholas.
6.	Buckenham Ferry, St Nicholas.
7.	Cockthorpe, All Saints.
9.	Coston, St Michael.
10.	Crownthorpe, St James.
11.	Dunton, St Peter.
13.	Forncett, St Mary.
14.	Frenze, St Andrew.
15.	Gunton, St Andrew.
19.	Illington, St Andrew.
47.	Islington, St Mary.
51.	Oxwick, All Saints.
79.	Ryburgh, Little, All Saints.
54.	Sco Ruston, St Michael.
26.	Shimpling, St George.
27.	Shingham, St Botolph.
61.	Tunstall, St Peter and St Paul.
85.	Whitlingham, St Andrew.
63.	Wiggenhall, St Peter.

Urban Decline/Reorganisation
143.	Bracondale, St Nicholas.
157.	Carrow.
124.	Lynn, King's, St James.
N1.	Norwich, All Saints, Fyebridgegate.
N2.	Norwich, All Saints, Timberhill.
N3.	Norwich, St Anne.
N4.	Norwich, St Bartholomew.
N6.	Norwich, St Botolph.
N8.	Norwich, St Clement Conesford.
N9.	Norwich, St Clement Fyebridge.
N10.	Norwich, St Crowche.
N11.	Norwich, St Cuthbert.
N12.	Norwich, St Edmund.
N13.	Norwich, St Edward.
N15.	Norwich, St Etheldreda.
N16.	Norwich, St Gregory.
N17.	Norwich, St Helen I.
N18.	Norwich, Holy Trinity.
N19.	Norwich, St James Pockthorpe.
N20.	Norwich, St John the Baptist Colegate.
N21.	Norwich, St John the Evangelist Conesford.
N22.	Norwich, St Laurence.
N23.	Norwich, St Margaret at Newbridge.
N24.	Norwich, St Margaret Fye Bridge.
N25.	Norwich, St Margaret Westwick.
N26.	Norwich, St Martin in Balliva.
N27.	Norwich, St Martin at Oak.
N28.	Norwich, St Martin at Palace.
N29.	Norwich, St Mary Coslany.
N30.	Norwich, St Mary in the Marsh.
N31.	Norwich, St Mary the Less.
N32.	Norwich, St Mary Unbrent.
N33.	Norwich, St Matthew the Apostle.
N34.	Norwich, St Michael Coslany.
N35.	Norwich, St Michael Conesford.
N36.	Norwich, St Michael at Pleas.
N37.	Norwich, St Michael at Tombland.
N39.	Norwich, St Olave Colegate.
N40.	Norwich, St Olave Conesford.
N42.	Norwich, St Peter Hungate.
N43.	Norwich, St Peter Parmentergate.
N44.	Norwich, St Peter Southgate.
N45.	Norwich, St Saviour.
N46.	Norwich, SS Simon and Jude.
N47.	Norwich, St Swithin.
N48.	Norwich, St Vedast.
N49.	Norwich, St Winwaloy.
N50.	Norwich, church in castle bailey.
222.	Thetford, All Saints.
223.	Thetford, St Andrew.
224.	Thetford, St Benet.
225.	Thetford, St Edmund.
226.	Thetford, St Etheldreda.
227.	Thetford, St George.
228.	Thetford, St Giles.

229.	Thetford, St Helen.		83.	Surlingham, St Saviour.
230.	Thetford, Holy Trinity.		221.	Swainsthorpe, St Mary.
231.	Thetford, St John.		129.	Tattersett, St Andrew.
232.	Thetford, St Lawrence.		60.	Tivestshall, St Mary.
233.	Thetford, St Margaret.		244.	Topcroft, St Giles.
234.	Thetford, St Martin.		A5.	Tottenhill.
235.	Thetford, Great St Mary.		A2.	Walpole, St Andrew.
236.	Thetford, St Michael.		62.	Walsham, South, St Laurence.
237.	Thetford, St Nicholas.		131.	Walsingham, Great, All Saints.
238.	Thetford, Church at Red Castle Site.		84.	Walton, East, St Andrew.
239.	Thetford, Church on site of Gas Works.		246.	Warham, St Mary the Virgin.
240.	Thetford, Church on site of St Michael's Close.		248.	Weasenham, St Paul.
34.	Yarmouth, Great, St George.		249.	Wicklewood, St Andrew.
255.	Yarmouth, Southtown.		86.	Wood Norton, St Peter.
			252.	Worstead, St Andrew.

Villages with two or more churches

Deserted Village

65.	Antingham, St Margaret.		133.	Alethorpe, All Saints.
110.	Barnham Broom, St Michael.		134.	Algarsthorpe, St Mary Magdalen.
137.	Barton Bendish, All Saints.		135.	Alpington/Apton, St Martin.
4.	Barton Bendish, St Mary.		35.	Appleton, St Mary.
138.	Barton Turf, B.		136.	Ashby, St Mary.
67.	Beachamwell, All Saints.		36.	Babingley, St Felix.
88.	Beachamwell, St John.		111.	Barwick, St Mary.
139.	Bedingham, St Mary.		66.	Bawsey, St James.
142.	Blo Norton, St Margaret.		37.	Bayfield, St Margaret.
144.	Bradcar, St Andrew.		140.	Beeston, St Andrew.
147.	Brundall, St Clement.		68.	Bickerston, St Andrew.
69.	Buckenham, New, St Mary.		141.	Bittering, Great, St Nicholas.
148.	Buckenham, Old, St Andrew.		39.	Bowthorpe, St Michael.
89.	Burgh, St Mary.		145.	Breccles, Little.
40.	Burlingham, St Peter.		146.	Broomsthorpe.
150.	Burnham, St Andrew.		149.	Buckenham Tofts, St Andrew.
151.	Burnham, St Edmund.		70.	Burgh Parva, St Mary.
114.	Burnham Sutton, St Ethelbert.		153.	Caldecote, St Mary.
152.	Burnham Thorpe, St Peter.		154.	Cantelose, All Saints.
90.	Caister, West, St Edmund.		156.	Carbrooke, Little.
155.	Carleton Rode, B.		158.	Choseley.
115.	Carlton, East, St Peter.		116.	Colveston, St Mary.
161.	Congham, All Saints.		165.	Doughton.
162.	Congham, St Mary.		167.	Dykebeck.
117.	Creake, North, St Michael.		92.	Egmere, St Edmund.
163.	Cressingham, Great, St George.		169.	Foston, St Peter.
164.	Dereham, West, St Peter.		73.	Gasthorpe, St Nicholas.
166.	Dunham, Great, St Mary.		95.	Godwick, All Saints.
12.	Feltwell, St Nicholas.		170.	Gowthorpe, St James.
168.	Fincham, St Michael.		172.	Hardwick.
119.	Foulden, St Edmund.		43.	Hargham, All Saints.
93.	Garboldisham, All Saints.		174.	Harling, Middle.
94.	Gillingham, All Saints.		17.	Harling, West, All Saints.
171.	Guist Thorpe, All Saints.		175.	Hautbois, Little, St Mary.
176.	Helmingham, St Mary.		121.	Hempton, St Andrew.
177.	Hempnall, St Andrew.		178.	Herringby, St Ethelbert.
18.	Hockwold, St Peter.		179.	Hockham, Little, St Mary.
183.	Itteringham, St Nicholas.		180.	Holm, St Andrew.
74.	Kirby Bedon, St Mary.		181.	Holverston, St Mary.
189.	Langham Parva, St Mary.		46.	Houghton-on-the-Hill, St Mary.
192.	Marham, St Andrew.		182.	Irmingland, St Andrew.
194.	Massingham, Great, All Saints.		48.	Kempstone, St Paul.
99.	Melton, Great, St Mary.		184.	Kenningham
195.	Melthwold Hythe.		185.	Kenwick, St Thomas.
76.	Mundham, St Ethelbert.		186.	Kerdiston, St Mary.
199.	Ormesby, St Andrew.		188.	Langhale, St Christopher.
200.	Ormesby, St Peter.		122.	Letton, All Saints.
204.	Pickenham, South, St Andrew.		123.	Leziate, All Saints.
78.	Raynham, West, St Margaret.		190.	Lynford.
102.	Ringstead, Great, St Peter.		49.	Mannington.
103.	Rockland, St Andrew.		193.	Markshall, St Edmund.
127.	Rockland, St Mary, St Margaret.		75.	Mintlyn, St Michael.
208.	Saxthorpe, St Dunstan.		196.	Moulton, Little, All Saints.
209.	Scratby, All Saints.		22.	Narford, St Mary.
210.	Seething, B.		197.	Nelonde, St Peter.
128.	Shotesham, St Botolph.		198.	Oby.
55.	Shotesham, St Martin.		202.	Palgrave, Little.
213.	Shouldham, St Margaret.		203.	Pattesley, St John the Baptist.
215.	Snetterton, St Andrew.		125.	Pensthorpe.
104.	Snoring, Little.		205.	Poringland, West, St Michael.
56.	Somerton, East.		101.	Pudding Norton, St Margaret.
216.	Stiffkey, St John the Baptist.		126.	Quarles.
217.	Stoke Holy Cross, B.		206.	Rackheath, Little, Holy Trinity.
218.	Stratton, St Peter.			

52.	Ringstead, Little, St Andrew.	130.	Thorpland, St Thomas.
207.	Roxham, St Michael.	243.	Thurketeliart.
80.	Saxlingham Thorpe, St Mary.	245.	Wacton, Little, St Mary.
211.	Setchey.	107.	Wallington, St Margaret.
81.	Snarehill.	247.	Waxham, Little, St Margaret.
82.	Stanninghall.	250.	Windle, St Andrew.
219.	Sturston, Holy Cross.	251.	Winston, St Andrew.
220.	Summerfield, All Saints.	109.	Wolterton, St Margaret.
105.	Testerton, St Remigius.	253.	Wreningham, Little, St Mary.
242.	Thorpeland, St Thomas.	64.	Wretham, West, St Laurence.
106.	Thorpe Parva, St Mary.		

Appendix XII

Additional Sites

The entries below consist of sites which should be included in this volume, but came to the author's attention too late to form part of the Catalogue of Sites or to be located on the map (Fig. 1). Nevertheless, it has been possible to make use of the data provided by these sites to complete the statistical Figures and Tables (Figs 2, 3, 5).

1. Booton, St Michael. One of the best 19th century churches in the county. Vested in the Redundant Churches Fund in 1987.
2. Walpole, St Andrew. Superb 15th century Marshland church. Vested in the Redundant Churches Fund in 1987.
3. Lynn, West, St Peter I. Original church washed away prior to 1271; new plot obtained for reconstruction of St Peter's.
4. Poringland, East, I. Church moved to a more convenient site in the reign of William II.
5. Tottenhill. Had a church (distinct from West Briggs) in the 15th century.

Bibliography

Addyman, P.V. and Morris, R.K., 1976 — *The Archaeological Study of Churches*, Counc. Brit. Archaeol. Res. Rep. 13

Allison, K.J., 1955 — 'The Lost Villages of Norfolk', *Norfolk Archaeol.* 31, 116-162

Astley, H.J.D., 1906 — 'The True Site of Markshall Church', *Norfolk Antiquarian Miscellany* 2nd Series, Pt.1, 39-45

Batcock, N.G., 1988 — 'The Parish Church in Norfolk in the 11th and 12th Centuries', *Minsters and Parish Churches: The Local Church in Transition 950-1200*, Oxford University Comm. Archaeol. 17, 179-190

Baty, E., 1987 — *Victorian Church Building and Restoration in the Diocese of Norwich* unpublished PhD. thesis, University of East Anglia.

Beckett, G., 1984 — 'The Barwicks: One Lost Village or Two?', *Norfolk Archaeol.* 39, 51-53

Beloe, E.M., 1899 — *Our Borough, Our Churches* (Wisbech)

Beresford, G., 1975 — *The Medieval Clay-Land Village: Excavations at Goltho and Barton Blount*, Soc. Medieval Archaeol.

Binney, M. and Burman, P., 1977a — *Change and Decay: The Future of Our Churches* (London)

Binney, M. and Burman, P., 1977b — *Chapels and Churches: Who Cares?* (London)

Blomefield, F., 1805-10 — *An Essay Towards a Topographical History of the County of Norfolk* 11 vols. (London)

Blyth, W., 1863 — *Historical Notices and Records of the Village and Parish of Fincham in the County of Norfolk* (King's Lynn)

Bond, F., 1905 — *Gothic Architecture in England* (London)

Bony, J., 1979 — *The English Decorated Style* (Oxford)

Brown, R.A., 1978 — *Castle Rising* (H.M.S.O.)

Byrant, T.H., 1898a-1915 — *The Churches of Norfolk* vols 1-19

Bullmore, W.R., 1917 — 'Notes on the Architecture and Wood-Carving of the Church of St Mary the Virgin, Wiggenhall', *Norfolk Archaeol.* 19, 314-332

Carthew, G.A., 1846 — 'Notices of the Saxon or Early Norman Church of Great Dunham', *Norfolk Archaeol.* 1, 91-99

Carthew, G.A., 1877 — *The Hundred of Launditch and the Deanery of Brisley in the County of Norfolk*, 2 vols (London)

Cattermole, P. and Cotton, S., 1983 — 'Medieval Parish Church Building in Norfolk', *Norfolk Archaeol.* 38, 235-279

Cautley, H.M., 1949 — *Norfolk Churches* (Ipswich)

Cautley, H.M., 1982 — *Suffolk Churches and their Treasures*, 5th edition (Woodbridge)

Chapman, C., undated — *Old St Margaret's Church, Hopton-on-Sea* (Guide)

Christie, H., Olsen, O. and Taylor, H.M., 1979 — 'The Wooden Church of St Andrew at Greensted, Essex', *Antiq. Journal* 59, 92-112

Clarke, R., 1935 — 'Notes on the Archaeology of Markshall', *Norfolk Archaeol.* 25, 360

Clarke, R., 1950 — 'Notes on Recent Archaeological Discoveries in Norfolk', *Norfolk Archaeol.* 30, 156-159

Clarke, R., 1955 — 'Archaeological Discoveries in Norfolk, 1949-54', *Norfolk Archaeol.* 31, 395-416

Clarke, R., 1960 — *East Anglia* (London)

Clarke, W.G., 1908 — 'Some Recent Finds in Norfolk', *Norfolk Antiquarian Miscellany*, 2nd Series, Pt.3., 94-107

Cocke, T., Findlay, D., Halsey, R., Williamson, E. and Wilson, G., 1982 — *Recording a Church: an illustrated glossary* (London)

Cooke, W.H., 1908 — *Eccles next the Sea*

Cotman, J.S., 1838 — *Architectural Etchings of the County of Norfolk* (London)

Cotton, S., 1987 — 'Medieval Roodscreens in Norfolk — Their Construction and Painting Dates', *Norfolk Archaeol.* 40, 44-54

Cox, J.C., 1911 — *The Churches of Norfolk*, 2 vols (London)

Crosby, A., 1986 — *A History of Thetford* (Chichester)

Cubitt, M., 1987 — 'The Churches of Hempnall', *Norfolk Archaeol. Res. Group* News 49, 1-7

Cushion, B., Davison, A., Fenner, G., Goldsmith, R., Knight, J., Virgoe, N., Wade, K. and Wade-Martins, P., 1982 — 'Some Deserted Village Sites in Norfolk', *E.Anglian Archaeol.* 14, 40-101

Dallas, C., forthcoming — 'Excavations in Thetford 1964-6 and 1969-70 by B.K. Davison', *E.Anglian Archaeol.*

Darby, H.C., 1973 — *A New Historical Geography of England before 1600* (Cambridge)

Dashwood, G.H., 1849 — 'Extracts from Wills', *Norfolk Archaeol.* 2, 104

Davison, A., 1972 — 'Some Aspects of the Agrarian History of Hargham and Snetterton as Revealed in the Buxton Mss', *Norfolk Archaeol.* 35, 335-355

Davison, A., 1980 — 'West Harling: A Village and its Disappearance', *Norfolk Archaeol.* 37, 295-306

Davison, A., 1983 — 'The Distribution of Medieval Settlement in West Harling', *Norfolk Archaeol.* 38, 329-336

Davison, A., 1984 — 'The Desertion of Caldecote: Some Further Evidence', *Norfolk Archaeol.* 39, 53-54

Davison, A., 1987 — 'Little Hockham', *Norfolk Archaeol.* 40, 84-93

Davison, A., 1988 — 'Six Deserted Villages in Norfolk', *E.Anglian Archaeol.* 44

De la Hey, C., 1984 — *The Fate of a Thousand Churches, Part One: East Anglia* (Save Britain's Heritage)

Dirsztay, P., 1978 — *Church Furnishings: A NADFAS Guide* (London)

Doubleday, H.A. and Page, W. (eds), — *Victoria History of the County of Norfolk* (London)

1901 (Vol.1) and 1906 (Vol.2)		James, S., Marshall, A. and Millett, M., 1984	'An Early Medieval Building Tradition', *Archaeol. Journal* 141, 182-215
Dunmore, S. and Carr, R., 1976	'The Late Saxon Town of Thetford: an archaeological and historical survey', *E.Anglian Archaeol.* 4	Jessop, A., 1879	'Bowthorpe Hall', *Norfolk Archaeol.* 8, 273-281
Dymond, D., 1985	*The Norfolk Landscape* (London)	Jessop, A., 1888	'The Condition of the Archdeaconry of Norwich in 1603', *Norfolk Archaeol.* 10, 166-184
Ecclestone, A.W., 1974	*A Yarmouth Miscellany*	Johnson, F., 1925	'The Chapel of St Clement at Brundall, Norfolk', *Norfolk Archaeol.* 22, 194-206
Erroll, A.C., 1970	*A History of Sheringham and Beeston Regis* (Norwich)	Joseph, H., 1879	'Stiffkey: A Sketch', *Norfolk Archaeol.* 8, 143-166
Faden, W., 1797 (reprinted 1975)	*Map of Norfolk* (Norfolk Rec. Soc. 42)	Kent, E.A., 1927	'The Saxon Windows in Hales Church, Norfolk', *Journal Brit. Archaeol. Assoc.*, 2nd Series, 33, 187-188
Farrer, E., 1890	*A List of Monumental Brasses remaining in the County of Norfolk* 3 vols (London)	Kinder, E.H., 1924	*Kirby Bedon* (Norwich)
Fawcett, R., 1975	*Later Gothic Architecture in Norfolk, and Examination of Some Individual Architects in the Fourteenth and Fifteenth Centuries* (unpublished PhD thesis, U.E.A.)	King, D., 1974	*Stained Glass Tours around Norfolk Churches* (Norfolk Society)
		Knocker, G.M., 1967	'Excavations at Red Castle, Thetford', *Norfolk Archaeol.* 34, 119-173
Fawcett, R., 1978	'A Group of Churches by the Architect of Great Walsingham', *Norfolk Archaeol.* 36, 277-294	Knowles, M.D. and Hadcock, R.N., 1971	*Medieval Religious Houses: England and Wales*
Fernie, E., 1983	*The Architecture of the Anglo-Saxons* (London)		
Greenwood, R. and Norris, M., 1976	*The Brasses of Norfolk Churches* (Norfolk Churches Trust)	Ladbrooke, R., 1843	*Views of the Churches of Norfolk* (Norwich; 7 Vols of lithographs, begun in 1822)
Gunn, J., 1879	'Saxon Remains in the Cloisters of Norwich Cathedral', *Norfolk Archaeol.* 8, 1-9	Lasko, P. and Morgan, N.J., 1974	*Medieval Art in East Anglia 1300-1530* (Norwich)
Gunn, J., 1884a	'Notice of a Stone Cross found on taking down the church of St Michael at Sidestrand, Norfolk, 1881', *Norfolk Archaeol.* 9, 180-183	Lee-Warner, H.J., 1884	'The Calthorps of Cockthorpe', *Norfolk Archaeol.* 9, 165-179
Gunn, J., 1884b	'Wheel Cross in the Church of St Peter, Barningham Northwood', *Norfolk Archaeol.* 9, 333-334	L'Estrange, J., 1874	*The Church Bells of Norfolk* (Norwich)
		Le Strange, R., 1973	*Monasteries of Norfolk* (King's Lynn)
Harrod, H., 1855	'Castle Rising', *Norfolk Archaeol.* 4, 59-91	Linnell, C.L.S., 1951	'Some Notes on the Blomefield Mss. in the Bodleian Library', *Norfolk Record Society* 22, 65-83
Harrod, W. (ed.), 1972	*Norfolk Country Churches and The Future* (Norfolk Society)		
Harvey, J.H., 1973	'Building Works by an East Anglian Priory', *Norfolk Archaeol.* 35, 505-510	Linnell, C.L.S. and Wearing, S.J., 1952	*Norfolk Church Monuments* (Ipswich)
Harvey, J.H., 1978	*The Perpendicular Style* (London)	Long, E.T., undated	*The Ruined Churches of Norfolk*, unpublished
Heywood, S., 1982	'The Ruined Church at North Elmham', *Journal Brit. Archaeol. Assoc.* 135, 1-10	Lunt, W.E., 1926	*The Valuation of Norwich* (Oxford)
Hill, G.F., 1939	*A History of North Burlingham Churches* (Norwich)	Mackerell, B., 1737	*History of King's Lynn*
Hillen, H.J., 1907	*History of King's Lynn* (Norwich)	Manning, C.R., 1892	'Buckenham Castle', *Norfolk Archaeol.* 11, 137-142
Hurst, D.G., 1962-3	'Medieval Britain in 1961, Pt.2: Post Conquest', *Med. Archaeol.* 313-349	Martin, T., 1771	Notes and Sketches of Norfolk Churches (NRO, Rye Mss. 17, 5 Vols)
Hurst, J.G., 1957	'Medieval Britain in 1956, Pt.2: Post-Conquest', *Med. Archaeol.* 1, 151-171	Martin, T., 1779	*The History of the Town of Thetford in the Counties of Norfolk and Suffolk from the earliest accounts to the present time*
Hurst, J.G., 1961	'Seventeenth-century Cottages at Babingley, Norfolk', *Norfolk Archaeol.* 32, 332-342		
Hudson, W., 1895	'The Assessment of the townships of the County of Norfolk for the King's tenths and fifteenths, as settled in 1334', *Norfolk Archaeol.* 12, 243-297	Messent, C.J.W., 1931	*The Ruined Churches of Norfolk* (Norwich)
		Messent, C.J.W., 1936	*The Parish Churches of Norfolk and Norwich* (Norwich)
Hudson, W., 1910	'The Norwich Taxation of 1254 so far as relates to the diocese of Norfolk and Norwich', *Norfolk Archaeol.* 17, 46-158	Messent, C.J.W., 1937	'Ruined Norfolk Churches', *E.Anglian Archaeol.* 2nd Series, No.6, 257-259, 308-310, 357-359
Hudson, W., 1921	'The Prior of Norwich's Manor of Hindolveston', *Norfolk Archaeol.* 20, 179-214	Millican, P., 1937	*A History of Horstead and Stanninghall* (Norwich)

Moralee, J., 1982	'Babingley and the Beginnings of Christianity in East Anglia' *Norfolk Archaeol. Res. Group News*, 31, 7-11	Rodwell, W. and Rodwell, K., 1977	*Historic Churches: A Wasting Asset*, Counc. Brit. Archaeol. Res. Rep. 19 (London)
Morant, A.W., 1872	'Notices of the Church of St Nicholas, Great Yarmouth', *Norfolk Archaeol.* 7, 215-248	Rodwell, W., 1981	*The Archaeology of the English Church* (London)
Morris, J. (ed.), 1984	*Domesday Book: Norfolk* 2 Vols (London)	Rogerson, A. and Dallas, C., 1984	'Excavations in Thetford 1948-59 and 1973-80', *E.Anglian Archaeol.* 22
Morris, R., 1983	*The Church in British Archaeology*, Counc. Brit. Archaeol. Res. Rep. 47 (London)	Rogerson, A., Ashley, S.J., Williams, P. and Harris, A., 1987	'Three Norman Churches in Norfolk', *E.Anglian Archaeol.* 32
Mortlock, D.P. and Roberts, C.V., 1981	*The Popular Guide to Norfolk Churches, 1: North-East Norfolk* (Fakenham)	Rose E. and Davison A., 1988	'St Catherine's Thorpe — The Birth and Death of a Myth', *Norfolk Arch.* 40, 179
Mortlock, D.P. and Roberts, C.V., 1985a	*The Popular Guide to Norfolk Churches, 2: Central and South Norfolk (including Norwich)* (Cambridge)	Rye, W., 1889	*Some Rough Materials for a history of the hundred of North Erpingham* (Norwich)
Mortlock, D.P. and Roberts, C.V., 1985b	*The Popular Guide to Norfolk Churches, 3: West and South-West Norfolk* (Cambridge)	Saunders, H.W., 1939	*The First Register of Norwich Cathedral Priory*, Norfolk Record Society, 11
Munford, G., 1858	*An Analysis of the Domesday Book in the County of Norfolk* (London)	Silvester, R. J., 1988	'The Fenland Project No.3: Marshland and the Nar Valley, Norfolk' *E. Anglian Archaeol.* 45
NCT (Norfolk Churches Trust), undated	*Ss Peter & Paul, Edgefield* (Guide)	Spencer, N., 1977	*Sculptured Monuments in Norfolk Churches* (Norfolk Churches Trust)
NRO (Norfolk Record Office)	FCB Faculty Books ANW Visitation Books	Stanton, P., 1971	*Pugin* (London)
Orange, A.J., 1970	*The Story of Feltwell*, 2 Vols	Stephenson, M., 1926	*A List of Monumental Brasses in the British Isles* (London)
Palmer, F.D., 1895	'Eccles by the Sea', *Norfolk Archaeol.* 12, 304-310	Sturgess, J.P., 1864	'Bickerston or Bixton Church', *The East Anglian or Notes and Queries 1*, 239
Parker, I.H., 1851	'Architectural Notes of the Churches and Other Buildings in the City and Neighbourhood of Norwich', *Proc. Archaeol. Inst., Norwich, 1847*, 157-197	Summerson, J., 1983	*Architecture in Britain 1530-1830*, 7th edition (Harmondsworth)
Pevsner, N., 1962a	*The Buildings of England: North-East Norfolk and Norwich* (Harmondsworth)	Tanner, N.P., 1984	*The Church in Late Medieval Norwich, 1370-1532* (Toronto)
Pevsner, N., 1962b	*The Buildings of England: North-West and South Norfolk* (Harmondsworth)	Taylor, H.M. and Taylor, J., 1965	*Anglo-Saxon Architecture*, 2 Vols (Cambridge)
Pevsner, N., 1975	*The Buildings of England: Suffolk* (Harmondsworth)	TBA (Thetford Borough Archives)	
Pugin, A. W., 1836	*Details of ancient houses of the 15th and 16th centuries selected from those existing at Rouen and Caen and Beauvais and Gisors and Abbeville and Strasburgh and etc..*	Tricker, R., 1981a	*All Saints, Stanford* (Guide)
		Tricker, R., 1981b	*Saint Mary's, West Tofts* (Guide)
		Tristram, E.W., 1955	*English Wall Painting of the Fourteenth Century*
		Tuck, D.W., undated	*The Parish of Fulmodestone and its Churches* (King's Lynn)
Purdy, R.J.W., 00	'Mannington Hall', *Norfolk Archaeol.* 14, 321-328	Tuck, D.W., 1981	*St James Chapel — Workhouse — Hospital* (King's Lynn Museum, unpublished)
Purdy, R.J.W., 1907	'Hautbois Magna', *Norfolk Archaeol.* 16, 147-152	Turner, D., 1846	'Letter from Dawson Turner to Henry Harrod transmitting A Crucifix and Alabaster Tablet', *Norfolk Archaeol.* 1, 243-251 and 300-304
RCF (Redundant Churches Fund), 1980	*Guide to the Churches at Barton Bendish, Norfolk*, Series B, No.2	Tymms, S. (ed.), 1866	'Ruined and Decayed Churches, 1602', *The East Anglian or Notes and Queries 2*, 75-76, 89-90, 223-225 and 231-233
RCF, 1983a	*Guide to the Church of St Margaret, Hales*, Series 2, No.2	Wade-Martins, P., 1980a	'Excavations in North Elmham Park, 1967-72', *E.Anglian Archaeol.* 9, 3-11
RCF, 1983b	*Guide to the Church of Wiggenhall St Mary the Virgin*, Series 2, No.14	Wade-Martins, P., 1980b	'Village Sites in Launditch Hundred, Norfolk', *E. Anglian Archaeol.* 10
Redstone, L.J., 1946	'Three Carrow Account Rolls', *Norfolk Archaeol.* 19, 41-88	Walters, H.B., 1938-1965	'Inventories of Norfolk Church Goods (1552)', *Norfolk Archaeol.* Vols 26-33
Richards, W., 1812	*The History of Lynn*, 2 Vols	Warner, P., 1986	'Shared churchyards, freemen church buildings and the development of parishes in eleventh-century East Anglia', *Landscape History* 8, 39-52
Rigold, S., 1962-3	'The Anglian Cathedral of North Elmham, Norfolk', *Med. Archaeol.* 6-7, 67-108		

Watkin, A., 1947, 1948	*Inventory of Church Goods temp. Edward III*, Norfolk Rec. Soc. 19, Part 1 (1947) and Part 2 (1948)	Wilson, D.M. and Moorhouse, S., 1970	'Medieval Britain in 1970', *Med. Archaeol.* 15, 130-131
Webb, G., 1965	*Architecture in Britain: The Middle Ages* (Harmondsworth)	Woodforde, C., 1950	*The Norwich School of Glass-Painting in the Fifteenth Century* (London)
Wilkinson, J., 1822	*The Architectural remains of the ancient town and borough of Thetford in the Counties of Norfolk and Suffolk*	Wortley, J.D., 1925	*The Parishes of Attlebridge and Morton-on-the-Hill* (Norwich)
Williams, J.F., 1945	'St Bartholomew, Heigham', *Norfolk Archaeol.* 28, 229-233	Wylam, A.R.B., 1958-61	'Monumental Inscriptions in North Burlingham St Peter', *Norfolk Archaeol.* 32, 82-84

Index

Placenames are in Norfolk unless otherwise indicated. This index covers the main text only. Page x at the front of the book gives a full guide to the microfiche reports.

Adam, Robert, 24, 50
Aelmer, Bishop of Elmham, 55
Aerial photographs, 53, 144, 145, 152, 153, 156, 158, 159, 161
Alabaster, panel of martyrdom of St Erasmus, 33
    Kervile monument, 34, 78
Alethorpe, All Saints, 12, 53
Algarsthorpe, St Mary Magdalen, 53
Alpington/Apton, St Martin, 53
Altar rails, wooden, 35, 51, 60
    brass, 71
Altar table, 60, 65, 71, 75, 113
    slab, marble, 101
Anguishe, family, 34, 50, (Pl. LI)
Antingham, St Margaret, 10, 46, 49 (note 21), 52, (Pl. XVII)
    St Mary, 52
Appleton, St Mary, 7, 12, 23, 24, 46, 47, 51 (Pl. VIII)
Apse, 23, 53, 54, 55, 114, 116, 132, 144, 156, 158, 160
    elliptical, 80
Apton, see Alpington
Arcade, 13th century, 23, 72, 74
    14th century, 61, 62, 85, 94, 120, 122
    15th century, 58, 59
Arch, chamfered, 63
    double chamfered, 62, 68, 76, 85, 120
    double hollow chamfered, 73, 110, 136
    four-centred, 68, 73, 98
    four-centred relieving, 150
    mitred, 144
    pointed segmental, 86, 94, 120, 135, 144
    relieving, 90, 134
    Romanesque, 114, 132
    round-headed, 134
    segmental, 56, 62, 77, 94, 102, 119
    triple chamfered, 99, 134
Archaeological recording of fabric, 46, 47, 91, 101, 107, 110, 113, 147
Arms, Royal, 35, 71, 79, 101, 113, 150
Ashby, St Mary, 48, 53, 156-157, 158, 159, (Pl. CXXIII)
    Hall, 156
Atthill family, 65
Aumbry, 66, 110, 124, 158

Babingley, St Felix I, 12, 23, 24, 41, 46, 47, 48, 49 (note 16), 51, 83-88 (Figs. 13, 14, Pls XX, LXXV, LXXVI, LXXVII, LXXVIII)
    St Felix II, 45, 49 (Note 2), 83, 88, 171
    River, 83
Bagthorpe, St Mary, 9, 33, 44, 50
Bakon, Robert, 60
Barmer, All Saints, 9, 41, 44, (Pl. X)
Barn, conversion of church to use as, 5, 51, 52, 53, 135, 136, 161, 162
Barnham Broom, St Michael, 10, 46, 53
    St Peter and St Paul, 52
Barningham, North, St Peter, 23, 24, 33, 34, 35, 44, 47, 50, 56-60 (Figs. 6, 7, Pls L, LXV, LXVI)
Barningham, Winter, 60
Barshams, North, East and West, 10, 49, (note 11)
Barton Bendish, 49 (note 11)
    All Saints, 49 (note 16), 50, 53
    St Andrew, 50
    St Mary, 23, 24, 33, 42, 44, 50
Barton Turf, 10, 49 (note 11), 53
Barwick, St Mary, 46, 53
Base course, 102, 125, 134, 136, 138, 140, 150
Base, clustered column, 138
    moulded, 94, 120, 138
    polygonal, 76, 98, 134
    water-holding, 77
Bastwick, St Peter, 46, 52
Bawdeswell, 49 (note 3)
Bawsey, St James, 11, 12, 23, 46, 47, 52, 114-116, 118, (Cover, PLs XCII, XCIII, XCIV, XCV)
Bayfield, St Margaret, 7, 46, 51
Beachamwell, 10
    All Saints, 24, 46, 52

    St John, 46, 52
    St Mary, 52
de Beaufo, Nicholas, 69
Beckham, East, St Helen, 46, 53
Beckham, West, All Saints, 41, 46, 53
Bedingham, St Andrew, 53
    St Mary, 10, 53
Beeston-next-Mileham, 88, 98, 101
Beeston St Andrew, 12, 53
Bell, Henry, 150
Bells, 33, 71, 72, 75, 77, 93, 144
    selling of, 63, 68, 74, 106, 123, 127, 135, 152
Bell cote, 72, 105, 107
Bell cupola, 107
Benches, medieval, 35, 51, 78
Bench-ends, medieval, with carved figures, 35, 51, 78, 93, (Pl. LIII)
    with poppy-heads 35, 60, 78, 93, 140
    17th century, 35
    19th century, 65, 71, 107
Berdewell chapel, 69, 72, (Fig. 11, Pl. LXIX)
    family, 33, 34, 71
    Hall, 71
Bible, illustrated, 79
Bickerston, St Andrew, 46, 52
Bier, 35, 101
Bigot, Roger, 127
Bircham, Great, 51
    Tofts, St Andrew, 46, 51
Bittering, Great, St Nicholas, 53
Black Death, 7, 11
Blackford Hall, 54
Blenerhaysett family, 33, 34, 50
Blickling, palace of Bishop of Norwich, 159, 160
Blofield, Deanery of, 12
    St Andrew, 93
Blomefield, Francis, 49, 66, 69, 77, 127, 132, 154, 160, 161
Blo Norton, St Andrew, 53
    St Margaret, 10, 11, 49 (Note 13), 83
Bookcase, 75
Boon, E.F., 149
Booton, St Michael, 44, 49 (note 4), 191
Boss, carved, 72, 75
Bowthorpe, St Michael, 12, 46, 69 (note 21), 51
Bracondale, St Nicholas, 53
Bradcar, St Andrew, 53
Brandiston, St Nicholas, 9, 23, 24, 33, 44, 47, 50, 60-65, (Figs 8, 9, Pl. LXVII)
    Hall, 65
Brasses, 33, 34, 60, 71, 139 (Pls XLIVa, b, XLVa, b)
    heart, 77
Brasyer, Richard, (bell founder), 33
Breckles, Little, 53
Breckland, Deanery of, 12
Brick, see Materials
Brisley and Elmham, Deanery of, 12
Broomsthorpe, 53
Brown, John, 173, (Pl. CXXX)
Brundall, St Clement, 53
Bryant, T.A., 49
Buckenham Ferry, St Nicholas, 9, 23, 34, 44, 50, (Pls XXVII, XLIX)
Buckenham, New, St Mary, 5, 10, 46, 52
    St Martin, 52
Buckenham, Old, St Andrew, 53
Buckenham Tofts, St Andrew, 53
Burgh Parva, St Mary, 41, 46, 49 (note 21), 52
Burgh St Mary, 23, 46, 52
Burgh St Peter, 10
Burlinghams, North and South, 10, 49 (note 11)
Burlingham, North, St Peter, 7, 8, 33, 42, 44, 45, 46, 47, 51, 88-94, (Fig. 15, 16, 17, Pl. LXXIX, LXXX, LXXXI, LXXXII)
    St Andrew, 89, 93
Burnham and Walsingham, Deanery of, 12
Burnhams, The, 9, 10, 147
Burnham, St Andrew, 53, 147
    All Saints, 53
    St Edmund, 53, 147

Sutton, St Ethelbert, 41, 46, 48, 53, 146-148 (Figs 40, 41, Pl. CXV)
Thorpe, St Peter, 53, 147
Ulph, 147
Burroughes family, 93
Buttresses with one set-off, 68
   with two set-offs, 56, 62, 63, 68, 72, 73, 76, 77, 102, 108, 114, 118, 140
   with three set-offs, 61, 62, 73, 102, 108
   angle, 63, 76, 77, 94, 108, 150
   clasping, 72, 119
   diagonal, 58, 62, 68, 72, 73, 86, 89, 98, 99, 105, 114, 115, 122, 138, 139, 140, 146, 149, 152, 154, 161
   sloping, 58, 102, 110

Caister, West, St Edmund, 46, 52
Caldecote, St Mary, 47, 53
Calthorpe, Sir James, 34, 50
Candelabra, 75
Candlestick, 65, 75
   brass, 71, 77
Cantelose (Cantley), All Saints, 10, 53
Capital, bell, 77
   Corinthian, 80
   cushion, 114, 115, 118, 150
   foliate, 73
   moulded, 58, 62, 85, 94, 98, 120
   polygonal, 58, 62, 76, 105, 139
   scalloped, 51, 114
Carbrooke, Great, 53
   Little, 53
Carleton Rode, 10, 49 (Note 11), 53
Carlton, East, St Peter, 10, 46, 49 (note 11), 53
Carrow, St James, 53
Castle Rising, castle, 52
   church in castle enclosure, 5, 23, 46, 52, 83 (Pl. VII)
   St Laurence, 52
Caston Hall, 76
Cautley, H. Munro, 49
Cawston, 88
Ceramic, pamments, 60, 63, 78, 96
   terracotta inlay, 60
   tiles, 19th century, 60, 75, 93, 107
   tiles, medieval, 77
Chair, 79, 93
Chalice, 75, 93, 101
Chandelier, brass, 71
Chapel-of-ease, 51, 53, 54
Chapel, mortuary, 50, 51, 52, 96, 101
Chapling, J., 34
Cheadle (Staffs.), St Giles, 72
Chests, 35, 71
Choir-stalls, 60, 75, 79
Choseley, 11, 53
Churchyard, 41, 42, 60, 65, 71, 75, 79, 82, 88, 93, 96, 101, 107, 113, 116, 118, 123, 127, 132, 136, 138, 140, 142, 143, 145, 147, 149, 152, 153, 154 (Pl. LVIII)
Clenchwarton, South, 8, 53
Clock, 93, 144
Cluny, (France), 130
Cockley Cley, All Saints, 53
   St Peter, 53
Cockthorpe, All Saints, 9, 34, 35, 41, 44, 50 (Pl. LVIII)
Coffin, stone, see Sarcophagus
Coin, Roman, 71, 148,
   medieval, 148
Colchester, garrison church, 75
Colhoun, William, 11
Column, Corinthian, 80
   Doric, 81
   marble, 75
Colveston, St Mary, 46, 53
Congham, All Saints, 53
   St Mary, 53
Corbel, 61, 136
   carved, 66, 72, 74, 119
   for statue, 58, 73
   table, 150
Cornice, brick, 62, 63
   stone, 77
Cotman, John Sell, 48-49, 117
Commandment boards, 35, 71
Consolidation of parishes, 7

Corpusty, St Peter, 35, 42, 45
Coston, St Michael, 9, 23, 44, 50 (Pl. XXVI)
Cox, J. Charles, 49
Coxford Priory, 97
Creake, North, St Mary, 53
   St Michael, 46, 53
   South, 75
Cressingham, 10, 49 (note 11)
   Great, St George, 53
Croftes family, 66, 71
Cropmarks, 161
Cross, brass, 77
   consecration, 77
   processional, 75
Crownthorpe, St James, 44, 45, 50 (Pls XLII, XLIII)
Croxton, St John the Baptist, 8, 46, 51
Crucifix, 75
   enamelled copper, 13th century, 33
Cupboard, 93

Decorated/Perpendicular 'overlap,' 24, 63, 65
Decorated style (c. 1280- c. 1380), 23
Defence, Ministry of, 45
Depwade, Deanery of, 12
Dereham, West, 10
   St Andrew, 53
   St Peter, 53
Deserted villages, 11-12, 51, 52, 53, 54, 71, 75, 88, 101, 116, 119, 134, 136, 138, 142, 143, 144, 156, 157, 159
Desk, prayer, 75
   reading, 65, 79, 93
Dole cupboard, 35, 79
Domesday Book, 10, 49, 50, 51, 52, 53, 54, 55, 127, 139, 141, 142, 143, 144, 145, 160
Donor plaques, 24
Door, medieval, 35, 51, 71, 107, 127, 139 (Pl. LIV)
   sill, wooden, 125
Doorway, Early English, 23, 77
   Romanesque, 23, 50, 51, 96, 114, 117
   triangular-headed, 23, 52, 114, 116
Doughton, 54
Dovehouse, 52
Draw-bar hole, 115, 119, 125, 134
Dunham, Great, St Andrew, 54
   St Mary, 54
Dunton, St Peter, 44, 50
Dykebeck, 54

Earlham, St Anne, 93
Early English style (c. 1170- c. 1310), 23
Easter sepulchre, 157
Eborard, Bishop of Norwich (1121-45), 149, 150
Eccles-next-the-sea, St Mary, 8, 46, 48, 53, 148 (Pls XII, CXVI, CXVII)
Edgefield, St Peter & St Paul, 8, 46, 47, 52
Edwards D., 160
Egmere, St Edmund, 46, 47, 48, 49 (note 21), 52, 134-136 (Pl. CIX, CX)
Elmham, North I, 5, 46, 52
   cathedral, 52, 130
Elsing, St Mary, 153
Ely, Deanery of, 49, (note 7)
Emparkment, 51, 144
Entablature, Doric, 81
Erpingham, 60
Essex, ruined churches, 1
Excavation, 54, 55, 147, 156

Faculty Bonds, 49
Fakenham, 12
Fawcett, R., 152, 153
Feltwell, Deanery of, 12, 49 (note 7)
   St Mary, 50
   St Nicholas, 8, 23, 24, 42, 44, 49, 50 (Pls XXVIII, XXXVI, LIX, LX)
Fincham, Deanery of, 12, 49 (note 7)
   St Martin, 157, 158
   St Michael, 48, 54, 157-158
   Rectory, 157
Fireplace, 72, 98, 150
Fitzroy family, 101
Flagon, 93
Flegg, Deanery of, 12
Flint Implements, 88
Flixton (Suffolk), 49 (note 8)

Floor slabs, 17th century, 75, 78, 107, 113, 123, 132, 154, 157
    18th century, 65, 71, 75, 78, 96, 107, 123
    19th century, 65, 71, 78, 96
    20th century, 96
Flooring, pamments or tiles, see Ceramic
    wooden, 63
Flushwork, 24, 50, 68, 138, 141
Font, 118, 120, 127
    Romanesque, 33, 50, 96, 158
    Early English, 34, 50 (Pl. XLVIII)
    Decorated, 34
    Perpendicular, 34, 50, 51, 71, 78, 101, 116, 139 (Pl. XLIX)
    19th century, 34, 60, 65, 75, 82, 107
    canopy, 35, 79
    foundation for, 159
Forncett St Mary, 42, 45, 47, 50
    St Peter, 50
Foston, St Peter, 54
Foulden, St Edmund, 46, 53
Foulsham, 10, 49 (note 11)
Fountaine family, 50
Framingham Earl, 159
Freeman J. (of Aylsham), 65
Frenze, St Andrew, 9, 33, 34, 35, 44, 50, 90 (Pl. XLIVa,b)
Friendless Churches, Friends of, 45, 50
Frieze, donor, 73
    triglyph, 80
Fritton, 49 (note 8)
Frontal, for altar, 75
Fulmodestone, St Mary, 8, 41, 46, 47, 51
Fuloflove, Ralph (priest), 33, 71
Furnishings, metal, 33
    wood, 35

Gable Cross, 65, 66, 102
    line, 114, 117
Gaffin, T. (of London), 71
Gallery, 80, 91, 93
Garboldisham, All Saints, 46, 52
    St John, 52
Gargoyle, 77, 141
Garrod, Sir Nicholas, 34, 50
Gasthorpe, St Nicholas, 46, 49 (note 21), 52
Gawdy, Judge, 12, 144
    family, 71
Gillingham, 10
    All Saints, 11, 46, 52
    St Mary, 52
Gipps, Richard, 34, 71
Glass, painted, 33, 50, 51, 63, 71, 75, 77, 78, 79, 113, 127
Godwick, All Saints, 11, 24, 46, 48, 52, 136-138, (Pl. CXI)
    Hall, 136, 137
Gorleston, 55
Gowthorpe, St James, 54
Gravestone, see Headstone
Great Ouse, River, 76
Greenhoe, South, Hundred of, 12
Grill, iron, 74
Grimshoe, Hundred of, 12
Grimston, 23
Guist, St Andrew, 11, 54
Guist Thorpe, All Saints, 11, 54
Gunton, St Andrew, 1, 2, 24, 44, 49 (note 3), 50 (Pls XXXVIII-XLI)

Hackford, All Saints, 11, 46, 48, 53, (Pls CXVIII, XVI, XIX)
Hainford, All Saints, 41, 46, 52
Hales, St Margaret, 8, 23, 33, 34, 35, 44, 50, 156, 158, 159, 161, (Pls XXIV, XXV)
'Hall church', 24
Hardwick, 12, 54
Hargham, All Saints, 11, 44, 51
Harleston, 8, 54
Harling, East, 65
    Middle, St Andrew, 54, 65
    West, All Saints, 23, 24, 33, 34, 35, 44, 47, 50, 54, 65-72, (Figs 10, 11, 12, Pls XLVa,b, LXVIII, LXIX)
    Hall, 71
Harmonium, 60, 71, 75
Harold, King (1066), 160
Harris, A., 159
Hautbois, Great, Castle, 97

hospital, 97
Holy Trinity, 33, 94, 96
St Mary, 23, 24, 33, 42, 46, 47, 48, 51, 94-97, (Figs 18, 19, Pls LXXXIII, LXXXIV, LXXXV)
Hautbois, Little, St Mary, 54
Heacham and Rising, Deanery of, 12
Headstones, 18th century, 65, 79, 88, 101, 113, 123, 140, 154
    19th century, 60, 65, 71, 75, 79, 88, 93, 96, 113, 123, 140, 142, 154
    20th century, 60, 65, 79, 96, 123, 142
Heigham, 49 (note 5)
    St Bartholomew, 33, 46, 52, (Pl. VI)
    St Philip, 45, 49 (note 2), (note 18), 170, 171, (Pls CXXVII, CXXVIII)
Helmingham, 10, 49 (note 11)
    St Mary, 54
Hempnall, 10, 49 (note 11)
    St Andrew, 54
Hempton, St Andrew, 12, 46, 53
Herringby, St Ethelbert, 54
Hethersett, 10, 49 (note 11), 53
Hewke, Andrew, 73, 74
Hilborough, 75
Hindolveston, St George (old church), 5, 8, 41, 42, 46, 48, 49, 52, 138-40, (Pls I, II)
    new church, 138
Hingham and Mitford, Deanery of, 12
Hobson, Thomas, 33
Hockham, Little, St Mary, 54
Hockwold, St Peter, 24, 33, 34, 44, 50, (Pls XXXI, XXXVII, LII)
Holl, Thomas, 33
Holm, St Andrew, 54
Holt, Deanery of, 12
Holverston, St Mary, 48, 54, 158-159
    Hall, 158, 159
Hopton, St Margaret, 8, 46, 47, 49 (note 8), 51
Horsnaile, Christopher (senior), 34
Houghton-on-the-Hill, St Mary, 23, 46, 47, 51
Hour-glass stand, 79
Hoveton, 10, 49 (note 11)
    St Peter, 49 (note 3),(note 15)
Humbleyard, Deanery of, 12
Hungerford, John and Maria, 34

Illington, St Andrew, 35, 45, 50
Image of Christ, 150
Incense burner, brass, 65
Ingworth, Deanery of, 12
Inscription, brass, 65, 139
    pewter, 71
    1st World War, 71
Irmingland, St Andrew, 54
Iron smelting, 118
Islington, St Mary, 9, 23, 42, 44, 51 ,(Pls XIV, XXIX)
Isolated site, 8, 50, 51, 71, 101
Itteringham, Nower's Manor, 160
    St Nicholas, 48, 54, 159-160, (Pl. III)
    St Mary, 159-160
Ivory, John (of Norwich), 34, (Pl. LII)

Jekyll, Thomas, 96
Jones, Inigo, 119

Kempstone, St Paul, 23, 35, 42, 46, 47, 51, 97-101 (Figs 20, 21, 22, 23, Pls XXI, LXXXVI, LXXXVIII)
    Lodge, 97, 99, 101
Kenningham, 54
Kenwick, St Thomas, 54
Kerdiston, St Mary, 54
Kervile, family, 77, 78
    Sir Henry and Mary, 34, 78
Keswick (nr Bacton), St Clement, 8, 54
Key, iron, 147
Keystone, 80
King, D., 127
King's Lynn, see Lynn
Kirby Bedon, St Mary, 23, 41, 46, 49 (note 21), 52, 75
    St Andrew, 52
Kirstead, 54
Kneeler, carved, 65
Knettishall (Suffolk), 49 (note 8)

Label-stops, carved, 65, 66, 68, 72, 73, 77, 83, 91, 108
Ladbrooke, John, 49, 56, 66, 74, 98, 105, 116, 123, 125, 132, 147
Lamp bracket, brass, 65
    iron, 65
Langford, St Andrew, 23, 33, 42, 46, 50
Langhale, St Christopher, 54
Langham, Magna, 10, 11, 49 (note 11)
    Parva, St Mary, 10. 11, 54
Lectern, brass, 33, 71, 77, (Pl. XLVI)
    wooden, 60
Leicester, Earl of, 101
de Lenne, Thomas (bellfounder), 33
Letheringsett, 60
Letton, All Saints, 46, 53
Leziate, All Saints, 11, 12, 41, 46, 53, 118
Limpenhoe, 8, 51
Lincoln, cathedral (Lincs.), 23
Lingwood, St Peter, 93
Litcham, church, 101, 137
    Priory farm, 101
Loddon, Deanery of, 12
London, Strand, St Clement Danes, 24, 81, 82
    St John's, Smith Square, 82
de Losinga, Herbert (Bishop of Norwich), 52, 55, 159
Lothingland, Deanery of, 49 (note 8)
Lowestoft, St John (Suffolk), 49 (note 8)
    St Peter (Suffolk). 49 (note 8)
Lynford, 54
Lynn, bellfoundry, 33
    Deanery of, 12
    King's, 12
    King's, St James, 10, 42, 46, 47, 48, 53, 149-152, (Pls CXIX, CXX, CXXI)
    King's, St James, (methodist chapel) 150
    King's, St Margaret, 10, 49, 52
    King's, mayor and corporation, 150, 152
    King's, museum, 118
    King's, St Nicholas, 10, 150, 152
    Marshland, Deanery of, 12, 49 (note 7)
    North, St Edmund, 8, 49 (note 9), 54
    South, St Michael, 45, 49 (note 2), (note 9), 171
    West, St Peter, 49 (note 9), 191

Mannington, 7, 46, 51
Manorial complex, 160
Marble, coloured, 72, 75
    Purbeck, 34, 50
March, Deanery of, 49(note7)
Marham, St Andrew, 54
Markshall, St Edmund, 12, 54
Martin, Tom, 63, 161
Mary I (1553-58), 135, 136
Massingham, Great, All Saints, 54
Materials
    arch, alternating brick and flint, 61, 62, 63, 66, 68, 74, 94
    arch, alternating limestone and flint, 58, 62
    brick, Roman, 58, 59, 63, 94, 95, 96
    brick, medieval, 68, 76, 77, 79, 85, 88, 90, 91, 94, 96, 99, 102, 106, 110 115, 117, 119, 120, 121, 122, 124, 125, 126, 131, 132, 134, 136, 138, 139, 144, 146, 149, 157, 161
    brick, 16th century, 116, 118, 120, 150
    brick, 17th century, 56, 85, 86, 88, 89, 98, 102, 129, 137
    brick, 18th century, 56, 58, 59, 61, 63, 68, 70, 85, 91, 94, 98, 102, 110, 138
    carstone, 76, 77, 83, 85, 86, 88, 114, 115
    clunch, 85, 129, 146
    conglomerate, 56, 58, 94, 95, 102, 117, 134, 142, 144
    courses, wide, 56, 58, 123, 125, 131
    erratic stone, 76, 77, 123, 124
    flint, 56, 58, 61, 62, 65, 66, 68, 71, 76, 83, 89, 90, 91, 94, 96, 102, 108, 110, 114, 117, 119, 120, 123, 124, 125, 129, 131, 134, 136, 138, 140, 142, 144, 146, 148, 150, 152, 154, 161
    flint, brick and limestone, 61, 98, 105
    flint, herringbone, 56
    flint, knapped, 56, 72, 120, 124, 125
    flint pebble, 136
    half-timber, 72
    iron, 83
    iron, smelting slag, 117
    lava, 77, 90, 99, 102, 110
    limestone, 56, 61, 63, 65, 66, 72, 76, 77, 80, 83, 85, 90, 91, 94, 102, 108, 114, 116, 117, 119, 120, 125, 129, 131, 134, 136, 139, 140, 142, 144, 150, 157, 161
    mortar, limestone, 110
    Sandringham stone, 83, 85, 86, 88
    tile, 134, 150
    wood, 125, 127, 141, 142
Matlaske, 60
Melton Constable, 52
Melton, Great, All Saints, 52
    St Mary, 10, 46, 52, (Pl. XVIII)
Messent, C.J.W., 49, 180
Methwold Hythe, 54
Mildenhall, Deanery of, 49 (note7)
Mileham family, 93
Mintlyn, St Michael, 11, 12, 46, 49, 52, 116-119 (Pls XCVI, XCVII, XCVIII, XCIX)
    Farm, 116, 118
Monument, funerary
    16th century, 139
    17th century, 34, 50, 60, 78, (Pl. LI)
    18th century, 34, 50, 60, 71, 78, 149, (Pl. LII)
    19th century, 34, 65, 71, 78, 85, 89, 91, 101
    20th century, 65
Morton-on-the-Hill, St Margaret, 10, 23, 35, 42, 44, 51, 54 (Pls LIV, LXI, LXII)
Mouchette, 73, 86
Moulton, Little, All Saints, 54
Moulton St Mary, 33, 34, 35, 44, 50, (Pls IX, XLVII, XLVIII, LI, LVI)
Mundford, 34, 75
Mundham, St Ethelbert, 41, 46, 52

Narford, St Mary, 46, 47, 50
National Monuments Record, 49
Nelonde, St Peter, 54
Niche, blank, 90, 96
    for piscina, 102, 117, 123
    statue, 58, 63, 66, 68, 89, 94, 139, 162
Nook-shaft, 72, 73, 77, 85, 114, 115
Norfolk Churches Trust, 44, 45, 50, 51
Norfolk, Duke of, 152
Norman style, see Romanesque
Norton (Durham), 130
Norwich, 12
    All Saints Fyebridgegate, 179
    All Saints Timberhill, 44, 45, 179
    Bridewell Museum, 33
    Cathedral cloister, 63
    Cathedral, dean and chapter, 150
    Cathedral Priory, 150
    church in castle bailey, 179
    Diocesan Board of Finance, 44, 45
    Historic Churches Trust 44, 45
    Holy Trinity, 179
    Palace of Duke of Norfolk, 152
    St Anne 9, 179
    St Bartholomew, 179
    St Benedict, 8, 179
    St Botolph, 179
    St Christopher, 9, 179
    St Clement, 44, 45, 179
    St Clement Conesford, 179
    St Crowche, 179
    St Cuthbert, 179
    St Edmund, 44, 45, 179
    St Edward, 9, 179
    St Ethelbert, 9, 179
    St Etheldreda, 44, 45, 179
    St Giles, 75
    St Gregory, 44, 45, 77, 179
    St Helen I, 179
    St James Pockthorpe, 44, 45, 179
    St John de Sepulchre, 45, 49 (note 17)
    St John Conesford, 9, 179
    St John Maddermarket, 45, 49 (note 17)
    St John the Baptist Colegate, 9, 179
    St Julian, 8
    St Laurence, 44, 179
    St Margaret at Newbridge, 9, 11, 179
    St Margaret Fyebridge, 179
    St Margaret Westwick, 44, 45, 179
    St Martin at Oak, 44, 45, 179

St Martin at Palace, 11, 44, 45, 49 (note14), 75, 179
St Martin in Balliva, 179
St Mary Coslany, 35, 44, 45, 60, 179
St Mary in the Marsh, 179
St Mary the Less, 7, 44, 45, 179
St Mary Unbrent, 179
St Matthew, 9, 11, 49 (note 14), 179
St Michael at Pleas, 44, 45, 179
St Michael at Thorn, 8, 179
St Michael Conesford, 9, 179
St Michael Coslany, 44, 45, 179
St Michael Tombland, 179
St Olave Colegate, 179
St Olave Conesford, 9, 179
St Paul, 8, 179
St Peter Hungate, 9, 33, 34, 35, 45, 93, 179
St Peter Parmentergate, 44, 45, 179
St Peter Southgate, 9, 179
St Saviour, 44, 45, 179
St Simon and St Jude, 45, 179
St Stephen, 49 (note 15)
St Swithin, 44, 45, 179
St Vedast, 179
St Winwaloy, 9, 11, 179
Nugent family, 71

Oby, 54, 156, 157
Orford, Earl of, 12
Ormesby, 48
    St Andrew, 54, 161
    St Margaret, 160, 161
    St Michael, 160, 161
    St Peter, 54, 160-161 (Pl. CXXV)
Ornament, architectural, chevron, 114, 118
    dentil frieze, 56
    dogtooth, 23, 96
Organ, 65, 75, 79, 82
    case, 75
    loft, 66, 72, 75
Overstrand, Christ Church, 45, 170
    St Martin I, 8, 49 (note 2), 54
Oxborough, St John, 52, 77
    St Mary Magdalen, 46, 52
Oxwick, All Saints, 42, 46, 51

Palgrave family, 33, 34, 58, 60
Palgrave, Little, 54
Panel, stone, 73
    wooden, Flemish, 71
Panelling, wooden, 60, 74, 79
Panxworth, All Saints, 42, 45, 46, 47, 48, 52, 140-142 (Figs 38, 39, Pls CXII, CXIII)
Parapet, 139
    brick, 80
    chequerboard, 149
    crenellated, 58, 68, 75, 77, 86, 137, 141, 144, 148
Parchmarks, 154, 160
Parfitt, H. (of Stalham), 65
Parkin, 49, 120, 157
Partridge family, 75
Pastoral Measure (1968), 1
Paten, 75, 93, 101
Pattesley, St John the Baptist, 54
Paving, stone, 78
Pediment, 81
    broken, 80
Pensthorpe, 12, 46, 53
Perpendicular style (c.1350-c.1540), 24
Pettus family, 34, 56
Pevsner, N., 49
Pews, 35, 50, 75, 82, 101, (Pl. LV)
Pickenham, South, 75
    St Andrew, 54
Piers, clustered, 23, 24
    Doric, 80
    giant, 139
    octagonal, 24, 58, 85, 94, 120, 139
    Perpendicular, 24
    quatrefoil, 23, 62, 73, 76
Pilaster, 80
    Doric, 80, 81

Pilaster-buttress, 131
Pilgrimage, to the image of St Theobald, 96
Piscina, 23, 73, 77, 83, 90, 98, 101, 102, 108, 114, 139, 158,
    angle, 66, 76
    column, 58
    double, 56, 66
Plinth, 66, 134
    course, flushwork, 68, 72
de la Pole, Michael, 88
Pope, Margaret, 56
Poringland, East I, 191
    West, St Michael, 54
Portal, see Doorway
Post-Medieval structures (c.1540 to today), 24
Pottery, Roman, 71, 88, 118, 132, 136, 158
    Middle Saxon, 88, 101, 116, 127, 136
    Late Saxon, 88, 101, 116, 127, 136
    Medieval, 88, 96, 101, 116, 127, 136, 144, 160
Power, Edward, 172, (Pl. CXXVIII)
Price, John (elder and younger), 24, 81, 82
Priest's door, 61, 66, 76, 89, 108, 119, 154
Pudding Norton, St Margaret, 12, 23, 46, 47, 48,
52, 142-144, (Pls XXII, CXIV)
    Hall, 142
Pugin, Augustus Welby, 24, 25, 34, 35, 47, 72, 73, 74, 76
Pulpit, 17th century, 35, 50, 51, 60, 79 (Pl. LVI)
    18th century, 35, 82 (Pl. LXXV)
    19th century, 107
    20th century, 65
    two-decker, 35, 51
    base of, 120

Quarles, 46, 53, (Pl. IV)
Quoins, ashlar and brick, 80
    conglomerate, 56, 58, 94, 96, 143
    flint, 63, 123, 125, 131
    limestone, 56, 58, 65, 66, 83, 85, 94, 102, 114, 117, 120, 131, 134, 138, 140, 143, 144
    machine-cut, 66
    Roman brick, 58, 63
    side-alternate, 129, 130
    upright-and-flat, 23, 66, 114, 116, 129, 130

Rackheath, All Saints, 24, 34, 44, 50
    Little, Holy Trinity, 54
Rawlins, Thomas, 34
Raynham, East, St Mary, 119, 123
    Hall, 119
    Old hall, 123
    South, 119
    West, St Margaret, 46, 52, 119-123, (Figs 32-33, Pls C, CI)
Redenhall, 54
    Deanery of, 12
Redundancy, procedure for, 1, 7
Redundant Churches Fund, 44, 45, 50, 51, 52, 56, 60, 61, 63, 65, 71, 76, 77
Reepham, 9, 10, 11, 41, 149, (Pls XVI, XIX)
Reformation, effects of, 7
Repps, 52
    Deanery of, 12
Reredos, stone, 75
    wooden, 35, 65, 71, 79
Respond, polygonal, 62, 72, 73, 77, 85, 86, 94, 98, 120
    round, 62, 76, 139
Ringstead, Great, St Peter, 23, 46, 52
    Little, St Andrew, 7, 11, 46, 49 (note 21), 51
Rising Haven, 83
Rockland St Mary, St Margaret, 10, 47, 53
Rockland All Saints, 52
    St Andrew, 41, 46, 52
    St Peter, 40, 41
Rogerson, Andrew, 47, 48, 99, 110
Romanesque style (c.1040-c.1180), 23, 50
Rood-loft, 75
Rood-stair, 56, 63, 68, 110
Roof, arch-braced, 24, 50, 56, 61, 90
    barrel, 66
    braced collar, 76
    collar and through-purlin, 81
    conical, 72
    crown post, 76
    gabled, 73

hammer-beam, 24, 68
lean-to, 73
Mansard, 80
waggon, 75
Roof-covering, copper, 80
lead, 76, 96, 122, 135
slate, 56, 76, 93, 141
thatch, 74, 101, 130, 161
tile, 56, 61, 65, 72, 74, 98, 102, 122, 161
Roof-line, 86, 134, 137, 143, 144, 149
Rose, Edwin, 76
Roudham, St Andrew, 8, 11, 24, 46, 47, 51 (Pl. XIII)
Rouen, 72
Roxham, St Michael, 54
Rudham, 49 (note 11)
East, 10
West, St Peter, 10, 23, 33, 44, 50 Ruddock (of Lopham), 71
Runcton, North, All Saints, 49 (note 3, 15), 54, 82
Runham, St Peter and St Paul, 45
Ruston, East, St Mary, 24, 33, 34, 35, 44, 50 (Pl. XXXII)
Ryburgh, Great, 52
Little, All Saints, 12, 41, 47, 52

Salhouse, 10
Salle, 9
Sandringham, Royal Estate, 83
Santon, 49 (note 3), 49 (note 7)
Sarcophagus, stone, medieval, 71, 86
stone, lid, 65, 116, 117, 118, 132
Saxlingham Nethergate, 33, 123, 126, 127
Thorpe, St Mary, 23, 41, 47, 52, 123-127 (Figs 34, 35, Pl. CII, CIII)
West Wood, 127
'Saxo-Norman' overlap, 130, 144
Saxthorpe, St Dunstan, 54
Sco Ruston, St Michael, 42, 45, 47, 51, 101-108 (Figs 24, 25, 26, 27, 28, Pls LXXXVIII, LXXXIXI)
Scoulton, 75
Scratby, All Saints, 54, 161
Screens, 35, 50, 51, 75, 79 (Pl. LVII)
medieval, painted, 79, 123
medieval, 93, 101, 158
Sedilia, 23, 66, 83, 98, 114, 158
Seething, 10, 54
Setchey, St Mary, 44, 49 (note 2), 172
chapel, 54
Shaft, mid-wall, 115
Sherborne (Dorset), Minster, 130
Shaft, octagonal, 150
Sheringham, Lower, St Peter I, 49 (note 2), 170
Shimpling, St George, 33, 34, 35, 44, 50, 51
Shingham, St Botolph, 23, 24, 35, 45, 51, (Pls XXIII, XXXIII)
Shipden, 8, 54
Shotesham, 10, 49 (note 11)
All Saints, 75
St Botolph, 47, 53
St Martin, 10, 41, 47, 51
Shouldham, 10
Shouldham Thorpe, 54
Shouldham, St Margaret, 54
Shropham, 53
Sidestrand, St Michael, 8, 54
Sill-sedilia, 56, 76
Singleton, R. (of Bury), 34
Snarehill, Great, 23, 47, 48, 52, 127-131, (Figs 36, 37, Pls CIV, CV, CVI)
Hall, 127
Snetterton, All Saints, 24, 44, 50
St Andrew, 54
Snoring, Little, St Andrew, 52
tower, 5, 49 (note 21), 52
Soakaway, for font, 120
Somerton, East, St Mary, 7, 47, 51
Southery, St Mary, 8, 42, 47, 51, 75, (Pl. XI)
Southwark (London), St George, 82
Southwood, St Edmund, 8, 46, 49, 51, (Pls LXIII, LXIV)
Spire, 68, 144
Spout, bronze, 144
Sprowston, New, St Cuthbert, 101
Squinch, 150
Squint, 72
Sparham, Deanery of, 12
St Edmundsbury and Ipswich, Diocese of, 49 (note 7)

St Felix, 83, 88
St Mary, statue of, 75
St Nicholas, statue of 63, 65
St Theobald, image of, 48, 96, 97
Stair-turret, 72, 74, 77, 105, 110, 138, 144, 154
Stairway, spiral, 72, 131, 135, 138, 154
Stanford, All Saints, 7, 23, 24, 46, 51
Training Area, 7, 8, 45, 47, 50, 51, 72, 74
Stanley, J. (of St Stephen's Norwich), 65
Stanninghall, 11, 12, 47, 52
Stiffkey, St John the Baptist/St Mary, 10, 54
Stoke Ferry, 10, 49 (note 11)
Stoke Holy Cross, 10, 49 (note 11), 54
Stone, carved : coffin lid, 53
fragments, 158
12th century, 54, 131, 132, 137, 138, 150, 152, 159, 161
roundel, 65
plaque in buttress, 102
springing at vault, 157
Stoup (Holy water), 65, 86, 102, 110, 162
Stove, 107
Stow (Lincs.), 130
Stowe (Bucks.), 24
Stratton, St Michael, 54
St Peter, 54
Sturston, Holy Cross, 11, 47, 54
Suffolk, ruined churches, 1
Summerfield, All Saints, 54
Sundial, 65, 68, 77, 81
Surlingham, St Mary, 131, 132
St Saviour, 23, 41, 47, 52, 130, 131-133, (Pls CVII, CVIII)
Sutton family, 24, 34, 72, 74
Sutton chapel/chantry, 72, 74
Swainsthorpe, St Mary, 54
Swift, John, 139

Table, 19th century, 71, 75
Tattersett, All Saints, 53
St Andrew, 10, 47, 53
Temouth, S.C. (of Pimlico), 71
Tendall, Amfelicie, 33
Terracotta, 33
Terringtons, The, 10
Testerton, St Remigius, 12, 47, 52
Themelthorpe, 10
Thetford, 130
All Saints, 9, 54
and Rockland, Deanery of, 12, 49 (note 8)
Church, Gasworks, site 55
Church, Red Castle site, 55
Church, St Michael's Close, 9, 55
Great St Mary, 9, 54
Holy Trinity, 9, 54
Martin's map of, (Pl. XV)
Priory, 54, 127
Priory Register, 130
St Andrew, 9, 54
St Benet, 9, 54, 55
St Cuthbert, 162
St Edmund, 9, 54, 55
St Etheldreda, 9, 54
St George, 9, 54
St Giles, 9, 48, 54, 161-162, (Pl. CXXVI)
St Helen, 9, 54
St John, 9, 47, 54
St Lawrence, 9, 54
St Margaret, 9, 54
St Martin, 9, 54, 55
St Mary the Less, 45, 49 (note 17)
St Michael, 9, 55
St Nicholas, 9, 55
St Peter, 161
The Canons, 162
Thorpe-by-Norwich, Old Thorpe Church, 55
St Andrew, 8, 47, 49 (note 21), 51, 55
Thorpe Hamlet, St Leonard, 49 (note 2), 170
St Matthew, 45, 49 (note 2), 170, 173, (Pls CXXIX, CXXX)
Thorpe Market, 49 (note 3)
Thorpe Parva, St Mary, 47, 52
Thorpeland, St Thomas, 55
Thorpland, St Thomas, 12, 47, 53

197

Thurgarton, All Saints, 35, 42, 44, 51
Thurketeliart, 55
Tie-beam, embattled, 76
Tiles, medieval (see also Ceramic), 33, 79, 96, 101, 126, 127, 135, 136, 150
    156, 158, 160, 161
    19th century, see Ceramic
Tilneys, 10, 54
Tivetshall, St Margaret, 10, 51, 108, 113
    St Mary, 10, 24, 42, 44, 45, 47 51, 108-113 (Figs 29, 30, 31, Pls XC, XCI)
Tomb canopy, 23, 73, 75, 85, 88
    recess, 72, 73, 85, 86
Topcroft, St Giles, 55
Torc, 116
Tottenhill, 191
Tottington, St Andrew, 7, 24, 35, 46, 50 (Pls LIII, LVII)
Tournus (France), 130
Tower, axial, 23, 114, 127, 129, 131, 132
    crossing, 150
    octagonal, 23, 52
    round, 23, 24, 50, 51, 52, 62, 63, 91, 94, 95, 96, 131, 132, 148, 156, 158, 161
    salient, 23, 129, 130
    square, 23
Tracery, see Window
Transept, continuous, 130
Transitional and Early English style (c.1170-c.1310), 23
Trench, robber, 157
Tuddenham, North and East, 10
Tunstall, St Peter and St Paul, 44, 47, 51
Tunstead, Deanery of, 12
Turbe, Bishop of Norwich (1146-74), 156
Tympanum, 118

de Ufford, Robert, 88

Vault, barrel, 23, 77, 86, 114, 116
    domical, 135
    plaster, 80, 81
    springer, 157
    tierceron, 72, 75
Vestments, 75

Wacton, Little, St Mary, 55
Wales, Prince of, 83, 88
Wall painting, 33, 50, 66, (Pl. XLVII)
    black lettered, 58, 91
Wall-post, 76
Wallington, St Margaret, 12, 46, 47, 48, 52, 144-155, (Pl. V)
    hall, 144, 145
Walpole St Andrew, 44, 191
    St Peter, St Peter's Lodge, 152
Walpole family, 52
Walsham, South, St Laurence, 8, 10, 11, 42, 45, 47, 51
Walsingham, Great, All Saints, 47, 48, 53, 152-154, (Pl. CXXII)
    St Peter, 88, 152, 153
    Priory, 135
Waltham Abbey, R.C. community, 82
Walton, East, St Andrew, 23, 46, 52
Walton, West, St Mary, 52
    Tower, 23, 44, 49 (note 6), 52, (Pl. XXX)
Warham, St Mary the Virgin, 55
Watson, James, 141
Waxham, 49 (note 11)
    Deanery of, 12)
    Great, 10
    Little, St Margaret, 10, 55
Weasenham, St Paul, 55
Weather cock, 81
Weeting, All Saints, 41, 47, 48, 53, 154-155 (Fig 42)
    St Mary, 154
West Tofts, St Mary, 7, 23, 24, 33, 34, 35, 45, 46, 47, 51, 72-76 (Pls LXX, LXXI)
Wheatacre, 10, 49 (note 11)
Whitlingham, St Andrew, 8, 12, 23, 42, 47, 52
Whitwell, St Michael, 11, 49 (note 16), 149

Wicklewood, 10, 50
    St Andrew, 55
Wiggenhall St German, 51, 76, 77
Wiggenhall St Mary the Virgin, 23, 24, 33, 34, 35, 44, 47, 51, 76-79, (Pls LVI, LXXII)
    St Mary's Hall, 79
Wiggenhall St Peter, 24, 42, 47, 51, (frontispiece, Pl. XXXIV)
Wilkinson J., 162
Wilton, 50
Wilton, Joseph, 34, 71
Windle, St Andrew, 55
Window
    four-centred, 56, 68, 76, 94, 136, 137
    elliptical head, 95
    lancet, 66, 69, 72, 86, 94, 123, 126, 130, 158
    lancet, cusped, 72, 99
    lancet, paired, 68
    lancets, stepped, 23, 56
    lunette, 80
    ogee, 68, 73, 141
    pointed segmental, 76, 117, 138
    round, 158
    round-headed, double-splayed, 23, 99, 101
    round-headed, single-splayed, 50, 114, 124, 125, 143
    segmental, 94, 98
    square-headed, 56, 58, 68, 91, 94, 98, 141, 150
    triangular-headed, 68
    wooden, mullioned and transomed, 150
Window tracery
    brick, 125, 126
    curvilinear, petal-motif, 62, 63, 72
    cusped intersected, 65, 76, 108 110
    drop-tracery, 71, 73, 94, 102, 105
    flowing, 83, 88
    intersected, 24, 51, 99, 102, 106, 120, 122
    intersecting ogee, 24, 58
    plate-tracery, 23, 66, 69, 72
    reticulated, 23, 24, 51, 63, 73, 85, 86, 89, 98
    supermullioned, 56, 61, 66, 71, 73, 76, 77, 89, 94, 99
    transomed, 58, 63, 138, 139
    Y-tracery, 24, 58, 59, 65, 72, 73, 74, 86, 102, 106, 108, 110, 120, 122, 137, 143
    Y-tracery, cusped, 74, 76, 144
Winston, St Andrew, 55
Winterton, 51
Wisbech, Deanery of 49, (note 7)
Wolterton, St Margaret, 12, 24, 46, 47, 52, (Pl. XXXV)
Wood Norton, St Peter, 47, 52
Wooden furnishings, 35
Workhouse, conversion of church to, 150, 152
Worstead, 49 (note 11)
    St Andrew, 10, 55
    St Mary, 10
Wren, Christopher, 24, 79, 82
Wreningham, Little, St Mary, 55
Wretham, East, 11
    West, St Lawrence, 7, 11, 12, 24, 41, 46, 47, 51
Wretton, 10
Wroxham, 10, 49 (note 11)
Wyche, Cyrill, 34, (Pl. LII)
Wymondham, 24
    Downham, St Edmund, 45, 49 (note 2), 171
    Silfield, St Helen, 45, 49 (note 2), 171

Yarmouth, Great, 12
    Borough Council, 45, 79 82
    St Andrew, 45, 49 (note 2, 19), 170
    St Benedict, 49 (note 10), 55, 79
    St George, 1, 2, 10, 24, 35, 45, 47, 49 (note 3), 51, 79-82, (Pls LXXIII, LXXIV)
    St James, 82
    St John, 82
    St Nicholas, 10, 35, 79, 82
    St Peter, 45, 49 (note 17)
Yarmouth, Southtown, St Nicholas, 49 (note 10), 55

East Anglian Archaeology

is a serial publication sponsored by the Scole Archaeological Committee Ltd. The Norfolk, Suffolk and Essex Units, the Norwich Survey and the Fenland Project will all be contributing volumes to the series. It will be the main vehicle for publishing final reports on archaeological excavations and surveys in the region.

Copies and information about the contents of all volumes can be obtained from:

Centre of East Anglian Studies,
University of East Anglia,
Norwich, NR4 7TJ

or directly from the Archaeology Unit publishing a particular volume.

Reports available so far:

Report No.1,	1975	Suffolk: various papers
Report No.2,	1976	Norfolk: various papers
Report No.3,	1977	Suffolk: various papers
Report No.4,	1976	Norfolk: Late Saxon town of Thetford
Report No.5,	1977	Norfolk: various papers on Roman sites
Report No.6,	1977	Norfolk: Spong Hill Anglo-Saxon cemetery
Report No.7,	1978	Norfolk: Bergh Apton Anglo-Saxon cemetery
Report No.8,	1978	Norfolk: various papers
Report No.9,	1980	Norfolk: North Elmham Park
Report No.10,	1980	Norfolk: village sites in Launditch Hundred
Report No.11,	1981	Norfolk Spong Hill, Part II
Report No.12,	1981	The barrows of East Anglia
Report No.13,	1981	Norwich: Eighteen centuries of pottery from Norwich
Report No.14,	1982	Norfolk: various papers
Report No.15,	1982	Norwich: Excavations in Norwich 1971–1978; Part I
Report No.16,	1982	Norfolk: Beaker domestic sites in the Fen-edge and East Anglia
Report No.17,	1983	Norwich: Waterfront excavations and Thetford-type Ware production, Norwich
Report No.18,	1983	Norfolk: The archaeology of Witton
Report No.19,	1983	Norfolk: Two post-medieval earthenware pottery groups from Fulmodeston
Report No.20,	1983	Norfolk: Burgh Castle: excavation by Charles Green, 1958–61
Report No.21,	1984	Norfolk: Spong Hill, Part III
Report No.22,	1984	Norfolk: Excavations in Thetford, 1948–59 and 1973–80
Report No.23,	1985	Norfolk: Excavations at Brancaster 1974 and 1977
Report No.24,	1985	Suffolk: West Stow, the Anglo-Saxon village
Report No.25,	1985	Essex: Excavations by Mr H.P. Cooper on the Roman site at Hill Farm, Gestingthorpe, Essex
Report No.26,	1985	Norwich: Excavations in Norwich 1971–78; Part II
Report No.27,	1985	Cambridgeshire: The Fenland Project No.1; Archaeology and Environment in the lower Welland valley
Report No.28,	1985	Norwich: Excavations within the north-east bailey of Norwich Castle, 1978
Report No.29,	1986	Norfolk: Barrow excavations in Norfolk, 1950–82
Report No.30,	1986	Norfolk: Excavations at Thornham, Warham, Wighton and Caistor St. Edmund, Norfolk
Report No.31,	1986	Norfolk: Settlement, religion and industry on the Fen-edge; three Romano-British sites in Norfolk
Report No.32,	1987	Norfolk: Three Norman Churches in Norfolk
Report No.33,	1987	Essex: Excavation of a Cropmark Enclosure Complex at Woodham Walter, Essex, 1976 and An Assessment of Excavated Enclosures in Essex
Report No.34,	1987	Norfolk: The Anglo-Saxon Cemetery at Spong Hill, North Elmham, Part IV: Catalogue of Cremations
Report No.35,	1987	Cambridgeshire: The Fenland Project No.2: Fenland Landscapes and Settlement between Peterborough and March
Report No.36,	1987	Norfolk: The Anglo-Saxon Cemetery at Morning Thorpe, Norfolk: Catalogue
Report No.37,	1987	Norwich: Excavations at St Martin-at-Palace Plain, Norwich, 1981
Report No.38,	1987	Suffolk: The Anglo-Saxon Cemetery at Westgarth Gardens, Bury St Edmunds, Suffolk: Catalogue
Report No.39,	1988	Norfolk: The Anglo-Saxon Cemetery at Spong Hill, North Elmham, Norfolk, Part VI; Occupation during the 7th-2nd millennia BC
Report No.40,	1988	Suffolk: Burgh: The Iron Age and Roman Enclosure
Report No.41,	1988	Essex: Excavations at Great Dunmow, Essex: a Romano-British small town in the Trinovantian *Civitas*
Report No.42,	1988	Essex: Archaeology and Environment in South Essex, Rescue Archaeology along the Gray's By-pass 1979/80
Report No.43,	1988	Essex: Excavation at the North Ring, Mucking, Essex: A Late Bronze Age Enclosure
Report No.44,	1988	Norfolk: Six Deserted Villages in Norfolk
Report No.45,	1988	Norfolk: The Fenland Project No. 3: Marshland and the Nar Valley, Norfolk
Report No.46,	1989	Norfolk: The Deserted Medieval Village of Thuxton, Norfolk
Report No.47,	1989	Suffolk: West Stow, Suffolk: Early Anglo-Saxon Animal Husbandry
Report No.48,	1990	Suffolk: West Stow, Suffolk: Prehistoric and Romano-British Occupation
Report No.49,	1990	Norfolk: The Evolution of Settlement in Three Parishes in South-East Norfolk
Report No.50,	1991	The Flatlands and Wetlands: Current Themes in East Anglian Archaeology
Report No.51,	1991	Norfolk: The Ruined and Disused Churches of Norfolk